In this new book, Anālayo builds on
work, *Satipaṭṭhāna: The Direct Path to*
our perspective on this seminal teaching by exploring the practices of mindfulness as presented in both the Pāli and Chinese versions of this important discourse. The brilliance of his scholarly research, combined with the depth of his meditative understanding, provides an invaluable guide to the liberating practices of the Buddha's teaching. This book is not for beginners looking for a general introduction to mindfulness. Rather, it is a work of profound research and investigation, offering a thorough, and often subtle, analysis of how we can understand the causes of suffering and realize the potential for freedom. – **Joseph Goldstein**, author of *Mindfulness: A Practical Guide to Awakening*, co-founder of the Insight Meditation Society, Barre, Massachusetts, USA

Anālayo shows that the practical instructions on Satipaṭṭhāna from these three traditions are sometimes identical, and sometimes different. The differences are often interesting, adding new perspectives to what we already knew; and affirming, where the traditions speak in one voice, the authenticity of the oral instructions and the likelihood that this was the actual teaching of the historical Buddha. This book will be useful for experienced seekers after truth who want to immerse themselves more deeply, and in more detail, in the core Buddhist practice of Satipaṭṭhāna. – **Kamalashila**, author of *Buddhist Meditation: Tranquillity, Imagination and Insight*, co-founder of Vajraloka Meditation Centre, Wales, UK

Anālayo's work is a treasury of impeccable scholarship and practice, offering a wise, open-minded and deep understanding of the Buddha's original teachings. His approach makes an inspiring contribution to the modern Dharma world. – **Jack Kornfield**, author of *The Wise Heart*, founding teacher of Spirit Rock Meditation Center, Woodacre, California, USA

Anālayo has offered us a work of great scholarship and wisdom that will be of immense benefit to anyone who wants to seriously study or to establish a practice of mindfulness. – **Sharon Salzberg**, author of *Lovingkindness*, co-founder of the Insight Meditation Society, Barre, Massachusetts, USA

PERSPECTIVES ON SATIPAṬṬHĀNA

Anālayo

Windhorse Publications

Published by
Windhorse Publications
169 Mill Road
Cambridge
CB1 3AN
UK

info@windhorsepublications.com
www.windhorsepublications.com

As an act of Dhammadāna, Anālayo has waived royalty payments for this book.
The index was not compiled by the author.
Cover design by Dhammarati

Typesetting and layout by Ben Cracknell Studios
Printed by Bell & Bain Ltd, Glasgow

British Library Cataloguing in Publication Data:
A catalogue record for this book is available from the British Library.

ISBN: 978 1 909314 03 0

CONTENTS

LIST OF FIGURES

ABOUT THE AUTHOR

Born in 1962 in Germany, Bhikkhu Anālayo was ordained in 1995 in Sri Lanka, and completed a PhD on the *Satipaṭṭhāna-sutta* at the University of Peradeniya, Sri Lanka, in 2000 – published in 2003 by Windhorse Publications under the title *Satipaṭṭhāna: The Direct Path to Realization.*

Anālayo is a professor of Buddhist studies at the Sri Lanka International Academy in Pallekele. He also teaches at the Center for Buddhist Studies of the University of Hamburg and researches at the Dharma Drum Buddhist College in Taiwan. His main research area is early Buddhism and in particular the topics of the Chinese *Āgama*s, meditation, and women in Buddhism. Besides his academic pursuits, he spends about half of his time in meditation under retreat conditions and regularly teaches meditation courses in Asia and the West.

ACKNOWLEDGEMENTS

I am indebted to Jake Davis, Sāmaṇerī Dhammadinnā, Aldo di Domenico, Sean Fargo, Robert Goodman, Kamalashila, Shi Kongmu, Ken Su, Shi Syinchen, Vishvapani, and Dhatvisvari for having helped me to improve my presentation. Any shortcomings in the following pages are entirely due to my own ignorance.

Contemplate the body by establishing mindfulness, diligently energetic, rightly knowing and rightly mindful, overcoming desires and discontent in the world. In the same way … feelings … mind … dharmas … This is called having oneself as an island by relying on oneself, having the Dharma as an island by relying on the Dharma, having no other island and no other reliance.

INTRODUCTION

This book is a follow-up to my study of *satipaṭṭhāna* as the "direct path to realization".[1] Originally I thought only of revising my earlier monograph, but eventually it became clear that a new publication would be the better solution. The main difference between the present work and the earlier study is that I take up in detail the discourse parallels to the *Satipaṭṭhāna-sutta* that have been preserved by other Buddhist traditions. In this way, with the present publication I approach matters of practice from the perspective that emerges through a comparative study of the parallel versions to the Pāli discourses, which are extant mainly in Chinese as well as in Sanskrit and Tibetan. While I base my presentation of the texts on academic methodology and in some parts of my discussions I need to take up matters that are of a more theoretical interest, as a whole this book is meant for practitioners and it is the relevance to meditation practice that informs my exploration.[2] In terms of the quotation given at the start of this book, I hope to make a small contribution to our understanding of the "Dharma" of *satipaṭṭhāna* meditation to be relied on when engaging in actual meditation practice.[3]

---

1 Anālayo 2003b.

2 A comparative study of the *Satipaṭṭhāna-sutta* geared towards an academic readership can be found in Anālayo 2011a: 73–97, which has more detailed references to other texts and to relevant secondary literature than my present study.

3 The quote is extracted from SĀ 639 at T II 177b3 which, unlike its parallel SN 47.14 at SN V 164,30 (translated Bodhi 2000: 1645), stipulates practice of each *satipaṭṭhāna* to be internal, external, and both. Another difference

As the present volume is a companion to my earlier publication, in what follows I do not cover comprehensively all relevant topics, primary sources, and secondary literature. Instead, I selectively take up what, in my opinion, is of practical significance and complements my previous book. Thus a basic familiarity with what I covered in my earlier study is needed to contextualize what I discuss in the present monograph.

My study is based on excerpts from the *Satipaṭṭhāna-sutta* found in the *Majjhima-nikāya* of the Theravāda Pāli canon and the two main canonical discourse parallels transmitted by other Buddhist schools. These two parallels are preserved in Chinese translation, found in the *Madhyama-āgama* and in the *Ekottarika-āgama*. I provide a continuous translation of these three canonical versions at the end of the book in Chapter 13.[4] Besides the *Satipaṭṭhāna-sutta* and its two discourse parallels, other discourses also give important indications on the practice of mindfulness. I have sought to incorporate a representative selection of this material by including translations of excerpts that are mostly taken from discourses in the Chinese *Āgama*s, but at times also from Sanskrit fragments or Tibetan parallels. Most of these have to my knowledge so far not been translated into English. All translations in the following pages are my own.

In translating the parallel versions preserved in Chinese and other languages, I do not intend to imply a judgement of any kind about the relative value of these discourses vis-à-vis the Pāli canon. Instead, I offer these translations merely as an expedient means to enable the reader to gain a first-hand impression of the situation in these parallel versions. The wealth of discourses preserved in the Chinese *Āgama*s is largely unknown to the general reader, mostly due to the lack of translations. Hence I attempt to provide translations of at least a selection of relevant passages. In the footnotes to my translations I give references to the standard English translations of the relevant Pāli passage in order to facilitate comparison beyond the selected observations that I give regarding variations between the parallels.

In addition to the material found in the discourses, several texts

---

is that in SN 47.14 the Dharma and oneself are qualified as being one's "refuge".

4 My translations are throughout based on the CBETA edition, and at times I have followed variant readings or emendations suggested by the CBETA team. Since the present work is aimed at a general readership, I have not marked such instances in my translations and only explicitly note my own emendations of the text.

of relevance for a comparative study of *satipaṭṭhāna* are found in the Abhidharma or *śāstra* literature of different schools. These texts are generally later than the early discourses, although in individual instances they may preserve an early presentation of some aspects of the teachings. As my interest is mainly in the information provided in the early discourses, I turn to these other texts only occasionally.[5] This is also not intended as a judgement on the value of those texts. It only reflects my attempt to explore first and foremost the early discourses as the type of text that in general reflects the earliest stages in the history of Buddhist thought. In this way, I hope to provide a reference point that enables others to delineate in detail the important contributions made by later traditions to *satipaṭṭhāna* practice.

The two Chinese parallels to the *Satipaṭṭhāna-sutta* of the *Majjhima-nikāya*, found in the *Madhyama-āgama* and the *Ekottarika-āgama*, stem from different Buddhist schools. The *Madhyama-āgama* was with considerable probability transmitted by Sarvāstivāda reciters. In the case of the *Ekottarika-āgama* the school affiliation is somewhat uncertain; the most frequently suggested affiliation is the Mahāsāṅghika tradition. Both collections were translated into Chinese towards the end of the fourth century of the present era. Some of the extracts translated below are taken from the *Dīrgha-āgama*, probably transmitted by Dharmaguptaka reciters, and from the *Saṃyukta-āgama*, which appears to have been transmitted within the Mūlasarvāstivāda tradition(s). With regard to Sanskrit fragments, a Sarvāstivāda / Mūlasarvāstivāda affiliation is often probable; nearly all material in Tibetan translation comes from the Mūlasarvāstivāda tradition.

In general terms, none of the *Āgama*s or *Nikāya*s can be considered to be invariably historically earlier than others. Each of these collections contains early and late material and it would be an oversimplification to consider one particular collection as in principle earlier than the others.[6] The same applies also to discourse length. While the tendency to expansion and addition during oral transmission has naturally resulted in several long discourses that show signs of having

5 An exception is Śamathadeva's compendium of canonical quotations found in the *Abhidharmakośabhāṣya*, D 4094 or Q 5595, which in spite of its *śāstra* nature in actual fact is mainly a source for canonical discourses. In the following pages, I regularly rely on parallels found in this important source for early discourse material in Tibetan translation.

6 For a critical examination of the main suppositions of the three-*aṅga* theory and the idea that the *Saṃyukta-āgama* and *Saṃyutta-nikāya* are earlier than other discourse collections, cf. Anālayo 2011a: 696–700.

combined material of different provenance, this does not mean that long discourses in general must be late and what is short is inevitably early. Later developments can also take the form of a new and short discourse. Such developments are also not confined to prose, but can express themselves as well in verse. Thus there is no hard and fast principle that short poetic sayings are invariably earlier and long prose expositions must be later in appearance. Such oversimplifications, in spite of their appeal, tend to obscure the situation rather than clarify it. A proper assessment of earliness or lateness needs to be based on a detailed comparative study of all extant versions of a particular passage, evaluated against the background of relevant teachings that are related to the same topic in other discourses and by keeping in mind the historical stages in the development of Buddhist thought that may have a bearing on the matter.

Thus material preserved in the Chinese *Āgama*s has in principle a similar claim to being an authentic record of the teachings of the Buddha and his disciples as that found in the four Pāli *Nikāya*s, although the fact of translation into Chinese obviously carries with it the possibility of translation errors. This makes itself felt in the case of the *Ekottarika-āgama* in particular, whose translation was carried out under difficult circumstances during a war and thus in an unstable situation.[7] The *Ekottarika-āgama* parallel to the *Satipaṭṭhāna-sutta* is in fact somewhat irregular and at times has inconsistent presentations, possibly reflecting the difficult circumstances of its translation. Nevertheless, at other times it does appear to preserve a state in the textual development that is earlier than the other two discourse versions.

In comparing the parallel versions, my aim is not to reconstruct "the original *Satipaṭṭhāna-sutta*". Instead, I mainly intend to explore the perspective that emerges when emphasis is given to those instructions that are common ground among the three canonical versions and thus can reasonably well be expected to be early.[8] While material shared by all three discourses naturally stands at the foreground of my study, some of the exercises not found in all versions can still make a good claim at being genuine mindfulness

7 This is reported in the introduction to the *Ekottarika-āgama* translation; cf. T II 549a18.

8 My position here is based on Anālayo 2012c, where I argue the historical value of the early discourses and the principle that parallelisms usually point to a common early core.

practices. The fact that I do not take these up in detail is not meant to dismiss these exercises. Rather, I suggest leaving them "on stage", but letting them stand somewhat more in the background compared to those modes of contemplation that are found in all versions. In other words, instead of a black-and-white perspective that oscillates between accepting and rejecting, in order to reflect the complexity of the situation that emerges through a comparative study of the *Satipaṭṭhāna-sutta* in the light of its canonical parallels, I would like to propose a three-dimensional perspective. In this way, the material that has come down to us in the different canonical discourse versions can be positioned in different ways in order to reflect their respective importance for the practice and their probable degree of earliness.

From an academic viewpoint it is not possible to reconstruct with certainty what the historical Buddha said.[9] Within the limits of the source material at our disposal, however, the comparative study of the early discourses takes us back as close as possible to the original delivery of a particular teaching. This thereby offers a window onto the earliest stages of Buddhist thought on mindfulness meditation. Given that this early stage would have been the common starting point of the different Buddhist schools and traditions, I hope that my examination will be of interest to followers of any Buddhist tradition. In order to present such a common ground, I have endeavoured to base my exploration predominantly on material that has been preserved in the canonical discourses of more than one school. On the rare occasions when I depart from this approach, I alert the reader to the fact that the passage taken up is only preserved in one tradition.

When a discourse has only been preserved in the Pāli canon, no firm conclusion can be drawn from the absence of a parallel. The *Āgama*s preserved in Chinese stem from different schools, therefore the lack of a parallel may at times just be due to the fact that we do not have a complete collection of the discourses of any other school to compare with the Theravāda collection. Where parallels exist, however, differences between the Pāli version and its counterparts do allow us to draw conclusions. In fact, it is precisely by comparing parallel versions that transmission errors can be detected.

9 The main change I would have made in revising my previous book would have been to replace expressions like "the Buddha said" with formulations of the type "the Buddha is reported to have said."

In the excerpt translations in the following chapters, I have tried to avoid gendered terminology, in order to ensure that my presentation does not give the impression of being meant for male practitioners only. The actual texts often have a monk as their protagonist and I have kept to the original formulation in the complete translations of the three canonical versions at the end of this book, so as to enable the reader to see the text as truthful to the original as possible within the confines of my translation abilities. In excerpts that come interspersed in my study, however, I have replaced "monk" with "... one", in order to ensure that the meditation instructions are of similar appeal to any reader, monastic or lay, male or female.

The translation terminology used here differs in some cases from my earlier monograph on *satipaṭṭhāna*. I have decided to follow the general custom of translating *saññā* as "perception",[10] and I render *paṭicca samuppāda* just as "dependent arising". When translating from the Chinese, here and elsewhere I employ Pāli terms in my translation for the sake of ease of comparison, without thereby intending to take a position on the language of the original manuscript used for translation into Chinese. Exceptions are terms like "Dharma" and "Nirvāṇa", both of which are now commonly used in Western publications.

---

10 The translation "(conceptual) identification" by Potter 1996: 128 seems to me to capture the nuances of *saññā* well. However, I realize that using translations that differ from the standard renderings employed in most publications simply results in making things more difficult for most readers, so I have decided to stick to the established usage "perception", following the example set by Skilling 1997: 477 n.31.

I

ASPECTS OF *SATIPAṬṬHĀNA*

As a starting point for my exploration of perspectives on *satipaṭṭhāna*, I would like to give an overview of the three main discourse versions employed in my study: the *Satipaṭṭhāna-sutta* of the *Majjhima-nikāya* and its two Chinese parallels in the *Madhyama-āgama* and in the *Ekottarika-āgama*. In Figure 1.1, I list the exercises found in each of these three versions, so as to give a first impression of the degree of difference between the parallels. The four *satipaṭṭhāna*s are listed on the left, and to the right of each are the corresponding contemplations in the three versions in order of increasing complexity.

Even a brief glance at Figure 1.1 shows that the three parallel versions differ considerably in regard to contemplation of the body and in relation to contemplation of dharmas. These and other variations will be a continuous theme in the coming chapters.

In this chapter, I first consider three general aspects of *satipaṭṭhāna*. I begin with the indication that *satipaṭṭhāna* is a "direct path". Then I survey variations in the parts of the discourse that I have dubbed the "definition" and the "refrain". In the next chapter, I look at the significance of mindfulness. Subsequent chapters are dedicated to exploring mindfulness in action, namely the *satipaṭṭhāna* meditation exercises listed in Figure 1.1.

satipaṭṭhāna	*Ekottarika-āgama*	*Majjhima-nikāya*	*Madhyama-āgama*
body	anatomical parts 4 elements bodily orifices corpse	breathing postures activities anatomical parts 4 elements corpse	postures activities counter unwholesome state forceful mind control breathing experience of 4 absorptions perception of light reviewing sign anatomical parts 6 elements corpse
feelings	3 and 6 types	3 and 6 types	3 and 18 types
mind	12 pairs	8 pairs	10 pairs
dharmas	awakening factors absorptions	hindrances aggregates sense-spheres awakening factors noble truths	sense-spheres hindrances awakening factors

Fig. 1.1 Overview of the *Satipaṭṭhāna-sutta* and its parallels

I.1 THE "DIRECT PATH"

The introductory passage in the three discourse versions reads as follows:

Majjhima-nikāya:

> This is the direct [literally: one-going] path for the purification of beings, for the surmounting of sorrow and lamentation, for the disappearance of *dukkha* and discontent, for acquiring the true method, for the realization of Nirvāṇa, namely, the four *satipaṭṭhāna*s.

Madhyama-āgama:

> There is one path for the purification of beings, for going beyond sorrow and fear, for eradicating *dukkha* and distress, for abandoning weeping and tears, for attaining the right Dharma, namely the four *satipaṭṭhānas*.

Ekottarika-āgama:

> There is a one-going path for the purification of the actions of living beings, for removing worry and sorrow, for being without vexations, for attaining great knowledge and wisdom, for accomplishing the realization of Nirvāṇa. That is: the five hindrances should be abandoned and the four *satipaṭṭhāna*s should be attended to.

The basic import of this passage is similar in the three versions: *satipaṭṭhāna* is a path of purification.[1] This path is qualified in the Chinese translations as "one" path or a "one-going" path, which as far as I can tell translates an original corresponding to the expression *ekāyana* in the Pāli version.

While the commentarial traditions envisage various nuances suggested by this expression,[2] I would opt for the sense of a "direct path", based on the usage of the same expression in one other canonical passage outside of the *satipaṭṭhāna* context. This is found in the *Mahāsīhanāda-sutta* and similarly in a partial Chinese parallel in the *Ekottarika-āgama*. In what follows, I translate the relevant section from the *Ekottarika-āgama* version:[3]

> It is just as a great pond that is not far away from a village, whose water is totally pure and clean, and suppose a person comes by one path straight [towards it]. A person, who has [good] eyesight and who sees from a distance this person coming, will know that this person will certainly reach the water pond, no doubt.[4]

The *Mahāsīhanāda-sutta* additionally indicates that the person walking on the *ekāyana* path to the pond is oppressed by heat and thirst.[5] This renders the prospect of reaching the pond rather attractive, making the whole simile come alive. The two versions continue by describing how a little later the observer sees that the other person has indeed reached the pond and taken a bath.

---

1 For a more detailed discussion of the notion of purification in early Buddhism, cf. Anālayo 2012f.

2 Cf. the survey in Anālayo 2003b: 27 and the discussion in Gethin 1992: 59–66.

3 EĀ 50.6 at T II 812a27 to 812b1.

4 The description of the attractive nature of the pond in the parallel MN 12 at MN I 76,28 (translated Ñāṇamoli 1995: 172) is more detailed, indicating that the water is cool and the banks are smooth and delightful, with a dense grove nearby.

5 MN 12 at MN I 76,29.

This simile is quite significant for appreciating *ekāyana* in its early Buddhist usage, because it has no direct relation to meditation practice and thus shows how the term was used in general in early Buddhist texts. The sense that emerges from this passage is that one path leads directly to the pond. Thus here *ekāyana* stands for "one direct path".

Several scholars have suggested alternative ways of understanding the expression *ekāyana*. Taking into account corresponding expressions in other ancient Indian texts outside of the Buddhist tradition, they suggest that the term conveys the sense of a "converging point", a "point of confluence", or "unification".[6] Understood in this sense, the *Satipaṭṭhāna-sutta* and its parallels would introduce the path of *satipaṭṭhāna* as a converging point for various types of practices, resulting in a unified or integrated path.

This suggestion is appealing from a practical perspective, as it reminds us that in early Buddhist thought *satipaṭṭhāna* is one of several practices to be cultivated, that it necessarily stands within the context of a cultivation of the noble eightfold path. However, it seems to me that the early discourses do not support the interpretation of *satipaṭṭhāna* as a converging point. While it is certainly important to consider the meanings a particular term has in ancient Indian texts in general, such an understanding needs to be tested by checking whether the same applies to the way the term is used in the early Buddhist texts.

The idea of a convergence or a confluence does make an appearance in the early discourses, but not in relation to *satipaṭṭhāna*. A discourse in the *Aṅguttara-nikāya* presents the power of wisdom as the converging point of the five mental faculties – which include the faculty of mindfulness – a role comparable to the peak of a roof.[7] While this discourse does not appear to have a parallel, the presentation of wisdom as the converging point for the other faculties, comparable to the peak of a roof that provides stability to the rafters, recurs in the *Saṃyutta-nikāya* and the *Saṃyukta-āgama*.[8] Judging from this simile, if a mental faculty were to be singled out

6 Kuan 2001: 164 and Nattier 2007: 196–9; cf. also Sujato 2005: 177–86, who develops a similar argument in an in my view unconvincing attempt to present *satipaṭṭhāna* as mainly an auxiliary for the development of absorption.

7 AN 5.12 at AN III 10,7 (translated Bodhi 2012: 636).

8 Cf., e.g., SN 48.52 at SN V 228,17 (translated Bodhi 2000: 1696) and its parallel SĀ 654 at T II 183b21.

as the "converging point", the one to choose would be wisdom. In contrast, mindfulness is one of the factors that converge on wisdom; it is one of the rafters, rather than being itself the roof peak or converging point.

A similar nuance emerges from the *Mahācattārīsaka-sutta* and its parallels, where the noble eightfold path leads up to the tenfold path of an arahant, which covers also right knowledge and right liberation.[9] That is, right knowledge and right liberation as representatives of the quality of wisdom would be the converging point of various types of practices, whose combination results in an integrated path. Another passage proclaims that, from an early Buddhist viewpoint, all things have liberation as their essence.[10] In other words, liberation could be considered a converging point of various practices in early Buddhist thought. In sum, as far as I can tell *satipaṭṭhāna* is not seen as the converging point of other practices in the early discourses. Instead, it is one of the practices that converge on wisdom and liberation.

The sense of a convergence would also not work for the simile in the *Mahāsīhanāda-sutta* and its parallel, where the situation depicts a single path that leads directly to the pond. There does not seem to be an allusion in the simile that this path is a converging point of other paths.

An idea that would fit the simile in the *Mahāsīhanāda-sutta* and its parallel would be the notion of a path that leads in one direction only. However, this would not work for *satipaṭṭhāna* meditation, which has a range of benefits. The first *satipaṭṭhāna* of body contemplation alone can have various results, ranging from overcoming discontent to experiencing deep concentration as well as gaining insight (a topic that I will discuss in more detail in Chapter 3). This is exemplified in the monk Anuruddha, who is often closely associated in the early discourses with the practice of *satipaṭṭhāna*. According to a discourse in the *Saṃyutta-nikāya* and its *Saṃyukta-āgama* parallel, Anuruddha's various attainments – which include supernormal powers resulting from deep concentration and liberating insight through the

---

9 MN 117 at MN III 76,1 (translated Ñāṇamoli 1995: 938) and its parallels SHT V 1125 R3, Sander and Waldschmidt 1985: 120, SHT VIII 1919 A1, Bechert and Wille 2000: 100, MĀ 189 at T I 736b20, and D 4094 *nyu* 46b4 or Q 5595 *thu* 86b2.

10 AN 8.83 at AN IV 339,8 (translated Bodhi 2012: 1232), with a similar indication found in the parallel MĀ 113 at T I 602c12; cf. also T 59 at T I 855c15.

destruction of the defilements – were the outcome of his practice of *satipaṭṭhāna*.[11] Thus *satipaṭṭhāna* does not lead in one direction only. Instead, *satipaṭṭhāna* is a practice that leads in more than one direction, as it builds a foundation for the development of insight as well as of tranquillity.

In sum, while alternative translations certainly add richness to our understanding of the expression *ekāyana*, it seems to me that the notion of a "direct path" fits the canonical usage best. Confirmation for this suggestion can be gathered from a discourse in the *Saṃyukta-āgama*, which qualifies the six recollections with the expression that in this collection functions as the counterpart to the Pāli term *ekāyano*, followed by an indication that this means a "straight path".[12]

Applying this sense to the present context, I understand *satipaṭṭhāna* to be the direct path for purifying the mind and thus proceeding towards liberation. Here mindfulness directly feeds into the development of insight, as it directly faces one's present-moment experience, uncovering its various features. Directly facing one's own condition right now is what informs progress along the path, being the appropriate attitude that one should maintain during formal practice and in everyday life. Summing up, in my view a central aspect of *satipaṭṭhāna* meditation is facing things directly with awareness.

I.2 THE "DEFINITION" OF SATIPAṬṬHĀNA

The part I refer to as the "definition" outlines the practice of *satipaṭṭhāna* in brief. This definition reads as follows in the three parallel versions:

---

11 SN 52.3 at SN V 298,5 (translated Bodhi 2000: 1754) and its parallel SĀ 537 at T II 139c22 report that Anuruddha's gain of supernormal knowledges was the outcome of his practice of *satipaṭṭhāna*. The commentary, Spk III 262,6, explains that the reference is to the six supernormal knowledges, i.e., supernormal powers, the divine ear, telepathic knowledge of the minds of others, recollection of past lives, the divine eye, and the destruction of the influxes.

12 SĀ 550 at T II 143b22+29 (on the translation terminology used in the first instance cf. Nattier 2007: 187f; that the reference to a straight path in the second instance would support an understanding of *ekāyano* as conveying straightness of direction has already been noticed by Harrison 2007: 208). While the Pāli parallel AN 6.26 at AN III 314,22 (translated Bodhi 2012: 885) does not use the qualification *ekāyana*, a Sanskrit fragment parallel, MS 2380/1/1+2 r1, Harrison 2007: 202, speaks also of the *ekāyano mārgaḥ*, but unfortunately has not preserved the part of the discourse corresponding to the section that has the gloss on the straight path.

Majjhima-nikāya:

> What are the four [*satipaṭṭhāna*s]? Here, in regard to the body ... one abides contemplating the body, diligent, clearly knowing, and mindful, free from desires and discontent with regard to the world. In regard to feelings ... the mind ... dharmas one abides contemplating dharmas, diligent, clearly knowing, and mindful, free from desires and discontent with regard to the world.

Madhyama-āgama:

> What are the four [*satipaṭṭhāna*s]? [They are] the *satipaṭṭhāna* of contemplating the body as a body ... feelings ... mind ... dharmas as dharmas.

Ekottarika-āgama:

> How to attend to the four *satipaṭṭhāna*s? Here ... [in regard to] one's own body one contemplates [the body] internally, and by removing evil thoughts and being free from worry and sorrow [one experiences joy in oneself] ... one contemplates the body externally ... the body internally and externally ... feelings internally ... feelings externally ... feelings internally and externally ... mind internally ... mind externally ... mind internally and externally ... dharmas internally ... dharmas externally... dharmas internally and externally, and [by removing evil thoughts and being free from worry and sorrow] one experiences joy in oneself.

Comparing the above passages, the *Majjhima-nikāya* and *Ekottarika-āgama* versions agree on stipulating mental balance as a key feature of mindfulness, expressed either in terms of being "free from desires and discontent with regard to the world" or as "removing evil thoughts and being free from worry and sorrow".

The *Ekottarika-āgama* discourse presents the additional qualification that in this way one "experiences joy in oneself", a recurrent indication made in this version elsewhere, even in relation to practices like reviewing the anatomical constitution of the body or the stages of decay of a corpse. This version also takes up the need to undertake *satipaṭṭhāna* internally and externally already at this point, something the parallel versions only mention in the part of the discourses that I have dubbed the "refrain". Notably, a presentation similar in this respect to the *Ekottarika-āgama* discourse can be found in an early Abhidharma text of the Theravāda tradition, the *Vibhaṅga*.[13]

The *Madhyama-āgama* version, however, merely lists the four *satipaṭṭhāna*s and thus gives no further indications at all. This absence needs to be considered in the light of the fact that a wide range of other texts speak of the need for *satipaṭṭhāna* practice to combine mindfulness with being diligent, with clearly knowing, and with removing desires and sorrow in regard to the world. Such passages occur in a variety of contexts not confined to a detailed exposition of *satipaṭṭhāna*. Often, as in the *Ekottarika-āgama* version, such passages stipulate that *satipaṭṭhāna* should be practised internally, externally, and internally and externally. This form of presentation occurs among discourses in the *Dīrgha-āgama* and the *Saṃyukta-āgama*,[14] in Sanskrit fragments whose topic is the four *satipaṭṭhānas*,[15] as well as in Sanskrit fragments of the *Mahāparinirvāṇa-sūtra*.[16] Looking beyond the early discourses, the same can be found in Abhidharma works of the Sarvāstivāda and Dharmaguptaka tradition, namely the *Dharmaskandha* and the **Śāriputrābhidharma*,[17] as well as in the *Śrāvakabhūmi* of the Yogācāra school.[18] Other occurrences are in works like the *Arthaviniścaya-sūtra*,[19] the *Daśabhūmika-sūtra*,[20] and in *Prajñāpāramitā* literature.[21]

In view of this range of texts supporting the form of presentation in the "definition" of the *Satipaṭṭhāna-sutta*, the absence of a counterpart in the *Madhyama-āgama* version is probably less weighty than it might first seem. That is, even though this part of the *Satipaṭṭhāna-sutta* does not recur in this form in both discourse parallels, it nevertheless probably reflects an early formulation of the essential aspects of *satipaṭṭhāna* meditation.

---

13 Vibh 193,2 (translated Thiṭṭila 1969: 251).

14 DĀ 4 at T I 35c27 and SĀ 639 at T II 177b3 (translated above at the outset of the book).

15 SHT I 614 aV+R, Waldschmidt 1965: 272, cf. also Pischel 1904: 1143, SHT III 862 V+R, Waldschmidt 1971: 111, SHT V 1180 A+B, Sander and Waldschmidt 1985: 174, and SHT IX 3039, Bechert and Wille 2004: 333.

16 S 360 folio 167R and folio 173V, Waldschmidt 1950: 15 and 18.

17 T 1537 at T XXVI 475c28 and T 1548 at T XXVIII 613a11.

18 Shukla 1973: 299,18.

19 Samtani 1971: 28,10.

20 Rahder 1926: 38,18.

21 Dutt 1934/2000: 204,4 and Ghosa 1914: 1427.

I would therefore conclude that properly undertaking *satipaṭṭhāna* does seem to require that mindfulness is established with continuity, corresponding to the quality of being "diligent" or more literally "ardent". Such mindfulness needs to be combined with an element of "clear knowing" or "clear comprehension" that understands what is being held present in the mind through mindfulness. Such a combination should lead to a balanced mental attitude that is not shaken by desires, worries, or dejection in regard to the world.

I.3 THE "REFRAIN" OF SATIPAṬṬHĀNA

The passage that I have dubbed the "refrain" provides instructions of general significance that are given in the *Satipaṭṭhāna-sutta* after each of the individual contemplations. In the *Ekottarika-āgama* version, this passage appears to have been preserved in full only for contemplation of feelings, mind, and dharmas. I take the lack of the full refrain in the case of the contemplation of the body to be the result of an error in transmission, which could easily have happened in view of the difficulties during the time of the translation of this collection. For the sake of comparison, therefore, in what follows I translate the "refrain" that in the three parallel versions occurs in relation to contemplation of feelings. This reads as follows:

Majjhima-nikāya:

> In regard to feelings one abides contemplating feelings internally … externally … internally and externally.
>
> Or one abides contemplating the nature of arising … the nature of passing away … the nature of arising and passing away in feelings.
>
> Or mindfulness that "there is feeling" is established in oneself just for the sake of bare knowledge and for the sake of continuous mindfulness. And one abides independent, not clinging to anything in the world.

Madhyama-āgama:

> In this way … one contemplates feelings as feelings internally and … externally. One establishes mindfulness in feelings and is endowed with knowledge, vision, understanding, and penetration.

Ekottarika-āgama:

> One [contemplates] their nature of arising ... of ceasing ... of arising and ceasing ...
>
> Further, one is able to know and able to see that these are feelings that manifest here and now, giving attention to their origination. Not depending on anything, one experiences joy in oneself [by removing evil thoughts and being free from worry and sorrow], not arousing worldly perceptions.
>
> Herein one is also not agitated, and because of not being agitated one attains Nirvāṇa, knowing as it really is that "birth and death have been extinguished, the holy life has been established, what had to be done has been done, there is no more experiencing of [another] existence."
>
> In this way ... one contemplates one's own feelings internally, discarding distracted thoughts and [experiencing joy in oneself by removing evil thoughts and] being free from worry and sorrow ... externally ... internally and externally ...

As in the case of the "definition" discussed earlier, central themes from the "refrain" of the *Satipaṭṭhāna-sutta* recur in the *Ekottarika-āgama* discourse, which in fact gives a more detailed account of what can be expected from successful *satipaṭṭhāna* meditation, namely the attainment of full awakening. In contrast to these two versions, the *Madhyama-āgama* parallel is again rather brief. In addition to the extract quoted above, the *Madhyama-āgama* discourse also indicates that a monk or a nun who contemplates in this way even for a short time can be reckoned to be practising *satipaṭṭhāna*.

Perhaps the most striking difference is that the *Madhyama-āgama* version does not mention contemplation of impermanence at all. As the need to be aware of arising and passing away is found in the *Satipaṭṭhāna-sutta* and in the *Ekottarika-āgama* version, this seems to me to be another case in which the *Madhyama-āgama* presentation should probably be given less weight. That is, I am inclined to follow the suggestion in the other two canonical discourses that contemplation of impermanence should be considered an integral aspect of *satipaṭṭhāna* practice. The fact that the indications given in the "refrain" rarely occur on their own, unlike the specifications provided in the "definition", makes it harder to locate parallels that support this conclusion. However, at least one supportive instance can be found in the description of *satipaṭṭhāna* meditation in the **Śāriputrābhidharma*, a Dharmaguptaka work, which also mentions contemplation of arising, passing away, and both.[22]

The relevance of contemplating impermanence for *satipaṭṭhāna* meditation also emerges from the description of mindfulness of breathing in the *Ānāpānasati-sutta* of the *Majjhima-nikāya*, which has similarly worded parallels in the *Saṃyukta-āgama* and in the Mahāsāṅghika *Vinaya*. (A more detailed discussion of these instructions can be found in Chapter 12.) The three versions agree on presenting various aspects related to the breath as a way of implementing the four *satipaṭṭhāna*s. All of these are undertaken against the background of awareness of the breath moving in and out. Such awareness is a continuous reminder of the impermanent nature of the breath and, by extension, of the impermanence of the whole of one's experience. Here awareness of the changing nature of observed phenomena is clearly integral to *satipaṭṭhāna* practice.

The three versions agree that *satipaṭṭhāna* should be undertaken not only internally, but also externally. Interpretations of this instruction vary in modern meditation circles as well as in Buddhist texts.[23] Attempting to evaluate these from the viewpoint of the early discourses requires a degree of inference, as explicit definitions only start with early Abhidharma literature. Here the *Vibhaṅga* of the Theravāda tradition and the *Dharmaskandha* of the Sarvāstivāda tradition indicate that "external" refers to contemplating other beings.[24]

A passage pointing to a similar understanding in the early discourses can be found in the *Janavasabha-sutta* and its *Dīrgha-āgama* parallel. Here is the relevant passage from the *Dīrgha-āgama* version:[25]

> What are the four [*satipaṭṭhāna*s]? In regard to the internal body one contemplates the body, diligently without remiss, with collected mindfulness that is not lost, removing lust and discontent in the world. In regard to the external body one contemplates the body, diligently without remiss, with collected mindfulness that is not lost, removing lust and discontent in the world. In regard to the internal and external body one contemplates the body, diligently without

22 T 1548 at T XXVIII 614b15.

23 Cf. Anālayo 2003b: 94ff; for a detailed study of interpretations of internal and external contemplation in various Buddhist texts cf. Schmithausen 2012.

24 Vibh 194,2 (translated Thiṭṭila 1969: 252) and T 1537 at T XXVI 475c28.

25 DĀ 4 at T I 35c27 to 36a3.

> remiss, with collected mindfulness that is not lost, removing lust and discontent in the world.
>
> Contemplation of feelings, the mind, and dharmas is just like that, being diligently without remiss, with collected mindfulness that is not lost, removing lust and discontent in the world.
>
> Having contemplated the body internally, one arouses knowledge of the bodies of others. Having contemplated feelings internally, one arouses knowledge of the feelings of others. Having contemplated the mind internally, one arouses knowledge of the mind of others. Having contemplated dharmas internally, one arouses knowledge of the dharmas of others.

The parallel in the *Janavasabha-sutta* additionally indicates that such knowledge and vision of the body, and so on, of others takes place after one has gained concentration through internal *satipaṭṭhāna* contemplation.[26] The two versions thus clearly agree that the progression from internal to external *satipaṭṭhāna* practice requires turning one's awareness from contemplating oneself to contemplating others.

The *Saḷāyatanavibhaṅga-sutta* and its parallels preserved in Chinese and Tibetan describe an actual instance of awareness of others as a form of *satipaṭṭhāna* practice. The passage in question depicts three *satipaṭṭhānas* practised by the Buddha as a teacher. (I take these up in more detail in Chapter 12.) With each of these three *satipaṭṭhānas* the objects are his disciples. The Buddha is aware when they all listen to him and follow his instructions, or when only some listen, or when none of them is paying proper attention.

While this particular mode of *satipaṭṭhāna* is a specific quality of the Buddha, the ability to recognize whether one's audience is paying attention to what one says is within the reach of anyone, even without previous training in meditation or concentration. One does not need telepathic powers to become aware of listeners' reactions, as one can deduce what is taking place from their bodily postures and facial expressions.

---

26 DN 18 at DN II 216,13 (translated Walshe 1987: 298). Another difference is a matter of sequence, as DN 18 just describes internal contemplation of the body before turning to contemplating the body of another, so that it has no preceding reference to external and internal-and-external contemplation of the body. DN 18 then takes up feeling, mind, and dharmas only after having described contemplation of the body of another. Another parallel, T 9 at T I 216a9, does not offer any specification about the nature of external contemplation.

According to the *Sampasādanīya-sutta* and its *Dīrgha-āgama* parallel, one of four ways of knowing the state of mind of another is precisely by looking at their body and taking into account the way they speak. The relevant passage in the *Dīrgha-āgama* version reads as follows:[27]

> Having on one's own observed the body or heard the speech of another, one says to that person: "Your mind is like this, your mind is like this."

The *Sampasādanīya-sutta* does not explicitly mention observing the body. According to its presentation of this way of knowing, one proceeds by reflecting on what one has heard and then comes to the conclusion that the mind of the other is in a certain way.[28]

Thus the following points emerge:

- The *Janavasabha-sutta* and its parallel concord with the early Abhidharma that external *satipaṭṭhāna* refers to others.
- The *Saḷāyatanavibhaṅga-sutta* and its parallels provide an explicit relationship between *satipaṭṭhāna* and knowing the attitude of others in a way that can be undertaken even without needing to rely on telepathy.
- The *Sampasādanīya-sutta* and its parallel confirm that knowledge of the mind of another can be gained by inference.

It thus seems safe to conclude that the original sense of external *satipaṭṭhāna* meditation was concerned with contemplating others.

I.4 SUMMARY

The practice of *satipaṭṭhāna* offers a "direct path" for the development of liberating insight by directly facing whatever happens with awareness. This requires an effort to ensure that mindfulness is established with continuity and in combination with the presence of clear understanding. Underpinned by the cultivation of these mental qualities, *satipaṭṭhāna* meditation takes place with a balanced mental attitude that remains aloof from reactive patterns of desire and aversion. Engaging in actual *satipaṭṭhāna* practice in this way eventually leads to awareness of the impermanent nature of

---

27 DĀ 18 at T I 78a3 to 78a4.

28 DN 28 at DN III 104,1 (translated Walshe 1987: 419). A Sanskrit fragment has preserved parts of a parallel version to this passage, Or. 15009/137r6, Kudo 2009: 189.

contemplated phenomena; whereby one "keeps calmly knowing change". An integral aspect of *satipaṭṭhāna* meditation is to proceed from observing phenomena in oneself to becoming aware of when and how they occur in others.

II

MINDFULNESS

In this chapter I examine the quality of mindfulness itself. First I survey passages in the discourses that describe a loss of mindfulness and its consequences. Then I explore the protective function of mindfulness. Finally I take another look at the relationship between mindfulness and memory, which I have already discussed to some degree in my earlier book on *satipaṭṭhāna*.[1]

II.1 LOSS OF MINDFULNESS

For an appreciation of the functions of mindfulness in early Buddhist thought, helpful indications can be gathered from passages that depict the results of the absence of mindfulness. Descriptions of what happens when mindfulness is lost indirectly show what functions mindfulness was held to perform. A recurrent theme in such passages is that the absence of mindfulness results in the mind being overwhelmed by sensual desire.

The "protective" function exercised by mindfulness in this way points to an important ethical dimension of mindfulness practice. A discourse in the *Saṃyutta-nikāya* and its *Saṃyukta-āgama* parallel illustrates this ethical dimension with the example of a monk who goes to beg for food without having established mindfulness. Here is the relevant part from the *Saṃyukta-āgama* version:[2]

1 Anālayo 2003b: 46ff.
2 SĀ 1260 at T II 345c14 to 345c17.

> A foolish and ignorant person, who dwells in dependence on a village, puts on the robes in the morning, takes the alms bowl, and enters the village to beg for alms without properly guarding the body, without restraint of the sense-doors, and without the mind being collected through mindfulness.[3]
>
> On seeing women, he arouses improper attention and, grasping the sign of their bodily form,[4] lustful sensual desires appear in his mind. Lustful sensual desires having appeared, he is ablaze with the fire of sensual desire, which burns his body and mind.[5]

Like its *Saṃyutta-nikāya* parallel, the *Saṃyukta-āgama* discourse indicates that eventually the monk disrobes. From a monastic perspective, his failure to establish mindfulness, together with his not guarding the body and loss of sense-restraint, is thus a rather grave matter.

The coexistence in this passage of mindfulness, guarding the body, and sense-restraint shows the close interrelation of these practices. In fact, mindfulness of one's present condition naturally comes with awareness of one's bodily activities and of what one experiences through the senses. Guarding the body and maintaining sense-restraint in turn collaborate with established mindfulness in making one aware as soon as something manifests through the senses that could disturb one's mental equipoise.

The point of the above description does not seem to be that the monk just forgets what he is about to do because he lacks mindfulness. The parallel versions do not report that he was no longer able to collect his almsfood or that he forgot the way back to his dwelling place. Rather, they highlight that he eventually disrobed. The *Saṃyukta-āgama* version is more detailed in this respect, as it describes that, once his body and mind were on fire with sensual desire, he was no longer able to delight in being in an empty place or at the root of a tree. That is, recalling his immediate purpose does not appear to

---

3 According to the parallel SN 20.10 at SN II 271,6 (translated Bodhi 2000: 711), besides not protecting the body, he also did not protect his speech or his mind.

4 A "sign" (*nimitta*) refers to the characteristic(s) of a particular object to which one pays attention; for a more detailed discussion, cf. Anālayo 2003a.

5 SN 20.10 additionally notes that the women were lightly clad; another difference is that SN 20.10 does not mention improper attention. SN 20.10 also does not explicitly indicate that as a result of what he has seen the monk is ablaze in body and mind.

be the problem. Instead, the problem is that his lack of mindfulness caused the arising of sensual desire that affected his subsequent life and practice to such an extent that in the end he decided to disrobe. This shows that the quality of mindfulness described in this passage would not represent the monk's ability to keep doing what he had set out to do.

Does the monk's loss of mindfulness then imply that he was no longer aware of his role as a monk? After all, if he had been aware of his role as a monk he would have avoided looking at women in a way that arouses lust in his mind. A similar passage in another discourse in the *Saṃyutta-nikāya* and in the *Saṃyukta-āgama* suggests that this is also not the central function of mindfulness in such a situation. This passage depicts a king who faces the same problem. When he enters his harem without sense-restraint, without protecting the body, and without having established mindfulness, he is overwhelmed by lust.[6] For a king to be aware of his role would not be of much help in such a situation, since that role is quite compatible with feeling lustful desires for the females in his harem. Thus, a loss of mindfulness leading to the arising of sensual desire does not appear to be necessarily related to forgetting one's role or what one is about to do.

The problem of a lack of mindfulness leading to the arising of lust recurs in a set of stanzas in a discourse in the *Saṃyutta-nikāya*, with parallels in the *Saṃyukta-āgama* and in a discourse quotation preserved in Tibetan translation. These stanzas elaborate on the meaning of a succinct teaching (also given, according to a discourse in the *Udāna*, on another occasion to the ascetic Bāhiya), instructing that one should remain just with what is seen, heard, etc.[7] Here is the relevant passage from the *Saṃyukta-āgama*:[8]

> If, on having seen a form with the eye,
> Right mindfulness has been lost,
> Then, in relation to the form that has been seen,
> The sign will be grasped with thoughts of craving.
> For one who grasps the sign with craving and delight,
> The mind will constantly be bound by attachment.

---

6 SN 35.127 at SN IV 112,28 (translated Bodhi 2000: 1199) and its parallel SĀ 1165 at T II 311b16.

7 Ud 1.10 at Ud 8,5 (translated Ireland 1990: 20); cf. Anālayo 2003b: 229ff.

8 SĀ 312 at T II 90a20 to 90a22.

In agreement with its parallels, the *Saṃyukta-āgama* discourse indicates that the same detrimental repercussions can be expected for being without mindfulness at the other sense-doors.[9] Given that in this stanza guarding the body and sense-restraint are not mentioned, it becomes clear that it is precisely the loss of mindfulness that is responsible for lust manifesting in the mind when one sees forms, etc. By contrast, when mindfulness is established one is able to remain just with what is seen, etc., without unwholesome reactions arising.[10]

This helps to explain the role of mindfulness in the passages depicting the repercussions of being without mindfulness. When mindfulness is established, one becomes fully aware of what is present, without getting carried away by mental reactions. Being mindful in this way, in what is seen there will truly be only what is seen. The task is not to avoid seeing things altogether, but to see them without unwholesome reactions. Being fully aware of what is taking place right now without reacting in unwholesome ways is central to the protective function of mindfulness.

II.2 PROTECTIVE MINDFULNESS

The notion of protection through establishing mindfulness finds an illustration in a simile in another discourse in the *Saṃyutta-nikāya* and the *Saṃyukta-āgama* that involves a monkey. In what follows, I translate the *Saṃyukta-āgama* version of the simile.[11]

> Among the Himalayas, there are icy and steep places, difficult to access even for monkeys, let alone humans. There are also mountains where monkeys dwell, but no humans. There are also mountains where people and animals dwell together.[12]

---

9 SN 35.95 at SN IV 73,18 (translated Bodhi 2000: 1176) and D 4094 *ju* 241b6 or Q 5595 *tu* 276a5; cf. also Sanskrit fragments SHT V 1311, Sander and Waldschmidt 1985: 215f, and SHT X 4097, Wille 2008: 265.

10 Brown et al. 2007: 212 explain that "a mindful mode of processing involves a receptive state of mind, wherein attention is kept to a bare registering of the facts observed. When used in this way to prolong that initial contact with the world, the basic capacities for awareness and attention permit the individual to 'be present' to reality as it is rather than to react to it."

11 SĀ 620 at T II 173b21 to 173b29.

12 The description of the location in the parallel SN 47.7 at SN V 148,8 (translated Bodhi 2000: 1633) does not mention coldness, instead characterizing these areas as being difficult to reach and rugged.

> The hunter takes sticky resin and puts it on top of some grass in a place where monkeys roam. Those monkeys who are clever keep far away from it and leave, but a foolish monkey is unable to avoid it. It touches it a little with a hand and the resin sticks to the hand. Using the second hand it then wishes to get off and tries to be free from it, so both hands stick to the resin. With the feet it tries to get off and the resin sticks to the feet. With the mouth it gnaws the grass and thereby the resin sticks to the mouth. The resin sticks to these five parts alike.[13]
>
> [The monkey] lies on the ground, joined together as if it were rolled up. The hunter comes, spears [the monkey] on a stick and, carrying it on his back, leaves.[14]

The parallel versions agree that the simile illustrates the need to beware of straying from one's ancestral domain: the four *satipaṭṭhāna*s. Straying out of this ancestral domain takes place when one pursues the pleasures of the five senses, which the *Saṃyutta-nikāya* version identifies as the domain of Māra,[15] the Buddhist personification of what obstructs the path to liberation.

The *Saṃyukta-āgama* discourse translated above then continues by illustrating how one strays from one's own domain of the four *satipaṭṭhāna*s with the example of a monk who goes begging without properly protecting the body and without sense-restraint. On seeing objects of the five senses, lust and attachment arise, whereby the monk is bound in five ways and at the mercy of Māra. This echoes the passage discussed above in which a monk who is without mindfulness becomes prey to sensual desire on seeing women during his almsround.

In terms of the simile of the monkey, without the protective distance afforded by established mindfulness, one is in danger of getting "stuck" in the world of the five senses. Once this happens, the tendency is to get ever more stuck through mental elaborations and associations, like the silly monkey who ends up with all its limbs stuck to the resin. To avoid getting stuck in the world of the

---

13 In SN 47.7 the monkey first uses one foot. After that gets stuck, it uses the other foot.

14 SN 47.7 reports that the monkey is screeching, but does not compare its predicament to being as if rolled up. It also precedes its description of the action taken by the hunter by indicating that, in this way, the monkey has met with calamity and is at the mercy of the hunter.

15 SN 47.7 at SN V 149,8.

senses, one had better stay in the high mountain areas of mindfulness practice.

Another simile on *satipaṭṭhāna* as one's proper domain describes a quail caught by a hawk. Here is the *Saṃyukta-āgama* version of the simile:[16]

> In the distant past there was a bird, [of the species] called quail. It had been caught by a hawk, who flew up high into the sky. Up in the sky [the quail] called out: "I was not alert and suddenly I met with this misfortune. Because I departed from my ancestral domain and journeyed to another place, therefore I met with this misfortune. How else could I today be put in this difficulty by him, unable to be free!"
>
> The hawk said to the quail: "What is the place of your own domain, where you are able to be free?" The quail replied: "My own domain is in the midst of a ploughed furrow in a farm field. There I am fully free from misfortunes; that is my home and ancestral domain."
>
> The hawk's pride was aroused. It said to the quail: "I set you free to leave, to return amidst ploughed furrows. Will you be able to escape me thereby?"[17]
>
> Then the quail got out from the claws of the hawk and returned to the ploughed furrow, to a big clod below which there was a safe place to stay. Then it went on top of the clod, wanting to give battle to the hawk.[18]
>
> The hawk was greatly enraged [thinking]: "That is [just] a little bird and it dares to give battle to me." Extremely angry, it quickly flew straight down to fight. Then the quail entered beneath the clod.

16 SĀ 617 at T II 172c25 to 173a8.

17 The parallel SN 47.6 at SN V 147,2 (translated Bodhi 2000: 1632) indicates that the hawk was confident of its strength, but did not boast of it. The reading known to the commentary Spk III 200,14, however, appears to have rather been that the hawk was confident of its strength and boastful; cf. also Bodhi 2000: 1918 n.131. The wording in SĀ 617 supports the reading reflected in the commentary, which also fits the context better.

18 SN 47.6 does not mention a safe place to stay below the clod. According to its description at SN V 147,13, when the hawk had come close, the quail got "inside" the clod. The idea of getting inside a clod is somewhat less straightforward, compared to the idea of getting into a small place below a big clod. Another version of this simile, T 212 at T IV 695a19, refers to a place between two clods or rocks, and then indicates that the quail got "inside" this space. After having reached the clod, according to SN 47.6 at SN V 147,7, the quail openly challenges the hawk to come and get it; the same is the case for T 212.

> The hawk, by the power of its flight, dashed with its breast against the solid clod, shattered its body and died.[19]

The *Saṃyutta-nikāya* parallel reports that, on being caught, the quail laments its lack of merit and luck, rather than blaming itself.[20] The *Saṃyukta-āgama* version in comparison gives more emphasis to the quail's negligence as the reason for its capture by the hawk. This accords with the main point of the simile in both versions, namely that one should not be negligent and stray out of one's proper domain – the four *satipaṭṭhāna*s – in order not to be "caught".

The simile's illustration of the protective function of *satipaṭṭhāna* as a safe ground that enables one to withstand the allure of sensually enticing objects concords with the passages discussed above that describe how a loss of mindfulness results in being overwhelmed by sensual desire. The fact that the weak quail is able to overcome the strong hawk seems to convey the message that by sticking to mindfulness one can withstand situations that, without mindfulness, could be quite overpowering.

The similes of the monkey and of the quail converge on the notion of protection through establishing mindfulness. Other discourses highlight that mindfulness is indeed the one factor that offers protection.[21] In this way, establishing mindfulness enables one to deal with the outside world without being swept away by the streams of desire or aversion.[22] This finds a succinct expression in a stanza from the *Sutta-nipāta* that, in a parallel that has been preserved in the *Yogācārabhūmi*, reads as follows:[23]

---

19 SN 47.6 does not describe the anger of the hawk and reports that the quail waited until the hawk had come close.

20 SN 47.6 at SN V 146,20.

21 Mindfulness is introduced as the one factor of protection in AN 10.20 at AN V 30,24 (translated Bodhi 2012: 1360) and EĀ 52.7 at T II 827a19.

22 The potential of mindfulness to prevent being carried away by the stream of aversion would receive support from the finding by Arch and Craske 2006: 1857 that "based on a 15 minute focused breathing induction with a sample that had no previous experience with mindfulness meditation" and where "no instructions were given regarding how to approach a picture stimuli viewed after the induction", the research showed that "the focused breathing induction lead to increased behavioral willingness and tolerance for remaining in contact with unpredictable, negative stimuli." For research showing that mindfulness promotes lower neural reactivity in the case of unpleasant as well as pleasant stimuli, cf. Brown et al. 2013.

23 Enomoto 1989: 34, parallel to Sn 1035 (translated Norman 1992: 116).

Those streams that are in the world,
Are held in check by mindfulness.

II.3 MINDFULNESS AS A GATEKEEPER

The notion of protection also comes up in a different way in two similes that compare mindfulness to a gatekeeper of a border town. In what follows, I translate the *Saṃyukta-āgama* version of one of these two similes:[24]

> It is just as a border-country king who has the walls of the city well kept in order, the gates with a firm foundation and the access roads level and straight. He has placed four gatekeepers at the four city gates, all of whom are clever and wise, knowing those who come and go. In that city there are four access roads towards the couch that has been prepared for the lord of the city to sit on.[25]
>
> Suppose from the eastern direction a messenger comes and asks the gatekeeper: "Where is the lord of the city?" He answers: "The lord is in the middle of the city, at the end of the four access roads, seated on a couch." Having heard this, the messenger approaches the lord of the city. [Having delivered his message],[26] he receives an instruction and returns by the road. From the southern … western … northern direction a messenger comes and asks the gatekeeper: "Where is the lord of the city?" He answers: "In the middle of the city, at the end of the four access roads." Having heard it, they all approach the lord of the city, [deliver their message], receive an instruction and return to their former place.[27]

---

24 SĀ 1175 at T II 315c19 to 315c28.

25 In the Pāli parallel, SN 35.204 at SN IV 194,11 (translated Bodhi 2000: 1252, given as number 245), the city wall has instead six gates. The Tibetan parallel, D 4094 *nyu* 43a4 or Q 5595 *thu* 82b1, agrees with SĀ 1175 in this respect. SN 35.204 and the Tibetan version concord, however, in describing the gatekeeper as competent in keeping out those who are unknown and allowing access to those who are known. SN 35.204 and the Tibetan parallel also do not describe the seating arrangement made for the lord of the city, only indicating that he is in the centre of the town.

26 My supplementation is guided by the context and by the fact that the explanation of the simile in SĀ 1175 at T II 316a4 refers to a true message, which is similarly mentioned in the parallel versions of the simile and in their later explanation of this simile.

27 In SN 35.204 and in the Tibetan parallel, a pair of messengers approaches the gatekeeper.

The *Saṃyukta-āgama* version continues by identifying the four gatekeepers with the four *satipaṭṭhāna*s. A parallel found in the *Saṃyutta-nikāya* describes only a single gatekeeper, who represents mindfulness.[28] A third parallel preserved in Tibetan translation also has only a single gatekeeper, which according to its presentation stands for mindfulness of the body.[29] Another difference is that, while the above-translated *Saṃyukta-āgama* version identifies the messenger as insight (*vipassanā*), the *Saṃyutta-nikāya* version and the Tibetan parallel speak of two messengers, representing insight and tranquillity (*samatha*).

Whether the messenger is insight alone or insight together with tranquillity, the task of the gatekeeper in this simile is to show the path by which the messenger(s) can reach the lord of the city who represents consciousness (*viññāṇa*) according to all versions.[30] Thus the gatekeeper in this simile seems to reflect the monitoring role of mindfulness in relation to insight and tranquillity. Through mindfulness – be this mindfulness in general, mindfulness of the body, or all four *satipaṭṭhāna*s – one is aware of the proper route to be taken in cultivating insight and tranquillity. This simile thus throws into relief the function of mindfulness as the mental quality that monitors progress on the path to liberation and thereby protects one from taking the wrong route.

Another simile that also takes up the motif of mindfulness as a gatekeeper occurs in a discourse in the *Aṅguttara-nikāya* and in its *Madhyama-āgama* parallel. Here is the *Madhyama-āgama* version of this simile:[31]

> It is just as if in the king's border town a chief officer has been appointed as gatekeeper, one who is sharp-witted and wise in making decisions, brave and resolute, of excellent counsel, who allows entry to the good and keeps out the bad, in order to ensure peace within and control outside enemies.
>
> In the same way, a noble disciple continuously dwells with mindfulness, achieves right mindfulness, always recalling and not forgetting what was practised or heard long ago.

28 SN 35.204 at SN IV 194,34.

29 D 4094 *nyu* 43b3 or Q 5595 *thu* 83a2.

30 Bodhi 2000: 1429 n.209 comments that the point of the simile would be "that consciousness is the functional centre of personal experience".

31 MĀ 3 at T I 423c14 to 423c19. Further parallels to this simile can be found in EĀ 39.4 at T II 730b6 and in T 212 at T IV 652c9.

> This is a noble disciple's gaining of mindfulness as the gatekeeper, as the chief officer, who removes what is bad and unwholesome and develops wholesome states.

A parallel in the *Aṅguttara-nikāya* similarly indicates that the gatekeeper of mindfulness represents the ability to recall and not forget what was done or heard long ago.[32] The reference in the two parallel versions to remembering what was done and what was heard points to different types of memories. The first type would be memory of autobiographical events. To recall what one has heard, however, points to an ability of considerable importance in an oral culture like ancient India, namely memorization. The early Buddhist reciters had to rely on precisely this ability to transmit the teachings of the Buddha and his disciples to future generations. Therefore it can safely be assumed that the practical need to be able to remember well what one has heard long ago must have exerted its influence on the early Buddhist theory and practice of mindfulness.

II.4 MINDFULNESS AND MEMORY

The relationship of these two types of memory to the situation depicted in the above simile is not immediately evident. There is a clear parallel between the gatekeeper's preventing the bad from entering the city and the task of mindfulness in keeping the bad out of the mind. The role that memory plays in this respect, however, needs further exploration.

In order to be able to distinguish those who are entitled to enter from those who are not, the gatekeeper needs to rely on his memory. However, such reliance on memory is something that is common to any of his states of mind; it is not specific to his task at the city gate. Going home after work he needs to remember the way home, and returning to work at the gate the next day he also needs to remember the meaning of concepts like "city gate", "my work duty", etc. The aspect of the mind that is responsible for this type of memory is perception (*saññā*).[33] Perception is what matches experience with concepts learned earlier,[34] something required for almost any

32 AN 7.63 at AN IV 111,1 (translated Bodhi 2012: 1078, given as number 67).
33 Ñāṇaponika 1949/1985: 69 explains that "ancient Buddhist psychology ascribed the main share in the process of recollecting to perception (*saññā*)."
34 Cf. Anālayo 2003b: 204.

state of mind. In fact it is hard to think of an intentional human activity that is not in some way informed by past experiences and does not depend on concepts and ideas learned earlier. It would be problematic to assign the memory of such past experiences, concepts, or ideas to mindfulness on its own, since it would follow that someone without any kind of meditative training is pretty much continuously mindful. In order to preserve the distinct function and meaning of mindfulness, it seems to me to reflect the canonical position better if this kind of basic remembering is considered a function of perception.

As the passages describing the consequences of a loss of mindfulness clearly show, from an early Buddhist viewpoint mindfulness is something that needs to be intentionally brought into being.[35] These passages do not give the impression that the mere ability to remember a concept is central to their notion of mindfulness. In fact, the passage quoted above does not just mention the gatekeeper's ability to recognize, but instead draws attention to his ability to allow entry to the good and keep out the bad.

Alternatively, perhaps the relation to memory in this simile can be found in the gatekeeper's need to remember what he is supposed to do. This would fit the simile, although it would not work so well with the subsequent explanation. According to this explanation, the purpose of the simile is to illustrate that through mindfulness one is able to recall what happened long ago. Such an ability does not have a straightforward relation to remembering what one is supposed to do. This much can also be seen from the passages that take up a loss of mindfulness, where the examples do not seem to be about forgetting what one had set out to do.

To execute his duty of allowing entry to the good and keeping out the bad, the gatekeeper needs, above all, to be fully aware of what is happening at the city gate. His task is to be aware of who is entering it right now and he must not be distracted from this present-moment awareness by dwelling on the past. It seems to me that the motif of the gatekeeper of mindfulness stands for being fully aware in the present moment at the gates of one's mind, which is precisely the quality that enables preventing the "bad" – desire and aversion – from entering the city of one's mind. That is, I would see the gatekeeper simile

35 As Bodhi 2011: 28 explains, "mindfulness ... does not occur automatically but is a quality to be cultivated (*bhāvetabba*)."

as pointing to the same protective functions of mindfulness as are illustrated in the similes of the monkey and the quail.

The relationship of mindfulness to memory then emerges naturally from the fact that being fully aware in the present moment is precisely the quality of the mind that facilitates later remembering. It will only be possible to remember that of which one has been aware. The more one has been aware, the better one will be able to remember. If mindfulness was established, it will indeed be possible to recall what was done or heard, even if it happened long ago.

In the case of the gatekeeper, his present-moment awareness needs to be somewhat broad or panoramic, as he has to remain alert to the whole situation at the gate. He cannot allow himself to focus on one particular person coming in at the expense of losing sight of others who are also moving through the gate. As the first gatekeeper simile shows, his overview of the entire situation is not limited to what happens at the gate, as he may also be required to inform messengers of the path from the gate to the lord of the city. But he nevertheless stays at the gate, fulfilling his task of being fully aware of whatever happens in the present moment, thereby being able to discern the good from the bad.

In practical terms, this means that, if one is doing something with such awareness that it can later be remembered easily, then one is indeed being mindful. Walking towards the meditation hall, for example, I could be mindful of my walking, or else be lost in thinking, perhaps dwelling on some memories of the past. The fact that at a certain point I have reached the meditation hall clearly means that I must have walked there. But if I have not been mindful of the walking, I will not be able to recall the experience of having walked. I will only be able to conclude that I must have walked to the hall by inference, since I am now in the meditation hall. If I have been mindful, however, I will be able to recall the walk. This does not necessarily mean remembering every minute detail of the path that I took, but the experience of having walked towards the hall will be available for my recall simply because I was aware when this experience happened.

Even without mindfulness, some degree of attention has to be with the walking, otherwise it will be impossible to keep on the path or even to take the next step. But the attention required for such semi-automatic actions can be quite superficial. Most of the mind can be involved with something else at the same time, such as daydreaming, dwelling in memories, or anticipating the future. When one is mindful of walking, however, and the mind is present with the experience of walking in an open and receptive manner, then one is fully with the experience of walking and thus more fully and accurately aware of it. With such a way of being mindful of one's walking, attention becomes somewhat panoramic, in the sense of being aware of the whole situation instead of singling out one of its details and focusing on it to the exclusion of anything else. Such broad and receptive awareness would indeed make it possible, if needed, for the experience of walking to be recalled later. This type of alert, broad, and receptive awareness is what makes the difference in one's ability to recall past actions.

While mindfulness is thus different from the basic form of attention that appears to be present in any state of mind,[36] attention is nevertheless closely related to mindfulness.[37] In fact in several discourses thorough attention (*yoniso manasikāra*) parallels aspects of *satipaṭṭhāna* meditation practice.[38] What makes the difference, however, is that the basic function of attention is present in any state of mind, unlike mindfulness or thorough attention, which have to be cultivated and intentionally brought into being.[39] The cultivation of a strengthened and thereby to some degree broadened form of attention makes it possible to remember easily what one did in the past.

These two aspects of strengthening and broadening are to some extent interrelated. Remaining firmly established in mindfulness without immediately reacting in a judgemental manner, and without being carried away by mental elaborations, allows for awareness of

---

36 The precedent in the early discourses for the notion of a universal factor of the mind, in the sense of being present in any state of mind, would be the definition of "name" in "name-and-form". SN 12.2 at SN II 3,34 (translated Bodhi 2000: 535) and EĀ 49.5 at T II 797b28 agree that attention is one of the factors that make up "name". Here "name" covers the mental factors that are required for understanding an object and hence responsible for the genesis of a concept. These, together with material objects subsumed under "form", are experienced by consciousness (which in this definition is not itself part of "name").

37 Griffiths 1992: 111 explains that mindfulness "consists essentially of paying attention to and taking note of objects of knowledge; it is an intentional act of the mind and thus overlaps in meaning considerably with *attention* (*manaskāra*)."

38 Anālayo 2003b: 59f; for a more detailed study of *yoniso manasikāra* cf. Anālayo 2010b: 69ff (reprinted Anālayo 2012b: 193ff).

39 Bodhi 2011: 30 warns of "confounding *sati* and *manasikāra*, deliberate mindfulness and the automatic act of advertence".

more aspects and details of the present situation.[40] Thus a broader range of data can be taken in by the mind. Expressed in terms of photography, being mindful is like taking a picture with a long exposure time and a wide-angle lens.

In sum, when considered from the viewpoint of *satipaṭṭhāna* meditation practice, I consider a central import of the memory nuance of mindfulness to be that an intensified and broadened form of attention given to what is occurring in the present enriches one's awareness of what is happening to such an extent that this strengthens one's ability to recall later what took place.[41] Precisely this enriched present-moment mindfulness forms a continuous theme throughout the different *satipaṭṭhāna* exercises, enabling awareness of the condition of one's body, the hedonic tone of feelings, the present condition of one's state of mind, etc.

As the mental quality that holds things in mind in the present moment, mindfulness is responsible not only for proper memory storage, but also for the quality of mind that makes it easy to retrieve things from memory later.[42] As I suggested in my earlier book,[43] this aspect of mindfulness becomes evident when one fails to remember

---

40 Bishop et al. 2004: 233 point out that "because attention has a limited capacity ... when it is released from elaborative thinking, more resources are made available to process information related to current experience. This increases access to information that might otherwise remain outside awareness, resulting in a wider perspective on experience."

41 Bodhi in Ñāṇamoli 1995: 1252 n.560 explains that "the relationship between the two senses of *sati* – memory and attentiveness – may be formulated thus: keen attentiveness to the present forms the basis for an accurate memory of the past." Griffiths 1992: 114 similarly points out that "the very act of paying close attention to the present contents of one's mind makes it possible to recall those contents at some later time." He explains (p.111) that mindfulness "has by itself nothing essentially to do with the remembering of some past object of cognition ... and it is perhaps more natural to take its primary sense as having a present reference. The fact that *smṛti* notes ... these objects, however, makes possible their preservation as objects of consciousness ... and thus explains the extension of the term to cover at least some of the same semantic grounds as the English word *memory* and its cognates. In other words, I suggest that the basic meaning of *smṛti* and derivatives in Buddhist technical discourse – basic in the sense that this meaning is both temporally and logically prior to other meanings – has to do with observation and attention, not with awareness of past objects."

42 As, e.g., Muzzio at al. 2009: 2837 note, "the recruitment of attention is important not only for optimal encoding but also for subsequent retrieval"; on the interrelation between attention and memory from a neurobiological perspective cf. also, e.g., Chun and Turk-Browne 2007.

43 Anālayo 2003b: 48f.

something because the mind is excessively focused. On laying the question aside and allowing the mind to return to a more open and broad-minded condition, one may find that the information arises in the mind on its own.

This aspect of mindfulness concerned with facilitating the actual remembering of information from the past is prominent in relation to the practice of recollection (*anussati*) and of less relevance to *satipaṭṭhāna* meditation. While these two modes of meditation have much in common, a chief requirement for *satipaṭṭhāna* is that the practitioner remains mentally anchored in the present moment.[44] The task is to examine one's bodily condition now, to recognize how one feels in the present and how one's mind is at this precise moment, rather than to recall what happened earlier. It is this type of mindfulness in the present moment, developed through *satipaṭṭhāna* meditation, that is an integral part of the noble eightfold path to liberation.

If mindfulness were just about remembering things from the past, there would have been no need for the scheme of four *satipaṭṭhāna*s as an elaboration of the path-factor of right mindfulness. In order to inculcate the ability to recall the past, the practice of memorizing texts that was undertaken anyway by the early Buddhist disciples to transmit what they considered to be the "word of the Buddha"

---

44 In the case of mindfulness of breathing, for example, as pointed out by Bodhi 2011: 32, "the breath is something occurring in the present, not in the past, which means that in this context *sati* is attentiveness to a present event, not recollection of the past." Thus when Gethin 2011: 270 conceptualizes the same practice to mean that "one has to remember that what it is one should be doing is remembering the breath", I think his usage of the term "to remember" is intended to be understood in a rather broad sense, as a way of reflecting the fact that mindfulness holds things in mind and thereby performs a function akin to remembering, but not in the sense that during mindfulness of breathing one is actually remembering something from the past. While I appreciate Gethin's attempt to bridge the sense of *sati* as present-moment awareness and its nuances related to memory, I think it can become problematic if the aspect of remembering is given excessive emphasis. An example is Ṭhānissaro 2012: 86, who having confined *sati* to memory then has to find another term for present-moment awareness, which he allocates to clear knowing, *sampajañña*. His take on *sati* then makes it difficult for him to appreciate the qualities of receptivity and bare observation in mindfulness to such an extent that the *satipaṭṭhāna* instructions on their own appear incomplete to him and in need of supplementation; cf. Ṭhānissaro 2012: 150. In order to avoid such problems, I think we have to handle the memory aspect of mindfulness in a way that allows for the essential qualities of *sati* as a receptive form of present-moment awareness to remain.

would have been amply sufficient. Following the Vedic model of oral transmission, this could have become their main training ground for cultivating the ability to remember. According to the *Manusmṛti*, the ability to recollect past lives requires recitation of the Vedas (which means their memorization), together with pure conduct and austerities.[45] Thus the very fact that a scheme of four *satipaṭṭhāna*s has come into existence makes it clear that in early Buddhist thought mindfulness is not just about recalling the past.

Not only does mindfulness not have the task of remembering things during *satipaṭṭhāna* meditation practice, it does not even appear to get actively involved in other ways. This suggests itself from the fact that the actual instructions for the individual exercises that are common to the parallel versions do not mention "mindfulness", *sati*, itself.[46] Only the part that I have dubbed the "refrain", which comes after the individual instructions, explicitly mentions mindfulness.[47] In this way, the exposition in the *Satipaṭṭhāna-sutta* and its parallels describes different meditation exercises, whose successful implementation leads to mindfulness becoming well established. In these different meditation exercises, however, mindfulness itself is not given an active task. Instead of being actively involved, mindfulness furnishes the basic condition of receptive and alert mental presence within which more specific meditative activities can take place.

Expressed in Pāli terminology, according to the actual instructions the activities required for *satipaṭṭhāna* meditation are that a practitioner "knows" (*pajānāti*), "examines" (*paccavekkhati*), and "compares" (*upasaṃharati*). The activities of examining and comparing are required for those exercises that are common to the three versions of the first *satipaṭṭhāna*, concerned with the

45 Bühler 1886: 152 (IV.148): "By daily reciting the Veda, by (the observance of the rules of) purification, by (practising) austerities, and by doing no injury to created beings, one (obtains the faculty of) remembering former births."

46 An exception is the listing of the seven awakening factors, where *sati* occurs as the first in the listing. Yet here, too, the actual meditative task is to "know" whether *sati* or any other awakening factor is present or absent.

47 I am indebted to Gil Fronsdal for drawing my attention to this pattern in relation to the *Satipaṭṭhāna-sutta* where, among the individual instructions, mindfulness is only mentioned in the introductory part for mindfulness of breathing: "having established mindfulness in front, one breathes in mindfully and breathes out mindfully." In the subsequent instructions for this exercise the term then no longer occurs, and the meditative task is that one "knows" (*pajānāti*) and that one "trains" (*sikkhati*).

comparatively gross object of the body. With the respectively subtler objects in the remaining three *satipaṭṭhāna*s, the meditative task is just that one "knows" (*pajānāti*).

Such knowing, examining, and comparing is based on, establishes, and strengthens the mental space of present-moment mindfulness, within which these activities take place. Thus *satipaṭṭhāna* is very much about what one does to establish and maintain mindfulness. In other words, mindfulness is not in itself something that one *does*. Rather, practising *satipaṭṭhāna* is all about *being* mindful.

Such *being* mindful then becomes a factor of awakening. Understood in this way, the four *satipaṭṭhāna*s are ways of bringing the mindfulness awakening factor into being so that it is well established. This is the foundation for the other awakening factors and therewith for progress to liberation. The central quality throughout is *being* mindful in the present moment.

Besides actualizing the awakening potential of the mind, once present-moment mindfulness has been established in this way, it also becomes possible to navigate the vicissitudes of everyday life without running into an accident. This aspect of mindfulness comes up in the context of a simile in the *Saṃyutta-nikāya* that likens various mental qualities to parts of a chariot, where mindfulness is the careful charioteer.[48] The *Saṃyukta-āgama* parallel expresses the same idea in terms of having "right mindfulness". The relevant passage is formulated in this way:[49]

> Being well protected by right mindfulness is like being a good charioteer.

Attempting to draw out the implications of this image, the good or careful charioteer is first of all fully aware in the present moment, not allowing any possible distraction to interfere with the task at hand. Being fully "present", the charioteer also has an overview of the whole traffic situation: he is aware of what is happening not only directly in front, but also to the sides and to some degree even behind. Driving

48 SN 45.4 at SN V 6,10 (translated Bodhi 2000: 1526) and a Sanskrit fragment counterpart, Waldschmidt 1967: 248.

49 SĀ 769 at T II 201a4. The same simile recurs in SĀ 98 at T II 27a28, SĀ² 264 at T II 466c1, and a Sanskrit fragment parallel, Enomoto 1997: 98. In this case, however, the Pāli parallel, SN 7.11 at SN I 172,30 (translated Bodhi 2000: 267), found also at Sn 77, instead compares mindfulness to a ploughshare and a goad.

in the present moment with a clear sense of direction, knowing where the journey should lead, a good charioteer is nevertheless able to adjust to the traffic without becoming restless because of an excessive goal-orientation. Just as lacking a sense of direction would be detrimental, as the charioteer would not know where to go, similarly being too preoccupied with reaching the final destination would diminish the ability to steer smoothly through the present situation.

Much of this applies to one's personal practice of *satipaṭṭhāna*, which requires combining a sense of direction with the absence of preoccupation with reaching the goal. The key is to remain in the present, with a broad mental attitude of receptivity and clarity; in short, to remain mindful. The different ways in which one can be mindful will be explored in the following chapters.

II.5 SUMMARY

A loss of mindfulness can result in getting stuck in the world of the five senses like a silly monkey, whereby one's attention can get caught by sensually alluring objects, much like a quail that has strayed out of its proper domain. The meditator's proper domain is well-established mindfulness as the wise gatekeeper of one's mind. Being fully aware in this way one will later be able to remember easily what has happened.

III

CONTEMPLATION OF THE BODY

The exercises for contemplating the body in the *Satipaṭṭhāna-sutta* of the *Majjhima-nikāya* and its two Chinese *Āgama* parallels show considerable variations, as can be seen from Figure 3.1, which lists the three versions of body contemplation in order of increasing complexity. The three meditation practices in **bold** font – contemplation of the body's anatomical parts, of the elements, and of a corpse in decay – are their common ground and these will be discussed in more detail in later chapters.

Ekottarika-āgama	*Majjhima-nikāya*	*Madhyama-āgama*
anatomical parts	breathing	postures
4 elements	postures	activities
bodily orifices	activities	counter unwholesome mental state
corpse	**anatomical parts**	forceful mind control
	4 elements	breathing
	corpse	experience of 4 absorptions
		perception of light
		reviewing sign
		anatomical parts
		6 elements
		corpse

Fig. 3.1 Contemplation of the body

In this chapter I survey the exercises found in addition to these three practices, beginning with those that occur in only one of the versions and not in the others. Then, after a comparative survey of contemplation of the body, I consider the benefits that can be expected from contemplation of the body.

III.1 BODY CONTEMPLATIONS FOUND IN ONLY ONE VERSION

III.1.1 CONTEMPLATION OF THE BODILY ORIFICES

The *Ekottarika-āgama* version includes an exercise concerned with the orifices of the body that is not found in the other two versions. The instructions are as follows:

> One contemplates the orifices that are found in this body that discharge impurity. It is just as a person who, contemplating a bamboo garden, contemplates clumps of reeds. In this way ... one contemplates the orifices that are found in this body and that discharge impurity.

A similar presentation occurs in the *Gaṇḍa-sutta* of the *Aṅguttara-nikāya*,[1] which compares the impure liquids that come out of the nine orifices of the body to a festering boil. The same motif is also taken up in the *Vijaya-sutta* of the *Sutta-nipāta*, which similarly refers to the nine orifices of the body that discharge impurity, such as mucus from the eyes, wax from the ears, snot from the nostrils, bile and phlegm from the mouth.[2] These together with the orifices responsible for discharging urine and faeces make up the nine openings of the body.

Thus the exercise in the *Ekottarika-āgama* discourse is similar to a way of viewing the body described in Pāli discourses that do not have an explicit relation to *satipaṭṭhāna* practice. The simile that illustrates this form of practice in the *Ekottarika-āgama* version appears to depict the contrast between a beautiful bamboo grove seen from afar and the discovery, on closer examination, of clumps of reeds in the grove that usually grow in shallow pools of stagnant and smelly water. This then illustrates the impure liquids that are discovered on close examination of the body.

1 AN 9.15 at AN IV 386,24 (translated Bodhi 2012: 1270). This discourse has a parallel in another *Ekottarika-āgama* collection of which only a part has been preserved in Chinese translation, EĀ[2] 29 at T II 880a30; for a study of this collection, cf. Harrison 1997.

2 Sn 197f (translated Norman 1992: 22). The **Śāriputrābhidharma*, T 1548 at T XXVIII 613c2, includes a comparable exercise in its exposition of contemplation of the body.

The topic of the impure liquids discharged by the orifices of the body fits the context in the *Ekottarika-āgama* discourse, where some of these liquids and the theme of impurity have already been introduced in the contemplation of the anatomical parts, mentioned previously in this discourse. The absence of this practice from the *Majjhima-nikāya* and *Madhyama-āgama* versions makes it probable that this exercise is a later addition to the *Ekottarika-āgama* account. From a practical perspective, however, this addition appears to offer a meaningful alternative approach to exploring the nature of the body.

III.1.2 COUNTERING UNWHOLESOME MENTAL STATES

Several other exercises are found only in the *Madhyama-āgama* version. After describing awareness of postures and activities, the *Madhyama-āgama* discourse gives the following instruction:

> [When] evil and unwholesome thoughts arise ... one rectifies, abandons, eradicates, and stops them by recollecting wholesome states. It is just as a carpenter or a carpenter's apprentice who might apply an inked string to a piece of wood [to mark a straight line] and then cut the wood with a sharp adze to make it straight.

The next exercise similarly addresses the mind:

> With teeth clenched and tongue pressed against the palate ... one uses [the will-power of one's own] mind to rectify the mind, to rectify, abandon, eradicate, and stop [evil thoughts]. It is just as two strong men who might grab a weak man and, turning him this way and that way, might beat him up as they wish.

Instructions on countering unwholesome thoughts or even subduing them with the use of force are found in the *Vitakkasaṇṭhāna-sutta* and its *Madhyama-āgama* parallel.[3] The theme of these discourses is

3 MN 20 at MN I 119,5 (translated Ñāṇamoli 1995: 211) and its parallel MĀ 101 at T I 588a10 (translated and discussed below in Chapter 8). This parallelism has already been noted by Kuan 2008: 86f, who then suggests that an indication regularly found in the *Kāyagatāsati-sutta*, MN 119 at MN III 89,22, according to which the mind becomes concentrated in this way, is also a borrowing from the *Vitakkasaṇṭhāna-sutta*. Yet the whole point of the *Kāyagatāsati-sutta* and its parallel is to show how contemplation of the body leads to various benefits, in particular to the gaining of concentration. Thus, as far as I can see, there is no need to assume that a borrowing occurred, as

the gradual removal of unwholesome thoughts, which would be a more appropriate setting for these instructions than contemplation of the body. Perhaps the image of physical effort in the description of rectifying one's mind "with teeth clenched and tongue pressed against the palate" led to relating this type of practice to body contemplation, and by association the other exercise found in the same context, together with the carpenter simile, came to be also part of the *satipaṭṭhāna* instructions in the *Madhyama-āgama*. Such an association of textual pieces is a natural occurrence during the oral transmission of a text.[4]

III.1.3 EXPERIENCING THE FOUR ABSORPTIONS

After describing mindfulness of breathing in four steps, the *Madhyama-āgama* version takes up the bodily experience of the four absorptions, together with similes that illustrate this experience. The instructions for the first absorption are as follows:

> One completely drenches and pervades one's body with joy and happiness born of seclusion [experienced in the first absorption], so that there is no part within one's body that is not pervaded by joy and happiness born of seclusion.
>
> Is it just as a bath attendant who, having filled a vessel with bathing powder, mixes it with water and kneads it, so that there is no part [of the powder] that is not completely drenched and pervaded with water.[5]

The *Madhyama-āgama* discourse continues by similarly taking up the pervasion of the body with joy and happiness born of concentration

---

the indication that the mind becomes concentrated in this way fits the context well. The same holds for the similes illustrating the benefits of mindfulness of the body in the *Kāyagatāsati-sutta*, which Kuan 2008: 95 also takes to be a borrowing. The assumption that these parts must be a borrowing then leads Kuan to a hypothesis that in my view is inconclusive, namely that the original meaning of *kāyagatā sati* goes beyond being mindful of the body.

4 Von Hinüber 1996/1997: 31 explains that "pieces of texts known by heart may intrude into almost any context once there is a corresponding key word."

5 The corresponding simile in MN 119 at MN III 92,32 (translated Ñāṇamoli 1995: 953) additionally specifies that the ball of bath powder does not ooze. Another difference is that, in addition to a bath attendant, MN 119 also speaks of his apprentice.

(second absorption), pervasion of the body with happiness born of the absence of joy (third absorption), and pervasion of the body with mental purity (fourth absorption). The respective similes illustrate this as follows:

Second absorption:

> It is just as a mountain spring that is full and overflowing with clear and clean water, so that water coming from any of the four directions cannot enter it, with the spring water welling up from the bottom on its own, flowing out and flooding the surroundings, completely drenching every part of the mountain so that there is no part that is not pervaded by it.[6]

Third absorption:

> It is just as a blue, red, or white lotus, being born in the water and having come to growth in the water, remains submerged in water, with every part of its roots, stem, flower, and leaves completely drenched and pervaded [by water], so that there is no part that is not pervaded by it.[7]

Fourth absorption:

> It is just as a man who covers himself from head to foot with a cloth measuring seven or eight units, so that no part of his body is not covered.[8]

The original place for contemplating the bodily experience of the absorptions would have been the *Kāyagatāsati-sutta* and its *Madhyama-āgama* parallel, which agree on describing the experience of the absorption from the perspective of its effect on the body. The *Kāyagatāsati-sutta* is even more detailed in this respect than its *Madhyama-āgama* parallel, as it precedes the depiction of the bodily pervasion with the standard description of the attainment of the respective absorption.

---

6 MN 119 at MN III 93,10 instead describes a lake whose water wells up from within.

7 According to MN 119 at MN III 94,1, the water that pervades the lotus is cool.

8 The simile in MN 119 at MN III 94,16 does not give the size of the cloth, but indicates that it is white.

III.1.4 PERCEPTION OF LIGHT AND THE REVIEWING SIGN

Another two exercises in the *Madhyama-āgama* parallel to the *Satipaṭṭhāna-sutta* that would have originally had a different placement are concerned with the perception of light and with grasping the reviewing sign (that is, reviewing the characteristics that one has seen with insight). The instructions regarding perception of light are as follows:

> One is mindful of the perception of light, properly taking hold of it, properly retaining it, and properly recollecting what one is mindful of, [so that] what is behind is like what is in front, what is in front is like what is behind, night is like day, day is like night, what is above is like what is below, and what is below is like what is above. In this way one cultivates an undistorted and undefiled mind, a mind that is bright and clear, a mind that is not at all obscured by impediments.

The instructions for the reviewing sign are as follows:

> One properly holds [in mind] the reviewing sign, recollecting properly what one is mindful of. It is just as a person who is seated and contemplates another person who is lying down, or while lying down contemplates another person who is seated. In the same way ... one properly holds [in mind] the reviewing sign, recollecting properly what one is mindful of.

The first of these two exercises is also found in a discourse in the *Aṅguttara-nikāya* as part of a set of five recollections, where it is preceded by the attainment of the first three absorptions and followed by contemplation of the anatomical parts of the body and of a corpse in decay.[9] Another discourse in the *Aṅguttara-nikāya* then mentions holding in mind the reviewing sign together with the four absorptions,[10] followed by similes that correspond to the similes used in the *Kāyagatāsati-sutta* and its *Madhyama-āgama* parallel.

While the two *Aṅguttara-nikāya* discourses appear to be without a known parallel, it may well be that such discourses were known within the Sarvāstivāda tradition, but have not been preserved among the material we currently have at our disposal. In such a case, during

9 AN 6.29 at AN III 323,14 (translated Bodhi 2012: 890); noted by Kuan 2008: 86 as probably being the original context for the instruction now found in MĀ 81.

10 AN 5.28 at AN III 27,13 (translated Bodhi 2012: 649); mentioned by Kuan 2008: 95 as the likely original context for the instruction now found in MĀ 81.

oral transmission the fact that perception of light occurs together with the absorptions, as well as with contemplation of the anatomical parts of the body and of a corpse in decay, could easily have led to its inclusion in another context where the absorptions occur together with contemplation of the anatomical parts and contemplation of a corpse, such as in a version of the *Kāyagatāsati-sutta*. Similarly, the fact that grasping the reviewing sign occurs in a context related to absorption and is accompanied by similes could easily have led to its inclusion in another context where the absorptions and these similes are found. In this way, a tendency which is often at work during oral transmission, namely to associate various originally unrelated textual pieces, would explain why these exercises are now found in the *Madhyama-āgama* parallel to the *Kāyagatāsati-sutta*.

In turn, this could then have influenced the *Madhyama-āgama* parallel to the *Satipaṭṭhāna-sutta*. The fact that the parallel to the *Kāyagatāsati-sutta* precedes the parallel to the *Satipaṭṭhāna-sutta* in the *Madhyama-āgama* might then, in the course of transmission, have caused the exposition in the previous discourse to be applied to the subsequent discourse. In this way, this exposition would have become part of contemplation of the body in the fourfold *satipaṭṭhāna* scheme.

In contrast, in the *Majjhima-nikāya* the *Satipaṭṭhāna-sutta* occurs first and the *Kāyagatāsati-sutta* comes later. Thus in the *Majjhima-nikāya* such a copying would not naturally have occurred. The two respective discourses in the *Majjhima-nikāya* in fact differ: the *Satipaṭṭhāna-sutta* does not cover the absorptions, which are only mentioned in the *Kāyagatāsati-sutta*.

In sum, the exercises found only in the *Madhyama-āgama* parallel to the *Satipaṭṭhāna-sutta* have no evident relation to the topic of contemplation of the body as a *satipaṭṭhāna* practice and appear to be later additions. Such additions would be in line with a general tendency for the first *satipaṭṭhāna* concerned with contemplation of the body to grow through the incorporation of other textual passages.

III.2 BODY CONTEMPLATIONS FOUND IN TWO VERSIONS

III.2.1 MINDFULNESS OF BREATHING

A body contemplation that is found in both the *Majjhima-nikāya* and *Madhyama-āgama* versions is mindfulness of breathing. The instructions are as follows:

Majjhima-nikāya:

> Gone to the forest, or to the root of a tree, or to an empty hut ... one sits down; having folded the legs crosswise, set one's body erect, and established mindfulness in front, one breathes in mindfully and breathes out mindfully.
>
> Breathing in long, one knows: "I breathe in long", breathing out long, one knows: "I breathe out long." Breathing in short, one knows: "I breathe in short", breathing out short, one knows: "I breathe out short." One trains: "I breathe in experiencing the whole body", one trains: "I breathe out experiencing the whole body." One trains: "I breathe in calming the bodily formation", one trains: "I breathe out calming the bodily formation" ...
>
> It is just as a skilled turner or a turner's apprentice who knows, when making a long turn: "I make a long turn"; he knows, when making a short turn: "I make a short turn."

Madhyama-āgama:

> One is mindful of breathing in and knows one is breathing in mindfully; one is mindful of breathing out and knows one is breathing out mindfully. Breathing in long, one knows one is breathing in long; breathing out long, one knows one is breathing out long. Breathing in short, one knows one is breathing in short; breathing out short, one knows one is breathing out short. One trains [in experiencing] the whole body when breathing in; one trains [in experiencing] the whole body when breathing out. One trains in calming bodily formations when breathing in; one trains in calming bodily formations when breathing out.[11]

The actual instructions in the two versions correspond quite closely. A difference between them is that the *Madhyama-āgama* discourse does not have the simile that illustrates awareness of the long and short breath with the example of a turner who makes a long or a short turn on his lathe. Unlike other similes in the *Majjhima-nikāya* version, which explain the whole practice of the contemplation in question, this simile only illustrates the first two of the four steps of

---

11 The passage actually speaks of the "verbal formations" when breathing out, which clearly seems to be a textual error, hence I have emended this to read "bodily formations", in line with what is to be experienced when breathing in.

mindfulness of breathing. Moreover, the turner simile is absent from the *Kāyagatāsati-sutta*, whose description of mindfulness of breathing in its other aspects closely follows the *Satipaṭṭhāna-sutta*.[12]

Another difference is that the *Madhyama-āgama* account does not describe the location where mindfulness of breathing is undertaken. According to the *Majjhima-nikāya* discourse, a meditator goes to a secluded place and sits down with legs crossed and with the body erect. Similar instructions can be found in descriptions of mindfulness of breathing in sixteen steps in the *Ānāpānasati-sutta*,[13] with parallels in the *Saṃyukta-āgama* and in the Mahāsāṅghika *Vinaya*.

The *Saṃyukta-āgama* discourse begins by describing how a monk goes begging on his almsround with the body guarded, the senses well restrained, and the mind settled. After completing his meal he puts away his bowl and robe, washes his feet, and approaches a place suitable for meditation, such as a forest or an empty hut. The monk then sits down at the root of a tree or in an open space, keeping his body erect and collecting mindfulness in front of himself.[14] At this point the *Saṃyukta-āgama* version mentions the removal of the five hindrances, following which the monk engages in the sixteen steps of mindfulness of breathing.

The description of the sixteen steps of mindfulness of breathing in the Mahāsāṅghika *Vinaya* similarly begins by depicting how a monk goes begging on his almsround with controlled activities, well-established mindfulness of the body, a settled mind, and sense-restraint. After completing his meal he goes to a secluded place to sit, such as an open space, a mountain cave, or a cemetery, puts down grass as a seat and sits down with straight posture. After overcoming the five hindrances, he engages in the practice of mindfulness of breathing in sixteen steps.[15]

Now, in the case of the *Satipaṭṭhāna-sutta*, the appropriate places and the posture for mindfulness of breathing are mentioned explicitly only in reference to this exercise, not in relation to any of the other body contemplations. Given that in the *Madhyama-āgama* parallel the instructions do not make any comparable specification regarding the appropriate posture or place, this may not be original

---

12 MN 119 at MN III 89,9 (translated Ñāṇamoli 1995: 949).
13 MN 118 at MN III 82,24 (translated Ñāṇamoli 1995: 943).
14 SĀ 803 at T II 206a20; parallel to SN 54.1 at SN V 311,7 (translated Bodhi 2000: 1765), whose presentation of the sixteen steps corresponds to MN 119.
15 T 1425 at T XXII 254c9.

to the *satipaṭṭhāna* context. Perhaps the instructions on the first four steps of mindfulness of breathing originate from a fuller exposition of the sixteen steps, similar to what is now found in the *Ānāpānasati-sutta* and its parallels. Since the scheme of sixteen steps is a whole way of practice in itself, instructions on the appropriate place and posture fit such a context more naturally than their appearance in only one of the several exercises in the *Satipaṭṭhāna-sutta*.

Another problem is that, according to the "refrain" that comes after the instructions on mindfulness of breathing in the *Satipaṭṭhāna-sutta*, the practice should be undertaken internally and externally. While the exercises found in all versions – the anatomical constitution, the elements that make up the body, and its decay at death – can easily be applied to the body of others, it is considerably less straightforward to think of a meaningful way to practise mindfulness in relation to the breath of another person.[16]

Moreover, the *Satipaṭṭhāna-sutta*'s listing of only the first four steps has the result that the dynamics underlying the scheme of sixteen steps is lost from sight. The whole purpose of the sixteen-step exposition is to show how mindfulness of breathing can be developed in such a way that it covers all four *satipaṭṭhāna*s, a topic I will discuss in more detail in Chapter 12. This rather remarkable presentation on how all *satipaṭṭhāna*s can be put into practice with a single object is lost when just the first four steps – being aware of the long breath, of the short breath, of the whole body, and calming bodily formation(s) – are removed from this wider context and presented on their own.

The extraction of a shorter passage from a longer exposition could easily have happened in the process of oral transmission. The qualification of the first four steps of mindfulness of breathing as being a form of contemplation of the body would naturally have led to associating them more explicitly to contemplation of the body as the first *satipaṭṭhāna*, which is what we now see in the *Majjhima-nikāya* and *Madhyama-āgama* versions.

In sum, the following points emerge:

- Mindfulness of breathing is absent from the *Ekottarika-āgama* version.

16 Gethin 1992: 53 comments that "the idea of watching another's body is no doubt clear enough if we are talking about the parts of a body or a corpse, but when we are talking of the breath the idea is perhaps a little harder to grasp."

- It has a different placing within the sequence of the body contemplations in the *Majjhima-nikāya* and the *Madhyama-āgama* discourse.
- The simile of the turner and the description of the appropriate place and posture are absent from the *Madhyama-āgama* version.
- The point made with these four steps emerges clearly only when they occur as part of the full scheme of sixteen steps.
- The four steps are not easily practised as an external form of *satipaṭṭhāna* meditation.

In the light of these points, it seems to me probable that the four steps of mindfulness of breathing are an addition to the original scheme of contemplation of the body in the *Satipaṭṭhāna-sutta* and its *Madhyama-āgama* parallel.

Suggesting that the four steps of mindfulness of breathing could be an addition to the *Satipaṭṭhāna-sutta* does not imply that the practice as such is late or that it should not be reckoned a form of *satipaṭṭhāna* meditation. In the light of the close similarity between descriptions of the sixteen steps of mindfulness of breathing in canonical texts of the Theravāda, Mūlasarvāstivāda, and Mahāsāṅghika traditions, there can be little doubt that this mode of developing awareness of the breath is an integral part of the early Buddhist teachings, in as much as we can access these through the canonical texts. Speaking of an addition therefore only means that an early passage was probably copied from its original place of occurrence and became part of the larger *satipaṭṭhāna* scheme at some point during oral transmission. Such copying must have happened at a comparatively early time, since both the Sarvāstivāda and Theravāda traditions agree on including mindfulness of breathing in their expositions of *satipaṭṭhāna*.

The suggestion that the first four steps of mindfulness of breathing may not have been part of the earliest formulation of contemplation of the body also does not imply in any way that mindfulness of breathing is not a form of *satipaṭṭhāna* meditation. On the contrary, the sixteen steps of mindfulness of breathing provide a full implementation of the entire scheme of four *satipaṭṭhāna*s, showing that the practice of mindfulness of breathing has a much broader compass than just being a way of practising only one *satipaṭṭhāna*. In other words, considering the four steps of mindfulness of breathing as an addition to the *Satipaṭṭhāna-sutta* restores this mode of meditation practice to its full position as a complete practice of all four *satipaṭṭhānas* with the explicitly stated potential of leading on its own to liberation. In chapter 12 of my study I will return to this topic, since the scheme of sixteen steps throws light on the overall significance of the four *satipaṭṭhānas*.

III.2.2 POSTURES AND ACTIVITIES

Two forms of body contemplation found in the *Majjhima-nikāya* and *Madhyama-āgama* versions are awareness of bodily postures and clear knowing of various activities. In the case of awareness of bodily postures the instructions read as follows:

Majjhima-nikāya:

> When walking, one knows: "I am walking"; or when standing, one knows "I am standing"; or when sitting, one knows "I am sitting"; or when lying down, one knows: "I am lying down"; or however one's body is disposed, one knows it accordingly.

Madhyama-āgama:

> Walking one knows one is walking, standing one knows one is standing, sitting one knows one is sitting, lying down one knows one is lying down, [falling] asleep one knows one is [falling] asleep, waking up one knows one is waking up, [falling] asleep [or] waking up one knows one is [falling] asleep [or] waking up.

The instructions in the *Majjhima-nikāya* discourse do not mention falling asleep or waking up.[17] Another difference is that, after listing the four postures, the *Majjhima-nikāya* version indicates that one should be aware of the body in whatever way it is disposed. In other words, the four postures explicitly mentioned are examples and not intended to restrict the practice to those moments only when one is properly seated, or stands fully straight, etc.

The instructions for clear knowing of various activities are as follows:

---

17 Jaini 1979/1998: 66 n.56 quotes instructions on an apparently similar form of practice among the Jains, which requires the practitioner to be aware while assuming any of the four postures and while eating or speaking; cf. also Schmithausen 1976: 254.

Majjhima-nikāya:

> When going forward and returning one acts clearly knowing; when looking ahead and looking away one acts clearly knowing; when flexing and extending [one's limbs] one acts clearly knowing; when wearing the outer robe and [other] robes and [carrying] the bowl one acts clearly knowing; when eating, drinking, consuming food and tasting it one acts clearly knowing; when defecating and urinating one acts clearly knowing; when walking, standing, sitting, falling asleep, waking up, talking, and keeping silent one acts clearly knowing.

Madhyama-āgama:

> One clearly knows one is going out and coming in, one contemplates and discerns it well; bending, stretching, lowering, or raising [any of one's limbs], one does it with appropriate deportment; wearing one's outer robe and [other] robes, and [carrying one's] bowl, one does it properly; walking, standing, sitting, lying down, [falling] asleep, waking up, talking, and keeping silent – all this one clearly knows.

The *Majjhima-nikāya* discourse thus extends clear knowing to looking ahead and away, to eating and drinking, and to defecating and urinating.[18] While the *Madhyama-āgama* version has fewer activities, it specifies more precisely the implications of what is meant by "clear knowing". Thus going out and coming in should be discerned well and movements of the limbs should be executed with appropriate deportment. One's robes and the bowl should be worn or carried properly.

These additional specifications are in line with an overall depiction of the proper conduct of a monastic, whose adoption of mindful and considerate behaviour is a distinct step in the gradual path of training that leads from going forth to liberation. In several discourses, clear knowing of bodily activities occurs separately from the four *satipaṭṭhāna*s, and in these contexts clear knowing is presented as something that leads up to the four *satipaṭṭhāna*s instead of being

18 A discourse in the *Dīrgha-āgama*, DĀ 2 at T I 14a3, mentions clear knowing when looking in different directions and in regard to eating and drinking, as is the case for the *Śrāvakabhūmi*, Shukla 1973: 11,12. A description of proper conduct in the Jain tradition, Deo 1956: 487, also covers defecating and urinating.

an integral part of them.[19] Given that this form of practice is also not mentioned in the *Ekottarika-āgama* version, it seems that clear knowing of activities could also be a later addition to the *satipaṭṭhāna* scheme.

The same holds for awareness of the postures, which is also not found in the *Ekottarika-āgama* version. The impression that these two practices may not have been part of the *satipaṭṭhāna* scheme from the outset is further strengthened by the difficulty of seeing the benefit of being aware that someone else is "walking", "standing", etc., or "bending" and "stretching", etc. That is, cultivating awareness in relation to bodily postures and activities only provides a way of anchoring mindfulness in the case of one's own postures and activities. An "external" application of these practices does not have such an effect. In contrast, an external form of practice does appear to be meaningful in the case of the three body contemplations that are found in all versions: anatomical parts, the elements, and a corpse in decay. Both one's own body and the bodies of others can be seen with insight as bereft of beauty, as simply a product of the material elements, and as bound to die and fall apart.

As with mindfulness of breathing, this hypothesis is not intended to suggest that awareness of postures and clearly knowing bodily activities are of later origin in themselves; nor does it imply that these are not excellent opportunities for developing mindfulness. What this suggestion entails is merely that a practice that was originally described in a different context may, at some comparatively early point of time during oral transmission, have been included in the description of contemplation of the body. This would have happened precisely because of the close relationship of this practice to, and its importance for, the cultivation of mindfulness.

III.3 BODY CONTEMPLATIONS FOUND IN ALL VERSIONS

The forms of contemplation of the body that are found in all versions are examining the body's anatomical parts and its elements, and comparing one's own body to a corpse in decay, which I will be

19 AN 10.61 at AN V 116,7 and AN 10.62 at AN V 119,17 (translated Bodhi 2012: 1417f), with parallels in MĀ 51 at T I 487c17, MĀ 52 at T I 489a18, and MĀ 53 at T I 489c21 (similar presentations in T 36 at T I 820b12 and T 37 at T I 821a9 only mention mindfulness, without explicitly bringing in clear knowing).

discussing in more detail in the next three chapters. The parallel versions agree not only in listing these three exercises, but also in the sequence in which they are presented. According to this sequence, the first of these body contemplations directly confronts notions of bodily beauty. This is a natural target, given that concern with beauty is such a prominent issue, whether in relation to one's own body or in relation to that of another. In fact in the *Vibhaṅga*, an early work in the Theravāda canonical Abhidharma collection, contemplation of the anatomical parts is the only exercise listed under contemplation of the body;[20] and in the *Dharmaskandha*, an early Sarvāstivāda Abhidharma work, contemplation of the body is concerned only with the anatomical parts and the elements.[21]

With the growing detachment developed through contemplation of the anatomical constitution of the body, the contemplation of the elements listed next in the *Satipaṭṭhāna-sutta* and its two parallels then turns to diminishing the sense of identification with the body. One comes to realize that one's body – as well as the bodies of others – is made up of the same elements as anything else outside in nature.

In the case of the body's death – the topic taken up in the third body contemplation found in all versions – one learns to accept the fact that one's own body is impermanent and bound to fall apart. In this way, one will no longer be affected by fear and attachment in the usual manner.

In doctrinal terms, the three topics that appear to be addressed through these three body contemplations would be:

- lack of beauty (*asubha*);
- not-self (*anattā*);
- impermanence (*anicca*).

The central aim of the contemplations of the body that are common to the three discourse versions would thus be to direct awareness to a clear understanding of the nature of the body from the viewpoint of its lack of intrinsic beauty, of its not-self nature, and of its inevitable destiny to end in death. This progression of themes begins with a survey of the anatomical parts in order to deconstruct the notion of

20 Vibh 193,17 (translated Thiṭṭila 1969: 251).

21 T 1537 at T XXVI 476a7; the anatomical parts and the elements are also the two aspects of contemplation of the body taken up from a variety of perspectives in the *Paṭisambhidāmagga*, Paṭis II 232,9 (translated Ñāṇamoli 1982: 398).

bodily beauty, a notion of considerable influence in many aspects of modern life. Behind concern with the attractiveness of the body stands one's tendency to identify with it; so the next exercise employs contemplation of the elements to undermine this sense of bodily identity. As long as one identifies with the body, the fact of its death remains an ever-present threat. The tendency to ignore and avoid one's own mortality is then countered with the third exercise.[22] The overall direction that contemplation of the body takes in this way is detachment from the body through understanding its true nature.

The resultant perspective is less evident when one considers the exercises listed under contemplation of the body in the *Satipaṭṭhāna-sutta* alone, which also cover, for example, mindfulness of breathing or awareness of postures. While such practices certainly have an important function as part of the path to awakening, the three exercises common to the parallel versions differ in so far as with them contemplation of the body is not just about using the body – or parts of it like the breath – to be mindful. Rather, these forms of contemplation of the body are first of all about understanding the nature of the body. That is, the emphasis is on insight to begin with, rather than just on mindfulness itself.

This, to my mind, is an important result deriving from a comparative study of the canonical parallels to the *Satipaṭṭhāna-sutta*, namely highlighting as an essential flavour of the first *satipaṭṭhāna* the cultivation of mindfulness to gain an insight into the nature of the body. While this does not in any way diminish the usefulness of those body contemplations that are not found in all versions, it does indicate that a central task of the first *satipaṭṭhāna* is to overcome the notion of bodily beauty, to let go of the idea of ownership of the body, and to counter the innate tendency to avoid the fact that the body will die.

III.4 BENEFITS OF CONTEMPLATION OF THE BODY

In the *Majjhima-nikāya* and *Madhyama-āgama* versions the passage that comes after each of these three exercises, which I have dubbed the

22 Harmon-Jones et al. 1997: 24 explain that "the fear of death is rooted in an instinct for self-preservation that humans share with other species. Although we share this instinct with other species, only we are aware that death is inevitable ... this combination of an instinctive drive for self-preservation with an awareness of the inevitability of death creates the potential for paralyzing terror."

"refrain", indicates that, by contemplating the nature of the body in this way, mindfulness becomes established and leads to knowledge. The two versions express this as follows:

Majjhima-nikāya:

> Mindfulness that "there is a body" is established in one just for the sake of bare knowledge and for the sake of continuous mindfulness.

Madhyama-āgama:

> One establishes mindfulness in the body and is endowed with knowledge, vision, understanding, and penetration.

Having directed mindfulness repeatedly to the body with the help of the three contemplations that are common to the parallel versions, the body as a whole becomes a more consciously registered part of one's experience. This natural consequence of engaging in body contemplation will result in a strengthening of awareness of one's body throughout any posture or activity. Thus, from a practical perspective, contemplation of the body undertaken with the aim of understanding the nature of the body does not dispense with awareness of bodily postures and activities, as these are much rather a natural result of such a form of practice. While contemplation of the body is not just about being aware of one's posture, such awareness remains a crucially important practice to enable continuity of mindfulness during various activities.

III.4.1 ANCHORING MINDFULNESS IN THE BODY

Awareness cultivated in this way leads to being centred in the body through mindfulness, which can serve as an important anchor for maintaining awareness during everyday activities. Such anchoring in the body through mindfulness finds an illustration in two similes in the *Saṃyutta-nikāya* and in the *Saṃyukta-āgama*. The first simile describes six animals bound to a strong post, while the second depicts a person carrying a container full of oil through a crowd that is watching a dancing girl. In what follows, I translate the *Saṃyukta-āgama* version of the simile of the six animals:[23]

---

23 SĀ 1171 at T II 313a15 to 313a24.

> It is just as a person who … had caught six types of animals: first he caught a dog, and taking hold of the dog he bound it to one spot. Then he caught a bird, then he caught a poisonous snake, then he caught a jackal, then he caught a crocodile, and then he caught a monkey. Having caught these animals, he bound them all to a single spot.[24]
>
> That dog desires to enter the village, that bird always wishes to fly up into the sky, that snake always wishes to enter a cave, that jackal delights in approaching a cemetery, the crocodile always wishes to enter a large lake, and the monkey wishes to enter a mountain forest.
>
> These six animals, being all bound to a single spot, with their different likes, each wishing to reach a peaceful place, are each in that place against their likes, because they are firmly bound. Each uses its strength to approach the direction they like, yet they are unable to get free.[25]

In agreement with its parallels, the *Saṃyukta-āgama* discourse indicates that the spot to which the animals are bound is a strong pillar, explaining that this pillar stands for mindfulness of the body and the six animals represent the six senses. This simile suggests that mindfulness of the body provides a centring comparable to a strong pillar that is able to withstand the pulling force of being attracted by this and that through the six senses.

The other simile about carrying a container full of oil on one's head takes up the same theme with a different example. Here is the *Saṃyukta-āgama* version of this simile:[26]

> Suppose there is a beauty in the world. This beauty of the world is in one place and smilingly performs various kinds of singing, dancing, music, and merriment. A great crowd has gathered in that

24 The sequence of listing the animals differs in the parallel versions: the Pāli parallel, SN 35.206 at SN IV 200,7 (translated Bodhi 2000: 1256, given as number 247), takes up a snake (not qualified as poisonous), a crocodile, a bird, a dog, a jackal, and a monkey. A Tibetan parallel, D 4094 *nyu* 80a2 or Q 5595 *thu* 125b6, lists a dog, a bird, a jackal, a crocodile, a snake (also not qualified as poisonous), and a monkey.

25 In SN 35.206 at SN IV 200,13 the snake wants to go into an anthill and the crocodile wants to go into the water. D 4094 *nyu* 80a5 or Q 5595 *thu* 126a3 agrees with SĀ 1171 that the snake wants to go into a cave (following the reading in D), but agrees with SN 35.206 that the crocodile wants to go into the water.

26 SĀ 623 at T II 174b21 to 174b29.

> place. Suppose there is a person who is not foolish and not silly, who likes joy and is averse to pain, who wants to live and is afraid of death.
>
> A person says to him: "Man, you take this bowl full of oil and pass through by the beauty of the world and the great crowd. I am sending a capable executioner to follow you with drawn sword. If you lose one drop of the oil, right away your life will be cut off." …
>
> Will that man carrying the bowl of oil be able to forget about the bowl of oil, forget about the executioner, and look at the dancing girl and at the great crowd?[27]

In such a situation the poor man will obviously not forget the task he has, since if he gets distracted by looking at the girl he might spill the oil and his life will come to an end. The *Saṃyutta-nikāya* discourse explains that the bowl full of oil represents mindfulness of the body in this simile.[28] Keeping in mind that in India containers are usually carried on the head, the image of the bowl of oil on one's head conveys a sense of being centred in the body through awareness.

Since the man has to be aware of the crowd around him in order to get through it without spilling the oil, the situation depicted in the simile makes it clear that the point is not to focus on one's own body to the exclusion of anything else. Instead, the field of attention is sufficiently broadened so that, while remaining centred in mindfulness of the body, one is also aware of one's environment and able to react to it meaningfully.

The similes of the six animals and of carrying a bowl of oil provide helpful indications of the benefits of mindfulness of the body in everyday life. The six "animals" of one's senses do pull in this or that direction often enough. Maintaining some degree of anchoring in awareness of the body can provide a crucial centring force. In this way, one would even be able to move safely through a great crowd that is watching the most beautiful girl singing and dancing, with an executioner at one's back who is ready to chop off one's head if mindfulness is "spilled" even for one moment.

---

27 The parallel SN 47.20 at SN V 170,3 (translated Bodhi 2000: 1649) reports a gradual building up of the great crowd: people first just gather to look at the beautiful girl, but when she starts singing and dancing more people come to join the crowd. Another difference is that SN 47.20 speaks of no longer attending to the bowl and out of negligence turning attention outwards.

28 SN 47.20 at SN V 170,18.

Such centring of mindfulness on the body while engaging in normal activities provides a helpful tool for maintaining awareness in an everyday setting. Attempting to bridge the gap between intensive practice and normal life, a common challenge is often that the more concentrated forms of attention developed in a retreat setting, along with the emphasis on stopping short at bare sense data, may not necessarily be functional in the outside world.

As a practical illustration I take the example of driving a car after emerging from a meditation retreat: if the traffic light has changed to red, one had better notice this clearly, instead of just remaining focused on the sensation of one's breath. Moreover, instead of merely noting "red, red", one also needs to recognize what a red traffic light means, in purely conventional terms. While this may seem patently clear on mere reflection, in actual experience it can take a little while before the mind has adapted itself to the requirements of being outside of a retreat setting.

A way of continuing practice in such situations could be to remain with an open mind, capable of engaging with the outside world, while at the same time also anchoring the mind through awareness of the body. That is, instead of fixing attention on anything in particular, such as the breath or the sensations of touch on the soles of one's feet, etc., awareness of the body as a whole can be used as a way of anchoring mindfulness in the present moment.

Such an anchor in fact provides a helpful check on whether one is actually being mindful or not, since on inspection it quickly becomes clear if this anchor has been lost. In contrast, trying to be mindful without any particular reference point, in the sense of just being mindful of whatever happens, is not necessarily easy to practise, however easy it may sound. For some practitioners, at least, there is a danger of self-deception. One might end up pretending to oneself that anything one does is being done mindfully, even when in reality one is no longer mindful.

Grounding oneself in awareness of the whole body not only provides a clear reference point that facilitates recognizing if one is really being mindful, it also naturally encourages a broad and open state of mind. Mindfulness of the body thus comes to function somewhat like a backrest, instead of resulting in a narrow focus, and therefore does not interfere with one's ability to handle things in the outside world. Moreover, awareness of the body facilitates becoming aware of feelings and thus of the potential arising of reactions by way of craving; this provides a lead over to contemplation of feelings, the second *satipaṭṭhāna*.[29] Thus, using the whole body to carry the "bowl" of mindfulness provides a strong "post" that can withstand the incessant pull of the six senses in this and that direction, enabling one to engage in the world without being carried away by it.

III.4.2 MINDFULNESS OF THE BODY AND DETACHMENT

Further perspectives on the benefits of mindfulness of the body can be gathered from the *Kāyagatāsati-sutta* and its *Madhyama-āgama* parallel. The two discourses are entirely dedicated to exploring the first *satipaṭṭhāna*, for which purpose they list the same exercises that make up contemplation of the body in the *Satipaṭṭhāna-sutta* and its *Madhyama-āgama* parallel.[30] After listing ways of developing mindfulness in regard to the body, the *Kāyagatāsati-sutta* and its *Madhyama-āgama* parallel survey the benefits that can be expected from this kind of practice.

The two versions illustrate the beneficial effects of mindfulness of the body with several similes that bring out in particular the positive effects of mental detachment through insight into the nature of the body. A chief benefit, mentioned after each of the body contemplations, is in fact the gaining of concentration of the mind. In what follows, I translate the similes illustrating the benefits of mindfulness of the body from the *Madhyama-āgama* version:[31]

> If one cultivates mindfulness of the body in this way, making much of it like this, then this completely includes all wholesome states, that is, the states that pertain to awakening. If one resolves on a state of

---

29 Hölzel et al. 2011: 549 explain that "heightened body awareness … helps to detect physiological aspects of the feelings present (e.g., body tension, rapid heartbeat, short shallow breath), and the provided information about the internal reaction to the stimulus is a prerequisite for accurate identification of the triggered emotional response."

30 In the case of MN 119, as mentioned above, the list of meditation practices also includes the bodily experience of the four absorptions, in addition to the exercises listed in MN 10.

31 MĀ 81 at T I 556c9 to 557b4 (translated Kuan 2008: 162). Kuan 2008: 131 points out that the image of the ocean as the converging point of all waters can also be found in the *Bṛhadāraṇyaka Upaniṣad* 2.4.11 (translated Radhakrishnan 1953/1992: 199).

> mind, it will reach completion. This is just as the great ocean. All of the small rivers will completely be included in the ocean.[32]

In other words, mindfulness of the body lays a foundation in mental culture that becomes as expansive as the great ocean, leading to the cultivation of other wholesome states comparable to rivers that flow into this ocean.

The two versions continue with a set of similes related to being able to withstand Māra. The *Madhyama-āgama* discourse provides the following similes for illustrating how one goes beyond the reach of Māra by cultivating mindfulness of the body:

> It is just as a water pot full of water that has been placed firmly upright on the ground. Suppose someone brings water and pours it into the pot ... will that pot take up the additional water in this way?

Of course, the water pot will not take up any extra water. This situation contrasts with the case of an empty water pot, into which extra water can be poured.

> It is just as a strong man who throws a light ball made of feather at a level door panel ... will it penetrate the door?

Obviously the ball will not stick to the door, contrary to the case when a strong man throws a heavy stone at a mound of wet mud.

> It is just as a person who, seeking fire, uses wet wood as a base and drills it with a wet drill ... will that person get fire in this way?

Needless to say, he will not be able to get fire, contrary to the case when he uses dry wood and a dry drill.

The presentation of these three images in the parallel versions is fairly similar, except for a difference in sequence. The *Kāyagatāsati-*

---

32 MN 119 at MN III 94,23 (translated Ñāṇamoli 1995: 954) identifies the wholesome states to be the states that partake of true knowledge. MN 119 does not mention the ability to accomplish whatever state of mind one may resolve on, although a similar statement does occur at a slightly later point in its exposition. The ocean simile in MN 119 then describes extending one's mind over the great ocean and thereby having included all the streams that flow into it – a simile also used in relation to mindfulness of the body in AN 1.21 at AN I 43,12 (translated Bodhi 2012: 129, given as number 575).

sutta first illustrates how those who have not cultivated mindfulness of the body will fall into the hands of Māra as easily as a heavy ball thrown at mud will stick, a fire made with dry wood will ignite, and water poured into an empty jug will be taken up. Next in the *Kāyagatāsati-sutta* comes the case of one who has cultivated mindfulness of the body, in which case Māra will not stand a chance. This compares to throwing a light ball at a door panel, trying to make fire with wet wood, and trying to pour water into a full jug. In the *Madhyama-āgama* version, however, the empty jug is followed by the full jug, the heavy ball thrown at wet mud is followed by the light ball thrown at a door panel, and the dry wood used for making fire is followed by the wet wood.

The *Kāyagatāsati-sutta* continues with three more similes, which compare the ease with which one who has cultivated mindfulness of the body can gain realization to the ease with which a strong man might tip over a full water jug, or loosen the embankment of a pond full of water, or the ease with which a skilled charioteer may drive a chariot wherever he likes.

The similes of the water jug, the ball, and the firewood that are common to the two versions vividly underscore the importance of mindfulness of the body for mental cultivation. The *Kāyagatāsati-sutta* and its *Madhyama-āgama* parallel continue by providing a list of the benefits that can be expected from successfully cultivating mindfulness of the body. While the listing shows some variations, the common ground between the two versions is that mindfulness of the body will enable one to endure patiently cold and heat, hunger and thirst, etc., as well as discontent and fear. These benefits reveal how detachment towards the body makes it possible to remain calm amidst bodily vicissitudes.

Benefits of a higher nature are that mindfulness of the body will facilitate the attainment of the four absorptions. This reflects the need to go beyond sensual desire in order to be able to access the happiness of the deeply concentrated mind. Further benefits are the attainment of the six supernormal knowledges, the last of which is the destruction of the influxes when attaining full awakening. In this way, mindfulness of the body becomes almost like a wish-fulfilling gem for those who have embarked on the path to liberation.

III.5 SUMMARY

A central theme of the first *satipaṭṭhāna* is insight into the real nature of the body as a way of developing detachment. Directing awareness to the body's anatomical constitution reveals its lack of beauty; contemplating the material elements found within oneself diminishes one's identification with the body; and facing the body's inevitable death drives home its impermanent nature. Repeatedly directing awareness to explore the nature of the body in this way enables mindfulness to remain centred in the body, providing a strong "post" that helps to carry the "bowl" of mindfulness through everyday activities without succumbing to distraction.

IV

THE ANATOMICAL PARTS

IV.1 INSTRUCTIONS

Examining the anatomical constitution of the body is the first of the three modes of body contemplation that are found in the *Satipaṭṭhāna-sutta* as well as in both of its Chinese *Āgama* parallels. In what follows I compare the relevant part of the instructions in the three versions and then explore their significance.

Majjhima-nikāya:

> One examines this same body up from the soles of the feet and down from the top of the hair, enclosed by skin and full of many kinds of impurity:
>
> "In this body there are head hairs, body hairs, nails, teeth, skin, flesh, sinews, bones, bone marrow, kidneys, heart, liver, diaphragm, spleen, lungs, bowels, mesentery, contents of the stomach, faeces, bile, phlegm, pus, blood, sweat, fat, tears, grease, spittle, snot, oil of the joints, and urine."
>
> ... it is just as a man with good eyes who has opened a double-mouthed bag full of different sorts of grain, such as hill rice, red rice, beans, peas, millet, and white rice, which he would examine: "This is hill rice, this is red rice, these are beans, these are peas, this is millet, and this is white rice."

Madhyama-āgama:

> One contemplates this body, according to its position and according to what is attractive and what is repulsive, from head

to foot, seeing that it is full of various kinds of impurities:

"Within this body of mine there are head hairs, body hairs, nails, teeth, rough and smooth epidermis, skin, flesh, sinews, bones, heart, kidneys, liver, lungs, large intestine, small intestine, spleen, stomach, lumps of faeces, brain and brain stem, tears, sweat, saliva, pus, blood, fat, marrow, mucus, phlegm, and urine."

It is just as a clear-sighted person who, on seeing a vessel full of various seeds, clearly distinguishes them all, that is, "rice, millet seed, turnip seed, or mustard seed".

Ekottarika-āgama:

One contemplates this body according to its nature and functions, from head to feet and from feet to head, contemplating all in this body that is of an impure [nature] as not worth being attached to.

One then contemplates that in this body there are body hairs, head hairs, nails, teeth, skin, flesh, tendons, bones, bone marrow, brain, fat, intestines, stomach, heart, liver, spleen, kidneys, one contemplates and knows them all. [There are also] faeces, urine, [whatever else] is produced by digestion in the two receptacles, tears in the eyes, spittle, mucus, blood in the veins, fat, and gall; one contemplates and knows them all as not worth being attached to.

When compared to the *Majjhima-nikāya* version, the introductory phrase in the *Madhyama-āgama* discourse makes an additional stipulation that the body should be contemplated "according to its position". This specification seems to imply that practice need not be confined to the sitting posture; in other words, reviewing the anatomical constitution can and perhaps even should be done according to whatever way the body is disposed at any time.[1] The *Majjhima-nikāya* discourse makes a comparable remark in relation to contemplation of the elements, where the body should be reviewed "however it is placed, however disposed".

The *Ekottarika-āgama* version instructs that the body should be examined "according to its nature and functions", where the Chinese term I have translated as "functions" could also be rendered as "activities". The instruction as a whole conveys a nuance of not only

1 A similar specification is made in a description of perception of the absence of beauty, *aśubha*, in a Gāndhārī fragment of a *Saṃyukta-āgama* discourse, Glass 2007: 150.

gaining insight into the constitution of the body, but also perhaps to some degree being aware of the function of the different anatomical parts. This is significant because not only dwelling excessively on the attractiveness of certain parts of the body but also feeling excessive repulsion towards other parts can result in losing sight of the fact that these bodily parts have a function simply in keeping the body alive and in working order.

The nuance of balance becomes explicit with the *Madhyama-āgama* version's injunction that the body should be examined "according to what is attractive and what is repulsive". While this stipulation is not made in the parallel versions, a similar attitude is to some extent inherent in the actual listing of parts. In all versions this listing mentions bodily parts like teeth, skin, and hair, which are commonly seen as attributes of attractiveness, alongside other parts of the body such as mucus, pus, faeces, and urine, which are generally experienced as repulsive. Thus the listing of bodily parts seems to exemplify what the *Madhyama-āgama* discourse makes explicit: contemplating in a balanced manner takes into account both what is usually seen as characteristic of bodily attractiveness and what is generally perceived as repulsive.[2] The basic lesson to be learned in this way is that, in the end, all these bodily parts are of the same nature, and that dividing them into what is attractive and what is repulsive is an evaluation of the mind.

The *Madhyama-āgama* account continues by indicating that the practice also requires "seeing that [the body] is full of various kinds of impurities". In the same vein, the *Ekottarika-āgama* discourse enjoins "contemplating all in this body that is of an impure [nature]", and the instructions found in the *Majjhima-nikāya* also speak of the body being "full of many kinds of impurity".

In the ancient Indian context, impurity was a quality quite naturally associated with the body.[3] Nevertheless, my rendering of the qualification in these passages from the Chinese *Āgama*s as "impure" is not the only way in which the original could be translated. Even though this is the most self-evident rendering of the

2 Commenting on the Pāli listing of anatomical parts, Hamilton 1995: 58 notes that its phrasing "clearly illustrates the extent to which each and every part is to be observed in the same objective light as part of the analytical meditation exercise. This is regardless of whether it is, say, a tooth or mucus or pus."

3 Olivelle 2002: 190 explains that, in ancient India in general, "ascetic discourse presents the body as impure in its very essence."

Chinese expression *bùjìng* (a sense evident in the corresponding Pāli expression *asuci*, which means "impure" or "unclean"), the Chinese term *bùjìng* can equally well render the qualification "unattractive", *asubha*.[4] This is clearly the case, for example, in the Chinese translations of a passage in the *Abhidharmakośabhāṣya*, which employ *bùjìng* to render what in the Sanskrit original is the term "unattractive", *aśubha*.[5]

Contemplation of the anatomical parts is in fact regularly subsumed under the heading of being concerned with what is "unattractive" in the early discourses, as well as in works like the *Arthaviniścaya-sūtra*, the *Śikṣāsamuccaya*, and the *Śrāvakabhūmi*.[6] Similarly, in a discourse in the *Aṅguttara-nikāya* the heading "unattractive" qualifies reviewing the anatomical parts of the body. This discourse nevertheless uses the qualification "impure" a little later, when introducing the actual listing of anatomical parts.[7] In other words, from the viewpoint of this discourse, the notions of lacking beauty and of being impure appear to be interchangeable.

Whatever term one might decide to use, the thrust of this exercise concerns disclosing the body's lack of beauty. The *Ekottarika-āgama*

---

4 Hirakawa 1997: 54 s.v. lists *aśubha* alongside *aśuddhi* and *aśuci* as possible Sanskrit equivalents for *bùjìng*.

5 *Abhidharmakośabhāṣya* 6.9, Pradhan 1967: 337,8, refers to *aśubha*, which its Chinese counterparts in T 1558 at T XXIX 117b6 and T 1559 at T XXIX 269c9 render as *bùjìng*; cf. also below note 38 and p.183, n.15.

6 The *Arthaviniścaya-sūtra*, Samtani 1971: 41,7, employs the term *aśubha* to qualify its listing of anatomical parts, notably introduced as an instance of right mindfulness in case a monk is passionate on seeing a woman (although an earlier passage in the same work employs the expression *aśuci*, cf. Samtani 1971: 23,5). The *Śikṣāsamuccaya*, Bendall 1902/1970: 209,7, introduces its listing of anatomical parts under the heading of *aśubhabhāvanā*. The *Śrāvakabhūmi*, Shukla 1973: 203,1, qualifies the listing of anatomical parts as a way of developing *aśubha*, in which case the Chinese translation, T 1579 at T XXX 428c24, employs the rendering *bùjìng*, although this is preceded by indicating that they are "rotten and impure".

7 AN 10.60 at AN V 109,18 (translated Bodhi 2012: 1412) introduces the listing of anatomical parts as a "perception of unattractiveness", *asubhasaññā*, but the listing itself then has the standard phrase on reviewing what is "impure", *asuci*. The only known parallel to this discourse is preserved in Tibetan, D 38 *ka* 277a1 or Q 754 *tsi* 293b5 (apparently translated from a Pāli original, cf. Skilling 1993), which speaks in both instances of impurity, *mi gtsang ba*. The narrative context of this instruction shows a sick monk being informed of various meditative modes of perception. As a result of the teaching, the monk recovers his health. Thus, at least in the early Buddhist setting, exercises like the present one were perceived as something that can generate inspiration.

version concludes its introductory description on how the actual contemplation should be carried out by indicating that this body is "not worth being attached to", a statement repeated again after the listing of anatomical parts. This remark clearly points to detachment and shows that, whichever of the two notions one might prefer – "impurity" or "lack of beauty" – the actual practice should be undertaken in such a way that it results in the balanced attitude of detachment.

For a proper appreciation of the nature of *satipaṭṭhāna* meditation, it is noteworthy that the present exercise involves a clear element of deliberate evaluation.[8] Whether "impure" or "unattractive", contemplation of the body from the perspective of its anatomical parts combines mindfulness with the use of concepts that clearly involve a value judgement. That is, mindfulness in early Buddhist thought is not just non-judgemental. Needless to say, such deliberate evaluation for the sake of progress on the path to liberation is quite different from compulsory reacting to experience in a judgemental way.[9]

Regarding the actual listing of anatomical parts, the parallel versions show some minor divergences. One example is the explicit reference to the brain in the two Chinese *Āgama* versions.[10] Such differences reflect the fact that the listings are probably best taken as exemplifying the anatomical constitution of the body by enumerating selected parts.[11] The actual parts would thus be less important than the overall realization of the true nature of the body.

The most prominent difference between the three versions is that the *Ekottarika-āgama* discourse does not have the simile illustrating the undertaking of this exercise with the example of looking at various

---

8 Bodhi 2011: 26 comments, in regard to "the common interpretation of mindfulness as a type of awareness intrinsically devoid of discrimination, evaluation, and judgment", that this "does not square well with the canonical texts and may even lead to a distorted view of how mindfulness is to be practiced".

9 Kabat-Zinn 2011: 291f in fact explains that to speak of mindfulness practice as "non-judgemental does not mean … that there is some ideal state in which judgements no longer arise". The point is only to avoid habitual judgemental reactions to what is experienced.

10 The brain is mentioned elsewhere in the Pāli discourses; cf. Sn 199.

11 Hamilton 1996: 10 points out that "the fact that the list is manifestly not comprehensive suggests that such descriptions are not intended to be understood as definite lists of what the body is made of; rather they indicate examples". For various listings of anatomical parts cf. also Dhammajoti 2009: 250–2.

grains. Judging from the description in the *Majjhima-nikāya* account, these grains are found in a kind of cloth bag employed for sowing.[12]

The simile in the *Majjhima-nikāya* and *Madhyama-āgama* discourses illustrates the proper attitude during meditation practice, thereby confirming the impression conveyed by the instruction in the *Ekottarika-āgama* version that none of the bodily parts is "worth being attached to". Just as looking at various grains would not stimulate attachment or aversion in the observer, in the same way examining the body's anatomical constitution should result in a balanced attitude that is aloof from attachment as well as from aversion.

Regarding the qualification of the body as "impure", the simile of looking at various grains would indeed illustrate a way of viewing something as bereft of beauty, whereas the same image does not appear to have any evident relation to impurity. Be it rice, beans, or other seeds, looking at these grains in their dry condition, ready for being sown, does not seem to illustrate impurity, for which other similes would have been more opportune. Thus the sense conveyed by the simile would fit an understanding of this exercise as concerned with lack of beauty, *asubha*.

IV.2 BALANCE

Now the balanced attitude required for proper practice does not automatically result from contemplating the body's anatomy. An unbalanced way of undertaking this exercise is in fact recorded in each of the main extant *Vinaya*s, according to which a group of monks, after contemplating the unattractive nature of their own bodies, were driven to commit suicide. The narration continues with the Buddha recommending that the monks should practise mindfulness of breathing instead.[13] Clearly, the development of loathing

---

12 Schlingloff 1964: 33f n.10.

13 This is reported in the Dharmaguptaka *Vinaya*, T 1428 at T XXII 576b7, the Mahāsāṅghika *Vinaya*, T 1425 at T XXII 254c6, the Mahīśāsaka *Vinaya*, T 1421 at T XXII 7c6, the Sarvāstivāda *Vinaya*, T 1435 at T XXIII 8a13, and the Theravāda *Vinaya*, Vin III 70,19 (= SN 54.9 at SN V 321,21, translated Bodhi 2000: 1774). The version of this tale in the Mūlasarvāstivāda *Vinaya* does not lead up to an instruction on mindfulness of breathing and instead has a ruling pronounced by the Buddha on this occasion; cf. T 1443 at T XXIII 923b24 and D 3 *ca* 134b4 or Q 1032 *che* 120b8. However, another Mūlasarvāstivāda version of this event, SĀ 809 at T II 208a3 (translated Anālayo in preparation), has instructions on mindfulness of breathing.

for the body to the extent of wishing to get rid of it was not the way the monks were expected to practise.

When attempting to make sense of this puzzling episode, it is perhaps significant that in none of the parallel versions did the Buddha deliver actual instructions on how perceiving the body as "impure" or as "bereft of beauty" should be undertaken. He is only on record for recommending such practice in general. Thus the point of this story seems to me to be that contemplating the anatomical parts can be harmful if it is undertaken in an unbalanced manner. Here the nuances conveyed by the simile in the *Majjhima-nikāya* and *Madhyama-āgama* discourses as well as the explicit recommendation of detachment in the *Ekottarika-āgama* account point in the same direction: mental balance and detachment are of central importance.

The overall importance of mental balance also emerges from another mode of presentation in the early discourses that describes a progressive training of perception in seeing something as repulsive or else as not repulsive, the final outcome of which is the poise of equanimity. A passage in the *Saṃyukta-āgama*, which relates this directly to establishing mindfulness, instructs as follows:[14]

> In relation to the body internally one arouses a perception of repulsiveness, and in relation to the body internally one arouses a perception of non-repulsiveness. With right mindfulness and clear knowing one has a perception of abandoning both repulsiveness and non-repulsiveness.

The passage then continues by applying the same instruction to the body externally as well as to the body internally and externally, and then in the same way to the other three *satipaṭṭhāna*s. The *Saṃyutta-nikāya* parallel to the above passage is considerably more detailed, as it describes perceiving what is not repulsive as repulsive and also what is repulsive as not repulsive, etc.[15] Its presentation makes it clear that the task is to develop a perception that runs counter to one's normal way of perceiving. But even this alternative mode of perception has no inherent value, apart from the fact that, if undertaken properly, it leads to equanimity and to being established in mindfulness and clear knowing. This sets the proper context for

---

14 SĀ 536 at T II 139b28 to 193c1.

15 SN 52.1 at SN V 295,11 (translated Bodhi 2000: 1751). Another difference is that SN 52.1 adds the presence of equanimity to mindfulness and clear knowing.

contemplation of the body's anatomy. Here the overall aim should similarly be arriving at detached equanimity with respect to the body, together with being established in mindfulness and clear knowing.

Besides the need for the proper attitude, another important aspect of contemplation of the anatomical parts is that actual practice is first of all concerned with one's own body. This is explicitly stated in the *Madhyama-āgama* version, which introduces the listing of bodily parts with the specification "within this body of mine". The same sense applies to the parallel versions, which use the expression "in this body". Since the passage is formulated from the perspective of the meditator, even without the explicit specification "of mine" it is clear that one's own body is intended. When listings of the anatomical parts are employed in other discourses for the purpose of contemplating the lack of beauty of the body, the question is similarly one of contemplating one's own body.[16]

A discourse in the *Saṃyutta-nikāya* and its *Saṃyukta-āgama* parallel explicitly tackles the issue of how young monks are able to live a life of celibacy. Besides looking at women as their relatives (mother, sister, or daughter) and undertaking the practice of sense-restraint, this discourse mentions contemplation of the anatomical constitution of the body as one of the tools that help young monks to rein in their sensual desires. In both versions, the instructions speak of the anatomical parts found in "this body"; that is, in the body of the practising monk.[17]

IV.3 THE DYNAMICS OF SENSUAL ATTRACTION

The logic behind this emphasis on contemplating one's own body first of all is clarified in a discourse in the *Aṅguttara-nikāya*, of which unfortunately no parallel seems to have been preserved. While in general in the present study I try to base myself on material preserved in more than one tradition, in this case I would like to make an exception and present my translation of the relevant passage, even though as far

16 The specification "in this body" is only absent when the listing of anatomical parts is used for contemplation of the elements, to which I will turn in the next chapter.

17 SN 35.127 at SN IV 111,17 (translated Bodhi 2000: 1198) and SĀ 1165 at T II 311a27. The same specification is also found in a Gāndhārī fragment of a *Saṃyukta-āgama* discourse, Glass 2007: 150.

as I am able to tell this is only preserved in the Theravāda tradition. This passage provides an important explanation of why contemplation of the anatomical parts needs to be first of all directed to one's own body. The *Aṅguttara-nikāya* proceeds as follows:[18]

> A female gives attention internally to the faculty of femininity: to feminine behaviour, feminine manners, feminine ways, feminine desire, feminine voice, and feminine adornments. She delights in them and enjoys them. Delighting in them and enjoying them she gives attention externally to the faculty of masculinity: to masculine behaviour, masculine manners, masculine ways, masculine desire, masculine voice, and masculine adornments. She delights in them and enjoys them. Delighting in them and enjoying them she yearns for union externally and she yearns for the happiness and joy that arise based on such external union.
>
> Living beings that enjoy femininity go into union with males … in this way a female does not transcend femininity …
>
> A male gives attention internally to the faculty of masculinity: to masculine behaviour, masculine manners, masculine ways, masculine desire, masculine voice, and masculine adornments. He delights in them and enjoys them. Delighting in them and enjoying them he gives attention externally to the faculty of femininity: to feminine behaviour, feminine manners, feminine ways, feminine desire, feminine voice, and feminine adornments. He delights in them and enjoys them. Delighting in them and enjoying them he yearns for union externally and he yearns for the happiness and joy that arise based on such external union.
>
> Living beings that enjoy masculinity go into union with females … in this way a male does not transcend masculinity.

The discourse then continues by explaining that in the opposite case, when one does not delight in the characteristics of one's own gender, one also does not delight in the characteristics of the other gender and thus there will be no yearning for external union.

The analysis offered in this passage provides a significant indication of the purpose and context of contemplation of the anatomical parts as a way of going beyond sensual desire. A passage like this makes it unmistakeably clear that, whatever may be the case in later Buddhist

---

18 AN 7.48 at AN IV 57,4 to 58,1 (translated Bodhi 2012: 1039, given as number 51).

literature, from an early Buddhist viewpoint the issue at stake is not a simplistic attribution of the problem of sensual attraction to the other sex. Rather, the roots of sexual desire are in one's own identification with and subsequent delight in the qualities and characteristics of one's own sex. The inability to transcend this narrow sense of identity based on being female or male is what leads to a search outside for what is experienced as lacking within. Letting go of that narrow sense of gendered identity and of the tendency to relish the characteristics of one's own sex opens up the path of transcendence that will lead to freedom.

This makes it clear why contemplation of the anatomical parts needs first of all to be undertaken in relation to one's own body. Contemplation of the body of another person falls into its proper place only after this foundational mode of practice concerned with one's own body has been well established.[19]

Actually contemplating the anatomical constitution of one's own body then can take the listing of anatomical parts as its starting point. Needless to say, the point of putting this into practice is not confined merely to memorizing or reciting the names of the parts, although this could be a starting point. Instead, successfully undertaking this form of meditation practice requires a basic anatomical knowledge of these parts and an attempt to imagine and ideally even get a physical sense of where at least the more evident of these anatomical parts are located within one's own body.

The *Sampasādanīya-sutta* and its *Dīrgha-āgama* parallel describe a progression of practice from contemplation of the anatomical parts to leaving aside skin and flesh in order to be aware just of the bones.[20] This gives the impression that actual practice does indeed

19 The *Vibhaṅga* begins its exposition of *satipaṭṭhāna* with the internal mode of practice, introduced at Vibh 193,18 (translated Thiṭṭila 1969: 251) with the phrase "in this body" and thus in reference to one's own body, in contrast to the external mode, which employs the expression "in that one's body", Vibh 194,4. The description of the external mode of contemplating the body of another is preceded by the explicit indication that, before embarking on such external contemplation, the internal contemplation of one's own anatomy must be well developed and cultivated, Vibh 193,23.

20 DN 28 at DN III 105,12 (the translation in Walshe 1987: 420 does not seem to do full justice to the original) mentions blood alongside the flesh. The parallel DĀ 18 at T I 77b18 mentions the teeth in addition to the bones. Another parallel, T 18 at T I 256a13, enjoins to contemplate skin, flesh, bones, and marrow. It is noteworthy that the description in DN 28 at DN III 105,12 employs the same verb *paccavekkhati* as used in the standard description of

have some relation to attempting to get a physical sense of bodily parts like the skin and the flesh, etc., eventually reaching the bones as the innermost part of the body that, with some training in bodily sensitivity, can in fact be felt.

IV.4 THE PROBLEMS OF SENSUAL ATTRACTION

In whatever way one implements these instructions, the principal aim of contemplating the anatomical constitution of the body is the removal of sensual desire. The reason why early Buddhism problematizes sensual desire becomes clear in the *Māgandiya-sutta* and its *Madhyama-āgama* parallel, which deliver the stark simile of a leper who scratches the scab off his wounds and cauterizes them over a fire.[21]

The relief he experiences in this way illustrates the enjoyment of indulging in sensual pleasures. The more the leper scratches his wounds the worse his condition becomes, just as the more one indulges in sensuality the stronger one's sensual desires will in turn become. In fact, according to the *Māgandiya-sutta* and its *Madhyama-āgama* parallel even a king, with all the sensual gratification at his beck and call, will not be at peace inwardly because of his thirst for sensual desires. In other words, gratification of sensual desires is not a real solution, as it only provides short-term relief at the cost of the long-term increase of sensual desire.

The *Māgandiya-sutta* and its *Madhyama-āgama* parallel indicate that, if a healed leper sees a sick leper cauterizing his wounds over a fire, the healed leper would certainly not find this attractive and would not feel any envy for the sick leper. If he is forcibly dragged to the fire, the healed leper would try with all his might to escape, as being no longer sick he would not want to come near to the fire that he had earlier approached so eagerly to cauterize his wounds.

The comparisons in the two parallels convey an emphatic rejection of indulgence in sensual pleasures. The final conclusion proposed in the *Māgandiya-sutta* and its *Madhyama-āgama* parallel is that, just as a

---

contemplation of the anatomical parts, mentioned in the preceding section of DN 28 and also in MN 10 at MN I 57,15, conveying the impression that both modes of practice involve the same basic mode of contemplation.

21 MN 75 at MN I 506,6 (translated Ñāṇamoli 1995: 611) and MĀ 153 at T I 671b25. My summary of the similes follows MĀ 153, which seems to me to present these in a preferable sequence.

leper only experiences the fire as pleasant because he is sick and has a distorted perception, so indulging in sensuality is only experienced as pleasant when one has a distorted perception – in other words, as long as one is, in a way, mentally sick with the contagious disease of sensual desire. Unless the proper medication is applied – such as contemplation of the anatomical constitution of one's body – this contagious disease of sensual desire threatens to disfigure the natural beauty of one's mind and turn one into a mental leper.

The theme of sensual pleasures is also tackled with a series of similes in the *Potaliya-sutta* and its *Madhyama-āgama* parallel. In what follows I translate the similes from the *Madhyama-āgama* version, each of which illustrates the nature of indulging in sensuality with a particular image:[22]

> It is just like a dog who, being hungry, emaciated, and exhausted, reaches a butcher's place. The chief butcher or the butcher's apprentice throws the dog a bone that has been cut clean of meat. Having got the bone, the dog chews it all over, even until it hurts its lips and damages his teeth or injures his throat, yet that dog does not get [anything] to satisfy its hunger ... [23]
>
> It is just like a small piece of meat that has fallen on the open ground not far away from a village. A crow or an owl takes the meat away and other crows, owls, and birds pursue it, competing [for the meat] ... [24]
>
> It is just like a person who holds a burning torch in the hand and walks against the wind ... [25]
>
> It is just like a great burning [charcoal] pit not far away from a village, which is full of fire but without smoke or flame. A man comes by who is not foolish, not stupid, not [mentally] deranged, who is in his right mind, free, and unconstrained, who wants pleasure and does not want pain, who abhors pain, who wants to live and does not want death, who abhors death ... would that man enter the burning [charcoal] pit? ... [26]

---

22 MĀ 203 at T I 774a20 to 775a13.

23 MN 54 at MN I 364,12 (translated Ñāṇamoli 1995: 469) does not mention that the dog hurts itself by gnawing the bone.

24 MN 54 at MN I 364,30 indicates that the other birds peck and claw the bird that has got the piece of meat.

25 According to MN 54 at MN I 365,5, the torch is made of straw.

26 MN 54 at MN I 365,16 indicates that the charcoal pit is deeper than the height of a man and without flames.

It is just like a huge poisonous snake that is not far away from a village and which is very vicious, exceedingly poisonous, black in colour, and terrifying. A man comes who is not foolish, not stupid, not [mentally] deranged, who is in his right mind, free, and unconstrained, who wants pleasure and does not want pain, who abhors pain, who wants to live and does not want death, who abhors death … would that man extend his hand or some other parts of his body, saying: "Bite me, bite me"? …

It is just like a person who dreams of being equipped with the five strands of sensual pleasure, amusing himself. On waking up, he does not see any of it at all …

It is just like a man who has borrowed goods for his pleasure, palaces with towers, a pleasure garden with bathing pools, a chariot drawn by an elephant or a horse, silk coverlets, rings for his fingers, bracelets for the arm, perfumed necklaces, golden ornaments and wreaths, or elegant clothes. On seeing him, many people exclaim to one another: "How good to be like this, how joyful to be like this, those who have wealth just amuse themselves to the utmost like this."[27]

[Later] the owner of those goods wants to take them back or gets someone else to take them back [for him]. As he is taking them back himself or gets someone else to take them back, on seeing this, many people say to one another: "He is a borrower and truly a deceiver. How bad is this borrower!" … [28]

It is just like a great fruit tree not far away from a village, and in this tree there are always many fine and appetizing fruits. Suppose a man comes by who is hungry, emaciated, and exhausted, wishing to get the fruits to eat them. He has the thought: "In this tree there are always many fine and appetizing fruits. I am hungry, emaciated, and exhausted, and I wish to get the fruits to eat them. Yet, below the tree there are no fruits that have fallen down by themselves, which I can get to eat my fill of and take back with me when I leave. I could climb the tree. Shall I now rather get up on this tree?" Having this thought, he heads up [the tree].

Another man comes by who is hungry, emaciated, and exhausted, wishing to get the fruits to eat them. He is carrying a very sharp axe. He has the thought: "In this tree there are always many fine and appetizing fruits. Yet, below the tree there are no fruits that have

27 MN 54 at MN I 366,1 only mentions a carriage and bejewelled earrings, equipped with which the borrower goes to the market place.

28 MN 54 does not describe how the people react.

> fallen down by themselves, which I can get to eat my fill and take back with me when I leave. I am not able to climb the tree. Shall I now rather cut down and topple this tree over?" He [starts to] cut down and topple it over ... if that man who is up in the tree does not come down quickly, then when the tree topples to the ground, won't he certainly break an arm or another limb of his body?[29]

The similes in the *Potaliya-sutta* show several minor variations, such as that falling into a charcoal pit happens because one is thrown into it by two strong men; and the dream is about seeing lovely parks and groves instead of being equipped with the five strands of sensual pleasure.[30] The most noteworthy difference is perhaps that the *Potaliya-sutta* does not have the simile of the poisonous snake at all.

After each of these similes, the parallel versions conclude that the little enjoyment provided by sensual pleasure contrasts with the much greater disadvantages that result from sensual indulgence. Thus, engaging in sensual pleasures is like a hungry dog gnawing a meatless bone and getting nothing that will assuage its hunger. Or else it is comparable to the predicament of a bird that, having got hold of a small piece of food, is immediately chased by others and has to let go of it to preserve its life; a simile that illustrates the competition that results from sensual pursuits. The same problem is addressed in greater detail in the *Mahādukkhakkhandha-sutta* and its parallel, according to which criminality and warfare can be traced back to the competition that results from desire for sensual gratification.[31]

Holding a burning torch against the wind in a way that one burns oneself portrays how the fire of sensuality will inevitably afflict oneself. The harm one can incur by indulging in sensuality is comparable to falling into a burning charcoal pit, perhaps an image meant to illustrate the karmic consequence of unwholesome conduct undertaken to gain sensual pleasures. Sensuality is better avoided, just as one would avoid a poisonous snake.

In the final analysis, sensual pleasure is an illusion, just like a dream. Engaging in sensual pursuits is like parading with borrowed

---

29 According to MN 54 at MN I 367,1, he might even die.

30 MN 54 at MN I 365,16.

31 MN 13 at MN I 86,28 (translated Ñāṇamoli 1995: 181) and its parallels MĀ 99 at T I 585a28, T 53 at T I 847b2, EĀ 21.9 at T II 605a28, and T 737 at T XVII 539c26.

goods or like climbing up a fruit tree, only to find that this tree is being cut down.

IV.5 HIGHER HAPPINESS

The net result of the perspective on sensual pleasures inherent in these images is not a denial of pleasure as such, but rather an emphasis on the dangers of indulging in pleasures of a sensual type and ignoring their inherent deficiencies. The *Māgandiya-sutta* and its parallel make it clear that the Buddha was able to gain a vastly superior pleasure that is independent of sensuality: the happiness of deep concentration. Therefore he had no interest in sensual pleasures and felt not the least desire for them.[32]

In the *Kāyagatāsati-sutta* and its *Madhyama-āgama* parallel, contemplation of the anatomical parts belongs to a set of practices whose purpose is to enable the mind to become concentrated.[33] A closer inspection of the various ways in which the body should be contemplated according to these discourses clarifies that in early Buddhist meditation practice the body is not simply seen as something negative.[34] Besides examining the body's anatomy, the *Kāyagatāsati-sutta* and its *Madhyama-āgama* parallel also describe awareness of the postures of the body. Here the task is to be with the body, in whatever posture, as continuously as possible. Such "being with the body" has nothing to do with disgust for the body. Aversion towards the body would make it difficult to undertake this exercise successfully, since its very purpose is to ground the practitioner firmly in his or her bodily experience in the present moment – the very opposite of an attempt to escape from the body.

The *Kāyagatāsati-sutta* and its *Madhyama-āgama* parallel also include the bodily experience of the four absorptions in their exposition. The instructions in both versions describe pervading the whole body with bliss and happiness to such an extent that every spot of the body is affected by such pervasion. Thus, during these meditative experiences the body becomes the focal point of intense forms of

32 MN 75 at MN I 504,34 (translated Ñāṇamoli 1995: 610) and MĀ 153 at T I 671b1.
33 MN 119 at MN III 90,33 (translated Ñāṇamoli 1995: 951) and MĀ 81 at T I 556a24.
34 For a more detailed examination of this topic cf. Anālayo forthcoming 2.

bliss and happiness. This seems a far cry from a total deprecation of the body.

The seemingly negative attitude towards the body that underlies contemplation of its anatomical parts thus stands within a meaningful meditative dynamic that leads up to bodily experiences of intense happiness and bliss gained through concentration. The rationale behind this is simply that sensual desire needs to be overcome so the mind can settle within and access such higher forms of happiness. Becoming aware of the body's anatomical constitution is thus a first step in gaining freedom from sensual desire, helping one to see the body from a detached perspective, free from attraction or aversion.

According to the standard description of the absorptions, the precondition for attaining the first absorption is that the mind is free from sensual desire, which is the first of the five hindrances that prevent one from gaining concentration. In this way, the rejection of sensual pleasure does not leave the practitioner in a dreary grey world bereft of joy and happiness. On the contrary, its purpose is to lead to freedom from the shackles of sensuality in order to be able to access a far superior source of happiness to be found within.

The discourses in fact regularly contrast the ignoble, ordinary, and filthy happiness of sensual pleasures to the superior happiness of the concentrated mind.[35] As a stanza in the *Dhammapada* proclaims:

> If, by giving up material happiness,
> One can discern an abundant happiness,
> [Then] the wise would give up material happiness,
> Beholding the abundant happiness.[36]

Just as the abandonment of sensual pleasures leads to a higher form of happiness, so the deconstruction of the notion of bodily beauty that informs contemplation of the bodily parts leads to a more refined concept of beauty. The clear rejection of the attractiveness of the body advocated in the present *satipaṭṭhāna* exercise does not mean

35 MN 66 at MN I 454,12 (translated Ñāṇamoli 1995: 557) and MĀ 192 at T I 743a12.

36 Dhp 290 (translated Norman 1997/2004: 43), with parallels in the Gāndhārī *Dharmapada* 164, Brough 1962/2001: 145, Patna *Dharmapada* 77, Cone 1989: 123f, and *Udānavarga* 30.30, Bernhard 1965: 399. My translation of Dhp 290 follows the explanation by Norman 1997/2004: 142; according to the commentarial exegesis, Dhp-a III 449,4, the stanza would not be concerned with giving up happiness that comes from "material" things, but rather with giving up a "lesser" happiness.

that early Buddhist thought rejects the notion of beauty altogether. Instead, the concept of beauty definitely does have a place in early Buddhist thought.

Behind this lies the doctrinal viewpoint that cultivating a mental condition free from aversion or ill will is one of the conditions that lead to having a beautiful body in a future life.[37] The relation to bodily beauty here is quite self-evident, as the arising of anger leads to facial expressions and bodily postures that are not particularly beautiful even in the present, without any need to wait for their results in future lives.

The notion of beauty is in fact directly applied to a condition of the mind in early Buddhist discourse: a concentrated mind that, being aloof from sensual desire and ill will, engages in the cultivation of *mettā* – "loving-kindness" or perhaps better "benevolence" – constitutes the acme of beauty. A discourse in the *Saṃyukta-āgama* explains:[38]

> A mind well cultivated in benevolence is supreme in beauty.

The parallel in the *Saṃyutta-nikāya* indicates that liberation of the mind by benevolence has beauty as its culmination.[39] In this way, the concept of beauty has its place in early Buddhist thought, a place that is based on a thorough analysis of the true significance of and the conditions for beauty. From an early Buddhist viewpoint, obsession with beautifying the body is a classical instance of mistaking the finger for the moon, as importance should instead be given to the mind as the source of beauty. Based on this shift of perspective, meditation could in a way be considered the proper means of beautification.

Just as the rejection of sensual pleasure underlying an examination of the body's anatomy has the function of leading to the experience of a higher form of pleasure, so the deconstruction of bodily beauty evident in the present exercise leads to another conception of

---

37 MN 135 at MN III 204,18 (translated Ñāṇamoli 1995: 1054) and its parallels MĀ 170 at T I 705a29, T 78 at T I 887c27, T 79 at T I 889c25, T 80 at T I 892a28, T 81 at T I 897a8, T 755 at T XVII 589a27, Lévi 1932: 37,18 and 185,25, and D 339 *sa* 301a4 or Q 1006 *shu* 312b8.

38 SĀ 743 at T II 197c11, notably an instance where the Chinese character *jìng* stands for "beauty", not for "purity".

39 SN 46.54 at SN V 119,17 (translated Bodhi 2000: 1609), following the explanation of the discourse's phrasing provided in the commentary Spk III 172,24.

beauty: the beauty of the mind, reached by eradicating attachment as well as aversion in regard to the body or anything else. Thus the deconstruction of bodily beauty does not leave the practitioner in a world in which beauty no longer has a place. Instead, it replaces a conception that depends on what current fashion designates to be the ideal external shape of a body with a timeless conception that is rooted in the cultivation of the mind.

IV.6 SUMMARY

Contemplation of the anatomical parts needs to be undertaken in a balanced manner and takes one's own body as the starting point. A chief aim of the practice is to counter the contagious disease of sensual desire, which in a way disfigures the natural beauty of one's mind and threatens to turn one into a mental leper. Having reached freedom from the shackles of sensuality, one is able to access a superior source of happiness to be found within: the beauty of the mind in deep concentration.

V

THE ELEMENTS

V.1 INSTRUCTIONS

The second of the three modes of body contemplation found in the *Satipaṭṭhāna-sutta* and in its two Chinese *Āgama* parallels examines the elements that are found in the body. In what follows I translate the instructions in the three versions and then study their implications.

Majjhima-nikāya:

> One examines this same body, however it is placed, however disposed, by way of the elements: "In this body there are the earth element, the water element, the fire element, and the wind element."
>
> ... it is just as a skilled butcher or a butcher's apprentice who, having killed a cow, were to be seated at a crossroads with it cut up into pieces.

Madhyama-āgama:

> One contemplates the body's elements: "Within this body of mine there are the earth element, the water element, the fire element, the wind element, the space element, and the consciousness element."
>
> It is just as a butcher who, on having slaughtered and skinned a cow, divides it into six parts and spreads them on the ground [for sale].

Ekottarika-āgama:

> One contemplates [reflecting]: "In this body, is there the earth element, the water [element], the fire [element], and the wind element?" In this way ... one contemplates this body.
>
> Again, [when] ... one contemplates this body by distinguishing the elements in this body as being the four elements, [then] this is just like a capable cow butcher or the apprentice of a cow butcher who divides a cow [into pieces by cutting through] its tendons. While dividing it he contemplates and sees for himself that "these are the feet", "this is the heart", "these are the tendons", and "this is the head."

When comparing these instructions, a prominent difference is that the *Madhyama-āgama* discourse lists two additional elements. While the listing of six elements, comprising space and consciousness alongside the four material elements, occurs elsewhere in the early discourses, in the present context this seems to be a bit of a misfit. Awareness of consciousness has little claim to be reckoned part of a contemplation of the body. Hence it seems safe to consider this a later addition in the *Madhyama-āgama* version and to conclude that the gist of this *satipaṭṭhāna* practice is contemplation of the four material elements.

The instructions in the *Ekottarika-āgama* discourse add a sense of inquisitiveness to the practice by formulating the contemplation as a question: "In this body, is there the earth element?", etc. The simile that illustrates the undertaking of this practice is also particularly graphic in the *Ekottarika-āgama* discourse, which in a way makes explicit what in the other versions would be implicit. While cutting up the cow and getting ready for sale, the butcher no longer thinks in terms of a "cow", but rather in terms of its various parts.[1] In the same way, a practitioner who views the body in terms of elements should come to see merely the elements. That is, the aim of the exercise is to undermine the perception of the body as a compact and discrete unit, thereby deconstructing the solid sense of "I" that so easily arises in regard to one's own body.

It is perhaps significant that the present context uses such a stark simile as a slaughtered and cut-up cow, whereas contemplation of the anatomical parts finds illustration in the comparatively more

1 This corresponds to the interpretation of the simile presented in the Pāli commentary, Ps I 272,1.

peaceful image of examining various grains. As can be seen from the case of the mass suicide of monks discussed in the previous chapter, giving attention to the impure or unattractive nature of the body needs to be carried out with a keen eye on mental balance. Hence the choice of the simile of looking at various grains may be deliberately intended to convey the sense of a balanced examination that is free from attachment or aversion.

In the present case of contemplation of the elements, perhaps the stark simile intends to give an edge to the practice. Understood in this way, the image of the butcher who slaughters and cuts up a cow would convey the message that the exercise should be taken up in such a way that it indeed results in mentally dissecting one's sense of the body as a compact unit, thereby "slaughtering" the cosy sense of a solid, embodied "I" that stands in the background of unawakened bodily experience.

Further information on contemplating the elements can be gathered from a discourse dedicated to an analysis of the elements, the *Dhātuvibhaṅga-sutta* and its parallels. Here is the corresponding section from the *Madhyama-āgama* version:[2]

> One discerns the body's elements: "In this body of mine there is the internal earth element, which was received at birth. What is it? It is head hair, body hair, nails, teeth, rough and smooth epidermis, skin, flesh, bones, sinews, kidneys, heart, liver, lungs, spleen, large intestine, stomach, and faeces", and whatever else like this is found in this body internally, whatever is contained in it internally that is solid, that is of a solid nature and found internally, having been received at birth ... this is the internal earth element ... [3]
>
> Whatever is the internal earth element and whatever is the external earth element, all of it is summarily called the earth element. All of it is not mine, I am not part of it, and it is not [my] self. On wisely contemplating it like this, knowing it as it truly is, the mind does not become defiled with attachment in regard to the earth element ... this is not neglecting wisdom ...
>
> One discerns the body's elements: "In this body of mine there is the internal water element, which was received at birth. And what is

2 MĀ 162 at T I 690c12 to 691a22.

3 The corresponding passage in the parallels MN 140 at MN III 240,27 (translated Ñāṇamoli 1995: 1089), T 511 at T XIV 780a15, and D 4094 *ju* 37a2 or Q 5595 *tu* 40a7 does not mention that the internal element was received at birth.

it? It is brain marrow, tears, sweat, saliva,[4] pus, blood, fat, marrow, mucus, phlegm, and urine", and whatever else like this is found in this body internally, whatever is contained in it internally that is watery, that is of a watery nature and moist internally, having been received at birth ... this is the internal water element ...

Whatever is the internal water element and whatever is the external water element, all of it is summarily called the water element. All of it is not mine, I am not part of it, and it is not [my] self. On wisely contemplating it like this, knowing it as it truly is, the mind does not become defiled with attachment in regard to the water element ... this is not neglecting wisdom ...

One discerns the body's elements: "In this body of mine there is the internal fire element, which was received at birth. And what is it? It is bodily heat, bodily warmth, bodily discomfort,[5] warmth in the body related to the digestion of beverages and food", and whatever else like this is found in this body internally, whatever is contained in it internally that is fiery, that is of a fiery nature and hot internally, having been received at birth ... this is the internal fire element ...

Whatever is the internal fire element and whatever is the external fire element, all of it is summarily called the fire element. All of it is not mine, I am not part of it, and it is not [my] self. On wisely contemplating it like this, knowing it as it truly is, the mind does not become defiled with attachment in regard to the fire element ... this is not neglecting wisdom ...

One discerns the body's elements: "In this body of mine there is the internal wind element, which was received at birth. And what is it? It is upward-moving winds, downward-moving winds, forceful winds, pulling and contracting winds, disturbing winds, irregular winds, winds in the joints, out-breath and in-breath", and whatever else like this is found in this body internally, whatever is contained in it internally that is windy, that is of a windy nature and moves internally, having been received at birth ... this is the internal wind element ...

---

4 The present rendering follows a suggestion by Glass 2007: 162 to read as one anatomical part what according to the punctuation in the Taishō edition would be two parts.

5 The reference to bodily discomfort, found also in D 4094 *ju* 37b4 or Q 5595 *tu* 41a2, has its counterpart in the second illustration in MN 140 at MN III 241,15, where the term employed shows some variations in the different editions, but which appears to refer to ageing.

> Whatever is the internal wind element and whatever is the external wind element, all of it is summarily called the wind element. All of it is not mine, I am not part of it, and it is not [my] self. On wisely contemplating it like this, knowing it as it truly is, the mind does not become defiled with attachment in regard to the wind element … this is not neglecting wisdom.[6]

These instructions provide helpful illustrations of the nature of each element, showing that the solid parts of the body exemplify the element earth, while its fluids correspond to the water element. The distinction between the two is not always self-evident. The above passage includes the brain stem under fluids,[7] while a discourse in the *Ekottarika-āgama* assigns the brain to the element earth.[8]

The recurrence of the listing of bodily parts, already found for contemplating the body's anatomy, as a way of also contemplating the elements shows that this contemplation has much in common with examining the anatomical constitution of the body. In as much as these two exercises are concerned, the difference is mainly the perspective adopted in regard to these bodily parts. Whereas in the previous exercise of contemplating the body's anatomy the issue was a deconstruction of the idea of bodily beauty, here the deconstruction is concerned with the sense of the body as a compact embodiment of a sense of "I", driving home the fact that the material out of which the body is made is just the same as anything else found in nature. One's own body is not essentially different from any other body or any other manifestation of matter.

The actual practice for the first two elements would thus be based on having acquired some basic anatomical knowledge, similar to contemplating the anatomical parts, enabling one to picture and, ideally, have a physical sense of the respective parts of the body. With the elements of earth and water being exemplified by the different bodily parts, the remaining two elements are fire and wind. Fire stands for all that is related to the production of heat in the body, whereas wind stands for motions within the body. In ancient Indian medicine, such winds are responsible for mobilizing the nervous

6 The parallel versions continue at this point by taking up the elements of space and consciousness.

7 This is also the case for a listing of the internal and external elements in the *Śrāvakabhūmi*, Shukla 1973: 213,8, which includes the brain under the internal water element.

8 EĀ 28.4 at T II 652a19.

system, and an imbalance in these bodily winds can cause disease.[9]

Contemplating the element of fire would imply becoming aware of bodily warmth in its various manifestations. Awareness of the body's skin temperature would be a practical option, or becoming aware of differences in the temperature of different parts of the body, such as cold feet or hot armpits, for instance. Such practice would require becoming more clearly aware of a natural sensitivity within the body whose function is to alert us to the need for more or less warmth.

In addition, awareness of the warmth of the body can also be undertaken when contemplating the breath, as the inhalation will usually be cooler than the exhalation. A discourse in the *Ekottarika-āgama* explicitly draws attention to the cool or warm nature of the breath as part of its instruction on mindfulness of breathing,[10] an aspect not mentioned in the standard expositions on mindfulness of breathing in the Pāli discourses.

Inhalations and exhalations are at the same time an obvious example for experiencing the wind element. Besides the breath, however, any of the various motions, subtle or coarse, that take place within the body could illustrate the wind element. In the same vein, small adjustments to the bodily posture during formal sitting as well as any motion of the body during various other activities could be contemplated as manifestations of the wind element.

The process of breathing in a way drives home the main lesson of the present form of contemplation in a fairly evident manner. The air taken in, so vital for the body's survival, needs to be returned right away to the outside world. In the same way, the whole body is a continuous process of material exchange with the outer environment, being incapable of independent existence. It is, in essence, nothing but a temporary crystallization of the four elements that are bound to be recycled soon, once again becoming part of the external environment.

The way in which the above-translated passage exemplifies the four elements makes it clear that the type of contemplation envisaged here is not concerned with atomic qualities. In fact a theory of atoms (*kalāpa* or *paramāṇu*) arose only at a later stage in the history of

---

9 On various wind diseases cf. Zysk 1991: 92–6 and 110–13.

10 EĀ 17.1 at T II 582a17 instructs the practitioner to become aware of the coolness of the out-breaths and in-breaths, or else of their warmth; cf. also T 1507 at T XXV 49c3.

Buddhist thought,[11] so the instructions in this passage or in other early discourses would not be based on such notions. Instead of referring to atomic qualities, the four elements stand simply for what is solid, fluid, warm, and moving in the obvious sense of what can be observed in outside nature as well as through turning awareness to oneself.

V.2 NOT-SELF

Another significant indication given in the above passage is that this way of contemplating not-self is to be applied comprehensively, covering not only oneself, but also any external manifestation of the elements. No instance of the four elements, whether within or without, in any way qualifies for being appropriated as "mine" or being identified with as "I am this", let alone stipulating some sort of a "self" in relation to it.

This is significant in that, during later developments in Buddhist thought, some degree of realism appears to have manifested, based on the notion that things have their own independent nature (*svabhāva*). Other later developments that would at least in part have been in reaction to this notion emphasized that everything is empty, at times moving to the opposite position of idealism, where the whole world is considered to be merely a projection of the mind.

The early Buddhist position represents a middle path between the two extremes of realism and idealism. The four elements as changing phenomena are considered to exist independent of the mind, yet the only way to experience them is through the mind. The world of experience that comes into being in this way is a reciprocally conditioning relationship between the experiencing mind and the impact of outer phenomena on the mind. Expressed in doctrinal terms, consciousness is that which experiences, while name-and-form (*nāma-rūpa*) is the impact of outer phenomena together with the recognizing and conceptualizing function of the mind. These stand in a reciprocally conditioning relationship to each other, out of which the whole chain of dependent arising (*paṭicca samuppāda*) evolves.[12]

11 Karunadasa 1967/1989: 142.

12 DN 15 at DN II 56,31 (translated Walshe 1987: 223) and its parallels DĀ 13 at T I 61b13, T 14 at T I 243c2, MĀ 97 at T I 580a1, and T 52 at T I 845b11. Here "name" does not stand for the mind in its entirety, as it does not include consciousness; cf. also p.33, n.36.

The world of experience that comes into being in this way is entirely devoid of a self or any lasting substance whatsoever. This is empasized in a discourse in the *Saṃyutta-nikāya* and its *Saṃyukta-āgama* parallel, which take as their starting point the dictum that the world is empty. In what follows I translate the explanation of this saying from the *Saṃyukta-āgama* version:[13]

> The eye is empty, it is empty of being permanent, of being perpetual, and of having an unchanging nature, and it is empty of anything belonging to a self. Why is that? This is its intrinsic nature. Forms ... eye consciousness ... eye-contact ... feeling, arisen in dependence on eye-contact that is painful, pleasant, or neutral, is also empty, it is empty of being permanent, of being perpetual, and of having an unchanging nature, and it is empty of anything belonging to a self. Why is that? This is its intrinsic nature.
>
> The ear ... nose ... tongue ... body ... mind ... are also like that. This is [the implication of] the saying: "The world is empty."

The abbreviations in the original imply that the same treatment should be applied to each of the other senses. In each case, the corresponding object, type of consciousness, contact, and whatever feeling arises should be seen as empty of anything pertaining to a self.

The definition of emptiness in the *Saṃyutta-nikāya* parallel is more succinct, as in relation to each organ, its objects, etc., it simply indicates that these are empty of a self and of what belongs to a self.[14] The basic agreement between the two versions makes it clear that the designation "empty" applies to each and every aspect of experience, inside and outside. That is, the dictum "the world is empty" needs to be understood in the most comprehensive manner possible, leaving no room for positing a self anywhere at all. As the more detailed exposition in the *Saṃyukta-āgama* clarifies, to qualify something as "empty" means the absence of anything that is unchanging, and thus of course the absence of a permanent self.

The corresponding qualification of "not-self" has a similarly comprehensive range of application. A succinct expression of the teaching on not-self can be found in a stanza from the *Udānavarga* that has similarly worded parallels in the different *Dharmapada* collections

13 SĀ 232 at T II 56b24 to 56b29 (translated Choong 2000: 93).

14 SN 35.85 at SN IV 54,7 (translated Bodhi 2000: 1163f). Baba 2004: 944 points out that the more detailed presentation in SĀ 232 is probably an addition; cf. also Lamotte 1973/1993: 18.

preserved in Indic languages. Here is the Sanskrit version from the *Udānavarga*:[15]

> "All phenomena are not-self".
> When one sees this with wisdom,
> One turns away from what is unsatisfactory.
> This is the path to purity.

The introductory phrase "all phenomena" (*dharmas*) makes it unmistakeably clear that there is nothing whatsoever that could be excluded from the qualification of not-self. The remainder of the stanza then succinctly depicts the results of insight into not-self. Wisely seeing and contemplating all phenomena as not-self lead to disenchantment and to detachment from what is, in the final analysis, unable to provide lasting satisfaction. This, in turn, purifies the mind, which reaches the culmination of purity with full awakening.

V.3 THE CHARIOT SIMILE

The significance of designating something as not-self receives a helpful illustration in the simile of a chariot, used by a nun in a discourse in the *Saṃyutta-nikāya*. This discourse has parallels in the two extant versions of the *Saṃyukta-āgama* and another parallel preserved in Tibetan translation. According to the introductory narrations, the nun had gone to meditate in seclusion and was challenged by Māra. He tried to unsettle her by questioning her about the "being", evidently meant in the sense of a substantial and permanent self, wanting to know who had created this being and from where it had come.

In order to appreciate the significance of this challenge by Māra, I need to take a brief look at his role in early Buddhist discourse. Tradition recognizes several aspects of Māra, ranging from a symbolic representation to an actually existing celestial being whose role is to act as an antagonist to the Buddha and his disciples. In this role, Māra is usually responsible for all kinds of mischief, such as trying to disturb meditating monks and nuns, or making a noise when the Buddha is giving a talk. The way to deal with him is invariably the same: Māra only needs to be recognized and seen for who he is. As soon as he is recognized, Māra loses his might, is defeated, and has to disappear.

---

15 *Udānavarga* 12.8, Bernhard 1965: 194, with parallels in Dhp 279 (translated Norman 1997/2004: 41), Gāndhārī *Dharmapada* 108, Brough 1962/2001: 134, and Patna *Dharmapada* 374, Cone 1989: 203.

A common interpretation of episodes where Māra acts as a challenger assumes that he acts out the inner uncertainties or defilements of those he challenges. Closer inspection of such episodes makes it clear that this interpretation is unconvincing.[16] In episodes where he approaches the Buddha or arahants, the issue at stake is rather that Māra personifies challenges posed to members of the Buddhist community by outsiders. In the present instance, Māra's queries about a "being" do not imply that the nun had any uncertainties or doubts about this issue. Māra's role in the present episode is thus only to portray – perhaps even caricature – the ideas and notions that were held by some ancient Indian contemporaries. Here is the reply given by the nun to Māra's queries according to one of the *Saṃyukta-āgama* versions:[17]

> You speak of the existence of a "being",
> This, then, is evil Māra's view.
> There is only a collection of empty aggregates,[18]
> There is no "being".
> Just as, when the various parts are assembled,
> The world calls it a chariot,
> [Similarly] in dependence on the combination of the aggregates
> There is the appellation: a "being".

In both versions the target of her reply is a substantialist notion of a being in the sense of a permanent self. The analysis of such notions of the self then proceeds in a way similar to taking apart a chariot. Once the different parts of a chariot are spread out on the ground, the situation has become similar to that of a butcher who has cut up the cow and spread its different parts on the ground for sale. The notion of a "chariot" or a "cow" no longer seems relevant, as only various parts are there.

This does not imply that the term "chariot" has no meaningful referent at all. The different parts spread on the ground are certainly

16 For a more detailed discussion cf. Anālayo 2013a.

17 SĀ 1202 at T II 327b7 to 327b10 (translated Anālayo 2013a), parallel to SN 5.10 at SN I 135,18 (translated Bodhi 2000: 230) and SĀ² 218 at T II 454c27 (translated Bingenheimer 2011: 171); cf. also Enomoto 1994: 42 and D 4094 *nyu* 82a1 or Q 5595 *thu* 128a2. While SN 5.10 identifies the nun as Vajirā, the parallels instead speak of Selā.

18 SN 5.10 at SN I 135,19 speaks of "formations" instead of "aggregates"; cf. also Vetter 2000: 157.

not a chariot, but once they are placed together in a way that enables them to function together, the result does become a "chariot", and it is possible to drive it. This simile does not deny that a chariot or a being exists at all. In fact, the nun does not say that there is no chariot, she only explains what the term "chariot" refers to, namely a functional assemblage of parts. Her point is that there is nothing substantial that corresponds to the notion of a chariot or a being. Whether one closely inspects a chariot or a being, all that can be found is a changing process of conditioned parts or aggregates whose mutual cooperation is responsible for the functional phenomenon referred to as a chariot or a being.

V.4 KARMA AND NOT-SELF

That the teaching of not-self needs to be distinguished from the idea that there is nothing at all can be seen from a misunderstanding reported in a passage in the *Mahāpuṇṇama-sutta* and its parallels. This passage describes a monk coming to the erroneous conclusion that the not-self teaching implies that there is nobody who will experience karmic retribution. According to the *Saṃyukta-āgama* version of this discourse, his reasoning was as follows:[19]

> If there is no self, and deeds are done by no self, then who will receive their retribution in the future?

This passage depicts a fundamental misunderstanding of the doctrine of not-self. Mistaking the not-self teaching to imply a denial of personal responsibility for one's deeds thoroughly misses the point. The not-self teaching is only about the absence of an unchanging, permanent self.[20] But the five aggregates as a process certainly exist and intentional actions, once performed, will inevitably have repercussions on future instances of the same flow of aggregates.

In terms of the butcher's simile, the fact that after cutting up the cow

19 SĀ 58 at T II 15a12f, with parallels in MN 109 at MN III 19,12 (translated Ñāṇamoli 1995: 890), SN 22.82 at SN III 103,27 (translated Bodhi 2000: 927), and D 4094 *nyu* 56a6 or Q 5595 *thu* 98a4.

20 Gombrich 2009: 9 comments on the "not-self" teaching that "all the fuss and misunderstanding can be avoided if one inserts the word 'unchanging', so that the two-word English phrase becomes 'no unchanging self' … for the Buddha's audience *by definition* the word *ātman*/*attā* referred to something unchanging."

the butcher no longer thinks in terms of a cow does not mean that there is nothing at all. The different parts of the cow are there right in front of him and he will be able to sell them to any customer that comes by. Moreover, even though he no longer thinks in terms of "a cow", he will still have to face the karmic results for his earlier killing of the cow.

Applied to the body, then, the vision that the present *satipaṭṭhāna* exercise attempts to arouse in the meditator is not that there is nothing at all. The aim is instead to replace the compact sense of a solid embodiment of oneself with a direct vision of the body as being just a combination of elements. With contemplation of the elements, the not-self strategy thus fosters de-identification by undermining the sense of ownership.

V.5 ELEMENTS AND NOT-SELF

Undermining the sense of ownership is also a central aspect in an instruction to the Buddha's son Rāhula on the topic of the elements. In what follows, I translate the *Saṃyukta-āgama* version of this instruction:[21]

> One knows as it truly is that whatever there is of the earth element, past, future, or present, internal or external, gross or subtle, sublime or repugnant, far or near, all of that is not-self … [whatever there is of] the water element … the fire element … the wind element … [22]
>
> For one who knows like this and sees like this there will be no "I", viewing as "mine", or underlying tendency connected to attachment to the I-conceit in relation to this body with consciousness and [in relation to] external objects and any signs …
>
> There being no "I", viewing as "mine", or underlying tendency connected to attachment to the I-conceit in relation to this body with consciousness and [in relation to] external objects and any signs, one is said to be eradicating the bondage of craving and the fetters.

---

21 SĀ 465 at T II 118c29 to 119a8.

22 SĀ 465 also brings in the other two elements of space and consciousness and, besides "not-self", also has counterparts to the reference to the denial of "mine" and "I am" in the Pāli parallel AN 4.177 at AN II 164,27 (translated Bodhi 2012: 542). The formulation of this reference in the corresponding Chinese text is cryptic and, while I have discussed this elsewhere (cf. Anālayo 2010a: 127 or Anālayo 2010c: 50), here I have abbreviated the passage in order to avoid the need for a detailed discussion of the intricacies of this Chinese formulation.

The *Aṅguttara-nikāya* parallel to this passage differs in not offering a detailed description of how the respective elements could be past, future, or present, etc. Instead, it simply speaks of the internal and external element.[23] According to the *Aṅguttara-nikāya* account, the result of wisely contemplating each element as it really is in terms of "not mine", "not I", and "not my self" is that one becomes disenchanted with the element and the mind becomes dispassionate. In this way one cuts off craving, becomes free from the fetters, and by fully understanding the I-conceit one makes an end of *dukkha*.

The main target in both versions is the tendency to identify, manifesting in the sense of "I am", and the tendency to appropriate, arising as the notion of "mine". These are a problem because they form the basis for the arising of craving. Letting go of such identifications and appropriations undermines the very ground on which craving thrives, and thereby leads to freedom.

V.6 ELEMENTS AND THE LIBERATED ONE

Needless to say, freedom from craving does not mean that an arahant no longer uses the term "I" or is unable to employ the expression "mine" to distinguish between his or her own body and that of another. The problem is not with words, but rather lies with the underlying attachment that usually accompanies their usage. This much can be seen from a description of an arahant's attitude in regard to the four elements given in the *Chabbisodhana-sutta*. Here is the *Madhyama-āgama* version of the relevant passage:[24]

> I do not see the earth element as mine, nor myself as pertaining to the earth element, nor the earth element as a self. That is to say, [in regard to these] three [modes of] clinging, which in dependence on the earth element come into existence, by the extinction, fading away, cessation, tranquillization, and calming of any underlying tendency to attachment I attained the knowledge that there is no clinging to anything and that by the destruction of the influxes the mind has been liberated ... I do not see the water [element] ... the fire [element] ... the wind [element] ... as mine, nor myself as pertaining to the ... element, nor the ... element as a self.[25]

23 AN 4.177 at AN II 164,26.
24 MĀ 187 at T I 733a2 to 733a6 (translated Anālayo 2012d: 233).
25 MĀ 187 applies the same also to the elements space and consciousness.

While the above passage presents the attitude of an arahant in relation to each element in terms of the absence of three modes of clinging, the *Chabbisodhana-sutta* takes up the same topic in just a twofold manner: an arahant neither takes the element as self nor has a sense of self based on the element.[26] The main point is the same: attachment and clinging have been overcome and thereby complete freedom has been gained. However, such freedom does not prevent the arahant from using the term "I". Thus the above strategy of seeing each element as "not I" and "not mine" is not aimed at the language one might use in regard to one's own body, but is intended to undermine and eventually eradicate completely any attachment or clinging in the form of "I am this" or "this is mine."

Having overcome attachment and clinging to the four elements, one's response to challenging and difficult experiences can change dramatically. This is illustrated in the *Mahāhatthipadopama-sutta* and its *Madhyama-āgama* parallel. The two versions describe in similar ways how someone has to face verbal abuse, or even is physically attacked with fists, stones, or sticks. One who has realized the not-self nature of the elements becomes able to bear these experiences with the thought that it is the nature of the body to be susceptible to such things.[27]

Another illustration of the attitude of one who has been fully liberated from the "I" conceit is found in a discourse in the *Aṅguttara-nikāya* and its parallels, which report how the arahant monk Sāriputta responded on being falsely accused by another monk. After calmly clarifying that someone like himself could not have perpetrated the alleged act, he depicts his mental attitude towards such false accusations with the help of the four elements. In what follows I translate the *Ekottarika-āgama* version of his declaration:[28]

> It is just like this earth, which receives what is pure and receives what is impure, such as faeces, urine, dirt, pus, blood, mucus, spittle, it receives all that without any resistance. Because of that the earth does not speak hateful or pleasing [words]. I am just like that …
>
> It is just like water that can be used to clean attractive things and can be used to clean unattractive things. That water does not think: "I am clean and am being put on them." I am just like that … [29]

26 MN 112 at MN III 31,23 (translated Ñāṇamoli 1995: 905).

27 MN 28 at MN I 186,5 (translated Ñāṇamoli 1995: 279) and MĀ 30 at T I 464c25.

28 EĀ 37.6 at T II 713a9 to 713a18.

29 In the parallels AN 9.11 at AN IV 375,6 (translated Bodhi 2012: 1262) and

> It is just like blazing fire that burns on a mountain or in an open country,[30] which does not choose between what is attractive and what is ugly, because it has no such perception or thought. I am just like that …

The *Ekottarika-āgama* version does not mention the wind element, which is probably a case of textual loss, as the parallel versions in the *Aṅguttara-nikāya* and in the *Madhyama-āgama* do mention the wind element and employ it in the same way as the other elements to exemplify the attitude of the arahant monk Sāriputta.[31] In fact, another discourse in the *Ekottarika-āgama* that also illustrates an attitude of patience with the help of the elements does take up the wind element alongside earth, water, and fire.[32]

In the present context, the elements are used to exemplify a mental attitude and thus function in a way different from the contemplation of the body. Nevertheless, the same theme underlies them, namely detachment through giving up the sense of "I".

In relation to the present *satipaṭṭhāna* exercise, then, in practical terms this mode of contemplation reveals that, however beautiful or ugly any particular material form may appear, it is just a combination of the four elements and therefore not essentially different from any other occurrence of matter in the world.

An image in the discourses compares the aggregate of material form to foam. This image occurs as part of a series of similes to illustrate the nature of the five aggregates. Here is the *Saṃyukta-āgama* version of the part of the simile that is concerned with bodily form:[33]

> It is just as a collection of foam that floats, following a great wave on the river Ganges, and a clear-sighted person carefully examines and analyses it. At the time of carefully examining and analysing, [the person finds that] there is nothing in it, nothing stable, nothing substantial, it has no solidity. Why is that? It is because there is nothing solid or substantial in a collection of foam. In the same way … on carefully examining, attending to, and analysing whatever

---

MĀ 24 at T I 453a25 the description of the other elements is similar to the description of the case of the earth.

30 AN 9.11 at AN IV 375,15 and MĀ 24 at T I 453b3 give no indication about the location of the fire.

31 AN 9.11 at AN IV 375,24 and MĀ 24 at T I 453b10.

32 EĀ 43.5 at T II 760a10.

33 SĀ 265 at T II 68c1 to 68c7.

> material form, past, future, or present, internal or external, gross or subtle, sublime or repugnant, far or near ... one [finds that] there is nothing in it, nothing stable, nothing substantial, it has no solidity.[34]

To sum up, this body as a combination of the four elements is devoid of anything substantial that could serve as a basis for an appropriation in terms of "I" and "mine". It is merely a mass of foam, carried away by the flow of change.

V.7 SUMMARY

Contemplation of the elements directs awareness to what is solid, fluid, warm, and moving in the body. Undertaking this exercise one in a way mentally dissects one's sense of the body as a compact unit. The resulting not-self strategy fosters de-identification with the body by undermining one's sense of ownership.

---

34 The parallel SN 22.95 at SN III 140,24 (translated Bodhi 2000: 951) does not mention a great wave.

VI

A CORPSE IN DECAY

VI.1 INSTRUCTIONS

Contemplation of the progressive stages of decay through which a dead human body passes if left out in the open is the last of the three forms of contemplating the body that are found in the *Satipaṭṭhāna-sutta* and in its two Chinese *Āgama* parallels. In what follows, I provide abbreviated translations of the instructions in the three versions and then examine their significance, especially in relation to contemplation of impermanence.

Majjhima-nikāya:

> As though one were to see a corpse thrown away in a charnel ground that is one, two, or three days dead, being bloated, livid, and oozing matter …
>
> … being devoured by crows, hawks, vultures, dogs, jackals, or various kinds of worms …
>
> … a skeleton with flesh and blood, held together by the sinews …
>
> … a skeleton without flesh, smeared with blood and held together by the sinews …
>
> … a skeleton without flesh and blood, held together by the sinews …
>
> … disconnected bones scattered in the main and intermediate directions, here a hand bone, elsewhere a foot bone, elsewhere a shin bone, elsewhere a thigh bone, elsewhere a hip bone, elsewhere a back bone, and elsewhere a skull …
>
> … bones bleached white, the colour of shells …

... bones heaped up, more than a year old ...

... bones rotten and crumbling to dust, and one compares this same body with it: "This body too is of the same nature, it will be like that, it is not exempt from that fate."

Madhyama-āgama:

One contemplates a corpse dead for one or two days, or up to six or seven days, that is being pecked at by crows, devoured by jackals and wolves, burned by fire, or buried in the earth, or that is completely rotten and decomposed ...

Similar to what one has formerly seen in a charnel ground, so ... one [recollects] a carcass of bluish colour, decomposed and half eaten [by animals], with the bones lying on the ground still connected together ...

... without skin, flesh, or blood, held together only by sinews ...

... disconnected bones scattered in all directions: foot bones, shin bones, thigh bones, a hip bone, vertebrae, shoulder bones, neck bones, and a skull, all in different places ...

... bones white like shells, or bluish like the colour of a pigeon, or red as if smeared with blood, rotting and decomposing, crumbling to dust. Having seen this, one compares oneself to it: "This present body of mine is also like this. It is of the same nature and in the end cannot escape [this fate]."

Ekottarika-āgama:

One contemplates a corpse that has been dead for one day, two days, three days, four days, five days, six days, or seven days, the body being bloated, a fetid place of impurity. One then contemplates that one's own body is not different from that: "My body will not escape from this calamity."

... a corpse that has visibly been fed on by crows, magpies, and owls, or that has visibly been fed on by tigers, wolves, dogs, worms, and [other] beasts. One then contemplates that one's own body is not different from that: "My body is not free from this calamity." This is reckoned how ... one contemplates the body and experiences joy in oneself [by removing evil thoughts and being free from worry and sorrow].

... a corpse that has been about half eaten and left scattered on the ground, a fetid place of impurity. One then contemplates that one's own body is not different from that: "My body is not free from this condition."

... a corpse whose flesh has disappeared, with only the bones remaining, smeared with blood ...

... a corpse [whose bones] are held together by the tendons, [like] a bundle of firewood ...

... a corpse whose joints have come apart, [with its parts] scattered in different places, here a hand bone, there a foot bone, or a shin bone, or the pelvis, or the coccyx, or an arm bone, or a shoulder bone, or ribs, or the spine, or the neck bones, or the skull. Again one uses the contemplation that one's own body is not different from that: "I will not escape from this condition. My body will also be destroyed."

... a corpse [whose bones] have become white, the colour of white agate. Again one contemplates that one's own body is not different from that: "I am not free from this condition."

... a corpse whose bones have become bluish, appearing as if they have been bruised, or of a colour that is indistinguishable from that of ash, as not worth being attached to.

In this way ... one contemplates one's own body and [experiences joy in oneself] by removing evil thoughts and being free from worry and sorrow: "This body is impermanent, of a nature to fall apart."

The parallel versions differ in the way they divide the actual stages of decay. The *Madhyama-āgama* description presents five, the *Ekottarika-āgama* version eight, and the *Majjhima-nikāya* discourse nine such stages. Nevertheless, the main import of the practice appears to be the same, in that contemplation proceeds from a dead and bloated body to a body that is eaten by various animals. Next the flesh completely disappears from the skeleton and then the tendons rot away, as a consequence of which the bones are no longer connected to each other. The bones then bleach in the sun and rot, and the *Majjhima-nikāya* and *Madhyama-āgama* versions note that their final condition is to turn into dust.

The *Madhyama-āgama* discourse begins the second of its stages of the decay of a corpse with the indication "similar to what one has formerly seen in a charnel ground". This specification is noteworthy in comparison to the *Majjhima-nikāya* version, which instructs: "as though one were to see a corpse thrown away in a charnel ground". In other words, the *Majjhima-nikāya* instructions could be read as recommending the use of visual imagination,[1] whereas the *Madhyama-āgama* instructions appear to require a recollection of what one has actually seen in a charnel ground.

The *Madhyama-āgama* version also mentions the additional options of contemplating a corpse "burned by fire, or buried in the earth". Bringing in cremation and earth burial – perhaps a later addition to the *Madhyama-āgama* discourse – would only be relevant to a general awareness of the mortality of the body. Once a corpse has been burned or buried in the earth, it would no longer be possible to develop distinct awareness of the body's gradual decomposition in the way this is described in common in the three parallel versions.

Regarding the actual instructions, the *Ekottarika-āgama* version differs in several ways from the other two discourse versions. In agreement with its parallels, the main point of the contemplation is to realize that one's own body is of the same nature as the corpse,[2] a contemplation that in the *Ekottarika-āgama* discourse is expressed vividly with the remark that "my body will not escape from this calamity" and, at a later point, "I will not escape from this condition. My body will also be destroyed."

Another and perhaps surprising indication is that through undertaking this practice one "experiences joy in oneself".[3] This is not the only place where the experience of joy is explicitly mentioned in the *Ekottarika-āgama* instructions for *satipaṭṭhāna* practice: the same occurs also in relation to the anatomical parts and in regard to the elements.

While this is a unique feature of the *Ekottarika-āgama* discourse and thus probably a later element, it nevertheless makes an important point from a practical perspective. What at first sight appears to be a

1 Ñāṇamoli 1956/1991: 760 n.27 comments that the present contemplations, based on the "progressive order of decay in order to demonstrate the body's impermanence, are not necessarily intended as contemplations of actual corpses so much as mental images to be created, the primary purpose being to cultivate impermanence".

2 This application to oneself fits the general thrust of mindfulness of death, which as Bowker 1991: 187 explains is concerned with "the fact that death (*maraṇa*) is approaching *me*. It is not a meditation on death in general, but on its application to me."

3 While I have supplemented the reference to experiencing joy in the final part of the cemetery contemplation in EĀ 12.1, as evident from the use of square brackets in the extract given above, this supplementation is guided by actual occurrences of this phrase in earlier parts of the same exercise.

fairly gruesome practice can produce joy if undertaken properly. This is simply because it leads to detachment. This becomes particularly evident with the last of the *Ekottarika-āgama* instructions, according to which the bones are to be seen as "not worth being attached to". As the discourse indicates, joy can arise because properly undertaken practice leads to removing unwholesome thoughts and thereby to a mental condition of becoming increasingly less affected by worries and sorrow. That is, the joy here is the joy of mental freedom from attachment to the body. In this way one becomes free from all the various negative mental reactions that, in one way or another, have a basis in one's attachment to bodily experience.

Another noteworthy feature is the *Ekottarika-āgama* version's conclusion of its description of this exercise, according to which "this body is impermanent, of a nature to fall apart." This in a way sums up the whole exercise. In spite of some similarity with contemplation of the anatomical parts, in as much as the corpse in its stages of decay reveals the "impure" or "unattractive" aspects of the body and thus counters sensual desire, the central aspect of contemplating a corpse in decay is driving home the truth of impermanence.

VI.2 THE DISADVANTAGE OF A BODY

The *Mahādukkhakkhandha-sutta* of the *Majjhima-nikāya* and its parallels employ the stages of a corpse in decay to describe the "disadvantage" inherent in a material body. This is preceded by a description of the "advantage", which is bodily beauty, and followed by indicating that the solution or "escape" from the dilemma is to give up desire and attachment in relation to the body. Here is the relevant part from the *Madhyama-āgama* parallel:[4]

> What is the gratification in relation to material form? Suppose there is a girl from the warrior, brahmin, merchant, or worker [class], aged fourteen or fifteen years, a time when her physical beauty is most exquisite. The pleasure and joy that arise caused by her physical beauty and conditioned by her physical beauty is the foremost gratification in material form, with nothing beyond it; [yet] it is beset by much danger.[5]

4 MĀ 99 at T I 585c17 to 586a1.

5 The parallels MN 13 at MN I 88,7 (translated Ñāṇamoli 1995: 183). EĀ 21.9 at T II 605b18, and T 737 at T XVII 540b5 do not mention the worker class,

> What is the danger in relation to material form? Suppose one sees that beautiful girl at a later time when she has become very old and feeble, her hair has become white and her teeth have fallen out, with hunched back and unsteady steps she walks leaning on a stick, her health is constantly deteriorating and her lifespan is approaching its end, her body is trembling and her sense faculties are deteriorating. What do you think, has her former physical beauty ceased and the danger [of material form] manifested? …
>
> Again, suppose one sees that beautiful girl lying on a bed, or sitting or lying on the ground afflicted with disease, with pain oppressing her body, experiencing extremely strong pain. What do you think, has her former physical beauty ceased and the danger [of material form] manifested? …
>
> Again, suppose one sees that beautiful girl dead for one or two days, or up to six or seven days, being pecked at by crows and hawks, devoured by jackals and wolves, burned by fire, or buried in the earth, or having become completely rotten and decomposed. What do you think, has her former physical beauty ceased and its danger manifested?

The discourse continues with further stages of decay of the corpse until the formerly attractive body has become rotting bones.

The parallel versions agree that the girl is at the peak of her beauty. The target of the analysis is thus clearly the ancient Indian conception of what makes a female supremely beautiful. Notably, elsewhere, when the question at stake is how one might feel about one's own beauty, often a boy is explicitly mentioned alongside a girl. Thus the *Anaṅgaṇa-sutta* and its *Ekottarika-āgama* parallel, for example, illustrate the willingness to follow an instruction with the image of girl or a boy who are freshly washed and dressed and who will joyfully receive a flower garland and put it on their head.[6]

The choice in the *Mahādukkhakhandha-sutta* and its parallels of taking up only the case of a girl would reflect what in ancient India was considered to represent the summit of human beauty. Judging

which is, however, mentioned in another parallel, T 53 at T I 847c17. MN 13 at MN I 88,8, EĀ 21.9 at T II 605b19, and T 737 at T XVII 540b6 also describe the girl as being neither too tall nor too short, neither too thin nor too fat, and neither too dark nor too fair.

6 MN 5 at MN I 32,26 and its parallel EĀ 25.6 at T II 634a6 (another two parallels, MĀ 87 at T I 569c5 and T 49 at T I 842a15, employ only a girl in their version of this simile).

from the descriptions in the two discourses, this was associated more with a young body at the age of fourteen or fifteen than with a body at a later age, say eighteen or twenty, and it was also associated more with a female body than with a male one.

A reason for seeing beauty exemplified in a young female body would be a conditioning prevalent in ancient India and elsewhere, according to which a male tends to look for beauty in a female, while a female tends to look for beauty in herself. As a result, a man's sensual interest in beauty expresses itself in a predominantly voyeuristic manner towards others' bodies,[7] while a female's concern with beauty has a more narcissistic leaning. From this viewpoint, then, the image of a pretty young girl becomes a natural illustration of the "advantages" associated with material form, reflecting the way beauty was perceived in ancient India. Needless to say, the whole point of the passage in the *Mahādukkhakhandha-sutta* and its parallels is to deconstruct such notions, not to confirm that they are appropriate.

This deconstruction, under the heading of revealing the "danger" in material form, draws attention to the temporal perspective – to impermanence – by depicting the same person becoming old, sick, and eventually dead. Several of the parallels are more detailed in their descriptions, explicitly mentioning that she has now become eighty, ninety, or a hundred years old.[8] In regard to the next stage of being afflicted by disease, the *Mahādukkhakhandha-sutta* and an *Ekottarika-āgama* parallel are also more graphic, as her illness has evolved to a stage where the body is lying in its own excrement and needs to be helped by others to be relieved of this condition.[9]

The example of a beautiful young girl who becomes old, sick, and eventually dead, whereupon her formerly attractive body undergoes the stages of decay that form the central theme of the present *satipaṭṭhāna* exercise, has a clear relation to sensual attraction. Nevertheless, impermanence is a central theme. In fact, in the *Mahādukkhakhandha-sutta* and its parallels the pretty girl illustrates the topic of material form, which is preceded by an examination

---

7 For a survey of research on how men and women react differently to visual sexual stimulation cf. Rupp and Wallen 2008.

8 MN 13 at MN I 88,15 and EĀ 21.9 at T II 605b23 indicate that she has become eighty, ninety, or a hundred years old, to which T 737 at T XVII 540b10 adds that she might even be a hundred and twenty years old.

9 According to MN 13 at MN I 88,23, she is lying in her own excrement and urine, being lifted up and set down by others. EĀ 21.9 at T II 605b29 similarly describes that she has lost excrement and urine, being unable to rise up.

of sensual pleasures and followed by investigating feelings. The "danger" of sensual pleasures is the need to toil and face competition in order to be able to indulge in them, while the "danger" of feelings is again the fact that they are impermanent.

Thus, as highlighted in the *Ekottarika-āgama* parallel to the *Satipaṭṭhāna-sutta*, the gist of contemplating a corpse in different stages of decay would indeed be the realization that "this body is impermanent, of a nature to fall apart." Needless to say, for such awareness to be fruitful it needs to be undertaken with a sense of imminence. It will not be enough to acknowledge that at some distant time in the future death might come. Instead, awareness that the body will certainly encounter death and fall apart needs to be combined with the realization that this may happen any time; in fact, it could happen soon, even right now ...

VI.3 RECOLLECTION OF DEATH

The immediacy that needs to accompany contemplation of the mortal nature of one's own body is brought home in a discourse in the *Aṅguttara-nikāya* and its *Ekottarika-āgama* parallel. The discourse begins with the Buddha enquiring if the monks are practising recollection of death. One monk replies that he regularly recollects death and, on being asked about how he undertakes this practice, according to the *Ekottarika-āgama* version he describes his way of contemplation as follows:[10]

> At the time of giving attention to perception of death, I have the aspiration to remain for seven days and give attention to the seven awakening factors. In the Tathāgata's teaching that would be of much benefit [for me] and I will not regret passing away after that. Blessed One, it is like this that I give attention to perception of death.
>
> The Blessed One said: "Stop, stop, monk, this is not an undertaking of the practice of perception of death, this is called being of a negligent nature."

Other monks then describe their practice, which involves periods of six, five, four, three, two, or a single day, or just the time period from getting ready to beg alms until returning to the monastic dwelling. Yet, none of them is able to satisfy the Buddha with their description.

10 EĀ 40.8 at T II 742a2 to 742a6.

The Buddha then explains that the commendable way of practice involves just the time taken by a single breath. Thus one who really practises mindfulness of death should be aware of the fact that even the next breath might not take place. In other words, the task is to bring awareness of mortality into the present moment, right into the here and now.[11]

The *Aṅguttara-nikāya* has two discourses that are parallels to this instruction. They differ in as much as here the time periods described begin with a single day and night,[12] followed by a day, half a day (only mentioned in the second version), the time of a meal, half a meal (only in the second version), the time of eating several morsels of food, the time of eating a single morsel of food, and the time of a single breath. The Buddha commends the last two cases and considers the others to be instances of negligence. The agreement among the parallel versions on what the Buddha considered as negligence clearly conveys the message that death is something one may encounter at any moment, thereby giving a sharp edge to awareness of the impermanent nature of one's own body.

VI.4 MOMENTARINESS

A quotation from this discourse can be found in a work preserved in Chinese that is generally known under the reconstructed title **Mahāprajñāpāramitāśāstra*. The quotation begins with the (somewhat improbable) option that one monk was practising recollection of death with the expectation that he would live for another seven years. After proceeding to shorter time periods until reaching the commendable way of practice where death is expected with the next breath, this discourse quotation then concludes by stating that all conditioned phenomena arise and pass away every moment.[13]

---

11 Such bringing of one's own mortality right into present-moment awareness runs counter to a common tendency described by Pyszczynski et al. 2004: 445 as follows: "when thoughts of death are in current focal attention, the individual responds with proximal defenses that attempt to deal with the problem of death … by either distracting oneself from the issue or pushing the problem of death into the distant future."

12 AN 6.19 at AN III 304,9 and AN 8.73 at AN IV 317,9 (translated Bodhi 2012: 876 and 1219). The fact that AN 8.73 mentions two more stages would be responsible for the allocation of the otherwise same instruction to the Sixes and Eights respectively in the *Aṅguttara-nikāya*.

13 T 1509 at T XXV 228b5; cf. also Lamotte 1970: 1424f.

The way in which discourse quotations have been preserved in later works sometimes shows the influence of later doctrinal developments, as can be seen in this case. The last part is clearly a later addition, as it reflects a development in Buddhist thought where the conception of impermanence led to the doctrine of "momentariness". The notion of the momentary dissolution of all phenomena has had a wide impact on different Buddhist traditions and thus often informs a specific understanding of impermanence. However, from a historical perspective the doctrine of momentariness is clearly a later development.[14]

Early Buddhist thought considers impermanence as including a period of continuous change that comes between the previous arising and the subsequent passing away. This threefold perspective is the theme of a discourse in the *Aṅguttara-nikāya*, which has a parallel in the *Ekottarika-āgama*. The *Ekottarika-āgama* applies this distinction to the human body and thus serves as a good example of how the notion of impermanence in early Buddhist thought is related to the overall theme of contemplating the body. The discourse proceeds as follows:[15]

> These three are the marks of conditioned existence. What are the three? One knows whence it arises, one knows that it will change, and one knows that it will cease and disappear.
>
> How does one know whence it arises? It is birth, the growing up and maturing of these five aggregates of clinging, the acquiring of all the elements and sense-spheres – this is whence it arises.
>
> What is its cessation? It is death, the passing away and discontinuity of life, its impermanence, the breaking up of the aggregates, one's being separated from one's clan and family, the life faculty being cut off – this is its cessation.
>
> What is its change? It is loss of teeth, whiteness of hair, exhaustion of one's energy and strength with the waxing and waning of the years, the falling apart of the body – this is its nature of being affected by change.

The parallel in the *Aṅguttara-nikāya* does not provide comparable illustrations, but simply distinguishes three marks of conditioned existence, which are an arising, a passing away, and an alteration

14 A detailed study can be found in von Rospatt 1995; cf. also Ronkin 2005: 59–65 and Karunadasa 2010: 234–61.

15 EĀ 22.5 at T II 607c14 to 607c21.

of what persists,[16] that is, a period of change that occurs between having arisen and passing away. The fact that what persists has the quality of alteration, in that it can be seen to undergo change, makes it clear that such persistence must be for more than just a single moment. In fact, in the passage from the *Ekottarika-āgama* change manifests as ageing, clearly involving a prolonged period of time.

The reference to an alteration of what persists in the *Aṅguttara-nikāya* discourse and the graphic description of change in its *Ekottarika-āgama* parallel show that the two versions agree in combining change with continuity. With the concept of momentariness, such continuity tends to be lost from sight. Once phenomena are taken to exist only for a single moment, disappearing right after they have appeared, it becomes difficult to account for the evident fact of continuity.

The concept of impermanence in early Buddhism does not face such a dilemma, since besides arising and disappearing it recognizes that phenomena do persist for some time, even though this persistence is obviously subject to the law of change. In other words, while all aspects of experience certainly undergo change, they do not necessarily disappear on the spot. This does not mean that some things may not disappear quickly, even at times right away. It only means that the doctrine that everything without exception passes away as soon as it has arisen is not the position taken in the early discourses.

The difference between the early Buddhist conception of impermanence and the later theory of momentariness can be illustrated by contrasting a flickering lamp with the steady flow of a river. The light of the lamp is experienced as disappearing as soon as it appears; the flowing water is experienced as a changing continuity, a constant flow of change. The impermanence with which the early discourses are concerned is best pictured as a flowing river. The image of a flowing mountain river is in fact used in a discourse in the *Aṅguttara-nikāya* and its *Madhyama-āgama* parallel to illustrate the nature of human life. The *Madhyama-āgama* version of this simile, which occurs as part of a series of illustrations of life's brevity, is as follows:[17]

---

16 AN 3.47 at AN I 152,7 (translated Bodhi 2012: 246).
17 MĀ 160 at T I 683c6 to 683c7.

> It is just as a mountain river which, having rapidly grown, flows quickly, with much that floats along on it. Its fast and swift flowing water does not stop for a moment.

The *Aṅguttara-nikāya* version of this simile emphasizes that the mountain river does not stop for a moment, for an instant, or for a second.[18] The first of the three similar terms employed in this description is *khaṇa*, precisely the word used to designate the theory of momentariness. There can be little doubt that at the time of the formulation of the simile in the *Aṅguttara-nikāya* discourse and its parallel the theory of momentariness was not yet in existence, and that human life was seen as a constant flow that does not stop for a moment. Instead of being a series of successive moments of disappearance, it was seen as a series of successive moments of change.

VI.5 CONSCIOUSNESS AND IMPERMANENCE

The dictum that everything is subject to change applies not only to the body, but also to the mind or consciousness. Realizing the impermanent nature of consciousness is a particularly challenging task. The experience of a constant form of awareness in the background of experience, independent of the actual content or affective mode of what is taking place in the mind, can easily be mistaken for a subtle form of awareness or mental luminosity that does not change. Close inspection, however, shows that even the most subtle form of awareness or of being conscious is definitely subject to the law of impermanence.

A discourse in the *Saṃyutta-nikāya* and its parallels preserved in Chinese translation and Sanskrit fragments illustrate the changing nature of the mind with the example of a monkey that roams through a forest. In what follows, I translate the relevant section from the *Saṃyukta-āgama*:[19]

> The mind, mentality, or consciousness, by day and night does not stop for a moment, but keeps on changing in various ways; having arisen in one way, it ceases in a different way. It is just as a monkey that journeys from tree to tree in a forest, from moment to moment it catches hold of a branch and lets go of it to catch another. The mind,

18 AN 7.70 at AN IV 137,19 (translated Bodhi 2012: 1096, given as number 74).
19 SĀ 290 at T II 82a11 to 82a15, with a Sanskrit fragment parallel in Tripāṭhī 1962: 116f.

> mentality, and consciousness is just like that, it keeps changing in various ways, having arisen in one way, it ceases in a different way.[20]

The simile of the monkey illustrates the constantly changing nature of the mind.[21] Just as the monkey keeps moving through the forest continuously, taking hold of one branch after the other, so too the mind constantly changes from moment to moment by turning to this or that object. However stable it may appear, consciousness is just a flux of conditionally arisen moments of being conscious.

VI.6 THE INEVITABILITY OF DEATH

Coming back to the topic of contemplation of death: insight into impermanence as a continuous change that underlies all aspects of one's existence (in that all experiences are just a flow of interrelated processes) has considerable potential to change one's attitude towards death. As long as the constant change inherent in life is not recognized, death is easily perceived as an abrupt end of all that has thus far been experienced as stable and lasting. Once sustained contemplation has made it clear that life is nothing but change, death becomes part of this process: a particularly drastic moment of change, yet, in the end, just another moment of change.

Without such insight, fear of death can result in focusing only on what is new, what is young, what is growing and developing, thereby turning a blind eye on what is old, decreasing, and about to pass away. Such a one-sided perspective prevents one from seeing reality as it is. Without seeing reality as it is, however, it is not possible to act according to what reality requires. That is, it is not possible to live properly and fully unless the inevitability of death is accepted as an integral part of life.

According to the *Ariyapariyesanā-sutta* and its *Madhyama-āgama* parallel, it was realizing the inevitability of death (as well as of old age and disease) that motivated the future Buddha to set out on his quest for awakening. The *Madhyama-āgama* version reports his reflection in the following manner:[22]

---

20 The parallel SN 12.61 at SN II 95,3 (translated Bodhi 2000: 595) indicates that the arising and ceasing of the mind takes place by day and by night.

21 The motif of the monkey who lets go of one branch to seize another one recurs in Sn 791 (translated Norman 1992: 92) to illustrate the letting go of one thing in order to take hold of something else.

22 MĀ 204 at T I 776a26 to 776b1 (translated Anālayo 2012d: 25f).

> Formerly, when I had not yet awakened to supreme, right, and complete awakening, I thought like this: "I am actually myself subject to disease and I naively search for what is [also] subject to disease, I am actually myself subject to old age and subject to death ... and I naively search for what is [also] subject to [old age and death] ... What if I now rather search for the supreme peace of Nirvāṇa, which is free from disease ... free from old age and death?"[23]

According to the *Saṅghabhedavastu* of the Mūlasarvāstivāda *Vinaya*, before his awakening the future Buddha had in fact been stirred by the vision of corpses in various stages of decay,[24] a description that provides a direct connection to the present *satipaṭṭhāna* exercise.

A discourse in the *Aṅguttara-nikāya* and its *Madhyama-āgama* parallel report the bodhisattva's reflection that people in the world react with disgust and aversion when they see someone else subject to old age, disease, and death, even though they are themselves subject to the same predicament. Going against the grain of this common reaction, the future Buddha lost any sense of pride or conceit in being endowed with youth, health, and life, once he realized that he too was subject to old age, disease, and death.[25]

A popular narration depicts the future Buddha being unaware of these predicaments of human existence until he went on pleasure outings and saw for the first time in his life an old person, a sick person, and a dead person. During a fourth outing he then saw a recluse. The famous tale of his four encounters is found in the introduction to the *Jātaka* commentary,[26] and in *Vinaya* texts of the Lokottaravāda-Mahāsāṅghika, Mahīśāsaka, and Mūlasarvāstivāda traditions. There are, however, some inconsistencies found in these *Vinaya* tales.

The *Mahāvastu*, a *Vinaya* text of the Lokottaravāda-Mahāsāṅghika tradition, precedes the four encounters by reporting that the bodhisattva had already at an earlier point of time informed his father of his wish to go forth, expressing his insight into the inescapability

---

23 MN 26 at MN I 163,20 (translated Ñāṇamoli 1995: 256) qualifies Nirvāṇa as the supreme security from bondage.

24 Gnoli 1977: 77,22.

25 AN 3.38 at AN I 145,23 (translated Bodhi 2012: 240, given as number 39) and MĀ 117 at T I 608a3, which in its prose part, however, does not explicitly mention death. Yet the same is part of a verse summary in MĀ 117 at T I 608a20, so that the lack of a reference to death in the prose is probably the result of a textual loss.

26 Jā I 58,31 (translated Jayawickrama 1990: 78).

of old age, disease, and death.[27] If at an earlier point in time he already had such insight and the wish to go forth, the episode of the four encounters and their impact on the mind of the young prince would be redundant.

The Mahīśāsaka *Vinaya* also reports that the bodhisattva, when still young, had the desire to go forth. When describing his fourth encounter with a recluse, however, according to the same Mahīśāsaka *Vinaya* account the bodhisattva asked his charioteer to explain what going forth meant.[28] Such a question would make little sense if at an earlier point of his life he already had the desire to go forth himself.

According to the *Saṅghabhedavastu* of the Mūlasarvāstivāda *Vinaya*, during the first and second encounter the bodhisattva enquired about the implications of being old or sick. In reply, his coachman informed him that to be old or to be sick entails that one will soon be dead.[29] The bodhisattva apparently understood this reply, since, instead of asking about the meaning of being dead, he asked if he was also subject to this same predicament. When during the next encounter the bodhisattva saw a corpse, he asked his driver what death meant. Not knowing this, the replies he had received during the previous outings would have been meaningless for him.[30]

The internal inconsistencies found in each of these three *Vinaya* accounts reveal the relatively late nature of this legend. The same can also be deduced from the fact that in the Pāli tradition this legend is not found in the discourses or in the *Vinaya*, but only in the *Jātaka* commentary. In fact it seems rather improbable that a person with such keen observational qualities as the Buddha displays elsewhere in the texts would have completely missed out on the fact that people grow old, become sick, and pass away. Thus, this aspect of the famous narration is best taken as the result of legendary embellishment.

Nonetheless, the central message conveyed by the tale conforms with the above-mentioned passage from the *Aṅguttara-nikāya* and its *Madhyama-āgama* parallel, in that old age, disease, and death appear

---

27 Senart 1890: 141,7 and 146,12 (translated Jones 1952/1976: 135 and 141). The present survey is based on extracts from Anālayo 2007a.

28 T 1421 at T XXII 101b20 and 101c17. Bareau 1962: 20 concludes that this internal inconsistency shows that the bodhisattva's desire to go forth belongs to an older textual stratum that remained when the later account of his four encounters was introduced.

29 Gnoli 1977: 65,25 and 68,12.

30 Gnoli 1977: 70,21.

to have been instrumental in stirring the future Buddha to go forth in quest of awakening.[31]

VI.7 DEATH AS A DIVINE MESSENGER

The role of these inevitable predicaments of life as a motivating force to perform wholesome deeds and avoid unwholesome ones also finds expression in the conception of the divine messengers. These are described in the *Devadūta-sutta* and its parallels, which depict an evil doer who has just passed away and, on arrival in hell, is brought before King Yama.[32] King Yama asks the culprit if he had seen the divine messengers. The evil doer denies this, whereon King Yama draws his attention to the fact that he did see them, but failed to realize their significance. The divine messengers whose significance the wrongdoer had been unable to appreciate are none other than old age, disease, and death, which in some form or another manifested around him. Yet the evil doer did not pay heed to them and did not have the good judgement to reflect that he too would be subject to the same predicaments.

The motif of death as a divine messenger is significant in the present context because trying to face death with the help of contemplation of a corpse – as described in the *Satipaṭṭhāna-sutta* and its parallels – raises the practical problem of having to find a human corpse that has been left out in the open to rot. Especially nowadays, this can be quite difficult. An alternative suggested in the *Śrāvakabhūmi* is that, instead of going to a charnel ground, one may also use a picture of a decaying corpse.[33] This is certainly a more easily available option for undertaking this form of contemplation.

Since contemplating an actual corpse in its various stages of decay even with the help of pictures may not always be possible for the average practitioner in the modern world, an approach to facing the fact of death could be simply reflecting on the divine messenger

---

31 Bodhi in Ñāṇamoli 1995: 1336 n.1207 suggests that AN 3.38 could be the nucleus out of which the legendary account of the bodhisattva's encounters developed.

32 MN 130 at MN III 179,13 (translated Ñāṇamoli 1995: 1029), AN 3.35 at AN I 138,12 (translated Bodhi 2012: 234, given as number 36), DĀ 30.4 at T I 126b21, MĀ 64 at T I 503c25, T 42 at T I 827a24, T 43 at T I 828c8, T 86 at T I 909b26, and EĀ 32.4 at T II 674c2; cf. also T 24 at T I 330c29, T 25 at T I 385c26, T 212 at T IV 668c3, and T 741 at T XVII 547a10.

33 Shukla 1973: 416,7.

of death. This would be within the purview of anyone willing to face the true nature of his or her bodily existence. Somewhere among one's relatives, friends, or acquaintances a death must have happened in the past. By engaging in such reflection, a meditator in a way follows the tracks of the Buddha during the time before his awakening, who, according to the texts surveyed above, was inspired by just such reflection on death to pursue the path to the deathless.

The theme of one's own impending death could also be developed with the help of a poetic reflection of the type found in a stanza in the *Udānavarga*. The stanza highlights the mortality of the body and its subsequent fate. Since from the Buddhist viewpoint the average case of death will be followed by rebirth, it is in fact the body in particular that will be affected by death, whereas the mind continues faring on in accordance with the deeds performed while still alive. Here I translate the Sanskrit version from the *Udānavarga*, which parallels a similar stanza in the different *Dharmapada* collections preserved in Indic languages:[34]

> Alas, ere long this body
> Shall lie on the earth,
> Devoid and bereft of consciousness,
> Like a discarded log of wood.

Seriously engaging in such a reflection will go a long way in preparing one for what is inevitable for any human being: facing one's own death.[35] This is the gist of the present *satipaṭṭhāna* exercise, namely the need to let death come alive. Only when death has become a natural part of life will it be possible to go beyond the deadening influence of existential fear and thereby become fully alive to life as it unfolds in the present moment. In addition, facing one's own death when still alive offers the best preparation for being able to live well the actual moment of death.

---

34 *Udānavarga* 1.35, Bernhard 1965: 108, with parallels in Dhp 41 (translated Norman 1997/2004: 7), Gāndhārī *Dharmapada* 153, Brough 1962/2001: 143, and Patna *Dharmapada* 349, Cone 1989: 195f.

35 Schmidt-Leukel 1984: 166 explains that, from a Buddhist viewpoint, the existential question that death poses human beings can be solved in life – in fact it can *only* be solved in life. It not only *can* be solved, it *must* be solved. Wayman 1982: 289 notes that mindfulness of death implies "a kind of conversion of the mind, a 'death' from previous ways of thinking by way of contemplating death".

VI.8 DYING

For handling properly the actual moment of death, this inevitable and yet most challenging of human experiences, the *Anāthapiṇḍikovāda-sutta* and its *Saṃyukta-āgama* parallel provide helpful instructions. The background to this discourse is that the householder Anāthapiṇḍika is gravely sick and has asked Sāriputta to come and pay him a visit. Having ascertained that the householder is on the verge of death, Sāriputta gives him the following instructions:[36]

> You should train like this: "I do not attach to the eye and do not give rise to a state of consciousness with lust and desire in dependence on the eye element. I do not attach to the ear … the nose … the tongue … the body … the mind and do not give rise to a state of consciousness with lust and desire in dependence on the mind element.
>
> I do not attach to forms and do not give rise to a state of consciousness with lust and desire in dependence on the form element. I do not attach to sounds … odours … flavours … tangibles … mind-objects and do not give rise to a state of consciousness with lust and desire in dependence on the mind-object element.
>
> I do not attach to the earth element and do not give rise to a state of consciousness with lust and desire in dependence on the earth element. I do not attach to the water [element] … the fire [element] … the wind [element] … the space [element] … the consciousness element and do not give rise to a state of consciousness with lust and desire in dependence on the consciousness element.
>
> I do not attach to the aggregate of form and do not give rise to a state of consciousness with lust and desire in dependence on the aggregate of form. I do not attach to the aggregate of feeling … of perception … of formations … of consciousness and do not give rise to a state of consciousness with lust and desire in dependence on the aggregate of consciousness."

The *Anāthapiṇḍikovāda-sutta* is more detailed in comparison, as it also takes up detachment from the six contacts and the six feelings (related to the six senses), as well as from the four immaterial attainments, this world and that world, and what is seen, heard, sensed, etc.[37] The need to detach from this world and the next world is also mentioned in an *Ekottarika-āgama* parallel to the above discourse.[38] In spite of

36 SĀ 1032 at T II 269c16 to 269c23 (translated Anālayo 2010d: 6f).
37 MN 143 at MN III 259,35 (translated Ñāṇamoli 1995: 1110f).
38 EĀ 51.8 at T II 819c9.

such differences, however, the main point of the instruction in the parallel versions is the same: detachment towards any aspect of experience is the medicine required at the time of death.

While the *Anāthapiṇḍikovāda-sutta* and its parallels phrase this crucial injunction in doctrinal terms, the same advice expressed in a more general manner can be found in a discourse in the *Saṃyutta-nikāya* and its *Saṃyukta-āgama* parallel. Here a lay disciple has asked how to edify another lay disciple who is seriously sick and appears to be about to pass away. After ascertaining if the sick person's confidence in the Buddha, the teaching, and the community is well established, the *Saṃyukta-āgama* version continues by recommending that the following advice be given:[39]

> "Are you emotionally attached to your mother and father?" If [the disciple] is emotionally attached to mother and father, [the disciple] should be taught to let go and should be told: "If by being emotionally attached to your mother and father you could stay alive, such emotional attachment would be acceptable. Since you will not stay alive because of being emotionally attached, what use is it to be emotionally attached?"

Once the person on the verge of death has been able to let go of emotional attachments related to parents, according to the *Saṃyukta-āgama* discourse one should continue instructing the disciple in the same way in relation to partner and children, in relation to employees, and in relation to possessions.

The reflection in the *Saṃyutta-nikāya* parallel expresses the same basic meaning by pointing out that one will pass away anyway regardless of whether or not one has fond feelings for one's parents.[40] Another difference is that the *Saṃyutta-nikāya* version does not mention employees or possessions and so does not explicitly cover the attachment one may have towards one's professional relationships and achievements as well as towards the material goods and property one had been considering as "mine".

The two versions continue by guiding the sick disciple towards detachment from the five sense pleasures and from celestial pleasures, culminating in inclining the disciple's mind towards the cessation of identity or Nirvāṇa. The parallels agree that a lay disciple

---

39 SĀ 1122 at T II 298a20 to 298a23.
40 SN 55.54 at SN V 409,6 (translated Bodhi 2000: 1835f).

who has gradually been led in this way to total detachment will be liberated in just the same way as a monk who reached liberation of the mind a long time before.

In this way, facing death with detachment has a remarkable potential for helping one make progress on the path to liberation. What can turn death into a moment of high realization is simply mindful detachment from all aspects of experience. Such detachment grows with the realization that with the inevitable passing away of the body it becomes meaningless to be attached. Hence it is better to overcome such attachments while one still has a chance to do so: while one is still alive.

All that is needed to prompt this sense of detachment is the realization that death cannot be avoided, that death is an inevitable aspect of life. This insight is neatly expressed in a poem found in the *Theragāthā*. Although I am not aware of a parallel version, I nevertheless would like to make an exception to my general procedure of basing myself on material preserved in more than one tradition, by presenting my translation of these stanzas to conclude the present chapter:[41]

> This is not [just] characteristic of today,
> It is not amazing and not even surprising,
> Who is born will die,
> What is so surprising about this?
> From the moment of birth
> Death is certain for those who live,
> All who are born die here,
> Such is the nature of living beings.

VI.9 SUMMARY

A central theme of contemplating a decaying corpse is to drive home the truth of the body's impermanence, making it clear that death will certainly occur. In fact, it could happen right now.

---

41 Th 552f (translated Norman 1969: 56).

VII

CONTEMPLATION OF FEELINGS

VII.1 INSTRUCTIONS

In this chapter I move on to the second of the four *satipaṭṭhāna*s. The instructions in the *Satipaṭṭhāna-sutta* and its two Chinese *Āgama* parallels for contemplation of feelings are as follows:

Majjhima-nikāya:

> When feeling a pleasant feeling ... one knows: "I feel a pleasant feeling"; when feeling a painful feeling, one knows: "I feel a painful feeling"; when feeling a neutral feeling, one knows: "I feel a neutral feeling."
>
> When feeling a worldly pleasant feeling ... an unworldly pleasant feeling ... a worldly painful feeling ... an unworldly painful feeling ... a worldly neutral feeling ... an unworldly neutral feeling, one knows: "I feel an unworldly neutral feeling."

Madhyama-āgama:

> At the time of experiencing a pleasant feeling ... one then knows one is experiencing a pleasant feeling; at the time of experiencing a painful feeling, one then knows one is experiencing a painful feeling; at the time of experiencing a neutral feeling, one then knows one is experiencing a neutral feeling.
>
> At the time of experiencing a pleasant bodily feeling ... a painful bodily [feeling] ... a neutral bodily [feeling] ... a pleasant mental [feeling] ... a painful mental [feeling] ... a neutral mental [feeling] ... a pleasant worldly [feeling] ... a painful worldly [feeling] ...

> a neutral worldly [feeling] ... a pleasant unworldly [feeling] ... a painful unworldly [feeling] ... a neutral unworldly [feeling] ... a pleasant sensual [feeling] ... a painful sensual [feeling] ... a neutral sensual [feeling] ... a pleasant non-sensual [feeling] ... a painful non-sensual [feeling]... a neutral non-sensual feeling, one then knows one is experiencing a neutral non-sensual feeling.

Ekottarika-āgama:

> Here, at the time of having a pleasant feeling ... one is aware of it and knows of oneself: "I am having a pleasant feeling." At the time of having a painful feeling, one is aware of it and knows of oneself: "I am having a painful feeling." At the time of having a neutral feeling, one is aware of it and knows of oneself: "I am having a neutral feeling."
>
> At the time of having a worldly pleasant feeling ... a worldly painful feeling ... a worldly neutral feeling ... an unworldly pleasant feeling ... an unworldly painful feeling ... an unworldly neutral feeling, one is also aware of it and knows of oneself: "I am having an unworldly neutral feeling" ...
>
> Again, at the time when ... one has a pleasant feeling, at that time one does not have a painful feeling; at that time one is aware and knows of oneself: "I am experiencing a pleasant feeling." At the time when one has a painful feeling, at that time one does not have a pleasant feeling; one is aware and knows of oneself: "I am experiencing a painful feeling." At the time when one has a neutral feeling, at that time there is no pain or pleasure; one is aware and knows of oneself: "I am experiencing a neutral feeling."

The instructions in these three versions agree on the basic distinction between pleasant, painful, and neutral feelings. Contemplation of feelings thus requires recognizing the affective tone of present-moment experience, before the arisen feeling leads to mental reactions and elaborations. Such reactions and elaborations tend to be influenced by the initial affective input of how one feels. From a practical perspective, this aspect of contemplation of feelings requires that one does not get carried away by the individual content of felt experience and instead directs awareness to the general character of experience in terms of its three affective tones: pleasant, painful, neutral.

The *Ekottarika-āgama* account adds the clarification that these three basic types of feeling do not coexist; that is, when one experiences one of them, neither of the other two can be present. While this clarification is not made in the other versions and may well be a later addition to the *satipaṭṭhāna* context, the *Mahānidāna-sutta* and the *Māgandiya-sutta*, as well as some of their parallels, have a similar presentation.[1] The implication of this presentation is that the ability to feel is a process that consists of a series of distinct moments of felt experience that are either pleasant, or painful, or neutral.

The parallel versions continue from the basic threefold distinction of feeling by directing awareness to the worldly or unworldly nature of these feelings. The *Madhyama-āgama* discourse introduces the additional category of bodily and mental feelings, as well as sensual and non-sensual feelings. Comparing the main instructions in the three versions results in the pattern shown in Figure 7.1, presented in order of increasing complexity:

Majjhima-nikāya and *Ekottarika-āgama*	*Madhyama-āgama*
pleasant, painful, neutral worldly, unworldly	pleasant, painful, neutral bodily, mental worldly, unworldly sensual, non-sensual

Fig. 7.1 Contemplation of feelings

VII.2 BODILY AND MENTAL FEELINGS

While bodily and mental feelings are not mentioned in the other versions and thus may be a later addition to the *satipaṭṭhāna* instructions, the basic distinction of feelings into bodily and mental type occurs in other early discourses. Since this distinction is of considerable practical relevance, in what follows I examine its implications before proceeding with a comparison of the instructions for contemplation of feelings in the *Satipaṭṭhāna-sutta* and its parallels.

Feeling is part of "name" in the definition of name-and-form as one of the links in the traditional exposition of the dependent

1 DN 15 at DN II 66,19 (translated Walshe 1987: 227) and its parallels DĀ 13 at T I 61c8, T 14 at T I 243c14, and MĀ 97 at T I 580a14. Similar presentations of an examination of the nature of feelings can be found in MN 74 at MN I 500,10 (translated Ñāṇamoli 1995: 605) and its parallels, found in the *Pravrajyāvastu* of the Mūlasarvāstivāda *Vinaya*, preserved in Tibetan, and in the *Avadānaśataka*, preserved in Sanskrit and Tibetan; cf. Eimer 1983: 101,8, Speyer 1909/1970: 192,2, and Devacandra 1996: 715,7.

arising (*paṭicca samuppāda*) of *dukkha*.[2] As part of "name", feeling is clearly a mental phenomenon and does not pertain to "form", or the material body. Therefore, to speak of bodily feelings as distinct from mental feelings does not mean that some feelings are not part of the mental side of experience. In fact a dead body, from which the mind has departed, will not be able to experience feelings. Thus, the distinction made in the texts between bodily and mental feelings refers to the type of contact that has led to the arising of the feeling itself, which could be either bodily or mental. This distinction is brought out with the help of a simile in the *Salla-sutta* and its *Saṃyukta-āgama* parallel. In what follows I translate the relevant part from the *Saṃyukta-āgama* version:[3]

> To a silly and unlearned worldling through bodily contact feeling arises that is increasingly painful, even leading to the ending of life. [The worldling] is worried and complains by crying and wailing, the mind giving rise to disorder and derangement. At that time, two feelings arise, bodily feeling and mental feeling.[4]
>
> It is just as a person whose body has been afflicted by two poisonous arrows and extremely painful feelings arise. The silly and unlearned worldling is just like this, giving rise to two feelings: bodily feeling and mental feeling, [when] extremely painful feelings arise. Why is that? It is because that silly and unlearned worldling lacks understanding.
>
> To a learned noble disciple through bodily contact painful feeling arises that is greatly painful and oppressive, even leading to the ending of life. [The noble disciple] does not give rise to worry or complain by crying and wailing, the mind does not become disordered or deranged. At that time, only one feeling arises, namely bodily feeling; mental feeling does not arise.
>
> It is just as a person, who is afflicted by one poisonous arrow, not being afflicted by a second poisonous arrow. [The learned noble disciple is just like that,] at that time only one feeling arises, namely bodily feeling; mental feeling does not arise.

---

2 SN 12.2 at SN II 3,34 (translated Bodhi 2000: 535) and its parallel EĀ 49.5 at T II 797b28.

3 SĀ 470 at T II 120a9 to 120a27.

4 The parallel SN 36.6 at SN IV 208,7 (translated Bodhi 2000: 1264) only indicates that the feeling is painful, without mentioning that it is oppressive and leads to the ending of life; it also depicts the worldling as beating his breast.

In the *Saṃyutta-nikāya* version the arrows are not poisonous.[5] Since the problem with a poisonous arrow occurs as soon as one is hit for the first time, the *Saṃyukta-āgama* version seems to offer a less apt presentation. When the question at stake is simply the pain of being hurt by a poison-free arrow, then there is indeed quite a difference between being hit by one arrow or by two arrows. The *Saṃyutta-nikāya* version of the simile thus better illustrates the distinction between the way a worldling and a noble disciple deal with bodily pain.

This exposition clarifies the distinction between bodily and mental feelings. Even in the case of the noble disciple the pain will be felt by the mind, simply because the mind is what experiences any sensation that arises in the body. However, the mind of the noble disciple just experiences the pain arisen from bodily affliction without reacting to that pain, and therefore without adding the second arrow of feelings aroused by mental distress, which only makes the situation worse.[6] In other words, the distinction between bodily and mental feelings reflects what has caused the arising of each feeling. But both bodily and mental feelings are experienced by the mind.

While feeling is invariably part of the mind, this does not imply that the experience of feelings is entirely mental and does not affect the body at all. In fact, common experience shows that the actual experience of pleasant or painful feeling does indeed influence the body. Joy can lead to the raising of the hair and create goose pimples, just as displeasure can show its effects through bodily tension and facial expressions. Obtaining or losing desirable objects can affect the heartbeat and blood circulation, and intense feelings can cause faster breathing, sweating, bodily tension, etc.

Several discourses in fact mention some aspects of the bodily effects of feelings. The *Kāyagatāsati-sutta* and its parallel depict how the pleasant feelings that arise during meditative absorption quite literally pervade the whole body. The effect of painful feeling on the body can be seen in passages that describe a monk being rebuked, as a result of which he sits in dismay with shoulders drooping and his

5 SN 36.6 at SN IV 208,11.

6 Salmon et al. 2004: 437 explain that "descriptions of chronic pain are riddled with judgmental evaluations (e.g., 'It's terrible', 'This will never end') that represent cognitive elaborations of the more fundamental somatotypic pain signals. It is often the case that the underlying physical sensations receive less attention than the accompanying cognitive evaluations, which promote anxious and depressive tendencies."

head hanging down, unable to speak.[7] The mental evaluation of the words he has just heard has aroused feelings that are experienced in the mind as the displeasure of dismay and perhaps shame, and which also manifest bodily to such an extent that the whole posture is affected.

Feelings can thus be seen as an intermediary between body and mind, with a conditioning effect in both directions. One aspect of this intermediary role is that whatever happens in the body is mentally experienced through the medium of feelings. The other aspect is that the affective tone of mental experience influences the body through the medium of feelings. The actual experience of feeling thus usually affects both body and mind. An exception is the attainment of the immaterial spheres, in which the bodily dimension of experience has been transcended and only neutral feelings are experienced. In the normal living situation of the average human being, however, the experience of feeling involves both the body and the mind. To sum up: bodily feelings (feelings that arise due to bodily contact) can have an effect on the body and on the mind, just as mental feelings (feelings that arise due to mental contact) can have an effect on the body and on the mind.

VII.3 WORLDLY AND UNWORLDLY FEELINGS

Turning from the topic of bodily and mental feelings back to the instructions on contemplation of feelings in the *Satipaṭṭhāna-sutta* and its two Chinese *Āgama* parallels, as mentioned above the three versions agree in distinguishing the three types of feeling into worldly and unworldly occurrences. The *Madhyama-āgama* version also introduces a distinction between sensual feelings and non-sensual feelings, whose practical implications appear to be similar to the categories of worldly and unworldly feelings.

Drawing attention to the worldly or unworldly nature of feelings introduces an ethical distinction between feelings that can lead to the arising of defilements and those that lead in the opposite direction. The central role that feelings have in this respect is particularly evident in the context of the dependent arising (*paṭicca samuppāda*) of *dukkha*, where feeling forms the crucial link that can trigger the

7 MN 22 at MN I 132,28 (translated Ñāṇamoli 1995: 226). The parallel MĀ 200 at T I 764a7 similarly describes the lowering of the head and the inability to speak.

arising of craving. Thus feeling affords an important opportunity for a direct contemplation of dependent arising.

VII.4 DEPENDENT ARISING

Such direct contemplation need not cover all of the twelve links that are enumerated in the common description of the dependent arising of *dukkha*. Traditional exegesis, found in works like the *Paṭisambhidāmagga* of the Theravāda tradition and the *Jñānaprasthāna* of the Sarvāstivāda tradition, interprets this twelve-link model as extending over three consecutive lifetimes.[8] This would obviously make it difficult to contemplate the whole series in the present moment. From the viewpoint of this explanation, ignorance (1) and volitional formations (2) pertain to the past, whereas with consciousness (3) the present life period begins that leads via name-and-form (4), the six senses (5), and contact (6) to feeling (7). Based on feeling arise craving (8), clinging (9), and becoming (10), after which come the links that tradition reckons as pertaining to a future life, namely birth (11), followed by old age and death (12).

The traditional mode of interpretation can find support from the early discourses. For example, the *Mahānidāna-sutta* and its parallels identify consciousness as that which enters the mother's womb.[9] This passage occurs in the context of an exposition of dependent arising. Thus the rebirth interpretation has its roots in the early discourses and it would not do justice to such passages if this mode of explanation were to be dismissed as being merely the product of later times.

According to modern scholarship, the formulation of dependent arising by way of twelve links appears to involve a criticism of a Vedic creation myth.[10] This would be in line with a general tendency in the early discourses to reinterpret ancient Indian ideas and conceptions in order to express Buddhist teachings. Rather than describing the creation of the world, however, the point made by this reinterpretation would be to reveal the conditioned genesis of *dukkha*.

Besides the three-life interpretation of this chain of twelve links, already the early Abhidharma traditions present an alternative

---

8 Paṭis I 52,19 (translated Ñāṇamoli 1982: 52) and T 1544 at T XXVI 921b17.
9 DN 15 at DN II 63,2 (translated Walshe 1987: 226) and its parallels DĀ 13 at T I 61b9, T 14 at T I 243b18, MĀ 97 at T I 579c17, and T 52 at T I 845b7.
10 Jurewicz 2000; cf. also Jones 2009.

mode of interpreting the standard depiction of dependent arising. This alternative mode, found in works like the *Vibhaṅga* of the Theravāda tradition or the **Mahāvibhāṣā* of the Sarvāstivāda tradition, applies each of the twelve links to a single mind-moment.[11] From this viewpoint, the reference to "birth" in the context of the twelve links refers to the arising of mental states. According to the *Abhidharmakośabhāṣya*, the operation of all twelve links can thus take place within a single moment.[12] This certainly makes the whole series more easily amenable to introspective analysis carried out in the present moment.

Traditional exegesis provides another interpretative tool, which divides the twelve links into causes and effects. Here ignorance (1) and volitional formations (2) are causes. The same is the case for the three links that arise after feeling: craving (8), grasping (9), and becoming (10). The other links are effects.

What causes the arising of *dukkha* are thus ignorant reactions (links 1 and 2), which manifest when feeling leads to craving, etc. (links 8, 9, and 10). This clearly puts a spotlight on feeling. It is at this juncture that ignorance needs to be deconditioned, so that reactions by way of craving can be avoided. In other words, feeling is the link where the presence of mindfulness can have a decisive effect on the dependent arising of *dukkha*.[13]

Expressed in practical terms, being mindful of feelings enables one to become aware of the conditioned genesis of *dukkha* right at its inception. Practice undertaken in this way would not be confined to feeling itself, but rather combines being rooted in awareness of feelings with taking into account in a broad manner the various conditions that influence the "feel" of present-moment experience, be these external causes that are part of the situation in which one finds oneself or internal conditions arising from within the mind.

This set of external and internal conditions is best approached

---

11 Vibh 144,2 (translated Thiṭṭila 1969: 189) and T 1545 at T XXVII 118c7.

12 *Abhidharmakośabhāṣya* 3.25, Pradhan 1967: 133,1.

13 Ñāṇaponika 1983: 5 points out that "Contemplation of Feeling can unfold its full strength as an efficient tool for breaking the chain of suffering at its weakest link." Hoffmann and Van Dillen 2012: 320 explain that "mindfulness- and acceptance-based interventions can reduce cravings in at-risk population … specifically, these interventions may empower people to mentally disengage from ongoing cravings by accepting them as transient events that will eventually fade rather than by trying to suppress them", whereas "wilful suppression of desire bears the potential to backfire."

in a constructive manner by skilfully turning "problems" into the path, instead of merely reacting to the feeling tone they have caused. Any problem becomes the path as soon as it is considered a learning opportunity, offering a chance to develop detachment. This shift of perspective, where one remains aware of feelings without giving in to their affective pull, will lead to a gradual emerging from the tendency to react to feelings and thereby fuel the dependent arising of *dukkha*. In this way, contemplation of feelings can become the decisive condition that ensures that the ever-changing process of causes and conditions that make up experience eventually leads to the experience of the unconditioned.

In the case of an arahant, volitional formations that are rooted in ignorance have been forever eradicated and feeling can no longer lead to craving. Needless to say, an arahant still has the fourth aggregate of volitional formations which, in spite of a considerable overlap, is not identical with the second link of volitional formations in the sequence of dependent arising. The crucial difference is the presence of ignorance, which gives rise to volitional formations in the form of reacting to feeling with craving, thereby leading to the dependent arising of *dukkha*. Such ignorance is present in dependent arising, but absent in the case of an arahant. The presence of mindfulness when feelings are about to lead to ignorant reactions is thus very helpful for progress on the path to becoming fully liberated.

A discourse in the *Saṃyutta-nikāya* and its parallels preserved in Chinese and Sanskrit describes an actual contemplation of dependent arising undertaken through being aware of feelings. Here is the relevant section from the Chinese *Saṃyukta-āgama*:[14]

> A learned noble disciple gives attention to dependent arising and contemplates it. That is, conditioned by pleasant contact, pleasant feeling arises. At the time of experiencing a pleasant feeling, one knows as it really is that one is experiencing a pleasant feeling. With the cessation of that pleasant contact, the pleasant feeling arisen in dependence on and conditioned by the pleasant [contact] ceases, stops, becomes cool, subsides, and disappears.[15]

---

14 SĀ 290 at T II 82a15 to 82a18.

15 The parallel SN 12.62 at SN II 96,23 (translated Bodhi 2000: 596) follows the introductory sentence with a short statement on specific conditionality. Another parallel preserved in Sanskrit fragments, Tripāṭhī 1962: 117, agrees in this respect with the presentation in SĀ 290.

Unlike the *Saṃyutta-nikāya* version, the *Saṃyukta-āgama* discourse and the Sanskrit fragment parallel employ a formulation similar to what is found in the context of *satipaṭṭhāna* practice, according to which "at the time of experiencing a pleasant feeling, one knows as it really is that one is experiencing a pleasant feeling." In this way, recognizing that one is experiencing a pleasant feeling right at the time of its occurrence affords an excellent opportunity for developing insight into dependent arising. This is noteworthy, since it reveals the deeper implications of contemplation of feelings as a *satipaṭṭhāna* practice, that is, as a way to contemplate dependent arising.

After indicating that the same instruction also applies to the other types of feelings,[16] the three versions then illustrate mindfulness of the conditioned nature of feelings with a simile. The *Saṃyukta-āgama* version of the simile is as follows:[17]

> It is just as fire that arises from the conjunction of two sticks, which are rubbed against each other. If the two sticks are separated from each other, the fire will accordingly also disappear. In the same way feelings arise conditioned by contact, are born of contact, and arise from contact.[18]
>
> Because of the arising of this or that contact, this or that feeling arises. Because of the cessation of this or that contact, this or that feeling also ceases, stops, becomes cool, subsides, and disappears.

This simile illustrates that the affective tone of feeling is conditioned by the type of contact from which it has arisen. The distinction in the first part of the *satipaṭṭhāna* instructions between pleasant, painful, and neutral feeling can be employed to recognize precisely this conditioned nature of feeling.

The second part of the *satipaṭṭhāna* instruction, concerned with the worldly or unworldly nature of feelings, inculcates an awareness of the type of feelings that are prone to lead to unwholesome reactions. This topic opens the vista towards the conditioning impact of feeling on later reactions.

---

16 While SN 12.62 at SN II 96,26 takes up pleasant, painful, and neutral feelings, SĀ 290 at T II 82a16 covers five types of feelings: physically pleasant and painful feelings, mentally pleasant and painful feelings, and neutral feelings.

17 SĀ 290 at T II 82a20 to 82a24.

18 SN 12.62 at SN II 97,13 simply indicates that, in dependence on the three types of contact, the corresponding feelings arise.

In sum, with the first and the second part of the instruction on contemplating feelings, practice can be seen to explore the *conditioned* nature of feelings as well as the *conditioning* nature of feelings.

VII.5 THE CONDITIONING NATURE OF FEELINGS

The conditioning nature of feelings comes in for closer examination in the *Cūḷavedalla-sutta* of the *Majjhima-nikāya*, which has a parallel in the *Madhyama-āgama* and another parallel preserved in Tibetan translation. The passage in question is part of a question-and-answer exchange between a lay disciple and the arahant nun Dhammadinnā. The first question relevant for the present context concerns the repercussions of pleasant, painful, and neutral feeling. In what follows, I translate the relevant parts from the Tibetan version.[19]

> Desire increases with pleasant feelings, aversion increases with unpleasant feelings, and ignorance increases with neutral feelings … [yet] not all pleasant feelings increase desire, not all unpleasant feelings increase aversion, and not all neutral feelings increase ignorance. There are pleasant feelings that do not increase desire, but [instead lead to] abandoning it; there are unpleasant feelings that do not increase aversion, but [instead lead to] abandoning it; and there are neutral feelings that do not increase ignorance, but [instead lead to] abandoning it.

While the Tibetan version speaks of what "increases" with each of these three types of feeling, in the parallel versions in the *Majjhima-nikāya* and *Madhyama-āgama* the issue at stake is rather what "underlying tendency" (*anusaya*) is related to these feelings.[20]

This passage in a way provides a gloss on the distinction introduced in the *satipaṭṭhāna* instructions concerning worldliness and unworldliness. The practical task is to recognize what type of feeling tends to lead to unwholesome reactions and what type of feeling does not have this tendency. Examples of the second type of pleasant feeling, those that do not lead to unwholesome repercussions, are given in the Tibetan version as follows:

19 Si 22,3 to Si 23,21 (translated Anālayo 2012d: 51; Si 22,3 corresponds to D 4094 *ju* 9b5 or Q 5595 *tu* 10b7).

20 MN 44 at MN I 303,9 (translated Ñāṇamoli 1995: 401) and MĀ 210 at T I 789c2.

> Here a noble disciple, being free from sensual desire and free from bad and unwholesome states, with [directed] comprehension and [sustained] discernment, and with joy and happiness arisen from seclusion, dwells having fully attained the first absorption.
>
> With the stilling of [directed] comprehension and [sustained] discernment, with complete inner confidence and unification of the mind, free from [directed] comprehension and [sustained] discernment, with joy and happiness arisen from concentration, [a noble disciple] dwells having fully attained the second absorption.
>
> With the fading away of joy, dwelling equanimous with mindfulness and comprehension, experiencing just happiness with the body, what the noble ones reckon an equanimous and mindful dwelling in happiness, [a noble disciple] dwells having fully attained the third absorption. Such pleasant feelings do not increase desire, but [instead lead to] abandoning it.

The *Majjhima-nikāya* and *Madhyama-āgama* parallels differ in so far as they illustrate the type of pleasant feeling that is not related to desire with the example of the first absorption alone,[21] without bringing in the second and the third absorption.

Here is the description of painful and neutral feelings that do not lead to unwholesome repercussions in the Tibetan version:

> Here a noble disciple generates an aspiration for supreme liberation: "When shall I dwell fully realizing that sphere, which the noble ones dwell having fully realized?" The mental displeasure and painful feeling [due to] that aspiration, that pursuit, and that longing do not increase aversion, but [instead] abandon it …
>
> Here a noble disciple, leaving behind happiness and leaving behind pain, with the earlier disappearance of mental pleasure and displeasure, with neither happiness nor pain, and with completely pure equanimity and mindfulness, dwells having fully attained the fourth absorption. Such neutral feelings do not increase ignorance, but [instead lead to] abandoning it.

The basic point made in the three versions is that feelings that arise when one experiences the joy or the equanimity of deep concentration do not "increase" desire and ignorance; such feelings are not related to the respective "underlying tendencies". The same holds for the feelings that arise when one experiences the sadness

---

21 MN 44 at MN I 303,30 and MĀ 210 at T I 789c11.

of knowing one has not yet reached liberation: these feelings do not "increase" aversion and are not related to the "underlying tendency" towards aversion. On the contrary, such feelings arise when someone is practising the path to liberation, and they are thus related to the abandonment of these three root defilements, not to their activation.

Expressed in *satipaṭṭhāna* terminology, these are "unworldly" types of feeling. Although even in relation to unwordly experiences attachment should be avoided, such experiences are nevertheless different from experiencing pleasant, painful, or neutral feelings of a worldly type.

The antidote to the activation of the underlying tendencies towards desire, aversion, and ignorance is mindful observation of the nature of the feeling that has arisen. Developing mindfulness in this way has the intriguing potential to enable one to become aware of the reaction to any feeling even before this reaction has fully started. Here a special effort is required to remain mindful of feelings even when the mind has been carried off by sensual fantasies, thoughts of aversion, or vain imaginings. Feelings that arise at such times are obviously worldly types of feeling, and contemplating them with awareness is the very means for breaking through their conditioning impact on the mind.

VII.6 COMMENDABLE FEELINGS

Another significant implication of the above analysis in the *Cūḷavedalla-sutta* and its parallels is that there are commendable pleasant feelings. The path to liberation, as it is described in early Buddhism, does not require rejecting pleasure altogether. That is, early Buddhist analysis does not assume that pleasure is in and of itself inevitably related to attachment. Rather, feelings of any affective type could either be commendable or else should be avoided. The distinction that marks the difference is their wholesome or unwholesome nature. According to the *Kīṭāgiri-sutta* and its *Madhyama-āgama* parallel, this crucial distinction is an outcome of the Buddha's personal realization. In what follows I translate the section from the *Madhyama-āgama* discourse that reports the Buddha presenting his own experience as the basis for his assessment of feelings.[22]

22 MĀ 195 at T I 750c27 to 751a3.

> If I had not known as it really is, had not seen, had not understood, had not arrived at, and not completely and rightly realized that there are pleasant feelings that increase unwholesome states and decrease wholesome states, it would not be proper for me to recommend the abandoning of these pleasant feelings.[23]
>
> If I had not known as it really is, had not seen, had not understood, had not arrived at, and not completely and rightly realized that there are pleasant feelings that decrease unwholesome states and increase wholesome states, it would not be proper for me to recommend the cultivation of these pleasant feelings.

The *Madhyama-āgama* discourse continues by applying the same analysis to painful feelings, an exposition that in the *Kīṭāgiri-sutta* also covers neutral feelings. According to both versions, the Buddha's own experience and understanding was what led to this rather crucial shift in the evaluation of feelings. Unlike the almost automatic tendency of the untrained mind to pursue pleasure and avoid pain, the question becomes one of pursuing wholesomeness and avoiding unwholesomeness. This, in short, is the gist of the whole path to freedom.

The distinction broached in the *satipaṭṭhāna* instructions in terms of worldly and unworldly types of feeling is formulated in the *Saḷāyatanavibhaṅga-sutta* and its parallels in a slightly different way, distinguishing between feelings related to attachment and those that are related to renunciation.[24] Here is the relevant section from the *Madhyama-āgama* parallel:[25]

> What is joy based on attachment? The eye comes to know forms that are conducive to joy and the mind reflects on them, craves for those forms and experiences happiness conjoined with desire. One desires to obtain those [forms] which one has not obtained, and, on having recollected those which one has already obtained, joy arises. Joy of this type is joy based on attachment.

---

23 MN 70 at MN I 475,34 (translated Ñāṇamoli 1995: 579) continues at this point with the same statement in the affirmative mode, i.e., the Buddha recommended the abandoning of pleasant feelings based on his own knowledge, etc.

24 MN 137 at MN III 217,13 (translated Ñāṇamoli 1995: 1067) differs in so far as it speaks of joy related to "the household life", instead of being related to "attachment", and of joy related to "renunciation", instead of "dispassion".

25 MĀ 163 at T I 692c21 to 693b2.

What is joy based on dispassion? One understands that forms are impermanent, changing, [bound to] disappear, fade away, cease, and subside; that all forms, both formerly and in the present, are impermanent, unsatisfactory, and bound to cease. Having recollected this, joy arises. Joy of this type is joy based on dispassion …

What is sadness based on attachment? The eye comes to know forms that are conducive to joy and the mind reflects on them, craves for those forms and experiences happiness conjoined with desire. Not obtaining those [forms] which one has not yet obtained, and those which one has already obtained being past and gone, scattered and decayed, having ceased or changed, sadness arises. Sadness of this type is sadness based on attachment.

What is sadness based on dispassion? One understands that forms are impermanent, changing, [bound to] disappear, fade away, cease, and subside; that all forms, both formerly and in the present, are impermanent, unsatisfactory, and bound to cease. Having recollected this one reflects: "When will I accomplish dwelling in that sphere, namely the sphere that the noble ones are accomplished in dwelling in?" This is one's aspiration for the highest liberation, [born of] being distressed by one's understanding of the sadness of *dukkha* and the sadness of birth. Sadness of this type is sadness based on dispassion … [26]

What is equanimity based on attachment? The eye comes to know forms and there arises equanimity. That is the indifference [of one] who is not learned, who lacks wisdom, a foolish and ignorant worldling. Such equanimity towards form is not separate from form. This is equanimity based on attachment.[27]

What is equanimity based on dispassion? One understands that forms are impermanent, changing, [bound to] disappear, fade away, cease, and subside; that all forms, both formerly and in the present, are impermanent, unsatisfactory, and bound to cease. Having recollected that, one is established in equanimity. If equanimity has been attained [in this way] through mental development, this is equanimity based on dispassion.[28]

---

26 The fearfulness of understanding the nature of *dukkha* is not mentioned in the parallels MN 137 at MN III 218,26 and D 4094 *ju* 167a1 or Q 5595 *tu* 192b5.

27 MN 137 at MN III 219,10 adds that such a person has not conquered his [or her] limitations or the results [of action] and does not see the danger.

28 MN 137 at MN III 219,25 instead indicates that such equanimity goes beyond forms.

In both versions the same treatment is then applied to the other sense-doors. Thus the type of joy that is related to attachment is the result of the pleasing and agreeable features of sense-objects, whereas joy related to renunciation arises from the detachment that comes when contemplating the impermanent and unsatisfactory nature of sense-objects. In the case of feelings of sadness, those related to attachment manifest when hankering for unobtainable sense-objects, whereas sadness related to renunciation occurs when generating a longing for liberation. Neutral feelings related to attachment are merely the outcome of the bland features of sense-objects, whose nature is such that it does not call up any particular interest or reaction in the mind. In contrast, neutral feelings related to renunciation are the result of equanimity gained through insight into the impermanent and unsatisfactory nature of sense-objects.

In other words, feelings of the attachment type are the outcome of the nature of the sense-objects, whereas feelings of the renunciation type, being related to insight, go beyond and transcend the limitations of the object they experience.

VII.7 THE NATURE OF FEELINGS

Besides these analytical presentations, the early discourses also offer similes that help inculcate a detached attitude towards feelings. Two discourses in the *Saṃyutta-nikāya* and their respective *Saṃyukta-āgama* parallels compare feelings to winds that blow in the sky and to visitors who come to a guesthouse. Here is the simile of the winds in the sky from the *Saṃyukta-āgama* discourse:[29]

> It is just as fierce winds that can suddenly arise in the sky, coming from the four directions: winds that are dusty or winds that are not dusty, world-pervading winds or world-destroying winds, weak winds or strong winds, even whirlwinds.[30]
>
> Feelings in the body are just like those winds. Various types of feeling arise one after the other: pleasant feelings, painful feelings, or neutral feelings.

29 SĀ 471 at T II 120b16 to 120b20, which unlike its parallel SN 36.12 at SN IV 218,13 (translated Bodhi 2000: 1272) continues by listing various additional distinctions of these three basic types of feeling, such as bodily and mental types, worldly and unworldly types, etc.

30 SN 36.12 at SN IV 218,8 also mentions winds that are cold or hot and does not refer to world-pervading winds, world-destroying winds, or whirlwinds.

The *Saṃyukta-āgama* version of the simile of the guesthouse is as follows:[31]

> It is just as various types of people who stay in a guest house, warriors, brahmins, householders, men from the countryside, hunters, those who keep the precepts, those who break the precepts, those who live at home, and those who are homeless, all come to stay therein.[32]
>
> This body is just like that [guest house]. Various types of feeling arise one after the other: pleasant feelings, painful feelings, or neutral feelings.

The evocative power of these similes can be of considerable practical help as a reminder to develop and maintain the appropriate attitude towards feelings. Just as it would be meaningless to contend with the vicissitudes of the weather, in the same way it is meaningless to react to feelings with desire and aversion. Feelings arise and pass away, just like different types of wind. Keeping the mind open, like the empty sky, allows the "winds" of feelings just to pass by.

The simile of the guesthouse further underscores the importance of a detached attitude in regard to feelings.[33] Contemplation carried out by becoming the friendly but uninvolved host, who knows only too well that it is meaningless to get too involved with those who will soon leave again, can allow feelings to come and go without a need to react to them and thereby without causing any further repercussions in the mind. Feelings become like guests, instead of being integral to "my" sense of identity and well-being.

VII.8 PAIN AND DISEASE

A particular challenge for the maintenance of detachment in relation to feelings comes when one is sick and in pain. Yet these are precisely the times when contemplation of feelings can show its strength. The

---

31 SĀ 472 at T II 120c9 to 120c12, which similarly to SĀ 471 continues by listing various additional distinctions of these three basic types of feeling, such as bodily and mental types, worldly and unworldly types, etc. In this case, the parallel SN 36.14 at SN IV 219,17 (translated Bodhi 2000: 1273) also takes up worldly and unworldly types of feeling.

32 SN 36.14 at SN IV 219,11 mentions only warriors, brahmins, merchants, and workers coming from any of the four directions.

33 The image of the guest as distinct from the host is a well-known motif in the Chan and Zen traditions, where it illustrates the nature of deluded thoughts; cf., e.g., Sheng Yen 2006: 96.

"magic wand" of mindfulness can turn even a dreadful experience into a powerful opportunity for progress on the path, for developing insight and detachment.

A discourse in the *Saṃyutta-nikāya* and its *Saṃyukta-āgama* parallel describes a visit paid by the Buddha to monks in the sick ward. In his advice to the ailing monks he at first reminds them of the practice of the four *satipaṭṭhāna*s and of the cultivation of clear knowing, followed by an instruction on how to deal with feelings. Here is the *Saṃyukta-āgama* version's description of how someone, who is established in mindfulness and clear knowing, contemplates the painful feelings that manifest at the time of being ill:[34]

> Being with right mindfulness and right comprehension, [one understands that] painful feelings arise in dependence on conditions, not independent of conditions. What are the conditions on which they depend? They depend in this way on the body. One reflects: "This body of mine is impermanent, it is conditioned. What arises in the mind depends on this condition. Painful feelings arisen in the mind in dependence on this condition are impermanent and conditioned."[35]
>
> One contemplates the body and the painful feelings as impermanent, [contemplates their arising and disappearance, contemplates being free from desire, contemplates cessation, and contemplates] letting go. Herein, the underlying tendency to irritation and anger in relation to this [body] and to the painful feeling will no longer be an underlying tendency.

As the *Saṃyutta-nikāya* parallel clarifies, by practising in this way the underlying tendency to irritation will be abandoned.[36] Practising in this way at the time of being afflicted by the pain of disease has a considerable potential to speed up one's progress in mental purification. The same applies, according to both versions, to undertaking this mode of contemplation in relation to pleasant and neutral feelings, which will enable one to abandon the underlying tendencies to lust and ignorance.

34 SĀ 1028 at T II 268c17 to 268c21, which abbreviates the description of the actual contemplation, hence I have supplemented this from the description of pleasant feelings in the same discourse at T II 268c14.

35 The parallel SN 36.7 at SN IV 212,10 (translated Bodhi 2000: 1267) at this point has the rhetorical question: "How could [the painful feeling] be permanent?"

36 SN 36.7 at SN IV 212,17.

In addition, mindfulness also offers an excellent way to face pain, because its very presence will make the actual experience of pain less oppressive. In terms of the simile of the two arrows, the presence of mindfulness goes a long way in avoiding the second arrow, that is, the mental anguish that is often enough added on top of the physical pain. This is exemplified in another discourse in the *Saṃyutta-nikāya* and the *Saṃyukta-āgama*, which reports how a group of monks visited Anuruddha, who had been ill. Anuruddha told his visitors that he had not been afflicted by the painful feelings caused by his disease because of his practice of the four *satipaṭṭhāna*s. His statement in the *Saṃyukta-āgama* version reads as follows:[37]

> Being established in the four *satipaṭṭhāna*s, any bodily pain is gradually appeased.

The *Saṃyutta-nikāya* parallel indicates that, because of dwelling with the mind well established in the four *satipaṭṭhāna*s, the arisen bodily feelings do not keep overwhelming the mind.[38]

The therapeutic effects of mindfulness practice are of considerable relevance in the modern-day clinical setting, and mindfulness-based approaches have proven their worth in a medical environment as methods for dealing with pain.[39] From the perspective of early Buddhism, such benefits do not exhaust the potential of the mindful contemplation of feelings. The central purpose of such practice is rather to lead to a state of complete mental health through awakening.

VII.9 FEELINGS AND AWAKENING

The degree to which contemplation of feelings has such an awakening potential can best be illustrated through the example of the two chief disciples of the Buddha: Sāriputta and Mahāmoggallāna. In the case of Mahāmoggallāna, the instruction that, according to the Pāli commentarial tradition, led to his awakening is recorded in a discourse in the *Aṅguttara-nikāya*, which has a parallel in the *Madhyama-āgama*. Both discourses report that, after having received instructions on the overcoming of mental torpor, Mahāmoggallāna

37 SĀ 541 at T II 140c19 to 140c20.
38 SN 52.10 SN V 302,18 (translated Bodhi 2000: 1757).
39 Cf., e.g., Kabat-Zinn et al. 1985.

asked the Buddha how to reach full awakening. This is the reply he received according to the *Madhyama-āgama* version:[40]

> When there are pleasant feelings, painful feelings, or neutral feelings, one contemplates such feelings as impermanent, contemplates their rise and fall, contemplates their eradication, contemplates dispassion towards them, contemplates their cessation, and contemplates letting them go.[41]
>
> Having contemplated feelings as impermanent, contemplated their rise and fall, contemplated eradication, contemplated dispassion, contemplated cessation, and contemplated letting go, one does not cling to this world. Because of not clinging to the world, one is not wearied. Because of not being wearied, one attains Nirvāṇa and knows as it really is: "Birth has been eradicated, the holy life has been established, what had to be done has been done. There will not be the experiencing of another existence."
>
> Mahāmoggallāna, in this way … one attains the ultimate, the ultimate purity, the ultimate holy life, the ultimate completion of the holy life.

According to the commentary on the *Aṅguttara-nikāya* parallel, putting this mode of contemplation into practice enabled Mahāmoggallāna's breakthrough to full awakening.[42] Even though this is not mentioned explicitly in the discourse versions, it is nevertheless clear that the formulation in both discourses presents contemplation of feelings as capable of leading to complete liberation.

The *Aṅguttara-nikāya* version precedes this instruction by explaining the implications of the dictum that nothing is worth adhering to.[43] This dictum succinctly sums up the results of proper contemplation of feelings, which removes the affective glue that coats experience until one discovers that nothing indeed is worth adhering to.

In the case of the other chief disciple of the Buddha, Sāriputta, contemplation of feelings again appears to have played a central role in his awakening. His realization is reported in the *Dīghanakha-sutta* and its parallels, which indicate that he reached full liberation

---

40 MĀ 83 at T I 560b5 to 560b12.

41 AN 7.58 at AN IV 88,18 (translated Bodhi 2012: 1061, given as number 61) speaks of contemplating impermanence, dispassion (or fading away), cessation, and letting go.

42 Mp IV 44,23.

43 AN 7.58 at AN IV 88,12.

when witnessing an instruction given by the Buddha to a wanderer. Here is the passage from the *Saṃyukta-āgama* version that records the Buddha's instruction to the wanderer:[44]

> There are three types of feeling, namely painful feeling, pleasant feeling, and neutral feeling. Regarding these three types of feeling, what is their condition, from what do they arise, from what are they born, from what do they evolve? These three types of feeling are conditioned by contact, they arise from contact, are born from contact, and evolve from contact. With the arising of this or that contact, feelings arise. With the cessation of this or that contact, feelings cease, are appeased, become cool, and are forever extinct.
>
> In regard to these three types of feeling – experienced as painful, experienced as pleasant, and experienced as neutral – one knows as it really is the arising of this and that feeling, their cessation, their advantage, their disadvantage, and the release from them. Knowing this as it really is, one contemplates these feelings as impermanent, contemplates their arising and disappearance, contemplates freedom from desire, contemplates cessation, and contemplates letting go.
>
> One knows as it really is that one is experiencing feelings that are limited to the body, and one knows as it really is that one is experiencing feelings that are limited to life. At the time when the body breaks up at death, all such feelings will forever become extinct, be forever extinguished without remainder.[45]
>
> One reflects: "A pleasant feeling experienced at that time will be destroyed together with the body, a painful feeling experienced at that time will be destroyed together with the body, a neutral feeling experienced at that time will be destroyed together with the body. All this is on the side of *dukkha*.
>
> Experiencing what is pleasant, one is free from bondage and is unbound; experiencing what is painful, one is free from bondage and is unbound; experiencing what is neutral, one is free from bondage and is unbound. From what bondage is one free? One is free from lustful sensual desire, from irritation, and from delusion; and I say one is equally free from birth, old age, disease, death,

44 SĀ 969 at T II 249c10 to 250a2.

45 The parallel MN 74 at MN I 500,27 (translated Ñāṇamoli 1995: 605) does not take up feelings limited to the body or to life.

> worry, sadness, vexation, and pain. This is reckoned freedom from *dukkha*." …
>
> At that time the venerable Sāriputta reflected: "The Blessed One recommends the eradication of desire in regard to this or that state, being free from desire, the cessation of desire, the giving up of desire."
>
> At that time the venerable Sāriputta contemplated that this or that state is impermanent, he contemplated its arising and disappearance, he contemplated freedom from desire, contemplated cessation, and contemplated letting go. With the non-arising of the influxes his mind attained liberation.

Instead of mentioning the dependence of feeling on contact, the *Majjhima-nikāya* version points out that, at the time of experiencing one feeling, one does not experience either of the other two.[46] Other parallels to the passage translated above cover both of these topics, the mutually exclusive nature of the three types of feelings, and their conditional dependence on contact.[47] The *Majjhima-nikāya* account also does not mention the gratification, danger, and release in relation to feelings, nor does it mention the feelings that are experienced when life comes to an end.

In agreement with its parallels, the *Dīghanakha-sutta* reports that Sāriputta reached full awakening at the end of this instruction. This happened according to its account when Sāriputta realized that the Buddha recommended the abandoning and letting go of those states through direct knowledge.[48] Thus, in as much as the potential of contemplation of feelings for liberation is concerned, the parallel versions are in close agreement.

The progression of ideas in the above passage from the *Saṃyukta-āgama* touches on several themes related to contemplation of feelings. The instruction begins with the basic threefold distinction that is also the basic mode of *satipaṭṭhāna* contemplation of feelings. Next it reveals that feelings are conditioned by contact. Then contemplation

46 MN 74 at MN I 500,10.

47 This is the case for a parallel in the Mūlasarvāstivāda *Vinaya*, preserved in Tibetan translation, Eimer 1983: 101,8, and for the *Avadānaśataka*, preserved in Sanskrit and in Tibetan translation, Speyer 1909/1970: 192,2 and Devacandra 1996: 715,7. Another parallel, SĀ² 203 at T II 449b12, and a Sanskrit fragment parallel, folio 165a1f, Pischel 1904: 815, agree with SĀ 969 in taking up only the dependency of feelings on contact.

48 MN 74 at MN I 501,2.

turns to the impermanent nature of all affective experience, which should be recognized as it really is.

This then leads to the situation where, in accordance with the *Salla-sutta*'s injunction to experience only the single arrow of bodily feeling, the experience of feelings is limited to the body, as negative mental reactions to what is felt at the body sense-door no longer manifest. This in turn enables facing death squarely; in fact all feelings are, in a way, limited by life and, in the case of one who has reached full liberation, will completely cease when the body meets death.

The resulting detachment leads to freedom – freedom from mental defilements and thereby freedom from *dukkha*. Putting into practice the relinquishment of desire in regard to any type of affective experience will enable the breakthrough to full awakening.

Considered together, the cases of Mahāmoggallāna and Sāriputta throw into relief the awakening potential of contemplation of feelings. The degree to which the second *satipaṭṭhāna* can thus become the occasion for the unfolding of the entire path to liberation receives a further highlight in the *Mahāsaḷāyatanika-sutta* and its parallels. The main topic of the exposition in this discourse is experience through the six sense-spheres. Here is the last part of the relevant section from the *Saṃyukta-āgama* version, namely its exposition of the case of the sixth sense-door, the mind:[49]

> Experiencing within what is painful, what is pleasant, or what is neutral, one knows and sees it as it really is. Because of knowing and seeing it as it really is, one is not defiled by attachment to the mind. One is not defiled by [attachment to] mental objects, to mind consciousness, to mental contact, and to the feelings that arise in dependence on and conditioned by mental contact, which are experienced within as painful, pleasant, or neutral.
>
> Because one is not defiled by attachment, one is not involved with their characteristics, is not bewildered by them, is not concerned with them, and is not in bondage to them. One's clinging to the five aggregates diminishes as well as one's craving, lust, and delight in relation to future becoming …
>
> One who knows and sees in this way is reckoned to be bringing to fulfilment through cultivation right view, right thought, right effort, right mindfulness, and right concentration. Right speech, right

49 SĀ 305 at T II 87b20 to 87c8.

action, and right livelihood are said to have been earlier purified and brought to fulfilment through cultivation. This is reckoned to be bringing the noble eightfold path to purity and fulfilment through cultivation. Having brought the noble eightfold path to fulfilment through cultivation, the four *satipaṭṭhāna*s are brought to fulfilment through cultivation, the four right efforts, the four bases for spiritual power, the five faculties, the five powers, and the seven factors of awakening are brought to fulfilment through cultivation.

The states that should be understood and should be comprehended, one completely understands and comprehends. The states that should be understood and should be abandoned, one completely understands and completely abandons. The states that should be understood and realized, one completely realizes. The states that should be understood and cultivated, one has completely cultivated.

The *Mahāsaḷāyatanika-sutta* and another parallel preserved in Tibetan translation add to the above presentation that by practising in this way tranquillity and insight come into being concurrently.[50]

The presentation in the three versions confirms the conclusion that can be drawn from the descriptions of how Mahāmoggallāna and Sāriputta reached full awakening: all the central aspects of the early Buddhist path to liberation can be developed through this particular mode of practice, that is, through contemplation of feelings.

By way of summarizing the main aspects of contemplation of feelings, in what follows I translate a poem from a discourse in the *Saṃyukta-āgama* that again highlights the potential of cultivating mindfulness in relation to feelings:[51]

At the time of feeling a pleasant feeling,
Yet not understanding it to be a pleasant feeling,
One tends towards the underlying tendency to lust,
Not seeing the way of release.
At the time of feeling a painful feeling,
Yet not understanding it to be a painful feeling,
One tends towards the underlying tendency to aversion,
Not seeing the way of release.

---

50 MN 149 at MN III 289,16 (translated Ñāṇamoli 1995: 1138) and D 4094 *ju* 205a4 or Q 5595 *tu* 234a4.

51 SĀ 468 at T II 119b23 to 119c4; cf. also fragment Or. 15009/206, Shaoyong 2009: 231.

[At the time] of feeling a neutral feeling,
The Fully Awakened One has taught,
That one who does not contemplate it well
Will in the end not cross over to the other shore.[52]
... One who makes an energetic effort
And has right knowledge, unshakeably,
Of all that is felt,
Such a wise one is able to experience [it] with understanding.
Being one who experiences all feelings with understanding,
One here and now eradicates all influxes.
At death the knowledgeable and wise one
Does not fall into various reckonings.
Having already abandoned various reckonings,
One has forever entered Nirvāṇa.[53]

VII.10 SUMMARY

Contemplation of feelings requires recognizing the affective tone of present-moment experience. This affective tone is the conditioned product of contact and in turn forms the condition for ignorant reactions to feelings by way of craving and clinging. Contemplation of feelings thus enables one to become aware of the conditioned genesis of *dukkha* right in the present moment. Feelings are like uninvited guests; by not reacting to them one can avoid being shot at by a second arrow.

---

52 The parallel to SN 36.3 at SN IV 205,24 (translated Bodhi 2000: 1261) indicates that, if one delights in it, one will not be released from *dukkha*.

53 According to the last stanza in SN 36.3 at SN IV 206,3, one who has fully understood feelings is without influxes here and now. At the breaking up of the body, being established in the Dharma, the knowledgeable one is beyond reckoning.

VIII

CONTEMPLATION OF THE MIND

VIII.1 INSTRUCTIONS

In this chapter I turn to the third of the four *satipaṭṭhānas*. The instructions in the *Satipaṭṭhāna-sutta* and its two Chinese *Āgama* parallels for contemplation of the mind are as follows:

Majjhima-nikāya:

> One knows a mind with lust to be "a mind with lust"; or one knows a mind without lust to be "a mind without lust".
>
> [Or one knows a mind] with anger … [a mind] without anger … [a mind] with delusion … [a mind] without delusion … a contracted [mind] … a distracted [mind] … [a mind that] has become great … [a mind that] has not become great … a surpassable [mind] … an unsurpassable [mind] … a concentrated [mind] … a not concentrated [mind] … a liberated [mind] … a not liberated mind to be "a not liberated mind".

Madhyama-āgama:

> Having a mind with sensual desire … one knows, as it really is, that one has a mind with sensual desire; having a mind without sensual desire one knows, as it really is, that one has a mind without sensual desire.
>
> Having a mind with anger … a [mind] without anger … a mind with delusion … a [mind] without delusion … a defiled [mind] …

> an undefiled [mind] ... a contracted [mind] ... a distracted [mind] ... an inferior [mind] ... a superior [mind] ... a narrow [mind] ... a great [mind] ... a cultivated [mind] ... an uncultivated [mind] ... a concentrated [mind] ... a not concentrated [mind] ... a not liberated mind ... a liberated mind one knows, as it really is, that one has a liberated mind.

Ekottarika-āgama:

> Here on having a mind with craving for sensual pleasures ... one is aware of it and knows of oneself that one has a mind with craving for sensual pleasures. Having a mind without craving for sensual pleasures, one is aware of it and knows of oneself that one has a mind without craving for sensual pleasures.
>
> Having a mind with anger ... a mind without anger ... a mind with delusion ... a mind without delusion ... a mind with thoughts of craving ... a mind without thoughts of craving ... a mind that has reached an attainment ... a mind that has not reached an attainment ... a mind that is distracted ... a mind that is not distracted ... a mind that is scattered ... a mind that is not scattered ... a mind that is pervasive ... a mind that is not pervasive ... a mind that is great ... a mind that is not great ... a mind that is boundless ... a mind that is not boundless ... a mind that is concentrated ... a mind that is not concentrated ... a mind that is not liberated ... a mind that is already liberated, one is aware of it and knows of oneself that one has a mind that is already liberated.

The actual instructions for contemplation of the mind in the three versions are fairly similar, although the formulation in the Chinese versions is somewhat more descriptive than the brief indications in the Pāli discourse. This is especially the case with the *Ekottarika-āgama* discourse, where "one is aware of it" and "knows of oneself that one has a [particular state of] mind". More marked differences can be found in relation to the states of mind listed. Figure 8.1 presents the various listings in order of increasing complexity, at times adjusting the sequence within a pair of mental states to facilitate comparison.

In Figure 8.1, "sensual desire" and "craving for sensual pleasures" are similar to the qualification "lustful". Likewise, "narrow" would correspond to the heading "not great". The "distracted" state of mind stands in the *Majjhima-nikāya* and the *Madhyama-āgama* listings in contrast with a "contracted" mental condition. The *Ekottarika-āgama* has two categories in this case: the "distracted" or "not distracted" state of mind and the "scattered" or "not scattered" state of mind. While the implications of a mental condition that is contracted are to some extent open to interpretation,[1] it seems clear that the parallel versions agree that a task of *satipaṭṭhāna* meditation is to recognize when the mind is distracted, that is, when a loss of mindfulness has occurred.[2]

Majjhima-nikāya	*Madhyama-āgama*	*Ekottarika-āgama*
lust / not ~	sensual desire / not ~	craving for sensual pleasures / not ~
anger / not ~	anger / not ~	anger / not ~
delusion / not ~	delusion / not ~	delusion / not ~
contracted / distracted	defiled / not ~	craving / not ~
great / not ~	contracted / distracted	attainment / not ~
surpassable / not ~	superior / not ~	distracted / not ~
concentrated / not ~	great / not ~	scattered / not ~
liberated / not ~	cultivated / not ~	pervasive / not ~
	concentrated / not ~	great / not ~
	liberated / not ~	boundless / not ~
		concentrated / not ~
		liberated / not ~

Fig. 8.1 Contemplation of the mind

The mental states common to all versions could be summarized as a set of four and a set of three. The first set of four covers unwholesome mental states as well as their absence:

- lustful and not ~
- angry and not ~
- deluded and not ~
- distracted and not ~

The set of three covers states of mind that would come about through successful meditative cultivation, together with their opposites:

- great and not ~
- concentrated and not ~
- liberated and not ~

1 Cf. Anālayo 2003b: 178 and n.19.
2 Brown et al. 2007: 214 explain that "recognizing that one is not being attentive and aware is itself an instance of mindfulness."

A set found only in the *Satipaṭṭhāna-sutta* is the "surpassable" state of mind and its counterpart, the "unsurpassable" state of mind. While the same term does not recur in the parallels, comparable conceptions could be the "cultivated" and the "uncultivated" states of mind in the *Madhyama-āgama* discourse and the mental conditions of having "reached an attainment" or "not reached an attainment" in the *Ekottarika-āgama* version. The task in each case would be the same: Recognizing the degree to which one's practice has developed and realizing if more can be done.

This constitutes a noteworthy aspect of the instructions for developing contemplation of the mind, showing that, from an early Buddhist viewpoint, enquiring if one has reached some degree of attainment is considered an integral part of knowing the nature of one's own mental condition. Such inculcating awareness of the degree of development of one's own mind is not meant to encourage an attitude of obsession with meditative attainments and goal orientation. The appropriate approach would be a middle way between excessive expectation, where the practice of mindfulness is undertaken only to reach attainments, and an attitude of disdaining any type of wholesome aspiration, considering mindfulness as something only truly practised when one remains in the present moment without any sense of a higher goal beyond what happens in the here and now.

VIII.2 WHOLESOME AND UNWHOLESOME STATES OF MIND

The instructions for contemplation of the mind in the *Satipaṭṭhāna-sutta* and its two parallels present the task of mindfulness in terms of distinguishing between two opposite conditions. Thus, for example, the presence of lust or sensual desire is mentioned together with its opposite, the absence of lust or sensual desire. This basic pattern reflects a crucial distinction that underlies the early Buddhist teachings, namely the difference between what is wholesome and what is unwholesome. This polar distinction, applied to the mind, finds a poetic expression in a twin stanza that occurs at the outset of the *Dhammapada* collection. In what follows I translate the corresponding stanzas from the *Udānavarga* preserved in Sanskrit.[3]

3 *Udānavarga* 31.23f, Bernhard 1965: 415, parallel to Gāndhārī *Dharmapada* 201f, Brough 1962/2001: 151, and Patna *Dharmapada* 1f, Cone 1989: 104. The version of this stanza in Dhp 1f (translated Norman 1997/2004: 1) differs

> Phenomena are preceded by the mind, they are led by the mind and [follow] the speed of the mind. Affliction will follow the one who speaks or acts with a corrupted mind, just as the wheel [follows] the foot of the ox [that draws the cart].
>
> Phenomena are preceded by the mind, they are led by the mind and [follow] the speed of the mind. Happiness will follow the one who speaks or acts with a pure mind, just as the shadow follows one along.

According to the *Dvedhāvitakka-sutta* and its *Madhyama-āgama* parallel, the basic distinction between wholesome and unwholesome states of mind was something the future Buddha had developed during his progress towards awakening. In what follows, I translate the relevant section from the *Madhyama-āgama* discourse:[4]

> Formerly, when I had not yet awakened to supreme, right, and complete awakening, I thought like this: "I should better divide my thoughts into two kinds, with thoughts of sensual desire, thoughts of ill will, and thoughts of harming as one kind, and thoughts without sensual desire, thoughts without ill will, and thoughts without harming as the other kind."
>
> After that, I divided all my thoughts into two kinds, with thoughts of sensual desire, thoughts of ill will, and thoughts of harming as one kind, and thoughts without sensual desire, thoughts without ill will, and thoughts without harming as the other kind.
>
> Practising like this, I went to stay in a remote and secluded place, practising diligently with a mind free from negligence. [When] a thought of sensual desire arose, I at once realized that a thought of sensual desire had arisen. [I realized that] this is harmful to myself, harmful to others, harmful in both respects; this destroys wisdom, causes much trouble, and does not [lead to] attaining Nirvāṇa. On realizing that this is harmful to myself, harmful to others, harmful in both respects, that this destroys wisdom, causes much trouble, and does not [lead to] attaining Nirvāṇa, [the thought] rapidly ceased.
>
> Again, [when] a thought of ill will … a thought of harming arose, I at once realized that a thought of ill will … a thought of harming had arisen. [I realized that] this is harmful to myself, harmful to others, harmful in both respects; this destroys wisdom, causes much

in as much as it speaks of dharmas being "mind-made"; cf. also Skilling 2007 and Agostini 2010.

4 MĀ 102 at T I 589a13 to 589b9.

trouble, and does not [lead to] attaining Nirvāṇa. On realizing that this is harmful to myself, harmful to others, harmful in both respects, that this destroys wisdom, causes much trouble, and does not [lead to] attaining Nirvāṇa, [the thought] rapidly ceased.

[When] a thought of sensual desire arose, I did not accept it, I abandoned it, discarded it, and vomited it out. [When] a thought of ill will ... a thought of harming arose, I did not accept it, I abandoned it, discarded it, and vomited it out. Why was that? Because I saw that innumerable evil unwholesome states would certainly arise because of [such thoughts].[5]

Is is just as in the last month of spring when, because the fields have been sown, the area where cows can graze is limited. A cowherd boy, having set the cows free in uncultivated marshland, will wield a cane to prevent them from straying into others' fields. Why is that? Because the cowherd boy knows that he would certainly be scolded, beaten, and imprisoned for such trespassing. For this reason, the cowherd boy wields a cane to prevent [them from straying into the fields].[6]

In the same way, [when] a thought of sensual desire arose, I did not accept it, I abandoned it, discarded it, and vomited it out. [When] a thought of ill will ... a thought of harming arose, I did not accept it, I abandoned it, discarded it, and vomited it out. Why was that? Because I saw that innumerable evil and unwholesome states would certainly arise because of [such thoughts] ...

In accordance with what one intends, in accordance with what one thinks, the mind takes delight in that ... one who often thinks thoughts of sensual desire abandons thoughts without sensual desire, and through often thinking thoughts of sensual desire, the mind takes delight in them ... one who often thinks thoughts of ill will ... thoughts of harming abandons thoughts without ill will ... thoughts without harming and through often thinking thoughts of ill will ... thoughts of harming, the mind takes delight in them.[7]

---

5 The parallel MN 19 at MN I 115,11 (translated Ñāṇamoli 1995: 207) does not mention the arising of innumerable evil and unwholesome states.

6 The time period in MN 19 at MN I 115,29 is the last month of the rainy season in autumn, close to harvest time. Although MN 19 does not explicitly indicate that the problem would be that the cows stray into the crops if they are not checked, the same is implicit in its presentation.

7 According to MN 19 at MN I 115,21, what one frequently thinks about will lead to a corresponding inclination of the mind.

A noteworthy difference when comparing this passage with the corresponding part of the *Dvedhāvitakka-sutta* is a matter of sequence, as in the Pāli version the simile of the cowherd comes after the indication that frequent thinking leads to a corresponding inclination of the mind. Here the *Madhyama-āgama* version seems to have a preferable progression of ideas, since the description of preventing the cows from straying into the cultivated fields illustrates the fear of unwanted consequences, not the relationship between thoughts and mental inclinations.

The two versions continue by applying the same exposition to the opposite case of having thoughts that are free from sensual desire, ill will, or harming, which are as unproblematic as the situation of the cowherd when the fields have been harvested. He will no longer need to make an effort to prevent the cows from straying into the fields and can just be aware of them from a distance. The two versions continue by pointing out that even having such wholesome thoughts will in the long run tire the body and the mind, hence developing mental tranquillity is preferable even to cultivating wholesome thoughts.

The above description gives a clear illustration of how the basic distinction introduced for contemplation of the mind in the *Satipaṭṭhāna-sutta* and its two parallels can be practically applied. At the same time, it hints at the development of mental tranquillity and concentration, which in the *satipaṭṭhāna* instructions for contemplation of the mind comes subsequent to recognition of the presence or absence of unwholesome states of mind.

Unlike the *satipaṭṭhāna* instructions, where the task is merely to recognize the condition of the mind, the *Dvedhāvitakka-sutta* and its *Madhyama-āgama* parallel envisage active measures to be taken in order to counter what is unwholesome. The absence of an explicit mention of such measures in the *Satipaṭṭhāna-sutta* needs to be considered in light of the fact that *satipaṭṭhāna* as right mindfulness is only one of the factors of the noble eightfold path and thus operates in conjunction with right effort, etc. The task of right effort is precisely to overcome what is unwholesome and cultivate what is wholesome. The indispensable basis for such overcoming is honest recognition of what is happening, however, and such recognition is only possible when the mind is receptive and open without immediately reacting – precisely the task performed by mindfulness.

VIII.3 DEALING WITH UNWHOLESOME THOUGHTS

A gradual approach comprising five ways to deal with unwholesome thoughts is described in the *Vitakkasaṇṭhāna-sutta* and its *Madhyama-āgama* parallel. In what follows, I translate the relevant sections from the *Madhyama-āgama* discourse:[8]

> If unwholesome thoughts arise, then ... one should instead attend to a different sign related to what is wholesome, so that the evil and unwholesome thoughts no longer arise.[9]
>
> For one who ... instead attends to a different sign related to what is wholesome, the arisen unwholesome thoughts will swiftly be extinguished. Evil thoughts having been extinguished, the mind will be continuously established in tranquillity within; it will become unified and attain concentration.
>
> It is just as a carpenter or a carpenter's apprentice who might apply an inked string to a piece of wood [to mark a straight line], and then cut the wood with a sharp adze to make it straight.

The *Vitakkasaṇṭhāna-sutta* instead illustrates this procedure with the example of a carpenter who removes a coarse peg with the help of a finer peg.[10] The illustrations in the two versions offer complementary perspectives on the same basic instruction, which is to replace the object that has led to the arising of unwholesome thoughts with a wholesome alternative. This in a way "straightens" out the mind, just as the carpenter trims the wood. It also replaces something coarse – the unwholesome thoughts – with something more subtle.

The Pāli simile additionally conveys the nuance of a gradual approach. The overall aim in the *Vitakkasaṇṭhāna-sutta* is to reach a condition of mental tranquillity and concentration, which cannot be achieved directly when the mind is full of unwholesome thoughts. A skilful approach in such a situation is to deal first of all with the unwholesome thoughts by replacing them with wholesome thoughts. After this has been achieved, it will be possible for the mind to settle into a tranquil state within.

However, at times this approach might not be sufficient, and, in

---

8 MĀ 101 at T I 588a10 to 588c21. For a comparison of the five methods described in the *Vitakkasaṇṭhāna-sutta* with modern psychology cf. de Silva 2001.

9 The parallel MN 20 at MN I 119,7 (translated Ñāṇamoli 1995: 211) specifies that such thoughts are connected with desire, anger, and delusion.

10 MN 20 at MN I 119,14.

spite of one's attempt to "straighten" out the mind by replacing the unwholesome thoughts with something subtler that is wholesome, the mind may continue to return to the issue that causes the unwholesome mental reactions. If it has not been possible to switch the mind from unwholesome to wholesome, it seems likely that the danger of allowing the mind to continue rolling in unwholesomeness has not been fully appreciated. In such a case, the second method can come to one's aid:

> If unwholesome thoughts [still] arise, then one should contemplate these thoughts as evil and beset by danger [thus]: "These thoughts are unwholesome, these thoughts are evil, these thoughts are abhorred by the wise. One who is filled with these thoughts will not attain penetrative [knowledge], will not attain the path to awakening, and will not attain Nirvāṇa, because of the arising of these evil and unwholesome thoughts."[11]
>
> For one who contemplates them in this way as evil, the arisen unwholesome thoughts will be swiftly extinguished. Evil thoughts having been extinguished, the mind will be continuously established in tranquillity within; it will become unified and attain concentration.
>
> It is just as a young and very handsome person, who has taken a bath and washed, dressed in clean clothes, applied perfume to the body, and combed the beard and hair, in order to be spotlessly clean. Suppose someone were to take a dead snake, or a dead dog, or a dead human that is half-eaten [by animals], of bluish colour, swollen and putrefied, with impurities oozing out, and put it around that [young person's] neck. That [young person] would abhor the filth, neither enjoying nor liking it.

The *Vitakkasaṇṭhāna-sutta* similarly takes up the case of a young man or a young woman who is fond of ornaments and finds a dead snake, a dead dog, or even a dead human body hung around his or her neck. While the *Vitakkasaṇṭhāna-sutta* does not describe the condition of the corpse, the *Madhyama-āgama* passage translated above depicts the corpse as half-eaten, putrefied, and with impurities oozing out. This further enhances the stark image of a corpse hung around one's neck to illustrate the peril in allowing such unwholesome thoughts to run on in the mind.

---

11 MN 20 at MN I 119,31 only highlights that such thoughts are unwholesome, blameworthy, and have *dukkha* as their result, without mentioning the attitude of the wise or the prospect of attaining Nirvāṇa.

At the time of being engrossed in an unwholesome thought a certain amount of pleasure may arise and one's sense of ego may find some gratification. Yet, viewed from a proper perspective, one is actually putting a dead carcass around the neck of one's own mind. Allowing the mind to be defiled in this way is similar to the impure substances that drip from the carcass, spoiling the clean appearance of a pretty young person who has washed and dressed up nicely.

This simile relates to a point I made earlier in relation to contemplating the anatomical constitution of the body, where I suggested that deconstructing the notion of bodily beauty leads on to another conception of beauty, namely the beauty of the mind. The present simile plays on the same idea. What is commonly regarded as exemplifying beauty – a pretty young person, dressed up and clean – represents mental beauty, a mind that has been cleaned from any mental dirt, even if only temporarily. How could one allow the carcass of unwholesomeness, which is oozing out impure thoughts, to remain around the "neck" of that beautiful mind?

While reflecting on the danger inherent in letting the mind run on in an unwholesome rut should go a long way in overcoming evil thoughts, at times this approach might still be insufficient. If unwholesome thoughts keep arising in spite of one's previous attempts to replace them with something wholesome or to realize the dangers of unwholesome thoughts, a third method can be employed. This method no longer relies on drawing attention to what is unwholesome – which in fact thus far has not been successful – and instead just sets things aside for the time being, until the mind has recovered sufficient composure in order to be able to see things in their proper perspective:

> One should not attend to these thoughts, because of which evil and unwholesome thoughts arise. For one who does not attend to these thoughts, the already arisen unwholesome thoughts will be swiftly extinguished. Evil thoughts having been extinguished, the mind will be continuously established in tranquillity within; it will become unified and attain concentration.
>
> It is just like a clear-sighted person who, not wishing to see forms that are out in the light, either closes the eyes or turns the body away and leaves.[12]

12 MN 20 at MN I 120,12 does not mention leaving, but only closing the eyes or looking at something else.

Clearly at this point the topic that has been obsessing one's mind is so prominent, so much engaging one's mind, that neither the attempt to replace it with something wholesome nor becoming conscious of the negative effects of one's unwholesome thoughts has been successful. At this point, then, the strategy is to set it aside consciously, to make an effort at dropping the issue at stake, rather like looking away or even walking away when one does not want to see something.

Often such recurrent unwholesome reactions take place when one is mentally reliving a situation that one has experienced, and the mind again and again returns to the same issue, perpetuating one's unwholesome reaction towards what took place. It should be clear that it will not be possible to deal with anything in an appropriate manner as long as the mind is overwhelmed by unwholesome thoughts and reactions in this way.

Thus the suggestion to set things aside for a while is not a form of escapism. On the contrary, it is a means for calming a mind that is in the firm grip of an obsessive thought pattern. In such a situation, this may be the best way to deal with a problem that creates overwhelmingly strong reactions in one's mind: one had better wait for a time when the mind has calmed down. Only from the vantage point of a calm and balanced mind will it be possible to deal with whatever may have happened in an appropriate manner. A practical way of implementing this method would be to tell oneself that now is not the time to deal with the issue at hand and that one will do so later, when conditions are appropriate for doing that. Consciously assuring oneself that the problem will at some time be taken up makes it easier to set it aside for the time being.

The *Vitakkasaṇṭhāna-sutta* and its parallel envisage the possibility that even this method might not be successful. If the unwholesome thoughts still continue, one can resort to a fourth method:

> One should employ intention and volitional formations to reduce those thoughts gradually, so that the evil and unwholesome thoughts no longer arise. For one who in regard to those thoughts employs intention and volitional formations to reduce the thoughts gradually, the arisen unwholesome thoughts will be swiftly extinguished. Evil thoughts having been extinguished, the mind will be continuously established in tranquillity within; it will become unified and attain concentration.

> It is just as a person who walks on a path, hurrying along quickly, and then reflects: "Why am I hurrying? Wouldn't I rather walk more slowly now?" and so the person walks slowly. Then that person reflects again: "Why am I walking slowly? Wouldn't I rather stand still?" and so the person stands still. Then that person reflects again: "Why am I standing? Wouldn't I rather sit down?" and so the person sits down. Then that person reflects again: "Why am I sitting? Wouldn't I rather lie down?" and so the person lies down. In this way that person gradually quietens the body's gross activities.

According to the *Vitakkasaṇṭhāna-sutta*, this method requires giving attention to "stilling the thought-formation".[13] Judging from the reference to "formation" (*saṅkhāra*) in both versions, perhaps the idea is to calm the volitional driving force behind those thoughts. In other words, once the strategy of setting aside the thoughts has not worked, one faces them straightaway and tries to look at the motivational force that stands behind them. Given that it was not possible to set them aside, this force must be quite strong, so turning toward this motivational force seems a natural next step after the previous methods have not produced the desired results.

Taking a lead from the simile, the point would be to ask oneself "why am I getting so agitated about this?", or "what is it that gets me so worked up about this?" This then can lead to the realization that there is no need to keep hurrying along mentally, but one may instead stand still, even sit or lie down, allowing the mind to relax, in order to come out of the strain and stress of mental obsession.

If even facing the unwholesome thoughts directly is unsuccessful, the *Vitakkasaṇṭhāna-sutta* and its parallel offer yet another alternative, which comes as a last resort. The purpose of this last resort would be to prevent the unwholesome thoughts from spilling over into unwholesome words and deeds. This fifth method is as follows:

> With teeth clenched and the tongue pressed against the palate one should use the mind to fix the mind, taking hold of it and subduing it, so that evil and unwholesome thoughts no longer arise. For one who uses the mind to fix the mind, taking hold of it and subduing it, the already arisen unwholesome thoughts will be swiftly

13 MN 20 at MN I 120,18.

extinguished. Evil thoughts having been extinguished, the mind will be continuously established in tranquillity within; it will become unified and attain concentration.

It is just as two strong men who grab a weak man, take hold of him, and subdue him.

This type of approach is often the first method that comes to one's mind when having to deal with unwholesome thoughts. Yet, in the *Vitakkasaṇṭhāna-sutta* and its *Madhyama-āgama* parallel this is the last resort only. This approach only has its place when all the other methods have failed, when one has been unable to replace the unwholesome thoughts with a wholesome object, stop them by reflecting on their danger, set them aside for the time being, or calm the situation by looking at what motivates the continued arising of these thoughts.

On its own, this type of forceful approach is not capable of leading forward on the path to liberation. In fact, the *Mahāsaccaka-sutta* and a parallel preserved in Sanskrit fragments include the use of such forceful control of the mind among the exercises that the bodhisattva Gotama tried and found incapable of leading him to awakening.[14] The point of this method is thus only to offer an emergency brake. Just as one who keeps engaging the brakes will not advance, so too the use of this method on its own will not result in substantial progress on the path. Nevertheless, emergency brakes have an important function in preventing an accident. The same holds true for this method, which can at least prevent an accident by word or deed when one is completely overwhelmed by unwholesome thoughts.

The five methods presented in the *Vitakkasaṇṭhāna-sutta* and its *Madhyama-āgama* parallel thus present a series of possible interventions that illustrate the need for a gradual approach in one's efforts to emerge from unwholesome thought processes. This gradual approach can be summarized under the following five steps:

- turn to something wholesome instead;
- realize the danger of what is going on;
- set aside the issue at hand;
- gradually relax the motivational force behind it;
- use forceful restraint as an emergency brake.

---

14 MN 36 at MN I 242,26 (translated Ñāṇamoli 1995: 337) and Liu 2010: 167ff.

VIII.4 A GRADUAL STILLING OF THOUGHTS

The notion of a gradual approach finds illustration in a simile that compares dealing with thoughts to the gradual refining of gold. In what follows I translate the *Saṃyukta-āgama* version of this simile:[15]

> Is is just as someone who is casting gold and who places a hoard of sand and earth into a trough and then rinses it with water, [so that] the rough [pieces] emerge and the contamination by solid stones and hard chunks flows away with the water. Yet there remains gross sand that is interspersed among [the gold]. By rinsing it again with water, the gross sand flows out with the water. After this the gold manifests.[16]
>
> Yet there is fine sand interspersed with black soil. By rinsing it again with water, the fine sand and the black soil flow out with the water. After that there is true gold that is pure, clean, and without admixture. Yet there still appears fine dross in the gold. After that the goldsmith places it into the furnace, heats it up, beating it and blowing on it, until it melts, in order to remove all dross and filth.
>
> Because the gold that has manifested is not light, not soft, does not send forth brilliance and would break if bent or straightened, the goldsmith or the disciple of the goldsmith places it again into the furnace, heats it up, beating it, blowing on it, turning it around on its sides, casting it, and smelting it. After that the gold that manifests is light, soft, and brilliant, and it will not break if bent or straightened. According to one's wish it can be made into a hairpin, an earring, a ring, a bracelet, into any type of ornament.
>
> In the same way ... one gradually removes the entanglement of gross defilements, evil and unwholesome deeds as well as any evil and wrong view, so that they cease. This is like the gold that manifested when the solid stones and hard chunks had been washed away ... [17]
>
> One in turn gets rid of gross dirt: thoughts of sensual desire, thoughts of ill will, and thoughts of harming. This is like the gold that manifested when the gross grit had been got rid of ...

---

15 SĀ 1246 at T II 341b26 to 341c24.

16 The description of the refining of gold in the parallel AN 3.100 at AN I 253,17 (translated Bodhi 2012: 335, given as number 101) is somewhat less detailed.

17 AN 3.100 at AN I 254,14 does not mention wrong view and distinguishes unwholesome deeds into bodily, verbal, and mental ones. AN 3.100 also proceeds straightaway to the next stage in the purification of the mind, without explicitly relating this and subsequent stages to a corresponding stage in the refining of gold.

> One in turn gets rid of fine dross, that is, thoughts about relatives and one's home country, thoughts about people, thoughts about being reborn in heaven. One gives attention to getting rid of them, so that they cease. This is like the gold that manifested when the filth and dross, the fine sand and the black soil, had been removed … [18]
>
> Having [still] wholesome thoughts about the Dharma, one gives attention to getting rid of them, so that they cease, in order for the mind to become pure. Just as the gold that manifested when the dross that appeared to be similar to gold had been removed, so that it became pure and clean …
>
> One who [then] is in the grip of the practice of any concentration is like a pond whose water is in the grip of the limits of the shore. Being in the grip of these states, one does not reach the supreme sublime peace, and does not reach appeasement and the eradication of all influxes. This is like the goldsmith or the disciple of a goldsmith who casts and smelts the gold that has manifested: having got rid of all dross, it is not [yet] light, not soft, does not send forth brilliance, would break if bent or straightened, and cannot be used according to one's wish for any type of ornament … [19]
>
> [But] one who attains any concentration without being in the grip of its practice reaches the supreme sublime peace, reaches the appeasement of awakening, with unified heart and unified mind such a one eradicates all the influxes that are there. This is like the goldsmith or the disciple of a goldsmith who has cast and smelted the gold that has manifested so that it becomes light and soft, will not break, is brilliant, and can be bent or straightened according to one's wish.

A prominent difference between the two versions is that in the *Aṅguttara-nikāya* discourse the attainment of concentration is not described as something that may hold the practitioner in its grip. Thus the *Saṃyukta-āgama* version stands alone in sounding a warning of possible pitfalls in the practice of concentration.

In spite of this difference, the main thrust in the two versions is similar, in that they show a gradual approach to thoughts that

18 Instead of thoughts about a heavenly rebirth, AN 3.100 at AN I 254,24 mentions thoughts about one's reputation.

19 A simile on being in the grip of some form of concentration is not found in AN 3.100, which instead at AN I 254,29 proceeds, after mentioning thoughts related to the Dharma, by indicating that such meditation (*samādhi*), i.e., reflection on the Dharma, is not peaceful and sublime, has not reached full tranquillity and unification of the mind, etc.

is similar to the gradual refining of gold. This gradual build-up provides an important perspective for actual practice. Sitting down to meditate with the unreasonable expectation of experiencing a completely thought-free mind is somewhat similar to trying to make ornaments from gold that is still mixed with sand and stones. It is no wonder that such attempts meet with frustration.

This does not mean that there is no true gold hidden in the recesses of one's mind – far from it. But a gradual refining process is required to uncover it, and one must learn the goldsmith's task. This task is to recognize the condition of one's mind at the present moment, to know where one is and then to aim just at the next step. If more washing is needed, then the time to approach the furnace has not yet come.

Thus, if one's present condition is not yet free from gross unwholesome conduct, one first of all aims at washing out that type of contamination, in which unwholesomeness manifests as solid stones and hard chunks. Once a basis in moral conduct has been established, the next step is to leave behind thoughts related to sensual desire or aversion. If unwholesome thoughts persist, the five methods from the *Vitakkasaṇṭhāna-sutta* and its parallel could be used at this juncture. However, this is not always necessary. Having recognized through mindfulness that these are unwholesome thoughts, one may sometimes be able just to let go of them, allowing this gross sand that obscures the gold in one's mind to be washed out by the current of change, to be carried away by the flow of impermanence.

Only after this has been achieved has the time come to address any distracted thoughts that roam about, taking hold of this or that; this is the fine dirt in the mind. In other words, having a distracted mind roaming here and there during one's meditation is already an achievement, as long as it does not get involved in the gross conditions of sensual desire and aversion. The stones and the sand have already been removed and, while more washing is needed, one is already moving close to the furnace stage in refining one's mind.

Even the removal of thinking about this and that is not yet the stepping stone for total mental quietude, as the next step still takes place within the arena of thinking, even though the type of thought that occurs at this stage is related to the Dharma.

From a practical perspective, it is important to remind oneself of the fact that the existence of thoughts in the mind is the most natural thing to happen when one meditates. The way to deal with them is not to try to force the mind to stop completely still. This naturally leads one to become frustrated – one might believe that everyone else must find this so easy, and that one is a hopeless case. Thinking is a natural tendency of the mind and the way to deal with it intelligently is to accept it for what it is and then adopt a gradual procedure in cultivating one's mind.

This gradual procedure could employ the first two of the states of mind mentioned for contemplation of the mind in the *Satipaṭṭhāna-sutta* as well as in its parallels as short labels to be used during actual meditation.[20] Gross unwholesome states of mind could be a mind "with lust" or else "with anger". The presence of lust or of anger is directly opposed to the path to liberation and thus requires that one extricates oneself from them. If when sitting in meditation one is no longer assaulted and overwhelmed by gross unwholesome states of sensual desire and aversion, much has already been accomplished. One has already made substantial progress if during one's meditation practice such gross states do not manifest in the way they did earlier, however much the mind may still be running here and there.

The tendency to distraction will be tackled only when the mind is firmly established in freedom from the gross unwholesome states of lust and anger, like the goldsmith who can only get rid of the fine dirt after all the gross stones and pieces have been washed away. The various ideas and reflections in which the mind likes to engage are less of a problem as they do not run opposite to the path. Instead, they are just horizontal to it, so to speak. There comes a time when these need to be washed out as well. But even with the mind running here and there the method is not to try to stop it all at once and have a thought-free mind on the spot. Instead, one directs the thinking tendency of the mind towards something that is related to the Dharma, thereby directing it to what is wholesome and engaging it in a type of mental reflection that leads in the direction of the path to liberation.

Eventually, then, there will be a time when even these wholesome reflections can be allowed to subside, making room for a mental stillness that has arisen naturally as the product of this gradual approach. This stillness is not something created forcefully by pushing out any thought and thus it is not in need of constantly being defended against the resurgence of the thinking activity. If on following the

20 On the efficacy of affect labelling cf., e.g., Creswell et al. 2007.

gradual procedure one has come to some degree of stillness, and then thought emerges again, often a smiling recognition can suffice to bring the mind back to stillness and tranquillity, to the condition of inner calmness that is simply so much more pleasant and attractive than any type of thought could be. The gold of one's own mind has emerged by now, and placing it in the furnace of meditation will in turn make it become soft and light, pliant and brilliant. This beauty of the mind has emerged from what earlier was just a mixture of sand, grit, and stones. The gold was there all the time. It just took the wisdom of a gradual approach and the patient effort of cleansing and refining the mind to uncover its hidden treasures.

VIII.5 POSITIVE STATES OF MIND

Employing the gradual approach illustrated in the simile of the goldsmith will be greatly facilitated if one makes a point of rejoicing in whatever level of the mind is within one's reach. If one's mind has a tendency to roll in unwholesome thoughts, every moment in which this does not happen is praiseworthy and deserves to be acknowledged in a positive light.

Acknowledgement of even small steps taken in the right direction is a central aspect of successful meditative culture. Importance should be given not only to what is negative (i.e., what should be avoided and abandoned), but also to what is positive (i.e., what should be cultivated and encouraged). This is in fact an underlying theme in the listing of mental states for *satipaṭṭhāna* contemplation, where a negative state comes accompanied by its positive counterpart. The task of mindful contemplation is clearly not only to recognize a mind *with* sensual desire or *with* anger, but also to recognize a mind that is *without* sensual desire or *without* anger.

Here states of mind without sensual desire or anger do not refer only to the mental condition of an arahant, who is forever free from desire and anger, etc. If that were the case, many of the mental states mentioned for *satipaṭṭhāna* practice would only be practicable for those who have already reached the final goal. Yet the discourses clearly indicate that even newly ordained monastics should be encouraged to engage in the practice of all four *satipaṭṭhāna*s.[21] The

21 SN 47.4 at SN V 144,15 (translated Bodhi 2000: 1630) and its parallel SĀ 621 at T II 173c16.

instructions do not seem to be only meant for advanced practitioners, but can safely be assumed to imply that even the temporary absence of a defilement is worthy of being noticed and acknowledged.

The rationale for the need to be aware not only of what is negative, but also of what is positive, finds an illustration in the *Anaṅgaṇa-sutta* and its parallels. The parallel versions of this discourse explain the need to recognize when a defilement is present as well as when one is free from a defilement with the example of a bronze dish. In what follows I translate the relevant simile from the *Ekottarika-āgama* version,[22] which takes up the four cases discussed in all versions in the following order:

- no awareness of having a defilement;
- awareness of having a defilement;
- no awareness of having no defilement;
- awareness of having no defilement.

> It is just as a person who has gone to the market and bought a bronze utensil which is dusty and dirty, being extremely unclean. That person does not rub and wipe it from time to time, does not clean and wash it from time to time, hence that bronze utensil becomes ever more dirty and extremely unclean.[23]

This simile illustrates the case of someone who has defilements and does not realize it. Not recognizing the presence of defilements obviously prevents one from making an effort to remove them. However, the situation is quite different when one is aware of the situation as it is, as then one can make an effort to purify the mind:

> It is just as a person who at the market has bought a bronze utensil which is soiled by dust and dirt. That person cleans it from time to time, washes and cleanses it, so that it becomes clean.

The *Anaṅgaṇa-sutta* and its parallels also examine the case of one who has no defilement within, a condition which the context shows to be concerned with the temporary absence of defilements, not with their final eradication. In the *Ekottarika-āgama* version the illustration

22 EĀ 25.6 at T II 632b14 to 632c18.

23 The parallels agree that the utensil is not cleaned. MN 5 at MN I 25,22 (translated Ñāṇamoli 1995: 109) adds that the dirty bronze dish is not made use of and instead put away in a dusty place. MĀ 87 at T I 566b11 specifies that it is put away in a dusty place instead of being put out in the sun. T 49 at T I 839b7 also notes that it is just put in a dusty place.

of not being aware of one's temporary freedom from defilements reads as follows:

> It is just as a person who has gone to the market and bought a bronze utensil which is [not] soiled by dust and dirt.[24] Yet, [that person] does not wash and cleanse it from time to time, does not clean it from time to time.

In this case, the problem is that one does not take care to maintain whatever degree of purity the mind has temporarily reached. In this way, the defilements get a chance to resurge in the mind and succeed in gaining control of it again. The case of one who is aware of being pure, however, is as follows:

> It is just as a person who has gone to the market and has got a bronze utensil which is very pure and clean. Moreover, [that person] cleans it from time to time, rubs it, and washes the utensil. Then that utensil will become ever more pure and attractive.

One who has reached some degree of purity and is aware of it will take care to protect it, and in this way makes further progress. This presentation highlights the need to recognize even temporary states of mental purity, an easily underestimated aspect of the path to liberation. The *Anaṅgaṇa-sutta* and its parallels make it clear that attention should not be given only to recognizing what is unwholesome in the mind. Instead, successful practice involves a balanced form of awareness, which acknowledges the presence of defilements just as much as it acknowledges their absence.

Practised in this way, contemplation of the mind becomes a middle path that avoids two extremes: the one extreme is seeing only what is bad within oneself and consequently getting frustrated, succumbing to feelings of inadequacy. As a result of this, inspiration can get lost and one no longer engages fully in the practice. The other extreme is pretending to oneself (and in front of others) that one is better than one really is, at the cost of ignoring one's own dark sides, those areas of the mind that are in need of purification. Such ignoring allows those dark sides to gather strength until they are able to overwhelm the mind completely. Steering a balanced middle path between these two extremes becomes possible through the simple

24 The addition of "not" suggests itself from the context and receives support from the parallel versions.

but effective element of honest recognition, introduced through mindfulness of the present condition of one's mind, which sees both one's shortcomings and one's virtues equally well.

VIII.6 MENTAL FREEDOM

The theme of recognizing what is wholesome becomes more prominent with the states of mind that are taken up in the remainder of the listing that is common to all *satipaṭṭhāna* versions of contemplation of the mind. Here the mind that has become great stands for the type of ornaments that one is able to fashion out of the gold of the mind, once it has been sufficiently refined. With the development of some degree of concentration the mind can emerge from the narrow recess of ordinary states of mind and get a taste of spaciousness and vastness. This can take place through various practices that are conducive to mental unification. A good example of engendering a boundless mental condition are the divine abodes (*brahmavihāra*s), whose meditative development the early discourses describe as a boundless radiation in all cardinal directions, resulting in a state of mind that has become "great".

Such a state of mind would be not only "concentrated", but also one that can be reckoned as "liberated". While final liberation from the defilements is clearly the ultimate goal in the early Buddhist scheme of mental purification, it is important to notice that the same scheme recognizes temporary states of mental freedom as integral aspects of the path.[25] A state of mind that is temporarily liberated can be developed by cultivating the *brahmavihāra*s of loving-kindness or perhaps better benevolence (*mettā*), as well as compassion, empathic joy, and equanimity. The early discourses illustrate the radiation of these *brahmavihāra*s in all directions with the example of a trumpeter who makes the sound of the trumpet heard in all directions.[26] Having accomplished such radiation one has reached a temporary liberation of the mind, which is liberated from any confines by having become boundless.

---

25 On different types of liberation cf. in more detail Anālayo 2009: 141ff (reprinted in Anālayo 2012b: 282ff).

26 The simile of the trumpeter to illustrate the radiation of the *brahmavihāra*s in all directions can be found, e.g., in MN 99 at MN II 207,22 (translated Ñāṇamoli 1995: 816) and its parallel MĀ 152 at T I 669c10.

The experience of a boundless state of mind, in which sensual desire and aversion are temporarily in abeyance, can become a powerful tool for making progress on the path. Such experiences, in a way, give a practical glimpse of the goal of practising meditation.

In modern-day Western society where rebirth is a novel doctrine for many, freedom from rebirth as a goal may at times fail to have an appeal, perhaps even fail to make sense. Even the concept of Nirvāṇa is not easily appreciated and thus can remain a somewhat remote ideal that does not exert a powerful attraction on the meditator. In contrast, having experienced a mental condition that is free and at peace, even just for a moment, can serve as a powerful inspiration towards the goal of being continuously free and at peace within. Such inner peace has found a poetical expression in a stanza in the *Dharmapada*. In what follows I translate the Chinese version:

> [When] the mind has become appeased,
> Tranquil, too, are [then] words and deeds.
> By being rightly liberated,
> One is stilled, with complete peace as one's refuge.[27]

VIII.7 SUMMARY

Contemplation of the mind inculcates the ability to distinguish clearly between wholesome and unwholesome mental conditions by seeing through the stream of thoughts that occurs at the surface level of the mind and recognizing the actual state of mind that stands behind them. By gradually washing out the grit of unwholesome thoughts, rather than just resorting to brute force, eventually the beauty of the still mind gradually emerges from the furnace of meditation. Progress towards uncovering the gold hidden in the mind requires that one directs mindfulness not only to one's shortcomings, but also to one's virtues, rejoicing in a temporarily liberated condition of the mind.

---

27 Stanza 15.7 in the Chinese *Dharmapada*, T 210 at T IV 564b10 (translated Dhammajoti 1995: 145), with parallels in Dhp 96 (translated Norman 1997/2004: 14), *Udānavarga* 31.45, Bernhard 1965: 424, and Patna *Dharmapada* 88, Cone 1989: 126.

IX

CONTEMPLATION OF DHARMAS

The exercises listed in the *Satipaṭṭhāna-sutta* and its two Chinese *Āgama* parallels for the fourth *satipaṭṭhāna*, contemplation of dharmas, show considerable variations. Figure 9.1 lists the three versions in order of increasing complexity. The contemplations in **bold** font are those that I will examine in greater detail in subsequent chapters.

Ekottarika-āgama	*Madhyama-āgama*	*Majjhima-nikāya*
awakening factors four absorptions	sense-spheres **hindrances** **awakening factors**	**hindrances** aggregates sense-spheres **awakening factors** four noble truths

Fig. 9.1 Contemplation of dharmas

In what follows, I survey the exercises that are not found in all versions, beginning with those that occur only in one version.

IX.1 CONTEMPLATIONS OF DHARMAS FOUND IN ONE VERSION

IX.1.1 THE FOUR ABSORPTIONS

The *Ekottarika-āgama* account of contemplation of *dharma*s includes the attainment of the four absorptions in its description of contemplation of dharmas. The instructions present the standard description of the attainment of the four absorptions, each time followed by the suggestion that this would be a form of *satipaṭṭhāna* practice. The full passage reads as follows:

> Again, free from craving for sensual pleasures, removing evil and unwholesome states, with [directed] awareness and [sustained] contemplation, being tranquil and mindful ... one enjoys the first absorption and experiences joy in oneself. In this way, [in regard to] dharmas ... one contemplates the characteristics of dharmas as a *satipaṭṭhāna*.
>
> Again, discarding [directed] awareness and [sustained] contemplation, arousing joy within, the mind being unified, without [directed] awareness or [sustained] contemplation, being mindful and tranquil, with joy and at ease ... one dwells in the second absorption and experiences joy in oneself. In this way, [in regard] to dharmas ... one contemplates the characteristics of dharmas as a *satipaṭṭhāna*.
>
> Again, mindfully discarding [joy] ... one cultivates equanimity in this respect, one constantly knows and experiences pleasant feelings oneself with the body, as sought after by noble ones, with purity of equanimity and mindfulness,[1] one engages in the third absorption. In this way, [in regard to] dharmas ... one contemplates the characteristics of dharmas as a *satipaṭṭhāna*.
>
> Again, discarding mental states of pain and pleasure and also being without sadness and joy, without pain and without pleasure, with purity of equanimity and mindfulness ... one enjoys the fourth absorption. In this way, [in regard to] dharmas ... one contemplates the characteristics of dharmas as a *satipaṭṭhāna*.

The inclusion of the four absorptions in the present context is unexpected. While the cultivation of mindfulness does provide an important basis for the development of mental tranquillity,[2] the attainment of absorption is not a form of *satipaṭṭhāna* practice in itself. A central characteristic of *satipaṭṭhāna* meditation is to be aware of variety,[3] as can be seen by briefly surveying the exercises in the three *satipaṭṭhāna*s studied thus far.

---

1 The present reference to purity of equanimity and mindfulness appears to be the result of an accidental copying of the phrasing appropriate for the fourth absorption.

2 Cf. Anālayo 2003b: 61ff.

3 Gunaratana 1991/1992: 165 explains that "concentration is exclusive. It settles down on one item and ignores everything else. Mindfulness is inclusive. It stands back from the focus of attention and watches with a broad focus, quick to notice any change that occurs." According to Olendzki

Contemplation of the anatomical parts requires reviewing the different parts of the body. While it is possible to take one of these parts and concentrate on it in order to develop unification of the mind up to absorption, this is not the way the practice is described in the parallel versions. The task is to become aware of the overall anatomical constitution of the body as a whole, by directing mindfulness to its various parts. This clearly requires staying within the realm of variety, and not focusing on one part to the exclusion of the others. In terms of the simile of the bag of grains, one surveys the various types of grain contained in the bag, instead of taking a single grain and concentrating solely on it.

The same holds for the case of contemplation of the four elements, where the point of the exercise is not to concentrate on a single element alone, but to be aware of all four as a way of "cutting up" the compact sense of an embodied self. Similarly, while the perception of a corpse in a particular stage of decay could be used for the purpose of developing mental tranquillity, the instructions for the cemetery contemplations require a form of reflection that is aware of the whole process of decay of a body and then compares this to the fate of one's own body.

With contemplation of feelings the task of *satipaṭṭhāna* is to be aware of differences that occur with changing experience, noting the present moment's affective tone of experience and being ready to notice when this changes into another affective tone.

While contemplation of the mind does cover the mind that is concentrated, etc., the point of the instruction is not about developing concentration, but rather about monitoring with mindfulness what is taking place, be this when the mind is concentrated or when the mind is not concentrated.

It seems clear that these *satipaṭṭhāna* contemplations take place within the realm of variety; their task is to be aware of differences and change. In contrast, absorption attainment requires unification

---

2009: 42, "like a floodlight rather than a spotlight, mindfulness illuminates a more fluid phenomenological field of ever-changing experience rather than isolating a particular object for intensive scrutiny. This alternative mode of observation is necessary because mindfulness practice is more about investigating a *process* than about examining an object. All mindfulness meditation requires a certain degree of concentration in order to gather and focus the powers of the mind, but the concentrated mind is then directed to a moving target – the flowing stream of consciousness – rather than being allowed to stabilize on a single point"; cf. also Lutz et al. 2008.

of the mind based on a single and stable object, a unification that is already a characteristic of the first absorption.[4] A mind that is unified on a single object is not capable of being aware of variety, just as being aware of variety prevents one from entering the first or a higher absorption.[5] It is precisely the awareness of variety that enables one to realize the impermanent and conditioned nature of the object(s) of contemplation, which in turn leads to liberating wisdom.

An extended poem in the *Aṅguttara-nikāya*, with a parallel in the *Madhyama-āgama*, compares mental qualities with parts of an elephant. In this poem, mindfulness corresponds to the elephant's neck, the natural support for the elephant's head, which represents wisdom in this simile.[6] This image reflects the principal purpose of *satipaṭṭhāna* practice: the engendering of liberating wisdom. As discussed in the introductory chapter to this book, wisdom and liberation are the converging point for *satipaṭṭhāna* meditation. This is also explicitly stated in the *Satipaṭṭhāna-sutta* and its parallels, according to which the purpose of *satipaṭṭhāna* meditation is to lead to the attainment of Nirvāṇa, not just to the attainment of mundane absorption, which is rather a by-product of the cultivation of mindfulness.[7]

The four absorptions are also mentioned in the *Mahāsatipaṭṭhāna-sutta*, which does not present these as a form of *satipaṭṭhāna* practice. Instead, the four absorptions only occur in its exposition of right concentration as part of the noble eightfold path.[8]

In descriptions of the noble eightfold path, right mindfulness does not only have the function of leading up to right concentration in the form of the four absorptions. If this were the case, by the same reasoning one would have to conclude that right effort also has

---

4 MN 43 at MN I 294,31 (translated Ñāṇamoli 1995: 391), MĀ 210 at T I 788c20, and D 4094 *ju* 8a1 or Q 5595 *tu* 8b8 list unification of the mind as one of the factors of the first absorption.

5 MN 125 at MN III 136,26 (translated Ñāṇamoli 1995: 995) omits the first absorption and thus, taken on its own, gives the impression that *satipaṭṭhāna* practice enables direct attainment of the second absorption. This is probably the result of a textual error, as the parallel MĀ 198 at T I 758b25 does mention the first absorption; cf. in more detail Anālayo 2012d: 414ff.

6 AN 6.43 at AN III 346,24 (translated Bodhi 2012: 909) and its parallel MĀ 118 at T I 608c11.

7 It seems to me that the suggestion by Sujato 2005: 186 that "the primary purpose of satipatthana is to lead to jhana" fails to appreciate the purposes and functions of *satipaṭṭhāna* meditation.

8 DN 22 at DN II 313,11 (translated Walshe 1987: 349).

the sole purpose of establishing the four *satipaṭṭhāna*s. While these three factors of the path certainly cooperate, build on each other, and even overlap to a considerable degree, they are nevertheless distinct aspects of the meditative culture of the mind, whose overall purpose is to arouse liberating insight in order to reach freedom from *dukkha*. Needless to say, right concentration is not the final goal of the noble eightfold path. Instead, the final goal is the attainment of full liberation, when the path becomes a ten-factored one, with right knowledge and right liberation as its culmination.

The attainment of absorption can of course become an occasion for the development of insight. In fact, according to the "refrain", which in the *Ekottarika-āgama* discourse also follows the description of the absorptions, one should contemplate the nature of arising, of ceasing, and of both arising and ceasing. On emerging from an absorption, directing one's awareness to the fact that this experience has come to an end offers a powerful occasion for the development of insight into the impermanent nature of even such sublime mental events. This is precisely why the contemplation of the mind in the *Satipaṭṭhāna-sutta* and its parallels mentions the concentrated mind, etc., as objects of mindfulness. However, this potential does not provide sufficient grounds for considering the actual attainment of the four absorptions to be a *satipaṭṭhāna* practice in itself.

Thus the presentation in the *Ekottarika-āgama* discourse gives the impression that a textual error has occurred. Judging from the parallel versions, what originally would have been a reference to the hindrances may have been replaced by what in the discourses usually comes after the removal of the hindrances, namely the attainment of absorption. Such an error could easily have happened during oral transmission and need not be seen as a sign of deliberate editing.

The hindrances are mentioned briefly in the *Ekottarika-āgama* version at the beginning of the discourse. After introducing the "one-going path" for the purification of beings and the realization of Nirvāṇa, the discourse states that "the five hindrances should be abandoned and the four *satipaṭṭhāna*s should be attended to." This is followed by explaining that the qualification "one-going" refers to "unification of the mind" and the "path" stands for the "noble eightfold path".

This explanation does not fit the context too well, since the one-going path only introduces the practice of one factor of the noble eightfold path, right mindfulness in the form of *satipaṭṭhāna*. Therefore the one-going path of *satipaṭṭhāna* cannot be identified with the whole noble eightfold path. Moreover, the purpose of the one-going path has just been clearly stated to be the realization of Nirvāṇa and thus not only the attainment of mental unification. While some degree of mental collectedness is certainly required for advanced stages of *satipaṭṭhāna* practice, remaining in a condition of deep concentration could become an impediment to the contemplations described in the discourses, because it would not permit awareness of variety and change.

The injunction that "the five hindrances should be abandoned and the four *satipaṭṭhāna*s should be attended to" also does not work well in the present context. According to the *Ekottarika-āgama* description of contemplation of the mind, mindfulness should be directed to the presences of mental states that are "with craving and sensual desire", "with anger", "with thoughts of craving", "distracted", and "scattered", etc. All of these would have little scope to arise in the first place if the five hindrances had already been successfully removed before engaging in *satipaṭṭhāna* meditation.

Thus, it seems to me that the *Ekottarika-āgama* presentation is the result of an error or a later addition, during which the contemplation of the five hindrances was lost from the section on contemplating dharmas, being replaced by the four absorptions, and a short reference to the five hindrances came to be part of the introductory section to the whole discourse.

IX.1.2 THE FIVE AGGREGATES

Other exercises that are found in only one version are the contemplation of the five aggregates of clinging and of the four noble truths in the *Majjhima-nikāya* discourse. The instruction for the first of these in the *Satipaṭṭhāna-sutta* of the *Majjhima-nikāya* directs mindfulness to recognizing each of the five aggregates and to contemplating their arising and their passing away. It reads as follows:

> One knows: "such is material form", "such is the arising of material form", "such is the passing away of material form"; "such is feeling" … "such is perception" … "such are volitional formations" … "such is consciousness", "such is the arising of consciousness", "such is the passing away of consciousness."

The "refrain" that follows each of the exercises in the *Satipaṭṭhāna-sutta* also mentions giving attention to impermanence, instructing that:

> one abides contemplating the nature of arising in dharmas, or one abides contemplating the nature of passing away in dharmas, or one abides contemplating the nature of arising and passing away in dharmas.

While at first sight this could appear a redundancy,[9] closer inspection shows that the actual instruction directs awareness to each aggregate individually, whereas the "refrain" speaks of "dharmas" in general. From a practical perspective, this offers a meaningful approach. At first, mindfulness recognizes each aggregate on its own and becomes aware of its impermanent nature. This way of practice then leads over to contemplating the five aggregates as a whole from the viewpoint of their changing nature. As the aggregates obviously fall into the broad category of "dharmas", this would be practice in accordance with the "refrain". Thus, while the absence of contemplation of the five aggregates of clinging from the Chinese parallels to the *Satipaṭṭhāna-sutta* is certainly significant, the way in which the exercise is formulated does not seem to be problematic in itself.

Elsewhere, the early discourses present contemplating the impermanent nature of the five aggregates of clinging as a particularly powerful mode of developing insight, with the potential to lead to full awakening. According to the *Mahāpadāna-sutta* and its parallel, the former Buddha Vipassī gained awakening through cultivating this contemplation.[10] In view of the dictum that all Buddhas of past, future, and present times reach awakening by overcoming the hindrances, practising *satipaṭṭhāna*, and cultivating the awakening factors,[11] there would seem to be good grounds for considering the Buddha Vipassī's contemplation of the five aggregates of clinging as an instance of *satipaṭṭhāna* practice.

From a practical perspective, in as much as the five aggregates of

9 Cf. Sujato 2005: 258.

10 DN 14 at DN II 35,15 (translated Walshe 1987: 212), with parallels in T 3 at T I 156b20 and in Sanskrit fragments S 462R and S 685V, Waldschmidt 1953: 50.

11 SN 47.12 at SN V 160,28 (translated Bodhi 2000: 1642) and its parallel SĀ 498 at T II 131a11.

clinging stand representative of attachment to body and mind, the four *satipaṭṭhāna*s can be seen to address precisely this issue. Practice of the four *satipaṭṭhāna*s, even without explicit attention given to the five aggregates, would undermine clinging to body, feelings, perceptions, volitional formations, and consciousness. Thus, even though the instructions for contemplation of the five aggregates are probably a later addition to the *Satipaṭṭhāna-sutta*, cultivating the four *satipaṭṭhāna*s in the way they are described in common in the parallel versions would still accomplish the aim of contemplation of the five aggregates.

IX.1.3 THE FOUR NOBLE TRUTHS

The other exercise found only in the *Satipaṭṭhāna-sutta* of the *Majjhima-nikāya* takes up the four noble truths in the following manner:

> One knows as it really is: "this is *dukkha*"; one knows as it really is: "this is the arising of *dukkha*"; one knows as it really is: "this is the cessation of *dukkha*"; one knows as it really is: "this is the path leading to the cessation of *dukkha*".

A similar mode of contemplation is found in the **Śāriputrābhidharma*, a canonical Abhidharma text of the Dharmaguptaka tradition.[12] The *Mahāsatipaṭṭhāna-sutta* in the *Dīgha-nikāya* tackles the same theme at considerable length. The discourse provides a detailed exposition of each aspect of the first and the fourth noble truth and explores the second and the third noble truth with the help of different stages in the perceptual process at each sense-door. This appears to be the result of the integration into the discourse of material that was originally of a commentarial nature.[13]

From a practical perspective, the scheme of the four noble truths is of considerable relevance to the practice of the four *satipaṭṭhāna*s. Helpful information in this respect can be found in the *Madhyānta-vibhāgabhāṣya* by Vasubandhu, which correlates the four *satipaṭṭhāna*s with the four noble truths. According to this correlation:

- contemplation of the body corresponds to the first noble truth;

---

12 T 1548 at T XXVIII 616b8.

13 Winternitz 1920/1968: 51, Bapat 1926: 11, Thomas 1927/2003: 252, Barua 1971/2003: 366ff; cf. also Anālayo forthcoming 1.

- contemplation of feelings to the second noble truth;
- contemplation of the mind to the third noble truth;
- contemplation of dharmas to the fourth noble truth.[14]

This suggestion fits the essential components of the four *satipaṭṭhāna*s that emerge from a comparative study. Contemplation of the body indeed reveals the unsatisfactory nature of the body by disclosing its lack of beauty, its not-self nature, and its impermanence, and thus can be considered a practical implementation of the perspective provided in the first noble truth.

Realizing the unsatisfactory nature of the body then leads to a closer consideration of the arising of craving, the theme of the second noble truth. This takes place with contemplation of feelings, which is precisely the aspect of personal experience that can lead to craving and thereby to the arising of *dukkha*. Insight into the arising of *dukkha* is closely related to the crucial distinction between what is wholesome and what is unwholesome, which underlies the distinction between worldly and unworldly feelings (the same basic distinction between what is wholesome and what is unwholesome also forms the background of the mental states listed in the third *satipaṭṭhāna*).

Contemplation of positive mental states as part of the third *satipaṭṭhāna* can give a foretaste of liberation, by making one aware of momentary experiences of mental freedom. Mental freedom will become continuous once *dukkha* has been fully eradicated. This aspect of contemplation of the mind can thus be seen to have a relation to the third noble truth of the eradication of *dukkha*.

A further refinement of insight into the nature of the mind comes with contemplation of the hindrances and of the awakening factors. Awareness of the conditions that lead to the removal of the hindrances and of the conditions that facilitate the cultivation of the awakening factors shows the practical path that will lead to the cessation of *dukkha*, the topic of the fourth noble truth.

Even though contemplation of the four noble truths does not feature in the parallels to the *Satipaṭṭhāna-sutta* and thus is probably a later addition, the four noble truths could nevertheless be considered as underlying the practice of the four *satipaṭṭhāna*s as a whole.

---

14 Anacker 1984/2005: 446,6 (translated ibid. 246); for other correlations cf. Anālayo 2003b: 25f.

IX.2 CONTEMPLATIONS OF DHARMAS FOUND IN TWO VERSIONS

IX.2.1 THE SIX SENSE-SPHERES

The *Majjhima-nikāya* and *Madhyama-āgama* versions of contemplation of dharmas direct mindfulness to the six sense-spheres. The instructions in the two versions read as follows:

Majjhima-nikāya:

> One knows the eye, one knows forms, and one knows the fetter that arises dependent on both; and one knows how an unarisen fetter arises, one knows how an arisen fetter is removed, and one knows how a removed fetter does not arise in the future.
>
> One knows the ear, one knows sounds ... one knows the nose, one knows odours ... one knows the tongue, one knows flavours ... one knows the body, one knows tangibles ... one knows the mind, one knows mind-objects, and one knows the fetter that arises dependent on both; and one knows how an unarisen fetter arises, one knows how an arisen fetter is removed, and one knows how a removed fetter does not arise in the future.

Madhyama-āgama:

> In dependence on the eye and forms a fetter arises internally. Actually having a fetter internally ... one knows, as it really is, that one has a fetter internally; actually not having a fetter internally ... one knows, as it really is, that one does not have a fetter internally. One knows, as it really is, how an unarisen fetter arises internally; and one knows, as it really is, how an internally arisen fetter ceases and does not arise again.
>
> In dependence on the ear ... the nose ... the tongue ... the body ... the mind and mind-objects a fetter arises internally. Actually having a fetter internally ... one knows, as it really is, that one has a fetter internally; actually not having a fetter internally ... one knows, as it really is, that one does not have a fetter internally. One knows, as it really is, how an unarisen fetter arises internally; and one knows, as it really is, how an internally arisen fetter ceases and does not arise again.

A difference between the two versions is that the *Madhyama-āgama* discourse does not direct mindfulness to the senses and their respective objects, which are simply mentioned as the condition for the arising of a fetter. Thus in its presentation the task is not so much to be mindful of a sense-door and its object as such, but to be aware of the presence or absence of a fetter. In other words, the fettering force of perceptual experience and its potential to lead to unwholesome mental reactions appear to be the main target of this exercise.

Another difference is a matter of sequence. The *Madhyama-āgama* version begins its exposition of contemplation of dharmas with the six sense-spheres and thus has these in the position where sense-restraint stands in the context of the gradual path to awakening, namely before the removal of the five hindrances. In the *Majjhima-nikāya* version, however, contemplation of the six sense-spheres occurs after contemplation of the five hindrances.

While such differences in sequence could be a sign of later addition, an impression supported by the fact that this exercise is not found in the *Ekottarika-āgama* discourse, such a form of contemplation would nevertheless seem to fit the present context. This is all the more the case since contemplation of the sense-spheres brings up the theme of causality, which is also central to contemplation of the hindrances and of the awakening factors. In the case of contemplation of the sense-spheres, the task is to be aware of – and to beware of – the conditions for the arising of a fetter.

As the main concern of this exercise is the fetter that arises in dependence on any of the six senses, from a practical perspective the main thrust of this contemplation could be captured with contemplation of the hindrances. Here the task is precisely to recognize when, in relation to what is experienced at any sense-door, a detrimental mental state arises that fetters the mind and quite literally "hinders" its progress along the path.

IX.3 CONTEMPLATIONS OF DHARMAS FOUND IN ALL VERSIONS

Strictly speaking, the hindrances are not a contemplation of dharmas found in all versions. Contemplation of the five hindrances occurs only in the *Majjhima-nikāya* and *Madhyama-āgama* versions under the heading of contemplation of dharmas, whereas in the *Ekottarika-āgama* account the hindrances are mentioned right at the outset of the discourse. On the assumption that the reference to the four absorptions found under contemplations of dharmas in the

Ekottarika-āgama version could be the result of a textual error that replaced an earlier passage on the five hindrances, it seems to me that contemplation of the hindrances should be considered an integral part of contemplations of dharmas, together with contemplation of the seven factors of awakening.

The hindrances in fact need to be overcome if the cultivation of the awakening factors is to lead to awakening. From a practical perspective, the need to recognize the hindrances and be aware of how to overcome them could therefore be considered as implicit in a successful cultivation of the awakening factors.

The exposition of contemplation of dharmas in the *Vibhaṅga* of the Theravāda Abhidharma mentions only contemplation of the hindrances and of the awakening factors.[15] This presentation clearly places these two exercises at the very heart of contemplation of dharmas.

The relevance of the hindrances to the fourth *satipaṭṭhāna* also emerges from a commentarial gloss on the *Samudaya-sutta* which, in agreement with its Chinese and Tibetan parallels, presents the conditions for the arising of each of the four *satipaṭṭhāna*s. In the case of contemplation of dharmas, the requisite condition is attention.[16] The Pāli commentary explains that wise attention leads to the arising of the awakening factors, whereas unwise attention leads to the arising of the hindrances.[17]

When considered in relation to the whole thrust of the three previous *satipaṭṭhāna*s, it seems a natural progression to proceed from contemplating the mind to contemplations of dharmas that stay within the mental realm.[18] Staying within the mental realm, these contemplations introduce a further refinement by directing awareness to the conditions for the removal or for the cultivation

---

15 Vibh 199,14 (translated Thiṭṭila 1969: 258).

16 SN 47.42 at SN V 184,22 (translated Bodhi 2000: 1660), SĀ 609 at T II 171b8, and D 4094 *nyu* 15b4 or Q 5595 *thu* 49a4.

17 Spk III 229,21.

18 This would not hold for contemplation of the five aggregates and of the six sense-spheres, as these involve the body in the form of the first of the aggregates and the fifth of the sense-doors. They thus do not take only mental phenomena as their object. To some degree, this even applies to the four noble truths. Manifestations of the first noble truth in the form of birth, old age, and death are not concerned only with what is mental, as they do have a relation to the body in the form of what is born, grows old, and passes away.

of those particular mental states that are of crucial importance for progress on the path: the hindrances and the awakening factors.

Considering the hindrances and the awakening factors to be the common ground of contemplation of dharmas in the three canonical versions would then place the main thrust of the fourth *satipaṭṭhāna* on the path to awakening. From this viewpoint, contemplation of dharmas is somewhat like a shorthand description of the path, which – after the hindrances have been overcome – requires the development of the awakening factors in particular. The task of mindfulness in the context of contemplation of dharmas would thus be to supervise the mind on the path to awakening, ensuring that the hindrances are overcome and the awakening factors are well established.

This is applicable to any practice, be that contemplation of the five aggregates, of the six sense-spheres, of the four noble truths, or any other form of contemplation that has the potential to lead to awakening. That is, contemplation of dharmas is not about being mindful of a particular topic. Instead, it involves a form of meta-awareness during contemplation, a being mindful of how the mind is progressing on the path.

IX.4 SUMMARY

The task of the fourth *satipaṭṭhāna* is to monitor the mind on the path to liberation. The two essential components of this path are overcoming the hindrances and cultivating the factors of awakening.

X

THE HINDRANCES

X.1 INSTRUCTIONS

With the present chapter I turn to the hindrances, those mental states that are singled out for their propensity to "hinder" the mind in its progress towards deeper concentration and liberation. The instructions for contemplating the hindrances in the *Satipaṭṭhāna-sutta* and its parallels are as follows:

Majjhima-nikāya:

> If sensual desire is present within ... one knows: "sensual desire is present within me"; or if sensual desire is not present within, one knows: "sensual desire is not present within me"; and one knows how unarisen sensual desire arises, one knows how arisen sensual desire is removed, and one knows how removed sensual desire does not arise in the future.
>
> If anger ... sloth-and-torpor ... restlessness-and-worry ... doubt is present within, one knows: "doubt is present within me"; or if doubt is not present within, one knows: "doubt is not present within me"; and one knows how unarisen doubt arises, one knows how arisen doubt is removed, and one knows how removed doubt does not arise in the future.

Madhyama-āgama:

> Actually having sensual desire internally ... one knows, as it really is, that one has sensual desire; actually having no sensual desire

> internally, one knows, as it really is, that one has no sensual desire; one knows, as it really is, how unarisen sensual desire arises; and one knows, as it really is, how arisen sensual desire ceases and does not arise again.
>
> In the same way, actually having anger ... sloth-and-torpor ... restlessness-and-worry ... doubt internally, one knows, as it really is, that one has doubt; actually having no doubt internally, one knows, as it really is, that one has no doubt; one knows, as it really is, how unarisen doubt arises; and one knows, as it really is, how arisen doubt ceases and does not arise again.

Ekottarika-āgama:

> What are the five hindrances that should be abandoned? That is, the hindrance of lustful sensual desire, the hindrance of ill will, the hindrance of restlessness[-and-worry], the hindrance of sloth-and-torpor, and the hindrance of doubt. These are reckoned to be the five hindrances that should be abandoned.

The instructions in the *Satipaṭṭhāna-sutta* and its *Madhyama-āgama* parallel are fairly similar. Regarding the recognition of a hindrance, it is worth noting that the formulations in both versions emphasize being aware of the actual presence of a hindrance. According to the *Majjhima-nikāya* version, "if [a hindrance] is present within, one knows: '[the hindrance] is present within me'"; according to the *Madhyama-āgama* instructions, "actually having [a hindrance] internally, one knows, as it really is, that one has [a hindrance]." These instructions clearly indicate that a central task of mindfulness is to be aware that a hindrance is present in the mind at this very moment.

X.2 MINDFULNESS AND DEFILEMENTS

This is significant in so far as later Theravāda tradition considers awareness of a hindrance to involve a retrospective form of mindfulness. In other words, one is not mindful of a hindrance when it is actually present in the mind, but rather of the fact that, just an infinitesimal fraction of time before one became aware, a hindrance had been in the mind.

Behind this notion stands the position taken in the Theravāda tradition that mindfulness is an invariably wholesome mental factor and thus does not occur in unwholesome states of mind.[1] Now there can be no doubt that establishing right mindfulness as one of the factors of the noble eightfold path has definite wholesome consequences. In fact, a passage in the *Saṃyutta-nikāya* and its *Saṃyukta-āgama* parallel identifies the four *satipaṭṭhāna*s as a heap of what is wholesome,[2] in contrast to the five hindrances, which are a heap of what is unwholesome. At the same time, however, the early discourses recurrently refer to wrong forms of mindfulness, which obviously cannot be considered wholesome.[3] Thus, from the perspective of the early discourses, it does not seem as if mindfulness should be considered an invariably wholesome mental factor.

According to the Theravāda theory of mind-moments, wholesome factors cannot coexist with anything unwholesome in the same state of mind. If mindfulness is considered as invariably wholesome, from the viewpoint of the theory of mind-moments it would be incapable of coexisting with the presence of any defilement in the same state of mind.[4] Since the presence of mindfulness would automatically mean that no defilement could be present at the same time in the mind, awareness of a hindrance or a defiled state of mind could only take place retrospectively, as an awareness of the fact that, just before mindfulness arose, a hindrance or defilement was present.

While this mode of presentation certainly has its significance within the parameters of the theory of mind-moments,[5] it can become problematic if it is taken to reflect actual meditation experience. The assumption that mindfulness cannot coexist with the presence

1 As 250,3 (translated Pe Maung Tin 1976: 333).

2 SN 47.5 at SN V 146,6 (translated Bodhi 2000: 1631) and SĀ 611 at T II 171b26.

3 For a survey of references to wrong mindfulness (*micchā sati*) in the Pāli discourses, cf. Anālayo 2003b: 52 n.31; in order not to overcrowd this footnote, I give only a single reference to each of the four main *Āgama*s: DĀ 10 at T I 55a11, MĀ 74 at T I 540c26, SĀ 271 at T II 71c4, and EĀ 16.6 at T II 580b10.

4 From the perspective of the Theravāda tradition, as formulated by Olendzki 2011: 61, "as a universal wholesome factor, mindfulness is exclusive of restlessness, delusion and all other unwholesome states, and cannot co-arise with these in the same moment." Olendzki 2011: 64 further notes that from this viewpoint "one cannot be angry and mindful at the same moment, so at whatever point true mindfulness arises the actual anger is already banished."

5 Gethin 1992: 43 explains that "the Theravāda conception of thought processes is such that it is quite possible to conceive of the mixing of skilful and unskilful consciousness in quick succession. In effect this conception of *sati* suggests that the stronger the quality of mind called *sati* becomes, the weaker unwholesome states of mind become, and the harder it is for these to take over and dominate thought, word and deed."

of anything unwholesome can give rise to the mistaken notion that the presence of a hindrance is a sign that one is not really practising mindfulness, since, as soon as one is truly mindful, any hindrance should disappear. This is not the case. According to the instructions for contemplation of the mind, discussed in the previous chapter, it is an integral part of *satipaṭṭhāna* practice to be aware of the fact that at the present moment one's mind is in a defiled condition. This is even more evident with contemplation of the hindrances, where the instructions clearly require one to be aware of the presence of a hindrance like sensual desire or anger within one's own mind right now, in the present moment.

In the case of a hindrance, such awareness needs to be sustained for some time, as the task is not only to be aware that a hindrance is present, but also to understand what led to its arising and how to remove it. Such practice requires an ability to face the presence of a hindrance in one's own mind without immediately reacting to it by trying to push it away, mistakenly believing that true meditation only takes place in the absence of any defilement. Much to the contrary, really transformative meditation takes place in precisely those moments in which the presence of a hindrance or a defilement in the mind is honestly recognized and made the object of one's awareness. This could be understood as to some degree involving an "embracing" of the fact that the mind is at present in a defiled condition. Such patient acceptance, allowing oneself to be exposed to the disconcerting experience of clearly seeing that one is quite different from what one would like to be,[6] can lead to a fuller understanding of how a defilement affects oneself.

The Sarvāstivāda tradition in fact differs from the Theravāda presentation by reckoning mindfulness to be a universal factor, present in all states of mind.[7] This definition also does not seem to fit with the canonical usage, already discussed above in the chapter on mindfulness, which clearly envisages a mental condition without

6 Hölzel et al. 2011: 545 draw attention to correspondences with modern therapy, pointing out that "practitioners are instructed to meet unpleasant emotions (such as fear, sadness, anger, and aversion) by turning towards them, rather than turning away ... parallels between the processes described here and exposure therapy are evident."

7 *Dhātukāya*, T 1540 at T XXVI 614b16, *Prakaraṇapāda*, T 1541 at T XXVI 634a25 or T 1542 at T XXVI 698c11; cf. also *Abhidharmakośabhāṣya* 2.24, Pradhan 1967: 54,17.

mindfulness, in which mindfulness is lost.[8] Since mindfulness can be lost, it follows that from the viewpoint of the early discourses it does not qualify as a universal factor of the mind.

A presentation that better reflects the position taken in the early Buddhist discourses in this respect comes from Vasubandhu's *Pañcaskandhaka-prakaraṇa*, according to which mindfulness is not a universal factor present in all states of mind, nor an invariably wholesome factor. Instead, it is an occasional factor. That is to say, mindfulness is present on certain occasions only, like concentration, for example.[9]

To sum up, mindfulness is a quality that needs to be consciously brought into existence. Contemplation of the hindrances then requires that mindfulness is cultivated in such a way that one is able to recognize the occurrence of an unwholesome condition in one's own mind right in the present moment.

X.3 REMOVAL OF THE HINDRANCES

The canonical instruction to be mindful of the presence of a hindrance does not, of course, mean that one should not try to overcome it. In fact, the need to abandon the hindrances is explicitly mentioned in the *Ekottarika-āgama* parallel to the *Satipaṭṭhāna-sutta*, which just lists the five hindrances as what "should be abandoned" (this appears at the beginning of the entire discourse and therefore is not formally part of contemplation of dharmas).

The need to remove the hindrances also becomes evident from a passage in the *Gopakamoggallāna-sutta* and its Chinese and Tibetan parallels, according to which the Buddha did not approve of a type of meditation in which the hindrances are just allowed free run. The Chinese version in the *Madhyama-āgama* presents this as follows:[10]

> Suppose a person is entangled in lustful sensual desire and does not know as it really is how to emerge from lustful sensual desire [when] it arises. As a result, such a person meditates, increasingly meditates, and repeatedly meditates being obstructed by lustful

8 Cf. the discussion above p.21ff.
9 Xuezhu and Steinkellner 2008: 4,7 and 5,1 (§4.1); for a translation of the Tibetan counterpart cf. Anacker 1984/2005: 66. The same position recurs in Sthiramati's commentary on Vasubandhu's *Triṃśikā*, Lévi 1925: 25,19 (§10).
10 MĀ 145 at T I 655b28 to 655c1.

> sensual desire … this is the first type of meditation that the Blessed One did not praise.

The discourse continues by making the same indication in relation to the other hindrances. Being entangled in these hindrances without knowing how to get out of them corresponds to the other types of meditation that the Buddha did not praise.[11] Clearly, the hindrances need to be removed and just to keep rolling in them is not the way to develop one's practice.

The instructions for contemplation of the hindrances in the *Satipaṭṭhāna-sutta* and its *Madhyama-āgama* parallel in a way put these two aspects into perspective. On the one hand, one needs to remain mindful in the presence of a hindrance; on the other hand, one needs to get out of it. At first, the receptive mode of just being aware has its proper place. Here one simply becomes aware of the fact that a hindrance is present in the mind. Sometimes, just that much may be sufficient for the hindrance to go into abeyance.

At other times, however, this is not enough. If the hindrance remains, mindfulness has the opportunity to gain a fuller picture of the situation, to develop a feel for the hindrance and for how it affects body and mind. The information gleaned in this way will help one in the future to detect the presence of a particular hindrance quickly. Gaining a fuller picture of the situation naturally leads to an understanding of how the hindrance arose in the first place, how one could come out of it, and how a recurrence of the hindrance in the future could be prevented. Needless to say, such understandings are not an idle gathering of information, but rather are meant to provide the basis for deploying right effort and overcoming the hindrance.

The actual removal of defiled states of mind or hindrances is the task of another factor in the eightfold path to liberation: right effort. Through right effort, arisen defilements are removed and their future arising is prevented. Mindfulness makes its contribution to such removal by exploring the situation to its fullest, gathering the type of information that will make the deployment of right effort efficient and successful. Such skilful use of mindfulness and effort

---

11 MĀ 145 at T I 655c7 actually does not mention the hindrance of restlessness-and-worry and thus lists only four hindrances. This is clearly an error in textual transmission. All five hindrances, including restlessness-and-worry, are mentioned in the parallels MN 108 at MN III 14,13 (translated Ñāṇamoli 1995: 885) and D 4094 *nyu* 68a2 or Q 5595 *thu* 112a2.

in combination is more likely to be successful in the long run than reacting to a hindrance immediately without giving mindfulness a chance to explore the situation at hand fully.

Even during the actual process of removing a hindrance or any unwholesome state of mind, mindfulness still has a task to fulfil. This task is described in the *Mahācattārīsaka-sutta* and its Chinese and Tibetan parallels, according to which mindfulness monitors the countermeasures taken by right effort to overcome any unwholesome mental condition.[12]

X.4 ANTIDOTES TO THE HINDRANCES

The second stage in the contemplation of the hindrances concerns the causes that have led to the arising of a particular hindrance and those that will lead to its removal. Additional information on what is helpful to overcome a hindrance is found in a discourse in the *Saṃyutta-nikāya* and its *Saṃyukta-āgama* parallel, as well as in a parallel preserved in Tibetan. The parallel versions examine the hindrances (and the awakening factors) from the perspective of what nourishes them. Here is the relevant section on the hindrances from the *Saṃyukta-āgama*:[13]

> Just as the body exists supported by nourishment, not without nourishment, in the same way the five hindrances exist supported by nourishment, not without nourishment ... [14]
>
> What is the de-nourishment for the hindrance of lustful sensual desire? Contemplating the absence of beauty,[15] giving attention to it, the not yet arisen hindrance of lustful sensual desire does not arise, the already arisen hindrance of lustful sensual desire is removed ...

---

12 MN 117 at MN III 71,24 (translated Ñāṇamoli 1995: 934) and its parallels MĀ 189 at T I 735c13 and D 4094 *nyu* 44b4 or Q 5595 *thu* 84a5 indicate that the overcoming of a wrong path-factor requires right view as the basis and then takes place through right effort in combination with right mindfulness.

13 SĀ 715 at T II 192a28 to 192c16.

14 A similar statement occurs in SN 46.2 at SN V 64,11 (translated Bodhi 2000: 1568), which only expounds what nourishes the hindrances and awakening factors, however, not what deprives them of nourishment. Such an exposition is found in SN 46.51 at SN V 105,15 (translated Bodhi 2000: 1599), which thus is the proper parallel for the remainder of SĀ 715.

15 The term used here is *bùjìng*, counterpart to "lack of beauty", *asubha*, in the Pāli parallel SN 46.51 at SN V 105,17 and *mi sdug pa* in the Tibetan parallel, D 4094 *ju* 285b6 or Q 5595 *thu* 30b8; cf. also the discussion above p.66.

> What is the de-nourishment for the hindrance of anger? Giving attention to a state of mind with benevolence (*mettā*), the not yet arisen hindrance of anger does not arise, the already arisen hindrance of anger is removed ... [16]
>
> What is the de-nourishment for the hindrance of sloth-and-torpor? Giving attention to clarity and illumination, the not yet arisen hindrance of sloth-and-torpor does not arise, the already arisen hindrance of sloth-and-torpor is removed ...
>
> What is the de-nourishment for the hindrance of restlessness-and-worry? Giving attention to calmness and tranquillity, the not yet arisen hindrance of restlessness-and-worry does not arise, the already arisen hindrance of restlessness-and-worry is removed ...
>
> What is the de-nourishment for the hindrance of doubt? Giving attention to dependent arising, the not yet arisen hindrance of doubt does not arise, the already arisen hindrance of doubt is removed.

The *Saṃyutta-nikāya* parallel differs in as much as in the case of sloth-and-torpor the de-nourishment is attention to the elements of arousal, endeavour, and exertion, and in the case of doubt the de-nourishment is frequent attention to wholesome and unwholesome states, blameworthy and blameless states, inferior and superior states, states pertaining to what is dark and what is bright.[17] In both cases, the Tibetan version concords with the above-translated *Saṃyukta-āgama* presentation.[18]

The parallel versions agree that attending to the lack of beauty counters lust, and that benevolence (*mettā*) counters anger. For sloth-and-torpor the differing presentations result in two recommendations. One is to give attention to what appears to refer to mental clarity and also illumination, in the sense of being in a well-lit place rather than being in the dark. The other is to energize one's practice by arousing the mind and exerting oneself. This could take place by giving emphasis to clarity in one's grasp of the meditation object. Thus the two propositions could be brought together under

16 The parallel SN 46.51 at SN V 105,23 speaks of liberation of the mind (*cetovimutti*) through benevolence (*mettā*); the Tibetan parallel, D 4094 *ju* 285b7 or Q 5595 *thu* 31a2, agrees with SĀ 715 in just mentioning benevolence as such, *byams pa*.

17 SN 46.51 at SN V 105,27.

18 D 4094 *ju* 286a1 or Q 5595 *thu* 31a3.

the heading of making an effort to increase one's mental clarity. Restlessness-and-worry requires the opposite, namely lessening one's mental energy by attending to what brings about calmness and tranquillity.

According to the *Saṃyukta-āgama* presentation, doubt can be dealt with by giving attention to dependent arising. Given that the present context is meditation practice, this could imply investigating the conditions that influence one's present meditative experience, and perhaps also the positive and negative effects of the meditation practice that one has undertaken so far. According to the *Saṃyutta-nikāya* parallel, doubt can be countered by clarifying to oneself what is truly wholesome or skilful and what is its opposite. From a practical perspective this could be similar to the *Saṃyukta-āgama* presentation, since doubt in relation to one's meditation practice could indeed be overcome if one were to reflect on the wholesomeness or skilfulness of one's present meditative practice as well as on one's meditative development thus far. These interpretations would result in the following summary presentation, as shown in Figure 10.1.

HINDRANCE:	DE-NOURISHMENT:
sensual desire	lack of beauty
anger	benevolence (*mettā*)
sloth-and-torpor	make effort to increase mental clarity
restlessness-and-worry	tranquillity
doubt	distinguish wholesome conditions from opposites

Fig. 10.1 De-nourishment for the hindrances

X.5 MANIFESTATIONS OF THE HINDRANCES

Further information on the hindrances can be gathered from the *Pariyāya-sutta*, which has parallels in Chinese and Tibetan translation. The parallel versions present an analysis that doubles the hindrances from their usual count of five to ten hindrances (this is also applied to the awakening factors, increasing them from seven to fourteen). In what follows, I translate the relevant passage on the hindrances from the *Saṃyukta-āgama* parallel to the *Pariyāya-sutta*.[19]

19 SĀ 713 at T II 191b11 to 191b20.

> How do the five hindrances become ten? There is lustful sensual desire for what is internal and there is lustful sensual desire for what is external. Lustful sensual desire for what is internal is a hindrance that is opposed to knowledge, opposed to awakening and which does not lead to Nirvāṇa.[20] Lustful sensual desire for what is external is a hindrance that is opposed to knowledge, opposed to awakening, and which does not lead to Nirvāṇa.
>
> There is anger and the sign of anger. Anger and the sign of anger are [each] a hindrance that ... does not lead to Nirvāṇa.
>
> There is sloth and there is torpor. Sloth and torpor are [each] a hindrance that ... does not lead to Nirvāṇa.
>
> There is restlessness and there is worry. Restlessness and worry are [each] a hindrance that ... does not lead to Nirvāṇa.
>
> There is doubt about wholesome states and doubt about unwholesome states. Doubt about wholesome states and doubt about unwholesome states are [each] a hindrance that ... does not lead to Nirvāṇa.

The *Pariyāya-sutta* in the *Saṃyutta-nikāya* differs in so far as it speaks of internal and external manifestations in the case of the second hindrance of anger and the fifth hindrance of doubt.[21] The Tibetan parallel agrees with the presentation in the *Saṃyukta-āgama* version translated above.[22]

According to the introduction to the discourse, the rationale for presenting this move from five to ten was to show a mode of analysis that distinguishes the Buddhist approach to the hindrances from the way these were apparently taught by other contemporaries. That is, this analysis intends to present aspects of the hindrances that reflect successfully working with them in a Buddhist meditative setting.

The cases of sloth-and-torpor as well as of restlessness-and-worry are fairly straightforward. In each case two somewhat different states appear to be presented together because their effect on the mind is similar.[23] In practical terms, lack of energy can become

20 While the Pāli parallel, SN 46.52 at SN V 110,5 (translated Bodhi 2000: 1603), does not indicate that each hindrance is opposed to knowledge, etc., a comparable indication is made in the Tibetan parallel, D 4094 *ju* 60a1 or Q 5595 *tu* 66a4.

21 SN 46.52 at SN V 110,7.

22 D 4094 *ju* 60a3 or Q 5595 *tu* 66a6.

23 The *Abhidharmakośabhāṣya* 5.59, Pradhan 1967: 318,14, explains that sloth-

an obstruction in the practice either because of being bored and listless, lacking inspiration, or else because of fatigue, having eaten too much, or being physically tired and worn out. The opposite problem of excess energy can come about due to excessive striving and agitation or else because of worrying about something done in the past or to be done in the future. Clearly distinguishing sloth from torpor and restlessness from worry will facilitate finding the appropriate remedy in each case.

With sensual desire, the point appears to be that such desire could be prompted by external stimulation or by internal imaginations, such as reliving sensual pleasures from the past or imagining what is still to come. A clear recognition of what originally triggered the sensual desire is helpful, as the action to be taken would be slightly different, even though in actual practice these external and internal aspects of sensual desire overlap to some degree. If external stimulation is the chief cause, the cultivation of sense-restraint is particularly required. If one is mentally reliving or imagining sensual pleasures, the antidotes to unwholesome thoughts described in the *Vitakkasaṇṭhāna-sutta* would come in handy.[24] In both cases, contemplating the anatomical nature of the body will certainly be beneficial.

According to the *Pariyāya-sutta* in the *Saṃyutta-nikāya*, the case of anger or aversion would be similar, in that irritation can arise either from external stimulation or from within one's own mind. The Chinese and Tibetan parallel versions differ, as according to them the distinction is between anger and the sign (*nimitta*) of anger. As an attempt at interpretation, when seen from a practical perspective the reference to the sign of anger could refer to the mental reliving of a particular situation or event – the "sign" – that has aroused one's anger. Following this interpretation, the distinction in the Chinese and Tibetan parallels would not differ greatly from the Pāli version's reference to what is internal and what is external.

In other words, one's present condition of anger may be aroused by an actual external situation, or it may be the product of the mind that imagines what might happen or revives what has happened in the past. In these two cases, again, slightly different antidotes

---

and-torpor is considered as a single hindrance because both sloth and torpor have the same effect, nutriment, and antidote; the same applies to restlessness-and-worry.

24 See above p.148ff.

can be employed. An external stimulation would require physical and verbal restraint, perhaps even avoiding the stimulus, if that is possible. The tendency of the mind to keep rolling in anger would again call for the methods described in the *Vitakkasaṇṭhāna-sutta*. In both cases, developing an attitude of loving-kindness or benevolence (*mettā*) will be very helpful.

In the case of doubt, the *Pariyāya-sutta*'s distinction between what is internal and what is external suggests that uncertainty can stem more from depending too much on what others say or else more from just lacking confidence in oneself. In the parallels the point at stake is that doubt can be about what is wholesome or about what is unwholesome. In other words, the distinction is about uncertainty in regard to what should be cultivated, and lack of clarity about what should be overcome or avoided.

The problem of doubt relates back to the quote I have placed at the outset of this book, according to which the practice of *satipaṭṭhāna* can become a way of relying on oneself and on the Dharma, without needing any other form of reliance. The sustained practice of mindfulness will make it ever clearer to oneself what is wholesome and should be cultivated, in contrast to what is unwholesome and should be avoided. From the perspective of contemplation of dharmas, what should be overcome are in particular the five hindrances and what should be cultivated are the seven awakening factors. Successful practice undertaken in this way will then build up inner confidence and a reliance on the Dharma that is increasingly less influenced by what others might say.

In practical terms, if doubt appears to be arising in particular due to comments made by others, investigating the Dharma taught in the discourses will be very helpful as a way of counterbalancing what others say. But if doubt is more the outcome of a lack of confidence in one's own abilities, repeated mindful recognition of the beneficial results of one's own efforts to practise the path offers a counterbalance. Contemplation of the hindrances leading up to their removal will clear out doubt about what is unwholesome, while cultivation of the awakening factors will lead to inner certainty about what is wholesome.

Combining the indications made in the parallel versions would result in the presentation of the manifestations of the hindrances shown in Figure 10.2.

HINDRANCE:	MANIFESTATIONS:
sensual desire	internal or external
anger	internal or external, anger or sign of anger
sloth-and-torpor	sloth or torpor
restlessness-and-worry	restlessness or worry
doubt	internal or external, about what is wholesome or unwholesome

Fig. 10.2 Manifestations of the hindrances

X.6 PRESENCE AND ABSENCE OF THE HINDRANCES

A clear understanding of the different ways in which the hindrances can manifest is relevant not only when one tries to meditate, but also in relation to more mundane tasks such as trying to learn something. As their very name indicates, the hindrances of sensual desire, anger, sloth-and-torpor, restlessness-and-worry, and doubt "hinder" the proper functioning of the mind.

Any attempt at study, whether of a language, a theory, or anything else, can be greatly enhanced by devoting some of one's awareness to one's mental condition while learning. Such awareness can alert one to the presence of any of the five hindrances. For example: indulging in sensual fantasies instead of being with the topic in hand, having aversion towards what one "has to learn", feeling bored, becoming restless in the wish to get it done quickly, or lacking confidence in one's ability to complete the task successfully. Each of these conditions will of course go a long way in frustrating one's efforts to learn effectively. Recognizing these conditions, however, makes it possible to overcome the mental condition that "hinders" one's attempt to learn effectively. In this way, contemplation of the hindrances has considerable potential in relation to education and study.

In the ancient Indian setting, the task of learning anything was inextricably related to memorizing, to learning something by rote. This was of considerable importance for the early Buddhist community, since all the teachings given by the Buddha and his disciples were passed on by oral transmission. Thus someone who is learned, in the ancient context, is one who quite literally "has heard much" and remembers it.

The *Saṅgārava-sutta* found in the *Saṃyutta-nikāya* and again in the *Aṅguttara-nikāya* takes this type of learning as its starting point: A brahmin asks why sometimes one is able to recall something even though one has spent little effort to learn it. Yet at other times, in spite of having earlier spent much dedicated effort, one is unable to recall it. The discourse reports the Buddha replying that this is so because of the presence or absence of the five hindrances. A mind free from the five hindrances learns easily, whereas for a mind overwhelmed by any of the hindrances it becomes difficult to learn anything. By way of illustration, the *Saṅgārava-sutta* offers similes for each of the five hindrances. Here are counterparts to these similes from Sanskrit fragments:[25]

> It is just as a bowl of water that is mixed with turmeric or ink, becoming turbid; then a clear-sighted person who examines the reflection of his [or her] own face would not see it [properly].[26]

The Sanskrit fragment continues by indicating that with a polluted mind one will not be able to know one's own benefit, the benefit of another, and the benefit of both, and one will also not be able to reach a higher meditative attainment. Instead of meditative attainments, the *Saṅgārava-sutta* version mentions the ability to recall what one has memorized, a direct reply to the question that stands at the outset of this discourse.[27] The remaining similes are as follows:

> It is just as a bowl of water that is heated by fire, greatly heated, boiling and bubbling up; then a clear-sighted person who examines the reflection of his [or her] own face would not see it [properly].

> It is just as a bowl of water that is covered with slimy moss and algae; then a clear-sighted person who examines the reflection of his [or her] own face would not see it [properly].

> It is just as a bowl of water that is stirred, impelled, and whirled by the wind; then a clear-sighted person who examines the reflection of his [or her] own face would not see it [properly].

25 Tripāṭhī 1995: 127 (§5.11) to 132 (§9.11).

26 The parallel SN 46.55 at SN V 121,25 (translated Bodhi 2000: 1611) mentions more dyes and indicates that due to the condition of the water the face cannot be seen as it really is; cf. also AN 5.193 at AN III 230,26 (translated Bodhi 2012: 807).

27 SN 46.55 at SN V 122,3; cf. also AN 5.193 at AN III 231,7.

> It is just as a bowl of water that has been put in a dark place; then a clear-sighted person who examines the reflection of his [or her] own face would not see it [properly].[28]

The *Saṅgārava-sutta* then correlates these five similes with the five hindrances. Thus the simile of the water mixed with dye represents sensual desire, the boiling water illustrates anger, water overgrown by algae corresponds to sloth-and-torpor, water agitated by wind exemplifies restlessness-and-worry, and water placed in the dark is the image used for doubt (see Figure 10.3).

HINDRANCE:	CONDITION OF THE WATER:
sensual desire	mixed with dye
anger	boiling
sloth-and-torpor	overgrown by algae
restlessness-and-worry	agitated by wind
doubt	placed in the dark

Fig. 10.3 The effect of the hindrances

The point made with these similes appears to be that sensual desire has a tendency to colour one's perception, making things appear more colourful than they really are and disabling one's recognition of their true nature. When the mind is boiling in anger and one is quite literally "heated up" by this hindrance, it will be impossible to see things in the proper perspective. With the stagnation of sloth-and-torpor the mind has become overgrown by sluggishness and dullness. Progress has come to a standstill, comparable to the stagnant condition of water overgrown by algae. The opposite is the case for restlessness-and-worry. Excessive agitation reigns in the mind and stirs up wave after wave of anxious thoughts, eventually even making it difficult to sit still. Finally doubt places one in the dark. The mind is devoid of clarity and one is unable to see for oneself what is appropriate to do and what should be avoided.

Another set of similes, found in the *Sāmaññaphala-sutta* and in a Sanskrit fragment parallel in the *Saṅghabhedavastu* of the Mūlasarvāstivāda *Vinaya*, illustrates the absence of the five hindrances.

28 In SN 46.55 at SN V 123,33 not only is the bowl in the dark, but the water is also turbid, disturbed, and muddy; cf. also AN 5.193 at AN III 233,10.

In what follows I translate the relevant parts from the Sanskrit fragments:[29]

> It is just as a person who had taken a loan to undertake a business and that business turned out successful for him, so that he could pay off the loan and still there would be wealth for him to support his wives.
>
> It is just as a person who is sick, suffering, diseased, and weak, the food swallowed by him is not digested by the body and the beverages drunk afflict the stomach.[30] After some time he would be well, healthy, and strong, the food swallowed by him is digested by the body and the beverages drunk do not afflict the stomach.
>
> It is just as a person who is a slave, sent around and commanded, dependent, and unable to act as he wishes. After some time he would no [longer] be a slave, not be sent around, not be dependent, and be able to act as he wishes.
>
> It is just as a person who has the hands fastened behind with tight bonds. Being freed from it he would be well, at ease, without fear, and safe.[31]
>
> It is just as a person who goes from danger to security, having journeyed from a place of famine he journeys to a place of abundance.[32]

The *Sāmaññaphala-sutta* adopts a different sequence, as the simile of the slave comes only after the simile of being in prison.[33] Since none

29 Gnoli 1978: 241,19 to 242,15, with emendations based on Wille 1990: 124,19.
30 The Pāli parallel DN 2 at DN I 72,6 (translated Walshe 1987: 101) does not mention beverages and additionally notes that he is weak.
31 DN 2 at DN I 72,15 indicates that he is bound in a prison.
32 According to DN 2 at DN I 73,3, he was travelling with wealth through a dangerous desert.
33 DN 2 at DN I 72,23. Another sequence can be found in DĀ 20 at T I 85a25 (parallel to an occurrence of the same five similes in DN 3, which at DN I 100,6 abbreviates and thus needs to be supplemented with the full description in DN 2). DĀ 20 has release from servitude as its first (fourth in DN 2), repayment of loan as it second (first in DN 2), recovery from disease as its third (second in DN 2), release from prison as its fourth (third in DN 2), and safe journey with wealth as its fifth (fifth in DN 2). Yet another sequence can be found in T 21 at T I 265c17 (parallel to DN 1), which begins with repayment of a loan (first in DN 2) and then has release from slavery as its second (fourth in DN 2), release from prison as its third (third in DN 2), recovery from disease as its fourth (second in DN 2), and safe journey with wealth as its fifth (fifth in DN 2).

of the versions provides an explicit relationship between a particular simile and a hindrance, the correlation between simile and hindrance depends on the sequence of enumeration.

Following the sequence adopted in the *Sāmaññaphala-sutta*, the following correlations would emerge: sensual desire is comparable to being in debt. Being "in debt" in this way one is constantly in search of something that will satisfy the pressing demands of the feeling of lack and longing that stands behind sensual desire. Anger is literally a dis-ease. This condition can be so bad that it becomes difficult to digest food properly. Sloth-and-torpor is like being in bondage, one is unable to act freely. Restlessness-and-worry results in acting compulsively and one is enslaved by mental agitation. Doubt is like being on a dangerous journey with scarce provisions.

According to the sequence in the *Saṅghabhedavastu*, however, sloth-and-torpor would be slavery and restlessness-and-worry a form of bondage. Combining the indications in the two versions would result in the presentation shown in Figure 10.4.

HINDRANCE:	PREDICAMENT:
sensual desire	being in debt
anger	disease
sloth-and-torpor	bondage or slavery
restlessness-and-worry	slavery or bondage
doubt	dangerous journey

Fig. 10.4 Predicaments that illustrate the hindrances

The parallel versions agree on describing the joy that arises in each case when the respective predicament has been overcome. Similarly, joy arises when the five hindrances are overcome, which then naturally leads the mind to concentration and, eventually, into the attainment of the absorptions.

This passage points to an important aspect of contemplation of the hindrances, namely that the instructions direct awareness not only to the presence of a particular defilement or hindrance, but also to its absence. Being aware of the mind free from the hindrances leads to joy, and such joy is an important condition for successful meditation practice. In fact, such joy is the key for reaching deeper levels of concentration, a feature to which I will return when examining the awakening factors in the next chapter.

The close relationship between the hindrances and the awakening factors receives attention in a passage found at the outset of the *Madhyama-āgama* parallel to the *Satipaṭṭhāna-sutta*, according to which Tathāgatas of past, future, and present times all attained or will attain unsurpassable and complete awakening in the following way:

> By abandoning the five hindrances, which defile the mind and weaken wisdom, by dwelling with the mind well established in the four *satipaṭṭhāna*s, and by cultivating the seven factors of awakening.

At first sight it may seem puzzling that the hindrances and the awakening factors are mentioned alongside the four *satipaṭṭhāna*s. Had these two sets been part of the fourth *satipaṭṭhāna* from the outset, there would be little reason for mentioning them separately. However, the point of the passage could be to depict a temporal progression. After abandoning the hindrances, it becomes possible to be "well established" in the four *satipaṭṭhāna*s, i.e., to practise these at an advanced level where states of desire and aversion etc. no longer manifest. This, in turn, becomes the basis for the cultivation of the seven factors of awakening.

X.7 SUMMARY

Mindfulness enables one to recognize the occurrence of a hindrance in one's own mind right in the present moment. This crucial element of receptive recognition provides the basis for subsequently overcoming a hindrance. Overcoming these hindrances with the appropriate remedies leads to joy, which is an important condition for successful meditation practice.

The hindrance of sensual desire colours the mind and through its pressing demands for satisfaction turns one into a debtor. Boiling in anger is quite literally a dis-ease. With sloth-and-torpor the mind stagnates, similar to water overgrown by algae. Restlessness-and-worry agitates the mind, stirring up wave after wave of anxious thoughts. Both are a form of bondage and result in a mind that is enslaved. Experiencing doubt is like being placed in the dark. The mind is devoid of clarity, whereby one's practice becomes a dangerous journey with scarce provisions.

XI

THE AWAKENING FACTORS

XI.1 INSTRUCTIONS

In this chapter I examine the instructions for contemplation of the awakening factors. In the *Satipaṭṭhāna-sutta* and its two Chinese *Āgama* parallels these instructions are as follows:

Majjhima-nikāya:

> If the mindfulness awakening factor is present within … one knows: "the mindfulness awakening factor is present within me"; or if the mindfulness awakening factor is not present within, one knows: "the mindfulness awakening factor is not present within me"; and one knows how the unarisen mindfulness awakening factor arises, and one knows how the arisen mindfulness awakening factor is perfected by development.
>
> If the investigation-of-dharmas awakening factor … the energy awakening factor … the joy awakening factor … the tranquillity awakening factor … the concentration awakening factor … the equanimity awakening factor is present within, one knows: "the equanimity awakening factor is present within me"; or if the equanimity awakening factor is not present within, one knows: "the equanimity awakening factor is not present within me"; and one knows how the unarisen equanimity awakening factor arises, and one knows how the arisen equanimity awakening factor is perfected by development.

Madhyama-āgama:

> Actually having the mindfulness awakening factor within ... one knows, as it really is, that one has the mindfulness awakening factor; actually not having the mindfulness awakening factor within, one knows, as it really is, that one does not have the mindfulness awakening factor. One knows, as it really is, how the unarisen mindfulness awakening factor arises; and one knows, as it really is, how the arisen mindfulness awakening factor is maintained without loss or deterioration, and how it is further developed and increased.
>
> In the same way, actually having the investigation-of-dharmas [awakening factor] ... the energy [awakening factor] ... the joy [awakening factor] ... the tranquillity [awakening factor] ... the concentration [awakening factor] ... the equanimity awakening factor within ... one knows, as it really is, that one has the equanimity awakening factor; actually not having the equanimity awakening factor within, one knows, as it really is, that one does not have the equanimity awakening factor. One knows, as it really is, how the unarisen equanimity awakening factor arises; and one knows, as it really is, how the arisen equanimity awakening factor is maintained without loss or deterioration, and how it is further developed and increased.

Ekottarika-āgama:

> One cultivates the mindfulness awakening factor supported by insight, supported by dispassion, and supported by cessation, discarding evil states.
>
> One cultivates the [investigation-of-]dharmas awakening factor... the energy awakening factor ... the joy awakening factor ... the tranquillity awakening factor ... the concentration awakening factor ... the equanimity awakening factor supported by insight, supported by dispassion, and supported by cessation, discarding evil states.

The instructions for contemplation of the awakening factors in the *Majjhima-nikāya* and the *Madhyama-āgama* are closely similar, in that the main task proceeds through two stages that are similar to the progression of practice when contemplating the hindrances: recognition of their presence or absence, followed by turning awareness to the conditions that are related to their presence or absence. This mode of exploring conditionality in a very practical and direct manner is a characteristic shared by these two contemplations of dharmas.

While in the case of the hindrances, the enquiry into their conditions is related to their removal, with the awakening factor the task is to "perfect them by development" according to the *Majjhima-nikāya* description, or to "further develop and increase" them according to the *Madhyama-āgama* account.

The *Madhyama-āgama* discourse covers the second stage of contemplation in a slightly more detailed manner. Besides knowing how a particular awakening factor comes to arise and how it can be further increased, according to this version one should also know how it can be maintained without loss or deterioration.

With the *Ekottarika-āgama* version a different perspective emerges. Here the instructions are not in accordance with the two-stage approach that is found in the other two canonical versions. Instead, the *Ekottarika-āgama* discourse describes how the awakening factors should be cultivated, which takes place by being supported by insight, dispassion, and cessation, so that they lead to overcoming any unwholesome condition in the mind. An important contribution made by the *Ekottarika-āgama* parallel to the *Satipaṭṭhāna-sutta* is thus the highlight it places on how the awakening factors should be developed.

The actual formulation in this *Ekottarika-āgama* passage, however, needs to be considered in the light of the fact that within the *Ekottarika-āgama* collection there are variant versions of this description.[1] This makes it quite possible that in the *Ekottarika-āgama* this formula suffered from transmission or translation errors. By contrast, the corresponding descriptions in the Pāli discourses and in other Chinese *Āgama*s show close agreement in indicating that the awakening factors should be cultivated "supported by seclusion, supported by dispassion, and supported by cessation, culminating in letting go". As an example, in what follows I translate a passage from the *Saṃyukta-āgama* that describes this central aspect of the cultivation of the seven awakening factors:[2]

> How does one cultivate the seven awakening factors, namely the mindfulness awakening factor ... up to ... the equanimity

1 Cf., e.g., EĀ 21.2 at T II 602c3 and EĀ 40.6 at T II 741b3.
2 SĀ 729 at T II 196a18 to 196a21.

> awakening factor? ... One cultivates the mindfulness awakening factor supported by seclusion, supported by dispassion, and supported by cessation, leading to letting go. Like this, one cultivates the investigation-of-dharmas [awakening factor] ... the energy [awakening factor] ... the joy [awakening factor] ... the tranquillity [awakening factor] ... the concentration [awakening factor] ... the equanimity awakening factor supported by seclusion, supported by dispassion, and supported by cessation, leading to letting go.

The *Saṃyutta-nikāya* parallel to this passage indicates that this mode of cultivation constitutes the path to the cessation of craving.[3] In other words, for the awakening factors to result in what their name promises – awakening and thus the cessation of craving and any other defilement – they need to be developed in the manner described here. While only the *Ekottarika-āgama* version of contemplation of dharmas explicitly highlights this feature, it can safely be assumed to be implicit in the reference to "developing" the awakening factors in the two other versions.

In fact the *Ānāpānasati-sutta* and its parallel in the *Saṃyukta-āgama* indicate in closely similar terms that these four qualities are what ensures that the cultivation of the awakening factors leads to liberation. Here is the relevant section from the *Saṃyukta-āgama* version:[4]

> One develops the mindfulness factor of awakening supported by seclusion, supported by dispassion, and supported by cessation, leading to letting go. Having developed the mindfulness factor of awakening [in this way], knowledge and liberation become fulfilled ... up to ... One develops the equanimity factor of awakening supported by seclusion, supported by dispassion, and supported by cessation, leading to letting go. Having developed the equanimity factor of awakening in this way, knowledge and liberation become fulfilled.

Thus these four meditative themes invest the seven mental qualities that have been collected under the heading of being awakening factors with the potential for resulting in awakening:

SECLUSION & DISPASSION & CESSATION → LETTING GO

3 SN 46.27 at SN V 87,11 (translated Bodhi 2000: 1586).
4 SĀ 810 at T II 208c2 to 208c6.

In what follows I attempt to draw out the practical aspects of this set of qualities: supported by seclusion, dispassion, and cessation, culminating in letting go. The first of these four themes, seclusion, can have a physical and a mental component. The early discourses often recommend retiring into seclusion for the purpose of meditative practice, which then leads to mental seclusion from unwholesome states and to the gaining of deeper concentration.[5]

The Pāli term for dispassion (*virāga*) can also mean "fading away". This brings out a central aspect of the meditative dynamics related to this term, in as much as on seeing the "fading away" of phenomena – in the sense of their passing away and disappearance – the attraction felt for them also starts to fade away, resulting in growing degrees of "dispassion".[6]

In passages describing the development of higher insight, dispassion often occurs together with disenchantment and cessation. Dispassion and cessation are also distinct steps in the development of contemplation of dharmas through mindfulness of breathing, which I will explore in the next chapter. The term cessation on its own is perhaps most prominently associated with the cessation of *dukkha* as the final aim of Buddhist practice.

The purpose of seclusion, dispassion, and cessation is to result in letting go or relinquishment. Such letting go of what is unwholesome underlies the whole compass of the path from its outset to its consummation, when the supreme letting go takes place with the breakthrough to liberation and the experience of Nirvāṇa.[7]

The *Abhidharmasamuccayavyākhyā* proposes a relationship between the four noble truths and cultivating the awakening factors "supported by seclusion, supported by dispassion, and supported by cessation, culminating in letting go".[8] It reasons that, when one is afflicted by *dukkha*, one will try to be "secluded" from it. When *dukkha* arises as a result of craving, one will aspire to "dispassion". Whenever the experience of *dukkha* ceases (temporarily), one will search for ways to realize such "cessation" (permanently). Hence the first three

5 On "seclusion", *viveka*, cf. in more detail Anālayo 2010b: 137ff (reprinted in Anālayo 2012b: 258ff).

6 On "dispassion" or "fading away", *virāga*, cf. in more detail Anālayo 2009: 36ff (reprinted in Anālayo 2012b: 45ff).

7 On "letting go" or "relinquishment", *vossagga*, and the closely related *paṭinissagga*, cf. in more detail Anālayo 2010b: 145ff (reprinted in Anālayo 2012b: 266ff).

8 T 1606 at T XXXI 740c18.

of the four noble truths correspond to the expressions "supported by seclusion", "supported by dispassion", and "supported by cessation". Finally experiencing the power of relinquishing *dukkha* makes one wish to cultivate the path to relinquishment or "letting go". From this viewpoint, the four meditative themes to be cultivated through the awakening factors would amount to an implementation of what in early Buddhist thought is considered the fundamental teaching delivered by the Buddha: the four noble truths.

XI.2 THE AWAKENING FACTORS AND THE HINDRANCES

In their role in leading to liberation, the awakening factors stand in direct opposition to the hindrances. The discourses regularly highlight the contrast between these two sets. Thus a discourse in the *Saṃyutta-nikāya* and its *Saṃyukta-āgama* parallel point out that the hindrances result in mental blindness just as the awakening factors lead to mental vision. Here is the relevant part from the *Saṃyukta-āgama* discourse:[9]

> There are five states which facilitate darkness, which facilitate a lack of vision, which facilitate the absence of knowing, which facilitate the weakening of wisdom, which are opposed to knowledge, which are opposed to awakening, and which do not lead to Nirvāṇa. What are the five? They are sensual desire, anger, sloth-and-torpor, restlessness-and-worry, and doubt ... [10]
>
> There are seven factors of awakening, which facilitate creating great knowledge, which facilitate vision, which increase wisdom, which result in knowledge, which result in right awakening, and which lead to Nirvāṇa. What are the seven? They are the mindfulness awakening factor, the investigation-of-dharmas awakening factor, the energy awakening factor, the tranquillity awakening factor, the joy awakening factor, the concentration awakening factor, and the equanimity awakening factor.[11]

---

9 SĀ 706 at T II 189c3 to 189c11.

10 The Pāli parallel SN 46.40 at SN V 97,14 (translated Bodhi 2000: 1593) does not explicitly mention that the five hindrances are opposed to awakening (or that the awakening factors result in right awakening), although this is implied by the fact that they do not lead to Nirvāṇa.

11 The sequence of the awakening factors seems to have become mixed up in this passage as, according to the standard enumeration, joy should come before tranquillity.

In spite of this opposition between the two sets – or perhaps because of it – the cultivation of some awakening factors can apparently already be initiated when some hindrances have not yet been fully overcome. This suggests itself from a discourse in the *Saṃyutta-nikāya* and its *Saṃyukta-āgama* parallel. In what follows I translate the relevant passage from the *Saṃyukta-āgama* discourse:[12]

> At the time of cultivating with effort the mindfulness awakening factor, on giving attention one understands: "The mind is not well liberated, sloth-and-torpor has not been destroyed, restlessness-and-worry has not been well suppressed. Thus, my establishing of the mindfulness awakening [factor] by attending to dharmas with diligence and effort is not balanced." It is like this for the investigation-of-dharmas ... energy ... joy ... tranquillity ... concentration ... equanimity awakening factor.

The description continues by taking up the positive case. When one has been able to get beyond these two hindrances, the mind becomes well liberated and without effort one is established in a particular awakening factor in a balanced manner. The *Saṃyutta-nikāya* parallel does not cover the negative case, but only presents the positive case as an illustration of how the seven awakening factors are well undertaken.[13] This presentation nevertheless implies that at other times the awakening factors are not well undertaken, which, according to the passage translated above, would occur when hindrances like sloth-and-torpor or restlessness-and-worry have not yet been fully overcome.

Thus, while the first two hindrances of sensual desire and anger need to be overcome in order for the cultivation of any of the awakening factors to be possible,[14] this may not fully apply to the hindrances of sloth-and-torpor or restlessness-and-worry. That this is indeed the case can be seen from the *Aggi-sutta* and its *Saṃyukta-āgama* parallel, as well as a third parallel preserved in Tibetan translation, which consider which awakening factors are commendable in certain situations. Here is the relevant part from the *Saṃyukta-āgama* discourse:[15]

12 SĀ 719 at T II 193c8 to 193c11.

13 SN 46.8 at SN V 76,23 (translated Bodhi 2000: 1578).

14 For a survey of various ways to counter these hindrances cf. Anālayo 2003b: 192ff.

15 SĀ 714 at T II 191c25 to 192a23.

> If at a time the mind is sluggish and one's mind has become stuck, it is not appropriate to cultivate the tranquillity awakening factor, the concentration awakening factor, and the equanimity awakening factor. Why is that? Because sluggishness has arisen in the mind, and being sluggish it has become stuck. The sluggishness would increase because of these states. It is just as a small fire that one wants to flare up by adding burned-out charcoal. What do you think ... would adding [burned-out] charcoal not make the fire die out?

The *Aggi-sutta* of the *Saṃyutta-nikāya* makes the same point by stating that these three awakening factors are not able to arouse the mind from its sluggishness, as trying to do so would be comparable to throwing wet grass, wet cowdung, or wet sticks, as well as water and earth, on a small fire which one wants to flare up.[16] The Tibetan parallel agrees with the *Saṃyukta-āgama* version that these awakening factors would actually increase the problem, rather than merely being insufficient to counter it.[17] The simile in the Tibetan version, however, corresponds to the illustration in the *Aggi-sutta* of throwing wet wood, wet grass, and wet dung on a small fire. The Tibetan version follows the same pattern for the rest of the discourse, agreeing with the *Saṃyukta-āgama* presentation in regard to the effect of the awakening factors and with the *Aggi-sutta* of the *Saṃyutta-nikāya* in regard to the simile.

> If agitation has arisen in the mind, if being agitated the mind has become stuck, at that time it is not appropriate to cultivate the investigation-of-dharmas awakening factor, the energy awakening factor, and the joy awakening factor. Why is that? Because agitation has arisen in the mind and the agitated mind has become stuck. This would increase because of these states. It is just as a blazing fire which one wants to extinguish by adding dry firewood. What do you think, would the fire not burn even more?

The *Aggi-sutta* of the *Saṃyutta-nikāya* indicates that it will not be possible to calm the mind through these three awakening factors, as trying to do so would be comparable to throwing dry grass, dry cowdung, or dry sticks on a great fire that one wants to extinguish.

---

16 SN 46.53 at SN V 112,28 (translated Bodhi 2000: 1605).
17 D 4094 *nyu* 52a6 or Q 5595 *thu* 92b8.

The *Aggi-sutta* also adopts a sequence that differs from the other two versions as, after indicating the time when tranquillity, concentration, and equanimity are inappropriate, it first mentions the time when these are appropriate, before turning to the time when investigation, energy, and joy are inappropriate.

> If sluggishness has arisen in the mind and, being sluggish, [the mind] has become stuck, this is the appropriate time for cultivating the investigation-of-dharmas awakening factor, the energy awakening factor, and the joy awakening factor. Why is that? It is because sluggishness has arisen in the mind and being sluggish it has become stuck. It can become clear, manageable, bright, and joyful because of these states. It is just as a small fire that one wants to get to flare up by adding dry firewood. What do you think ... will this fire flare up and burn?

According to the *Aggi-sutta* the sluggish mind can easily be aroused with the help of these awakening factors, like throwing dry grass, dry cowdung, or dry sticks on a small fire that one wants to flare up.

> If agitation has arisen in the mind and being agitated the mind has become stuck, [this is the appropriate time] for cultivating the tranquillity awakening factor, the concentration awakening factor, and the equanimity awakening factor. Why is that? Because agitation has arisen in the mind and the agitated mind has become stuck. Through these states one can settle the mind within, unify it, and collect it. It is just as a blazing fire that one wants to extinguish by adding burned-out charcoal. That fire will indeed die out.

The *Aggi-sutta* explains that the agitated mind can easily be calmed with the help of these awakening factors, just as a great fire can be extinguished by throwing wet grass, wet cowdung, or wet sticks, as well as water and earth on it.

The presentation in the *Aggi-sutta* and its parallels confirms that the cultivation of certain awakening factors can become an antidote to either sluggishness or else to agitation, which would be manifestations of the hindrances sloth-and-torpor or restlessness-and-worry. Another aspect of this exposition is that some awakening factors should not be developed in a state of mind that is sluggish, while others are not appropriate when one is agitated. In other words, bringing all seven awakening factors into being requires that even the more subtle hindrances are completely left behind. This gives the impression of a gradual progression in the cultivation of the awakening factors. Individual factors are being developed according to what the situation requires, until with increased purification of the mind it eventually becomes possible to establish all of the awakening factors.

Speaking of the whole set, it is remarkable that the *Aggi-sutta* and its parallel have so far not mentioned mindfulness. The reason for this is simple, as the *Saṃyukta-āgama* discourse concludes its survey of the awakening factors by stating:

> The mindfulness awakening factor is always of use.

This statement, found similarly in the parallel versions, seems to reflect in particular the crucial role of mindfulness as the factor that recognizes the present condition of one's mind, thereby providing the all-important foundation for the cultivation of the other awakening factors. Unless by establishing mindfulness of one's mental condition one recognizes that the mind is sluggish or agitated, the recommendations given in the *Aggi-sutta* and its parallels will be of little use. Thus mindfulness is indeed always of use, always required, and always to be relied on.

In view of this centrality of mindfulness, a chief purpose of the practice of the four *satipaṭṭhāna*s would be to establish the kind of mindfulness that can serve as the basis for cultivating the other awakening factors. From this viewpoint, it would also be understandable why many discourses simply mention the four *satipaṭṭhāna*s without going into a detailed exposition of the ways they can be practically undertaken, as is the case for the *Satipaṭṭhāna-sutta*. What really matters, it seems, is that through *satipaṭṭhāna* meditation mindfulness is established in regard to the body, feelings, mind, and dharmas in such a way that it leads on to the other awakening factors. This appears to be the gist of *satipaṭṭhāna* meditation as the direct path to awakening.

By way of summing up the indications provided in the *Aggi-sutta* and its parallels, once one has emerged from the two gross hindrances of sensual desire and anger, progress could take place as shown in Figure 11.1.

MENTAL CONDITION:	CULTIVATE:
either sluggish or agitated	mindfulness
sluggish	investigation, energy, joy
agitated	tranquillity, concentration, equanimity
neither sluggish nor agitated	all seven awakening factors

Fig. 11.1 Countering sluggishness and agitation

This flexible approach, adapting to the particular requirements of the situation at hand, requires the ability to cultivate various awakening factors individually. Mastery in such ability is described in a discourse in the *Saṃyutta-nikāya* and its *Saṃyukta-āgama* counterpart, which reports how the arahant monk Sāriputta illustrated his skills in this respect with the help of a simile. Here is the relevant part from the *Saṃyukta-āgama* discourse:[18]

> By way of decision I attain [any of] these seven awakening factors, attaining it without effort. In accord with my wish to attain an awakening factor during the morning time, the middle of the day, or the evening of the day, if I wish to be in its attainment, according to my wish I enter its attainment.
>
> It is just as a king or a great minister who dresses in various clothes that have been placed in a chest, according to his needs [in the morning], his needs in the middle of the day, and his needs in the evening of the day, freely, according to his wishes.[19]

In the *Saṃyutta-nikāya* parallel Sāriputta simply mentions that whichever awakening factor he wishes to dwell in during morning, noon, or evening time, he will dwell in it.[20] While the *Saṃyutta-nikāya* discourse does not explicitly note that this takes place effortlessly, this seems to be implied in its presentation.

XI.3 NOURISHING THE AWAKENING FACTORS

Returning to the basic opposition between the hindrances and the awakening factors, the presentation in the *Aggi-sutta* and its parallels shows how the cultivation of certain awakening factors can become a way of overcoming sluggishness and agitation, representing mental

18 SĀ 718 at T II 193b17 to 193b22.

19 The parallel SN 46.4 at SN V 71,25 (translated Bodhi 2000: 1574) indicates that the clothes are of different colours.

20 SN 46.4 at SN V 71,7.

conditions that would correspond to the third and fourth of the five hindrances. A topic thus far not explored is if any of the awakening factors may also be of help in regard to the hindrance of doubt.

This is indeed the case, as cultivating the second awakening factor of investigation-of-dharmas offers a way of emerging from doubt. The opposition between these two – as part of the basic opposition between the hindrances and the awakening factors – emerges from an exposition in a discourse in the *Saṃyutta-nikāya* and its parallels, part of which I already took up in the preceding chapter on contemplation of the hindrances. This discourse describes what deprives the hindrances of nourishment and what gives nourishment to the awakening factors. In what follows, I translate the *Saṃyukta-āgama* description of what nourishes the awakening factors:[21]

> It is just as the body, which is established supported by nourishment, exists supported by nourishment, in the same way the seven awakening factors are established supported by nourishment, exist supported by nourishment.[22]
>
> What is the nourishment for the mindfulness awakening factor? Having given attention to the four *satipaṭṭhāna*s, the not yet arisen mindfulness awakening factor arises, the already arisen mindfulness awakening factor is aroused further so as to increase and augment ...
>
> What is the nourishment for the investigation-of-dharmas awakening factor? There is investigation of wholesome states and there is investigation of unwholesome states; having given attention to this, the not yet arisen investigation-of-dharmas awakening factor arises, the already arisen investigation-of-dharmas awakening factor is aroused fully so as to increase and augment ...
>
> What is the nourishment for the energy awakening factor? Giving attention to the four right efforts, the not yet arisen energy awakening factor arises, the already arisen energy awakening factor is aroused fully so as to increase and augment ...
>
> What is the nourishment for the joy awakening factor? There is joy and there is the establishing of joy; giving attention to it, the not yet arisen joy awakening factor arises, the already arisen joy awakening factor is aroused fully so as to increase and augment ...
>
> What is the nourishment for the tranquillity awakening factor? There is bodily tranquillity and mental tranquillity; giving attention

21 SĀ 715 at T II 192c16 to 193a6.
22 Cf. above p.183, n.14.

> to it, the not yet arisen tranquillity awakening factor arises, the already arisen tranquillity awakening factor is aroused fully so as to increase and augment ...
>
> What is the nourishment for the concentration awakening factor? There are the four absorptions; giving attention to them, the not yet arisen concentration awakening factor arises, the already arisen concentration awakening factor is aroused fully so as to increase and augment ...
>
> What is the nourishment for the equanimity awakening factor? There are three elements. What are the three? The element of eradication, the element of dispassion, and the element of cessation; giving attention to them, the not yet arisen equanimity awakening factor arises, the already arisen equanimity awakening factor is aroused fully so as to increase and augment.

The *Saṃyutta-nikāya* discourse shows several differences when compared to this presentation. In the case of mindfulness the nourishment is "things that are the basis for the mindfulness awakening factor".[23] This could be supplemented with the reference in the *Saṃyukta-āgama* parallel to the four *satipaṭṭhāna*s, which are also mentioned in the Tibetan parallel.[24] The presentation in these two versions receives confirmation from the *Ānāpānasati-sutta* and its parallel, according to which the mindfulness awakening factor comes into being through the practice of *satipaṭṭhāna*.[25]

Clear discrimination between what is wholesome and what is unwholesome is according to all versions the nourishment for investigation-of-dharmas. This completes the topic of how the awakening factors counter the hindrances, since it shows that the investigation-of-dharmas awakening factor can counter doubt. The ability to discriminate between what is wholesome and what is unwholesome that nourishes this awakening factor is precisely what according to the *Saṃyutta-nikāya* version de-nourishes the hindrance of doubt. That is, overcoming doubt does not so much require faith, but instead calls for thorough investigation.

In the case of energy the parallel versions differ. The *Saṃyutta-nikāya* presentation speaks of giving attention to the elements of

---

23 SN 46.51 at SN V 103,32 (translated Bodhi 2000: 1598).
24 D 4094 *ju* 286b1 or Q 5595 *thu* 31b5.
25 MN 118 at MN III 85,8 (translated Ñāṇamoli 1995: 946) and its parallel SĀ 810 at T II 208b15.

arousal, endeavour, and exertion, whereas the *Saṃyukta-āgama* parallel and the Tibetan version bring in the four right efforts. Taken together, the two presentations thus point to qualities that energize and to how to utilize them: by countering what is unwholesome and cultivating what is wholesome.

In the case of joy the descriptions are fairly similar. The *Saṃyutta-nikāya* discourse speaks of "things that are the basis for the joy awakening factor", while its parallels mention "joy" and what "establishes joy".

The three versions agree that bodily and mental tranquillity nourish the tranquillity awakening factor. Thus calm behaviour and remaining mentally at peace cooperate in providing the appropriate environment for the growth of this factor of awakening.

A difference manifests again in relation to concentration, where the *Saṃyutta-nikāya* version mentions the sign of tranquillity and the sign of non-distraction,[26] whereas the *Saṃyukta-āgama* parallel stipulates the four absorptions, which in a way exemplify success in tranquillity and non-distraction. In this case the Tibetan version is closer to the *Saṃyutta-nikāya* presentation, as it refers to concentration and the sign of concentration.[27]

The nourishment for equanimity is "things that are the basis for the equanimity awakening factor" according to the *Saṃyutta-nikāya* presentation, whereas its *Saṃyukta-āgama* counterpart and the Tibetan parallel mention the element of "eradication", "dispassion", and "cessation", thus pointing to the meditative themes whose cultivation will result in the establishment of equanimity.

Summing up and to some degree combining the indications in the parallel versions, the presentation in Figure 11.2 could be developed.

AWAKENING FACTOR:	NOURISHMENT:
mindfulness	4 *satipaṭṭhānas*
investigation	distinguish wholesome from unwholesome
energy	make endeavour through 4 right efforts
joy	establishing joy
tranquillity	bodily and mental tranquillity
concentration	non-distraction, sign of concentration, 4 absorptions
equanimity	eradication, dispassion, and cessation as a basis for equanimity

Fig. 11.2 Nourishment for the awakening factors

26 SN 46.51 at SN V 105,3.
27 D 4094 *ju* 287a2 or Q 5595 *thu* 32a7.

XI.4 MANIFESTATIONS OF THE AWAKENING FACTORS

Another discourse that also takes up the hindrances and the awakening factors, part of which I already discussed in the preceding chapter, presents them in a way that doubles their usual count. Here is the passage on the doubling of the awakening factors from the *Saṃyukta-āgama* parallel to the *Pariyāya-sutta*:[28]

> How can the seven awakening factors be spoken of as fourteen? There is the establishing of mindfulness in relation to internal phenomena and there is the establishing of mindfulness in relation to external phenomena. That establishing of mindfulness in relation to internal phenomena is the mindfulness awakening factor that conforms with knowledge, conforms with awakening, and is able to lead to Nirvāṇa; and that establishing of mindfulness in relation to external phenomena is the mindfulness awakening factor that conforms with knowledge, conforms with awakening, and is able to lead to Nirvāṇa.[29]
>
> There is investigation of wholesome states and there is investigation of unwholesome states. That investigation of wholesome states is the investigation-of-dharmas awakening factor ... and that investigation of unwholesome states is the investigation-of-dharmas awakening factor ...
>
> There is effort to remove unwholesome states and there is effort to make wholesome states grow. That effort to remove unwholesome states is the energy awakening factor ... and that effort to make wholesome states grow is the energy awakening factor ...
>
> There is joy and there is the establishing of joy. That joy is the joy awakening factor ... and that establishing of joy is the joy awakening factor ...
>
> There is bodily tranquillity and there is mental tranquillity. That bodily tranquillity is the tranquillity awakening factor ... and that mental tranquillity is the tranquillity awakening factor ...
>
> There is concentration and there is the sign of concentration. That concentration is the concentration awakening factor ... and that sign of concentration is the concentration awakening factor ...

28 SĀ 713 at T II 191b21 to 191c13.

29 The Pāli parallel SN 46.52 at SN V 110,31 (translated Bodhi 2000: 1604) does not mention the attainment of Nirvāṇa and instead indicates that in this way the awakening factor becomes twofold. The Tibetan version, D 4094 *ju* 60b7 or Q 5595 *tu* 67a4, agrees with both versions, as it mentions the attainment of Nirvāṇa and the fact that the awakening factor becomes twofold.

> There is equanimity towards wholesome states and there is equanimity towards unwholesome states. The equanimity towards wholesome states is the equanimity awakening factor that conforms with knowledge, conforms with awakening, and is able to lead to Nirvāṇa; and the equanimity towards unwholesome states is the equanimity awakening factor that conforms with knowledge, conforms with awakening, and is able to lead to Nirvāṇa.

The *Pariyāya-sutta* of the *Saṃyutta-nikāya* accords with the above-translated *Saṃyukta-āgama* version that mindfulness can be directed to internal or external phenomena, which would refer to the distinction between internal and external introduced in the canonical versions of the *Satipaṭṭhāna-sutta*. The Tibetan version offers a different presentation, as it instead speaks of being mindful of wholesome or unwholesome phenomena.[30]

The *Pariyāya-sutta* adopts the same mode of explanation for the next awakening factor, indicating that wise investigation could be concerned with internal phenomena or external phenomena. The *Saṃyukta-āgama* presentation instead differentiates between investigating states that are wholesome and states that are unwholesome, a presentation also found in the Tibetan parallel. Thus, in the *Saṃyutta-nikāya* account, the distinction appears to be between introspective investigation of what happens within oneself and examination of how the outside world relates to and influences one's experience. In the two parallel versions, however, investigation could be concerned either with unwholesome states and becoming aware of how they arose, etc., or else with wholesome states and investigating how they can be further cultivated.

In the case of energy, the *Saṃyutta-nikāya* discourse distinguishes between bodily and mental manifestations of this awakening factor. This could be referring to the difference between, for example, sitting with determination to remain stable in one's sitting posture without moving as an exemplification of bodily effort, and the mental diligence required for remaining with one's meditation practice without allowing the mind to move around. The *Saṃyukta-āgama* parallel and its Tibetan parallel instead mention the removal of unwholesome states and the development of wholesome states. This could be exemplified through

30 D 4094 *ju* 60b6 or Q 5595 *tu* 67a3.

the example of any practice that is related to either cultivating what is wholesome or overcoming what is unwholesome.

When it comes to joy as an awakening factor, the *Saṃyutta-nikāya* version distinguishes between joy accompanied by initial and sustained application of the mind (*vitakka* and *vicāra*), two factors found in the first absorption, and joy without these, a condition characteristic of the second absorption. The formulations in the *Saṃyukta-āgama* presentation and the Tibetan parallel are less specific in this case, as they just refer to joy and to what establishes joy.

The three versions agree on mentioning bodily and mental tranquillity. Bodily manifestations of tranquillity would include tranquil bodily behaviour, verbal behaviour, and a calm sitting posture. Its mental counterpart could be achieved by establishing and maintaining tranquillity in the mind, either during formal practice or when engaging in everyday activities.

In the case of concentration, the *Saṃyutta-nikāya* version again distinguishes between what is accompanied by initial and sustained application of the mind (*vitakka* and *vicāra*) and what is without these, thus covering any level of concentration up to the first absorption and any level of concentration starting from the second absorption onwards (this case differs from joy, where the third and fourth absorption were not included, as these take place in the absence of joy). Here, too, the presentation in the *Saṃyukta-āgama* and the Tibetan version is more general, as they just mention concentration and the sign of concentration.

For equanimity the *Saṃyutta-nikāya* discourse again takes up the distinction between what is internal and what is external, whereas the *Saṃyukta-āgama* version and the Tibetan parallel mention the difference between what is wholesome and what is unwholesome. This is similar to investigation-of-dharmas, where the three versions have the same respective explanations. From a practical perspective, the cultivation of equanimity could be towards what arises from within oneself or in relation to what arrives from the outside world, and maintenance of mental balance would be required with what is wholesome as well as with what is unwholesome.

Summing up and combining the indications in the parallel versions would result in the presentation in Figure 11.3, showing how a particular awakening factor can manifest.

AWAKENING FACTOR:	MANIFESTATIONS:
mindfulness	internal or external of what is wholesome or unwholesome
investigation	internal or external of what is wholesome or unwholesome
energy	bodily or mental in relation to what is wholesome or unwholesome
joy	establishing joy up to first absorption or second
tranquillity	bodily and mental tranquillity
concentration	concentration up to first absorption or higher
equanimity	internal or external in regard to what is wholesome or unwholesome

Fig. 11.3 Manifestations of the awakening factors

XI.5 HEALING AND THE AWAKENING FACTORS

The potential benefits of cultivating the awakening factors even cover medical healing. This can be seen in a discourse that records an occasion when the Buddha was sick. Versions of this discourse are found in the *Saṃyutta-nikāya* and in the *Saṃyukta-āgama*, with parts of this discourse preserved also in Sanskrit and Uighur fragments. In what follows I translate the *Saṃyukta-āgama* version, which begins by reporting that the Buddha was on a journey and became ill. Ānanda prepared a place for him to rest, a description that gives the impression that the affliction must have been quite strong. After lying down, the Buddha addressed Ānanda:[31]

> [The Buddha] said to Ānanda: "Proclaim the seven factors of awakening." Then the venerable Ānanda said to the Buddha: "Blessed One, they are the mindfulness awakening factor, which the Blessed One realized himself through full awakening and taught as being supported by seclusion, supported by dispassion, and supported by cessation, leading to letting go. The investigation-of-dharmas … energy … joy … tranquillity … concentration … equanimity awakening factor which the Blessed One realized himself through full awakening and taught as being supported by seclusion, supported by dispassion, and supported by cessation, leading to letting go."
>
> The Buddha said to Ānanda: "Did you say: energy?"
>
> Ānanda said to the Buddha: "I said energy, Blessed One, I said energy, Well-gone One."

31 The present and the next two extracts are taken from SĀ 727 at T II 195c7 to 196a5.

The Buddha said to Ānanda: "Energy indeed, which I cultivated and made much of to reach supreme and full awakening." Having said this, he sat up with straight body and mindfulness established.

The parallel in the *Saṃyutta-nikāya* has a somewhat different setting. Instead of being on a journey, the Buddha is in the Squirrels' Feeding Place and the monk who recites the awakening factors for him is Mahācunda.[32] The actual recitation then highlights that the seven awakening factors have been well expounded and lead to direct knowledge, to awakening, and to Nirvāṇa. The *Saṃyutta-nikāya* version concludes by reporting that on hearing this recitation the Buddha recovered from his disease and was cured.[33]

The *Saṃyukta-āgama* discourse continues by reporting that a monk, who apparently had witnessed what happened, composed a poem on the spot to commemorate the Buddha's recovery. Parts of his stanzas have also been preserved in Sanskrit and Uighur fragments. In what follows I translate extracts from the version of his poem found in the *Saṃyukta-āgama*:

Delighting in hearing the wonderful Dharma,
[While] enduring a disease, [the Buddha] told someone to proclaim it.
A monk proclaimed the Dharma,
The unfolding of the seven awakening factors …
"Mindfulness, investigation-of-dharmas, energy,
Joy, tranquillity, concentration, and equanimity, [leading to] awakening,
These are the seven awakening factors,
They are sublime and well taught."
Hearing the seven awakening factors being spoken,
Thoroughly experiencing the taste of full awakening,
[Although] the body had been twisted and afflicted by great pain,
Enduring the illness, [the Buddha] sat up straight to listen.

---

32 SN 46.16 at SN V 81,1 (translated Bodhi 2000: 1581).

33 The *Saṃyutta-nikāya* has two similar discourses, where chief disciples also recover their health on hearing the Buddha recite the awakening factors for them, SN 46.14 and SN 46.15. The first of these two has a parallel in Tibetan, D 40 *ka* 281b1 or Q 756 *tsi* 298a8, a discourse apparently translated from a Pāli original, cf. Skilling 1993.

The Sanskrit fragments confirm that it was indeed the taste of the awakening factors that had such a remarkable effect at the physical level.[34] These descriptions suggest that recollecting what the Buddha had been able to gain through the awakening factors led to a powerful feeling of joy and an arousal of inner energy, which affected his body so much that it had visible effects on the illness. The poem continues by describing what happens in general when one properly listens to the Dharma:

> Hearing the Dharma being spoken, as it really is,
> Listening with a collected mind, intelligently, and with
> wisdom,
> To the Dharma proclaimed by the Buddha
> One attains delight and joy that are removed from sensuality.
> With delight and joy the body becomes tranquil,
> The mind also becomes happy on its own,
> The happy mind properly gains attainments,
> And right insight into existence, phenomena, and formations.

This poem shows that the development of the awakening factors is not confined to formal meditation only. Listening with a collected mind to the teachings leads to a type of joy that is removed from sensuality, whereby the body becomes tranquil and the happy mind attains concentration. Clearly, several of the awakening factors arise in this particular situation and then lead on to right insight.

While these stanzas do not have a counterpart in the Pāli parallel, a similar presentation can be found in another discourse in the *Saṃyutta-nikāya*, according to which all of the seven awakening factors can be aroused when one is listening to the Dharma with full attention.[35]

As mentioned earlier, according to the *Pariyāya-sutta* of the *Saṃyutta-nikāya* joy and concentration as awakening factors could be accompanied by initial and sustained application of the mind. These two factors are characteristic of the first absorption and of stages of tranquillity that lead up to the first absorption. Alternatively, joy and concentration could be without these, a condition characteristic of the higher absorptions. Once awakening factors can be aroused while listening to the Dharma, it becomes clear that awakening factors

34 Waldschmidt 1967: 244; cf. also the Uighur version in von Gabain 1954: 13.
35 SN 46.38 at SN V 95,19 (translated Bodhi 2000: 1592).

like joy and concentration are not confined to deep concentration during formal meditation. Thus the reference in the *Pariyāya-sutta* to joy and concentration accompanied by initial and sustained application of the mind is best taken as including types of wholesome joy and concentration that fall short of full absorption attainment. This conclusion is supported by the parallels to the *Pariyāya-sutta*, which do not refer to absorption at all when describing joy and concentration as awakening factors.

XI.6 SATIPAṬṬHĀNA AND THE AWAKENING FACTORS

Nevertheless, it is clearly in the context of formal meditation practice that the awakening factors are of special relevance. How the awakening factors arise out of *satipaṭṭhāna* meditation can be seen in the *Ānāpānasati-sutta* and its *Saṃyukta-āgama* parallel. The parallels show that the sequence in which the awakening factors are listed corresponds to the way they unfold their awakening potential. This sequence reflects an underlying progression in which the factor mentioned earlier supports the arising of the factor that comes next. Here comes the relevant part from the *Saṃyukta-āgama* version that describes this dynamic, a description that also provides some helpful indications regarding the significance of each awakening factor:[36]

> [In regard to] the body one establishes mindfulness by contemplating the body; one has established mindfulness [so that] mindfulness is firmly established and without forgetfulness. At that time one diligently develops the mindfulness factor of awakening. Having developed the mindfulness factor of awakening [in this way], the mindfulness factor of awakening becomes fulfilled.
>
> [When] the mindfulness factor of awakening has been fulfilled, one investigates and examines that state. At that time one diligently develops the investigation-of-dharmas factor of awakening. Having developed the investigation-of-dharmas factor of awakening [in this way], the investigation-of-dharmas factor of awakening becomes fulfilled.[37]
>
> [When] one has investigated, distinguished, and examined that state, one gains diligent energy. At that time one diligently develops

36 SĀ 810 at T II 208b15 to 208c6.

37 The Pāli parallel, MN 118 at MN III 85,17 (translated Ñāṇamoli 1995: 946), specifies that one investigates with wisdom.

> the energy factor of awakening. Having developed the energy factor of awakening [in this way], the energy factor of awakening becomes fulfilled.[38]
>
> [When] one has become diligent and energetic, the mind becomes glad and joyful. At that time one diligently develops the joy factor of awakening. Having developed the joy factor of awakening [in this way], the joy factor of awakening becomes fulfilled.[39]
>
> [When] one has become glad and joyful, body and mind are tranquil and calm. At that time one diligently develops the tranquillity factor of awakening. Having developed the tranquillity factor of awakening [in this way], the tranquillity factor of awakening becomes fulfilled.
>
> [When] body and mind have become happy, one gains concentration. At that time one diligently develops the concentration factor of awakening. Having developed the concentration factor of awakening [in this way], the concentration factor of awakening becomes fulfilled.[40]
>
> [When] the concentration factor of awakening has been fulfilled, then covetousness and sadness cease and one attains balance and equanimity. At that time one diligently develops the equanimity factor of awakening. Having developed the equanimity factor of awakening [in this way], the equanimity factor of awakening becomes fulfilled.[41]

The same procedure then applies to any of the other *satipaṭṭhāna*s; that is, with mindfulness as the starting point, the above dynamics could be established with any of the four *satipaṭṭhāna*s and lead to a cultivation of the awakening factors in the same manner.

Drawing out the implications of this description, mindfulness cultivated through the first *satipaṭṭhāna* proceeds beyond the superficial perception of the body as beautiful and penetrates to its less attractive inner parts. Mindful contemplation of the same body can also result in "cutting up" the compact sense of identity,

38 According to MN 118 at MN III 85,26, the energy is unshaken.

39 MN 118 at MN III 85,32 indicates that the joy arisen at this stage is non-worldly.

40 The formulation in MN 118 at MN III 86,10 is slightly different, in that it indicates that, when the body has become tranquil and one is happy, the mind becomes concentrated.

41 MN 118 at MN III 86,16 instead states that one looks with equanimity at the mind that has been concentrated in this way.

revealing that the whole body is merely a combination of the four elements. In the case of death, often a theme habitually avoided in modern-day society, the task is to pay full attention to one's own mortality as an inevitable and integral aspect of one's life. In each of these – or any other – *satipaṭṭhāna* meditation practices, based on having established mindfulness one investigates with energy so that the resulting detachment leads to joy and tranquillity, and the mind becomes concentrated and equanimous. In this way being secluded from unwholesome mental attitudes towards the body one develops dispassion for it, attachment gradually ceases and one increasingly learns to let go of one's sense of identification with the body.

The same dynamic applies to the other *satipaṭṭhāna*s, where based on established mindfulness the other awakening factors come into being, whose cultivation leads to seclusion, dispassion, and cessation, culminating in letting go. The only difference is the basic task of each *satipaṭṭhāna*. Mindful contemplation of feelings brings about knowledge by ensuring that one clearly registers the affective quality of one's present experience instead of reacting to it in a compulsory manner. In the case of the mind, contemplation penetrates the jungle of thought and uncovers the underlying mental condition at any given moment. In relation to the hindrances and the awakening factors, then, the task is not only to recognize what is happening, but also to uncover the conditions responsible for the presence or absence of the hindrances or awakening factors.

The *Ānāpānasati-sutta* agrees with its *Saṃyukta-āgama* parallel that, based on the practice of any of the four *satipaṭṭhāna*s, the awakening factors can be cultivated in such a way that they result in knowledge and liberation. It is this potential of resulting in awakening that places the awakening factors at the very heart of contemplation of dharmas and at the culmination point of *satipaṭṭhāna* meditation in its entirety. Their importance in this respect is reflected in a comparison in the discourses of the seven awakening factors to the seven precious possessions of a universal monarch.

XI.7 THE WHEEL-TURNING KING

The notion of a universal monarch is a recurrent theme in the early Buddhist discourses, a theme which has its roots in conceptions of kingship that predate the advent of Buddhism in India.[42] In the early discourses, the universal monarch functions as a worldly counterpart to the Buddha, who as a Tathāgata holds the supreme position in the spiritual realm.

Tradition depicts the universal monarch as endowed with seven treasures of magic potency. The first of these is a wheel of magical qualities, whose manifestation in the sky confirms to the king his role as a wheel-turning monarch (*cakkavattin*). The wheel then guides the king in his peaceful conquest of the whole world. In this peaceful conquest, the king is aided by a magical elephant and a magical horse, who are able to fly him wherever he wishes to go, and by a magical jewel that illuminates all directions. The other treasures are of a human type, comprising a queen of unsurpassable beauty and kind character, a steward able to produce wealth at will, and a general capable of accomplishing all orders.

A discourse in the *Saṃyutta-nikāya* and its *Saṃyukta-āgama* parallel applies the imagery of this depiction to the awakening factors. Here is the relevant passage from the *Saṃyukta-āgama*:[43]

> When a wheel-turning king emerges in the world, there are seven treasures that [also] appear in the world: the golden wheel treasure, the elephant treasure, the horse treasure, the supernatural jewel treasure, the woman treasure, the steward treasure, and the general treasure.[44] In the same way, when a Tathāgata emerges in the world, the treasures of the seven awakening factors appear.

While the *Saṃyutta-nikāya* discourse stops after making a similar comparison, the *Saṃyukta-āgama* parallel continues by describing how the king, when being on top of his palace on an observance day (*uposatha*), sees the golden wheel coming towards him in the sky with a thousand spokes. On seeing this, he realizes that he is indeed a wheel-turning king. The wheel comes close and he is able to take hold of it and start turning it. With the turning wheel up in space as his guide, the wheel-turning king and his army march in all four directions to conquer the world peacefully, being welcomed by the local kings who are eager to submit themselves to his rule.

---

42 Anālayo 2011b: 54f.

43 SĀ 721 at T II 194a6 to 194a9.

44 The Pāli parallel, SN 46.42 at SN V 99,3 (translated Bodhi 2000: 1594), does not indicate that the wheel is golden or that the jewel is supernatural.

While the discourse itself does not provide a one-by-one correlation, it seems safe to follow the commentarial tradition that the wheel corresponds to the mindfulness awakening factor.[45] Drawing out the implication of this imagery, with well-established mindfulness leading the way, the path is cleared for a peaceful conquest of the universe of one's own mind. The conquest that is led by mindfulness enables one to become a spiritual emperor in the world of one's experiences through having set in motion one's own wheel in the space of one's mind, the wheel of mindfulness. Mindfulness as an awakening factor in this way becomes the crown jewel of *satipaṭṭhāna* meditation.

The image of the treasures of the wheel-turning king throws into relief the central position and importance of the awakening factors in the early Buddhist path to freedom. The reason is simply that these factors – as their name indicates – lead to awakening.

XI.8 THE AWAKENING FACTORS IN PRACTICE

In view of this potential and the evident importance of the awakening factors, in what follows I attempt to summarize essential aspects of their development from a practical perspective, drawing on the passages discussed so far. I first take up the four meditative themes that need to be brought into being with the cultivation of the awakening factors, namely the need to be supported by seclusion, by dispassion, and by cessation, leading to letting go. Following the discussion of these four, I turn to the awakening factors themselves.

One possible way of putting these four aspects of the cultivation of the awakening factors into practice – certainly not the only one – would be by taking the theme of seclusion to refer in particular to "seclusion from what is unwholesome". As part of the introductory formula for attaining absorption, this constitutes a frequent occurrence of the term seclusion in the early discourses. "Seclusion from what is unwholesome" could then be seen as a summary of those stages of moral training that enable experiencing the happiness of seclusion through deep concentration. Such seclusion would stand for having developed a firm foundation in moral conduct and a healthy degree of inner detachment so that one is no longer carried away by the things in the world.

45 Spk III 154,19.

The Pāli term for dispassion often occurs in relation to the cessation of craving in the third noble truth, where it carries its other sense of "fading away", meaning the fading away of craving. Thus dispassion as the step-by-step "fading away of craving" could summarize the implications of this term in relation to the awakening factors. This would point to the need to recognize craving wherever it manifests and proceed, step-by-step, towards its fading away.

Finally, cessation occurs most prominently in references to the cessation of *dukkha*, which, according to the teaching of dependent arising (*paṭicca samuppāda*), is the outcome of the cessation of ignorance. While the total cessation of *dukkha* is only reached with full awakening, temporary cessations of particular manifestations of *dukkha* can be experienced right here and now.

In sum, without intending to exclude other possible interpretations, following this mode of understanding the first three aspects would be:

- seclusion from what is unwholesome,
- dispassion as the fading away of craving,
- the gradual cessation of *dukkha*.

These three could be visualized as the three legs of a tripod. On being supported by these three legs, "letting go" or "relinquishment" comes into its proper place, since these three ensure that the letting go is of the appropriate type. So the resultant picture could look somewhat like Figure 11.4.

Fig. 11.4 Essential aspects of the cultivation of the awakening factors

This tripod needs to be brought into being in regard to each of the awakening factors. From mindfulness to equanimity, each awakening factor should be supported by seclusion, supported by dispassion, and supported by cessation, leading to letting go.

While these qualities have a clear slant towards insight, which is precisely why they actualize the awakening potential of the awakening factors, the awakening factors themselves appear to cover both insight and tranquillity. According to the *Śrāvaka-bhūmi*, investigation-of-dharmas, energy, and joy pertain to insight, whereas concentration, tranquillity, and equanimity pertain to tranquillity, and mindfulness takes part in both.[46] This matches the division of the awakening factors into those that energize and those that calm.

Investigation and energy are, to some extent, similar to central qualities of *satipaṭṭhāna* contemplation mentioned in the "definition" part of the *Satipaṭṭhāna-sutta*, according to which one should contemplate "diligently" (= energy) and "clearly knowing" (= investigation).

While the first two awakening factors that come after mindfulness could indeed express a more insight-oriented perspective, the case of joy differs, since joy is also an important basis for the development of tranquillity and concentration. Thus joy as an awakening factor would not be restricted to the cultivation of insight.

Similarly, while equanimity has an important role in absorption attainment, the same quality is also of considerable significance in relation to insight. The relevance of equanimity to insight is reflected in the definitions of what nourishes equanimity as an awakening factor and in the descriptions of its different manifestations. Unlike the cases of joy and concentration, these definitions and descriptions do not bring in absorption at all. Thus equanimity can be in relation to what is internal or external and in regard to what is wholesome or unwholesome, and it has a close relation to the meditative themes of eradication, dispassion, and cessation. Taken together, these indications clearly express an emphasis on insight.

In the thought of early Buddhism, insight and tranquillity are complementary qualities, both of which need to be brought into being if the path to liberation is to bear fruit. Hence it is only natural to find that both insight and tranquillity underlie the awakening factors and it would not do justice to the early discourses if one

46 *Śrāvakabhūmi*, Shukla 1973: 326,5.

were to assume that the awakening factors are either only concerned with cultivating liberating insight or else just a way of developing concentration and entering absorption.

In Figure 11.5, I attempt to bring together the main aspects of the development of the awakening factors as a way of cultivating both tranquillity and insight. The seven awakening factors are given in the sequence of their cultivation according to the *Ānāpānasati-sutta* and its *Saṃyukta-āgama* parallel, using arrows to illustrate how they build on each other. The assigning of + and – reflects the indication in the *Aggi-sutta* and its *Saṃyukta-āgama* parallel of the energizing or calming effect of an awakening factor. The tripod as the placeholder for each awakening factor is meant to represent the need to develop each factor supported by seclusion, dispassion, and cessation, leading to letting go. The right half of the diagram moves through the realm of insight; the left half proceeds through the realm of tranquillity.

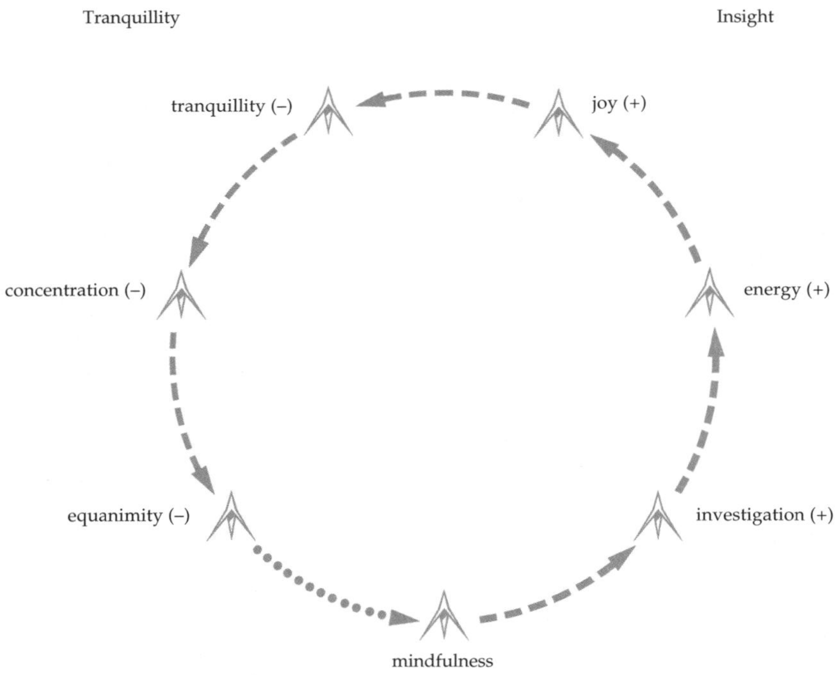

Fig. 11.5 Survey of the cultivation of the awakening factors

Mindfulness stands at the bottom as the one awakening factor that is commendable on all occasions. Pictured in a system of coordinates, mindfulness is the 0 point, the foundation for the whole system. Combining the information found in the *Aggi-sutta* and the *Pariyāya-sutta* as well as their parallels (Figures 11.2 and 11.3), this awakening factor has come into being through practising the four *satipaṭṭhāna*s internally or externally, and it has the task of being aware of what is wholesome or what is unwholesome.

Moving upwards from mindfulness into what in a system of coordinates is the + area come the factors that according to the *Aggi-sutta* and its parallel are energizers in case the mind is sluggish (+). The factors investigation and energy are closely related to insight. Both can be concerned with what is wholesome or what is unwholesome. Investigation can be brought into being internally or externally, and energy can be bodily and mental.

Joy leads over from insight on the right side of the diagram to tranquillity on the left side. Joy is still a factor that energizes (+). At the same time, joy is the basis for the ensuing development of mental tranquillity. Such joy could be of any level up to and including the first absorption, and also the joy of the second absorption.

The remaining awakening factors calm the mind (–). Most prominently related to the development of mental tranquillity are the two awakening factors of tranquillity and concentration. Tranquillity could be bodily and mental; concentration could be up to and including the first absorption, or else the higher absorptions.

These lead on to equanimity, which takes its inspiration from qualities like eradication, dispassion, and cessation. Equanimity may be related to what is wholesome or what is unwholesome, and it may be towards what is internal or what is external.

According to the instructions in the *Satipaṭṭhāna-sutta* and its *Madhyama-āgama* parallel, supervising the establishment of the equanimity awakening factor is an aspect of *satipaṭṭhāna* practice. In practical terms, this points to an interrelationship between equanimity and mindfulness. An important aspect of this interrelationship is that the presence of equanimity strengthens mindfulness.[47] In the diagram this is represented by the arrow that moves from equanimity to mindfulness. As equanimity feeds back into mindfulness, the cycle

47 Ṭhānissaro 1996: 154 explains that "equanimity as a factor of Awakening on the mundane plane can feed back into the process of meditation, providing a steady basis for more continuous mindfulness."

of cultivating the awakening factors continues, all the time being supported by seclusion, dispassion, and cessation, leading to letting go (reflected in the tripods in the figure).

A closer look at individual stages in the sequence of the awakening factors reveals further aspects of practical relevance. Regarding the development of insight, mindfulness should lead to investigation and this in turn should result in energy, which in the present context I take to stand especially for continuity of the practice, for the effort to persist with the task in hand. This sequence suggests that adding a quality of inquisitiveness to one's contemplation, a keenness to know, can enhance the continuity of one's mindfulness practice.

An example of this type of attitude can be found in the *Ekottarika-āgama* version's instruction for contemplation of the elements, which phrases the way one should contemplate in this way: "In this body, is there the earth element, the water [element], the fire [element], and the wind element?" In the same way, instead of contemplating the body as bereft of beauty, for example, one might look at it with the question: "Is it really attractive?" Or else, instead of seeing something as impermanent, contemplation could be undertaken by enquiring: "Is it changing?" Such an inquisitive mode can lend a sense of real investigation to the practice and makes it easier for mindfulness to remain with the object, which in this way has become naturally interesting.

With progressive practice one may just have such a questioning attitude, without going so far as to verbalize mentally a particular question. In fact, investigation is better not overdone in such a way that it leads to prolonged intellectual reflection, as energy gets dispersed in this way. If this can be avoided, investigation that takes off from mindfulness can produce the energetic momentum that maintains the practice smoothly. Practice flows almost effortlessly in this way, based on this combination of mindfulness with investigative interest.

Successfully undertaking such *satipaṭṭhāna* practice can at times be unpleasant, for example when one has to face one's own shortcomings, or when assumptions held for a long time are being questioned. In the long run, however, a healthy development of insight should result in joy. In terms of Figure 11.5, mindfulness, investigation, and energy should lead on to joy. This is another significant indication that helps to provide a check for the way in which one's practice is developing over longer periods of time. Genuine practice will sooner or later lead to the joy of letting go.

Joy, in turn, is a key for the development of mental tranquillity. No matter what meditation object one may chose for concentrating the mind, as long as one successfully brings into being wholesome types of joy while engaging with that object, tranquillity and concentration will naturally result. Here tranquillity serves as a counterbalance to the high energetic charge of joy, thereby ensuring that the mind can become concentrated. The transition from joy to tranquillity requires navigating the shift from what energizes (+) on the right side of the figure to what calms the mind (–) on its left side.

A natural result of wholesome joy and tranquillity is concentration, with which the true inner beauty and the power of the mind unfolds. Equanimity comes next as the culmination point of the cultivation of the seven awakening factors. Such equanimity comprises the balance needed to achieve deeper levels of concentration and the detachment that is required at the time of emerging from any concentrative attainment and turning to the cultivation of insight.

If the overall emphasis at a particular point in one's practice is on mental tranquillity, the first steps on the right side of Figure 11.5 that lead from mindfulness to joy may take up less space in one's actual practice. These may perhaps be merely a check to see if the hindrances are present (investigation), overcoming those that are present (energy), and then rejoicing in the mind that is free from the hindrances (joy) as the basis for cultivating tranquillity and concentration.

If at another time the cultivation of insight has become the prominent theme in one's practice, the emphasis will naturally be more on using mindfulness to cultivate investigation with continuity (energy). Factors that are on the left side of the figure, like tranquillity and concentration, will be more in the background in the form of stillness of the body and the mind, which does not succumb to distractions.

What remains as the backbone of practice throughout is the need to be firmly grounded in mindfulness and to keep aiming at the balance of equanimity. This is relevant for formal practice as well as for everyday life, where keeping up mindfulness and maintaining the mental balance of equanimity are cornerstones. What endows the establishment of any awakening factor with awakening potential, no matter what situation, is when seclusion, dispassion, and cessation lead to letting go.

XI.9 SUMMARY

When the wheel of well-established mindfulness is set in motion through *satipaṭṭhāna* practice, the path is cleared for a peaceful conquest of the universe of one's own mind through cultivation of the seven awakening factors. Such cultivation emphasizes investigation, energy, and joy when the mind is sluggish, or else deals with an agitated mind through tranquillity, concentration, and equanimity. The awakening potential of these seven mental jewels is activated once they are supported by seclusion from what is unwholesome, supported by dispassion as the fading away of craving, and supported by the gradual cessation of *dukkha*, so that they culminate in increasing levels of letting go until the supreme letting go takes place with the experience of Nirvāṇa.

XII

SATIPAṬṬHĀNA MEDITATION

In what follows, I proceed beyond the *Satipaṭṭhāna-sutta* and its parallels to other canonical passages related to *satipaṭṭhāna*. I begin with the scheme of sixteen steps of mindfulness of breathing as a way of developing all four *satipaṭṭhāna*s. Then I look at an alternative set of three *satipaṭṭhāna*s practised by the Buddha himself. This leads me to the theme of *satipaṭṭhāna* as a way of combining self-development with concern for others. I conclude by taking up the prediction found at the end of the *Satipaṭṭhāna-sutta* and its *Madhyama-āgama* parallel regarding the gradual nature of the *satipaṭṭhāna* approach to the realization of Nirvāṇa.

XII.1 INSTRUCTIONS FOR MINDFULNESS OF BREATHING

Looking back at the four *satipaṭṭhāna*s as they emerge from a comparative study of the three extant canonical versions, the following key points emerge: through cultivation of mindfulness one becomes more fully aware of aspects of the body that are commonly ignored, namely its lack of inherent beauty, its not-self nature, and the fact that it is inevitably going to die and fall apart. Contemplating the body in this way naturally anchors mindfulness in the body. With contemplation of feelings the task is to remain receptively aware of their affective input instead of immediately reacting to them. In the case of the mind, awareness penetrates the stream of thoughts on the mind's surface and recognizes one's underlying mental condition. In the case of contemplation of dharmas, mindfulness oversees the

...moval of the hindrances and the establishment of the awakening factors, directly fostering progress towards liberation.

The four *satipaṭṭhāna*s can also be cultivated with a single object. An example illustrating this possibility can be found in the instructions for mindfulness of breathing in sixteen steps in the *Ānāpānasati-sutta* of the *Majjhima-nikāya*, which has parallels in the *Saṃyukta-āgama* and in the Mahāsāṅghika *Vinaya*. In the closely similar presentation in the parallel versions, the sixteen steps of mindfulness of breathing exemplify the practice of the four *satipaṭṭhāna*s, with each *satipaṭṭhāna* being implemented by four of the sixteen steps. This shows in a very practical manner how to interrelate the four *satipaṭṭhāna*s in a single form of practice.

The *Saṃyukta-āgama* presentation describes how one first of all becomes aware of the breath coming in and going out and then proceeds through the sixteen steps as follows:[1]

> One is aware of the breath coming in, training well to keep being mindful of it, and one is aware of the breath going out, training well to keep being mindful of it.
>
> ... (1) long breath ... (2) short breath ... (3) experiencing the whole body when breathing in, one trains well [to experience] the whole body when breathing in; experiencing the whole body when breathing out, one trains well [to experience] the whole body when breathing out; (4) experiencing the calming of all bodily formations when breathing in, one trains well [to experience] the calming of all bodily formations when breathing in; experiencing the calming of all bodily formations when breathing out, one trains well [to experience] the calming of all bodily formations when breathing out.
>
> (5) Experiencing joy ... (6) experiencing happiness ... (7) experiencing the mental formations ... (8) experiencing the calming of the mental formations when breathing in, one trains well to experience the calming of the mental formations when breathing in; experiencing the calming of the mental formations when breathing out, one trains well to experience the calming of the mental formations when breathing out.
>
> (9) Experiencing the mind ... (10) experiencing the gladdening of the mind ... (11) experiencing the concentrating of the mind

1 SĀ 803 at T II 206a27 to 206b11, abbreviations are in the original. Here and below I have added numbers to the translated text to facilitate recognizing the different steps.

> … (12) experiencing the liberating of the mind when breathing in, one trains well to experience the liberating of the mind when breathing in; experiencing the liberating of the mind when breathing out, one trains well to experience the liberating of the mind when breathing out.
>
> (13) Contemplating impermanence … (14) contemplating eradication … (15) contemplating dispassion … (16) contemplating cessation when breathing in, one trains well to contemplate cessation when breathing in; contemplating cessation when breathing out, one trains well to contemplate cessation when breathing out.

The sixteen steps of mindfulness of breathing in the Mahāsāṅghika *Vinaya* follow a similar pattern, after the initial awareness of the breath coming in and out has been established. This is described as follows:[2]

> At the time of breathing in, one knows one is breathing in; at the time of breathing out, one knows one is breathing out.
>
> (1) At the time of breathing in long, one knows one is breathing in long; at the time of breathing out long, one knows one is breathing out long.
>
> (2) At the time of breathing in short, one knows one is breathing in short; at the time of breathing out short, one knows one is breathing out short.
>
> (3) At the time of breathing in pervading the body, one knows one is breathing in pervading the body; at the time of breathing out pervading the body, one knows one is breathing out pervading the body.
>
> (4) At the time of breathing in letting go of the bodily formations, one knows one is breathing in letting go of the bodily formations; at the time of breathing out letting go of the bodily formations, one knows one is breathing out letting go of the bodily formations.
>
> (5) At the time of breathing in with joy, one knows one is breathing in with joy; at the time of breathing out with joy, one knows one is breathing out with joy.
>
> (6) At the time of breathing in with happiness, one knows one is breathing in with happiness; at the time of breathing out with happiness, one knows one is breathing out with happiness.
>
> (7) At the time of breathing in [aware of] mental formations, one knows one is breathing in [aware of] mental formations; at the time

2 T 1425 at T XXII 254c14 to 255a4.

of breathing out [aware of] mental formations, one knows one is breathing out [aware of] mental formations.

(8) At the time of breathing in and letting go of mental formations, one knows one is breathing in and letting go of mental formations; at the time of breathing out and letting go of mental formations, one knows one is breathing out and letting go of mental formations.

(9) At the time of breathing in knowing the mind, one knows one is breathing in knowing the mind; at the time of breathing out knowing the mind, one knows one is breathing out knowing the mind.

(10) At the time of breathing in gladdening the mind, one knows one is breathing in gladdening the mind; at the time of breathing out gladdening the mind, one knows one is breathing out gladdening the mind.

(11) At the time of breathing in concentrating the mind, one knows one is breathing in concentrating the mind; at the time of breathing out concentrating the mind, one knows one is breathing out concentrating the mind.

(12) At the time of breathing in liberating the mind, one knows one is breathing in liberating the mind; at the time of breathing out liberating the mind, one knows one is breathing out liberating the mind.

(13) At the time of breathing in [being aware of] impermanence, one knows one is breathing in [being aware of] impermanence; at the time of breathing out [being aware of] impermanence, one knows one is breathing out [being aware of] impermanence.

(14) At the time of breathing in [being aware of] eradication, one knows one is breathing in [being aware of] eradication; at the time of breathing out [being aware of] eradication, one knows one is breathing out [being aware of] eradication.

(15) At the time of breathing in [being aware of] dispassion, one knows one is breathing in [being aware of] dispassion; at the time of breathing out [being aware of] dispassion, one knows one is breathing out [being aware of] dispassion.

(16) At the time of breathing in [being aware of] cessation, one knows one is breathing in [being aware of] cessation; at the time of breathing out [being aware of] cessation, one knows one is breathing out [being aware of] cessation.

XII.2 THE SIXTEEN STEPS

The instructions in the *Saṃyukta-āgama* discourse and in the Mahāsāṅghika *Vinaya* are fairly similar to those in the *Ānāpānasati-sutta* of the *Majjhima-nikāya*. Given that these texts represent the Mūlasarvāstivāda, the Mahāsāṅghika, and the Theravāda traditions respectively, this shows an impressive degree of correspondence and makes it safe to conclude that the sixteen steps are an integral part of the early teachings.

The instructions proceed from the long breath (1) to the short breath (2), to the whole body (3), and to the bodily formations (4). The parallel versions differ about whether these steps should be regarded as a form of training. The *Saṃyukta-āgama* discourse mentions training throughout, the Mahāsāṅghika *Vinaya* does not mention training at all, and in the *Majjhima-nikāya* version the training begins with the third step.[3]

The formulation in the Mahāsāṅghika *Vinaya* provides a helpful indication in understanding this third step, as it speaks of "pervading the body". This supports an understanding of this step as involving a broadening of awareness from having experienced the breath in its whole length in the previous two steps to becoming aware of the whole physical body as one is breathing. Another noteworthy aspect of the Mahāsāṅghika *Vinaya* text is that, instead of a "calming" of the bodily formations, it speaks of "letting go" of them. Both formulations appear to refer to the same aspect of practice from complementary perspectives, since the calming at this stage comes about precisely through an attitude of letting go.

The next set of four steps covers joy (5), happiness (6), the mental formations (7), and the calming or abandoning of the mental formations (8). The three versions set these steps against the background of continuous awareness of the incoming breath and the outgoing breath, giving the impression that this progression is not confined to actual absorption attainment. Instead, a more compelling interpretation, at least to my mind, is that these steps are accessible to any practitioner who is able to arouse some degree of wholesome joy or happiness in the mind, without necessarily entering absorption.

The same holds for the next four steps of training, which are concerned with experiencing the mind (9), gladdening the mind (10), concentrating the mind (11), and liberating the mind (12). The

3 MN 118 at MN III 82,32 (translated Ñāṇamoli 1995: 945).

parallel versions agree closely, except for the recurrent difference regarding whether these steps should be considered a form of training. In the fourth step in this part, the notion of "liberating" the mind need not be taken in an absolute sense,[4] but can simply be interpreted as referring to any temporary form of liberation from mental obstructions and unwholesome states.

A substantial difference emerges in regard to the last set of four. The *Saṃyukta-āgama* discourse and the Mahāsāṅghika *Vinaya* text proceed from impermanence (13) to eradication (14), dispassion (15), and cessation (16).[5] According to the *Ānāpānasati-sutta* of the *Majjhima-nikāya*, the themes of the last four steps are impermanence (13), dispassion (14), cessation (15), and letting go (16).[6] Here are the two patterns placed beside each other for ease of comparison:

impermanence – eradication – dispassion – cessation
(Mahāsāṅghika and Mūlasarvāstivāda)

impermanence – dispassion – cessation – letting go
(Theravāda)

Three topics emerge as the common ground among the parallel versions in regard to this last tetrad of mindfulness of breathing:

impermanence – dispassion – cessation

From a practical perspective, "dispassion" would comprise "eradication" in the form of the eradication of passion, and "cessation" would be closely related to "letting go". Thus the aspects that are not mentioned in every version would nevertheless conform, at least to some extent, with the basic three topics common to all three descriptions.

This set of three topics has considerable affinity with a recurrent pattern for the development of insight in the early discourses, which proceeds from perception of impermanence to seeing *dukkha* in what

4 See the discussion above p.162.
5 The *Śravakabhūmi*, Shukla 1973: 231,6, has a similar presentation; cf. also the so-called *Yogalehrbuch*, Schlingloff 1964: 82f. For variations in the sixteenfold scheme in other texts preserved in Chinese cf. Deleanu 1992: 51f.
6 The *Arthaviniścaya-sūtra*, Samtani 1971: 45,1, and the *Vimuttimagga*, T 1648 at T XXXII 430a5, agree in this respect with MN 118.

is impermanent, and then perceiving the absence of a self in what is *dukkha*.[7] In this way a meditative dynamic unfolds wherein the three characteristics build on each other:

impermanence – *dukkha* – not-self

The impermanent nature of the breath is the common starting point of the last set of four steps in all versions. Awareness of impermanence in fact forms a background theme throughout the whole set of sixteen steps, being inculcated by awareness of the distinction between breathing in and breathing out. The first of the final four steps gives additional emphasis to the fact that the breath is invariably changing, so now this impermanent nature moves from backstage right to the forefront of one's attention. In this way, breathing could even be used to engage in one of the commendable ways of practising mindfulness of death, mentioned in the chapter on contemplation of a corpse: one becomes aware of the fact that the present breath may be one's last.

With the next step, this impermanent experience is seen as something towards which one becomes dispassionate, as something that is not capable of yielding lasting satisfaction. That is, it is *dukkha*. Dispassion arises precisely because awareness of impermanence deepens. The detachment that sets in with this progression is a key to cultivating an understanding of not-self. Such understanding is a natural outcome of the preceding insight into impermanence and *dukkha*. In other words, once what is impermanent has been seen with dispassion as *dukkha*, it is natural that one's ingrained patterns of identification diminish and cease, and the whole of one's experience reveals itself as devoid of anything that could justify the conceit "I am" or an appropriation in terms of "this is mine". In this way, the mind becomes ready for cessation in its ultimate sense with the experience of Nirvāṇa.

XII.3 THE SIXTEEN STEPS AND THE FOUR SATIPAṬṬHĀNAS

Another discourse in the *Saṃyukta-āgama* that also covers the sixteen steps explains their correlation with the four *satipaṭṭhānas*.[8] The

7 Cf., e.g., AN 7.46 at AN IV 46,21 (translated Bodhi 2012: 1031, given as number 48); the same dynamic occurs in, e.g., DĀ 2 at T I 11c28, MĀ 86 at T I 563c17, SĀ 747 at T II 198a20, and EĀ 37.10 at T II 715b4; for a more detailed discussion cf. Anālayo 2012a: 42ff.

8 SĀ 810 at T II 208a29 (translated Anālayo 2007b).

discourse notes that each of these tetrads has as its object the body, feelings, mind, and dharmas respectively. Therefore each tetrad is an instance of practising one of the four *satipaṭṭhāna*s.

While agreeing on this basic correlation, in the case of the second, third, and fourth tetrads the *Ānāpānasati-sutta* differs in the way it explains the rationale behind this correlation. According to its explanation, the second tetrad – experiencing joy, happiness, and mental formations, as well as calming mental formations – fulfils contemplation of feelings because giving close attention to the breath can be reckoned as a certain feeling among feelings.[9] This explanation is not entirely straightforward, since elsewhere the discourses do not reckon attention (*manasikāra*) to be a type of feeling.[10]

The third tetrad – experiencing, gladdening, concentrating, and liberating the mind – corresponds according to the *Ānāpānasati-sutta* to contemplation of the mind because mindfulness of breathing cannot be properly developed when one has a loss of mindfulness and is without clear knowledge.[11] While this is certainly the case, mindfulness and clear knowledge would similarly be required for the other steps of mindfulness of breathing. Thus it is not clear why this requirement should provide a link between contemplation of the mind and this particular set of four steps of mindfulness of breathing.

The *Ānāpānasati-sutta* indicates that the final tetrad – contemplating impermanence, dispassion, cessation, and letting go – corresponds to contemplation of dharmas because at this stage one looks on well with equanimity, having seen with wisdom that covetousness and discontent have been overcome.[12] Why this should qualify contemplation of dharmas in particular is also not clear, since according to the *Satipaṭṭhāna-sutta* freedom from covetousness and discontent should be developed with all four *satipaṭṭhāna*s. Thus the absence of covetousness and discontent as such would not bear any specific relation to contemplation of dharmas alone.

According to the Pāli commentary, the relationship between the final four steps of mindfulness of breathing and contemplation of dharmas can be found in the reference to having seen the absence of

---

9 MN 118 at MN III 84,9.
10 Ps IV 140,14 recognizes the difficulty with this passage and explains that it is just a figurative way of speech and does not refer to attention itself, but only to its objects.
11 MN 118 at MN III 84,23.
12 MN 118 at MN III 84,33.

covetousness and discontent "with wisdom". The wisdom referred to here should be understood to represent the insight that arises through contemplation of impermanence, etc.[13]

Contemplation of impermanence, etc., certainly does invest the practice of mindfulness of breathing with a strong emphasis on the development of wisdom. Yet, according to the *Satipaṭṭhāna-sutta* contemplation of impermanence is relevant for each of the four *satipaṭṭhāna*s. In each case the nature of arising and of passing away should be contemplated in such a way that this leads to abiding "independent, not clinging to anything in the world". Although the formulation differs from the terms used in relation to mindfulness of breathing, the basic implications appear to be the same. Hence seeing "with wisdom" could in principle be developed with each of the four *satipaṭṭhāna*s, and not just with the fourth *satipaṭṭhāna* of contemplation of dharmas.

The explanations given in the *Saṃyukta-āgama* parallel appear more straightforward compared to those given in the *Ānāpānasati-sutta*. With each of the four tetrads the object of mindfulness is the body, feelings, mind, and dharmas respectively, therefore these four tetrads correspond to contemplating body, feelings, mind, and dharmas as a *satipaṭṭhāna* practice.

The *Ānāpānasati-sutta* and its *Saṃyukta-āgama* parallel agree that each of these four tetrads of mindfulness of breathing – standing for the practice of one *satipaṭṭhāna* – can on its own lead, via the cultivation of the awakening factors, to the attainment of liberation.[14] In other words, practice of any of the four *satipaṭṭhāna*s has the potential of leading directly to liberation.

XII.4 PRACTICE OF THE SIXTEEN STEPS

In what follows I briefly survey the sixteen steps from a practical perspective, without thereby in any way intending to present my interpretation as the only possible approach. A possible way of implementing this mode of practice could begin by contemplating the duration of the breath and its relation to the body. Becoming aware of the nature of the breath and of the body in this way would be similar

---

13 Ps IV 142,4.

14 MN 118 at MN III 85,8 and its parallel SĀ 810 at T II 208b15 indicate that any of the four *satipaṭṭhāna*s can become the basis for fulfilling the seven factors of awakening, etc.

in type to contemplating the nature of the body by contemplating the anatomical parts, the elements, and the stages of decay, although in these cases the exploration of the body's nature is undertaken in more challenging ways.

Awareness of joy and happiness as results of the inner calm generated through mindfulness of breathing would then be an instance of contemplation of feelings, especially pleasant feelings of an unworldly type. In terms of the second *satipaṭṭhāna*, at this juncture mindfulness appears to have the task of being aware of the presence of these feelings and perhaps also of alerting the meditator as soon as these have been replaced by other feelings due to, for example, mental distraction. Further progress would take place when awareness of joy and happiness leads on to becoming aware of mental formations and of their calming down. All this takes place against the background of constant awareness of the impermanent nature of the breath, as each feeling is experienced along with mindfully taking note when the breath comes in or when the breath goes out.

Continuing practice leads to a further refinement through awareness of the mind, gladdening, concentrating, and freeing it as a way of practising contemplation of the mind. This correlates with the mind that has become concentrated and the mind that has become liberated in the list of mental states that is common to the *Satipaṭṭhāna-sutta* and its parallels.

Contemplation of dharmas would then require giving attention to impermanence and other perspectives related to insight, thereby introducing central themes of the path to awakening. These bear a close resemblance to the four aspects that should ideally accompany the cultivation of the awakening factors, namely, being developed supported by seclusion, dispassion, and cessation, culminating in letting go.

In this way, the sixteen-step scheme of mindfulness of breathing can provide a model of practice that skilfully brings the four *satipaṭṭhāna*s into being, based on a single object of meditation. This shows that the question here is not so much the object that is chosen – which in this case is the breath and thus an aspect of the body – but rather to contemplate this object from the four perspectives underlying the four *satipaṭṭhāna*s.

Needless to say, putting this into practice would not simply be a by-product of being aware of the breath. Rather, implementing the sixteenfold scheme appears to require a conscious effort at broadening one's awareness. Based on having established mindfulness of the breath, practice is intentionally cultivated in such a way that it proceeds to awareness of the whole physical body, of feelings, of the condition of the mind, and of impermanence, etc.

XII.5 A FLEXIBLE APPROACH TO PRACTICE

The discourses give the impression that the sixteen-step approach to mindfulness of breathing was not the only form of practice in use among the Buddha's disciples for being aware of the breath. A discourse in the *Saṃyutta-nikāya* and its parallel reports how the Buddha enquired from a group of monks if they were practising mindfulness of breathing.[15] On being given a relatively simple description of practice that emphasizes having a mind free from desires, the Buddha approved. Then, apparently as a way of broadening the perspective on the same meditation subject, he expounded the sixteen steps. In another discourse in the *Majjhima-nikāya* and its *Ekottarika-āgama* parallel, the Buddha's son Rāhula is told to engage in mindfulness of breathing, and the sixteen-step scheme is only taught to him when he comes back for more detailed instructions.[16]

Such passages give the impression that the Buddha's disciples were left free to develop their own approaches to meditation practice. Another example is the instruction on contemplation of death, discussed earlier. Here, too, the Buddha is on record for broaching the topic by enquiring from a group of monks how they were undertaking this practice, receiving a variety of different replies.[17]

The impression conveyed by such passages is that in the early discourses meditation instructions were flexible. These were open invitations to practice, often given only in a succinct manner, instead of a fixed script that each and everyone had to enact to the last detail. This would further explain why detailed instructions on mindfulness are only given in the *Satipaṭṭhāna-sutta* and its parallels, in contrast to the more frequently found brief instructions in other discourses that just mention the four *satipaṭṭhāna*s and leave it to the individual

15 SN 54.6 at SN V 314,25 (translated Bodhi 2000: 1768) and its parallel SĀ 805 at T II 206b26.

16 MN 62 at MN I 421,24 (translated Ñāṇamoli 1995: 527) and its parallel EĀ 17.1 at T II 582a6.

17 See above p.104f.

practitioner how to implement these.[18] That the *Satipaṭṭhāna-sutta* and its parallels are not a fixed prescription of the one and only way to engage in *satipaṭṭhāna* meditation is in fact implicit in the presentation in the *Ānāpānasati-sutta* and its parallels, as here all four *satipaṭṭhāna*s are implemented with the single object of the breath.

The sixteen-step scheme of mindfulness of breathing can thus be read as an open invitation to enrich one's practice through a flexible employment of the four *satipaṭṭhāna*s, thereby revealing their cooperative effect. This cooperative effect of the four *satipaṭṭhāna*s finds an illustration in a simile in the *Saṃyutta-nikāya*, with a parallel in the *Saṃyukta-āgama*. Here is the relevant passage from the *Saṃyukta-āgama* discourse:[19]

> Just as a person coming by a chariot from the northern direction would run over a mound of earth at a junction of four roads, would he be able to flatten the mound?

As the person coming from the northern direction would indeed be able to flatten the mound, so too a person coming from any of the other three directions would be able to do the same. Practising the four *satipaṭṭhāna*s is similar. According to the *Saṃyukta-āgama* account each of them will lead to coming to know what is wholesome within, or else, according to the *Saṃyutta-nikāya* parallel, each of the four *satipaṭṭhāna*s will be able to flatten unwholesome states.[20] This simile suggests that, while each *satipaṭṭhāna* on its own makes a substantial contribution to flattening unwholesome states, combining the four *satipaṭṭhāna*s can have an even stronger effect in flattening the mound of defilements accumulated in one's mind, just as the mound will quickly be reduced to nothing if chariots come from all four directions.

By showing how the four *satipaṭṭhāna*s can be cultivated in conjunction, the description of the sixteen steps of mindfulness of breathing provides a remarkable example of the approach to mental culture in the early discourses. By interweaving and skilfully combining aspects of meditation practice in a flexible way, the whole path to liberation can unfold through a simple object like the breath.

A simile in a discourse in the *Saṃyutta-nikāya* and its *Saṃyukta-āgama* parallel illustrates the need for a skilful approach to mental

18 See above p.204.
19 SĀ 813 at T II 209a17 to 209a19.
20 SN 54.10 at SN V 325,7 (translated Bodhi 2000: 1777).

culture with the example of a cook. In what follows I translate the relevant passage from the *Saṃyukta-āgama* discourse:[21]

> Just as, for example, a foolish cook, who does not distinguish and is not skilful at combining various tastes, who waits upon his master with what is sour, salty, or bland in a way that does not suit his [master's] mind, who is unable to grasp well his master's preferences properly in regard to what is sour, salty, or bland, in regard to combining these various tastes.
>
> He is unable to wait on his master intimately [while standing by his] left and right sides, to serve him as he should do, to be receptive to his wishes, to well grasp his [master's] mind. Following his own ideas he combines the various tastes and presents them to his master. As these do not suit his [master's] mind and the master is not pleased, because of not pleasing [his master, the cook] will not receive a noble reward and will not be thought of fondly.

The *Saṃyutta-nikāya* parallel indicates that the foolish cook fails to notice whether the king or minister he is serving took much of something, or whether he reached for a particular dish and praised it.[22] In both versions the example of the foolish cook illustrates a form of practice of the four *satipaṭṭhānas* that is not successful in overcoming defilements and in settling the mind so as to lead it into concentration.

Applying this simile to mindfulness of breathing, the breath as such is a bland object, devoid of intrinsic interest. Some meditators may be naturally capable of successfully directing their mind to this object and sustaining it there, but others find this difficult, simply because the breath as such does not attract one's attention. Their predicament could be compared to being given a plate of plain rice, which on its own is tasteless. Just as with only plain rice, one would soon be on the lookout for something to add flavour to the meal, so the mind directed to an insipid object like the breath can find it boring and naturally turns to something tastier, like reviving memories of the past or devising plans for the future. When this happens, one need not stoically continue to swallow down plain rice, perhaps even counting each morsel of rice eaten as an additional measure to enforce the meal. Instead, with the help of the sixteen-steps scheme,

---

21 SĀ 616 at T II 172b27 to 172c4.
22 SN 47.8 at SN V 150,2 (translated Bodhi 2000: 1634).

ιe can take an alternative approach that keeps the mind more easily engaged with its object.

In order to please the mind, the skilful cook can accompany the plain rice of the breath with sixteen different dishes, according to the recipe given in the *Ānāpānasati-sutta* and its parallels. This would ensure that the breath becomes tasty enough for the mind to be pleased and remain interested. Appetizing the breath in this manner, by introducing a variety of perspectives and encouraging the arising of wholesome types of pleasure and joy, will go a long way in helping the mind to stay with the breath. The reason is simply that this approach naturally arouses interest in the object chosen for meditation practice.

As with the awakening factors, mindfulness and joy are important "kitchen appliances". Mindfulness not only attends to the breath, but is also aware of various aspects related to the breath. Most importantly, mindfulness is aware of how the mind is taking to the present practice, just as the skilful cook needs to be aware of what dish the master prefers. With established mindfulness one realizes what pleases the mind, what arouses wholesome types of joy and what makes the mind become interested and engaged. This can then be used skilfully to promote progress in the practice. Needless to say, the same applies to practice of the four *satipaṭṭhāna*s that is not based on the breath. Skilfully working in line with the natural tendencies of the mind in this way can go a long way in speeding up one's progress on the path.

XII.6 THREE SATIPAṬṬHĀNAS

Besides the perspectives on the scheme of four *satipaṭṭhāna*s that can be gathered from the *Satipaṭṭhāna-sutta* and the *Ānāpānasati-sutta*, together with their parallels, the early discourses also mention a set of three *satipaṭṭhāna*s. These are concerned with the Buddha himself in his role as a teacher. The three *satipaṭṭhāna*s are described in the *Saḷāyatanavibhaṅga-sutta* and parallels preserved in Chinese and Tibetan. Here is the relevant part from the Chinese translation of the *Madhyama-āgama* parallel to the *Saḷāyatanavibhaṅga-sutta*:[23]

> The Tathāgata teaches the Dharma to his disciples with thoughts of sympathy and consideration, seeking their benefit and welfare, seeking their peace and happiness, with a mind full of benevolence

23 MĀ 163 at T I 693c24 to 694a19.

> and compassion, [telling them]: "This is for your welfare, this is for your happiness, this is for your welfare and happiness."
>
> If the disciples are not respectful and do not act accordingly, do not become established in knowledge, their minds do not incline towards the Dharma, they do not follow the Dharma, they do not accept the right Dharma, they disregard the Blessed One's instruction and are unable to attain certainty in it – then because of this the Blessed One is not sad or sorrowful. Instead, the Blessed One is equanimous and unaffected, constantly mindful and constantly knowing. This is the first establishment of mindfulness that is cultivated by the Noble One. Having cultivated it, the Noble One is capable of teaching the assemblies …
>
> If the disciples are respectful and act accordingly, become established in knowledge, their minds surrender and incline towards the Dharma, they follow the Dharma, they accept and uphold the right Dharma, they do not disregard the Blessed One's instruction and are able to attain certainty in it – then because of this the Blessed One is not glad or joyful. Instead, the Blessed One is equanimous and unaffected, constantly mindful and constantly knowing. This is the second establishment of mindfulness that is cultivated by the Noble One. Having cultivated it, the Noble One is capable of teaching the assemblies …
>
> Some disciples are not respectful and do not act accordingly, do not become established in knowledge, their minds do not incline towards the Dharma, they do not follow the Dharma, they do not accept the right Dharma, they disregard the Blessed One's instruction and are unable to attain certainty in it; some disciples are respectful and act accordingly, they become established in knowledge, their minds surrender and incline towards the Dharma, they follow the Dharma, they accept and uphold the right Dharma, they do not disregard the Blessed One's instruction and are able to attain certainty in it – because of this the Blessed One is not sad or sorrowful and he is also not glad or joyful. Instead, the Blessed One is equanimous and unaffected, constantly mindful and constantly knowing. This is the third establishment of mindfulness that is cultivated by the Noble One. Having cultivated it, the Noble One is capable of teaching the assemblies.

While this is less evident in the formulation in the *Madhyama-āgama* version above, the *Saḷāyatanavibhaṅga-sutta* and the Tibetan parallel make it clear that the main problem is that the disciples do not listen properly when the Buddha is delivering his instructions.[24] Thus the three establishments of mindfulness or *satipaṭṭhāna*s refer to the following three situations:

- the disciples do not listen;
- the disciples listen;
- some listen, some do not listen.

In the *Madhyama-āgama* account, in each of these three situations the Buddha is fully aware of what is happening, but is not affected by it. He is neither disappointed on realizing that he is not being listened to, nor does he become elated when his teachings are well received. The Tibetan parallel is similar to the *Madhyama-āgama* presentation.

According to the *Saḷāyatanavibhaṅga-sutta* of the *Majjhima-nikāya*, however, when the disciples do not listen, the Buddha is not satisfied,[25] when some listen, the Buddha is neither satisfied nor dissatisfied, and when all listen, the Buddha is satisfied. In other words, according to the Pāli account there appears to be a difference in the Buddha's attitude, depending on whether his disciples listen or not.

Besides being found in the *Saḷāyatanavibhaṅga-sutta* and its parallels, the three *satipaṭṭhāna*s also occur in a range of other works, such as the *Abhidharmakośabhāṣya*, the **Mahāprajñāpāramitāśāstra*, the **Mahāvibhāṣā*, as well as the *Mahāvyutpatti*. These works all support the presentation in the *Madhyama-āgama* version, in as much as the Buddha's attitude remains unaffected in each of these three cases.[26]

The presentation in the *Saḷāyatanavibhaṅga-sutta* of the *Majjhima-nikāya* not only differs from its parallels and these other works, but also differs to some extent from a discourse in the *Saṃyutta-nikāya*, belonging to the Pāli canon of the same Theravāda tradition. According to this discourse, the Buddha's attitude when instructing

---

24 MN 137 at MN III 221,8 (translated Ñāṇamoli 1995: 1071) and D 4094 *nyu* 59a3 or Q 5595 *thu* 101b3 begin their respective description by indicating that the disciples do not (or do) "listen" and "give ear".

25 MN 137 at MN III 221,10.

26 The *Abhidharmakośabhāṣya*, T 1558 at T XXIX 140c26 and T 1559 at T XXIX 292a6 (the Sanskrit version, Pradhan 1967: 414,11, does not give all three cases in full), the *Mahāprajñāpāramitāśāstra*, T 1509 at T XXV 91b24, the **Mahāvibhāṣā*, T 1545 at T XXVII 160b20 and again T XXVII 942b16, and the *Mahāvyutpatti* 188–90, Sakaki 1926/1962: 16f; for further references cf. Anālayo 2011a: 787 n.147.

others was free from attraction or repulsion.[27] While attraction and repulsion are stronger reactions than being satisfied and dissatisfied, it nevertheless seems probable that the *Saḷāyatanavibhaṅga-sutta* has suffered from a transmission error. That is, the proper presentation would probably be that the Buddha's reaction remains the same, whether his disciples listen or not.[28]

Comparing these three *satipaṭṭhāna*s with the four *satipaṭṭhāna*s, it is noteworthy that the set of three does not bear any explicit relation to the common fourfold presentation by way of body, feelings, mind, or dharmas. This set of four does not naturally fit awareness of the three situations while giving a talk, where one may receive attention, one may be ignored by the audience, or one may be confronted with an audience where only some are attentive.

In evaluating this difference, however, it needs to be kept in mind that the four *satipaṭṭhāna*s describe the path to realization, whereas the three *satipaṭṭhāna*s depict the attitude of a fully awakened teacher.[29] Nevertheless, it is remarkable that these three attitudes of the Buddha as an awakened teacher are referred to with the same term *satipaṭṭhāna* that is elsewhere used for establishing mindfulness by contemplating body, feelings, the mind, and dharmas.

What appears to be common to both schemes is thus not the object of which one is mindful, but rather the mental attitude that ideally comes with properly established mindfulness. This attitude requires a form of mental presence that does not easily give rise to reactions coloured by likes and dislikes. This appears to be a key characteristic common to both the three and the four *satipaṭṭhāna*s.

The notion of mental balance also emerges in the passages describing a loss of mindfulness that I surveyed earlier.[30] With mindfulness properly established, one is able to see things without giving rise to likes and dislikes. In the seen there will be just the seen. In sum, it seems to me that *satipaṭṭhāna* requires a combination of being fully aware of what is happening with the maintenance of mental equipoise.

---

27 SN 4.14 at SN I 111,20; noted by Kuan 2008: 29 as standing in contrast to the presentation in MN 137.

28 For a brief discussion of the type of transmission error that may have occurred cf. Anālayo 2011a: 786 n.145.

29 Although, as already pointed out by Weber 1994: 68, the attitude depicted in the three *satipaṭṭhāna*s should ideally be emulated by any practising Buddhist.

30 See above p.21ff.

XII.7 SATIPAṬṬHĀNA AND BALANCE

The theme of maintaining balance through *satipaṭṭhāna* practice receives an illustration in a simile that describes the cooperation of two acrobats. This simile is found in the *Sedaka-sutta* of the *Saṃyutta-nikāya* and its *Saṃyukta-āgama* parallel. Here is the *Saṃyukta-āgama* version of the simile:[31]

> In former times, there was a teacher of acrobatics done in dependence on a pole. He placed the pole straight up on his shoulder and told his disciple: "Getting up and down on the pole, you protect me and I will also protect you. Protecting each other we will put on a show and gain much wealth."[32]
>
> Then the disciple of acrobatics said to the teacher of acrobatics: "What you said won't do. Instead, we should each take care to protect ourselves. [In this way] we will put on a show and gain much wealth. We will be physically at ease and yet I will get down safely." The teacher of acrobatics said: "As you said, we will take care to protect ourselves, this is correct and is also the meaning of what I said."
>
> [The Buddha said]: "Having protected oneself, one right away protects the other; when protecting the other and oneself, this is protection indeed.[33]
>
> [How does protecting oneself protect others]? Becoming familiar with one's own mind, developing it, protecting it accordingly and attaining realization – this is called "protecting oneself protects others".[34]

---

31 SĀ 619 at T II 173b7 to 173b18; for a more detailed study cf. Anālayo 2012e.

32 SN 47.19 at SN V 168,18 (translated Bodhi 2000: 1648) does not give further specification about where the pole was put. Another parallel in the *Bhaiṣajyavastu* of the Mūlasarvāstivāda *Vinaya*, T 1448 at T XXIV 32b11, reports that it was placed on the shoulder. SN 47.19 also does not mention that the protecting of each other should be done while getting up and down the pole, in fact in its account the teacher at first told the disciple to get up on his shoulders, SN V 168,20, which the latter then did, so that in SN 47.19 their discussion takes place with the disciple already standing on the shoulders of the teacher.

33 In SN 47.19 at SN V 169,11 the Buddha at first recommends the practice of *satipaṭṭhāna* to protect oneself and to protect another, and then indicates that by protecting oneself one protects others and by protecting others one protects oneself.

34 SN 47.19 at SN V 169,16 does not explicitly specify that the mind is the object of development. The *Bhaiṣajyavastu*, T 1448 at T XXIV 32b22, also does not mention becoming familiar with the mind.

> How does protecting others protect oneself? By the gift of fearlessness, the gift of non-violation, the gift of harmlessness, by having a mind of benevolence and empathy for the other – this is called "protecting others protects oneself".[35]
>
> For this reason … one should train oneself like this: "Protecting myself I will develop the four *satipaṭṭhānas*, protecting others I will develop the four *satipaṭṭhānas*."

Alongside a few minor variations, a noteworthy difference between the two versions is that according to the *Sedaka-sutta* the teacher does not reply to the disciple, and the Buddha comments that the remark by the disciple is the right method.[36] This gives the impression that this teacher was not really up to the position of teaching that he had assumed, since in relation to so fundamental a matter as how to perform properly, he needed to have the priorities clarified by his own disciple.

In the *Saṃyukta-āgama* version, however, the teacher himself acknowledges the correctness of what the disciple has said, after which he adds that this "is also the meaning of what I said"; that is, this much was implicit in his original statement. Here the teacher indicates that he had already been aware of the point made by the disciple. Even though his concern for the disciple had led him to express his advice in terms of protecting the other, the need for both to protect themselves by keeping their own balance was implied in his statement. In this way, the disciple's remark does not imply ignorance on the side of the teacher, but only highlights a principle that is implicit in the teacher's proposal that they protect each other.

Now for the two acrobats to perform their feat successfully, the teacher would have to keep the pole firmly upright and the disciple would have to maintain balance while on top of the pole.[37] In view of this need for cooperation, the teacher's suggestion that "you protect

---

35 Instead of fearlessness, non-violation, and harmlessness, SN 47.19 at SN V 169,19 speaks only of patience and harmlessness. The *Bhaiṣajyavastu*, T 1448 at T XXIV 32b24, mentions not annoying, not angering, and not harming another.

36 SN 47.19 at SN V 169,9.

37 Olendzki 2010: 127f explains that the image of the acrobat needing to pay attention to his or her own physical sense of balance mirrors the task of a meditator, in that "the acrobat, like the meditator, is bringing conscious awareness to a process that is always occurring but is generally overlooked." The simile thus exemplifies that "mindfulness is a tool for looking inward, adjusting our balance."

me and I will also protect you" is quite meaningful. He will protect the disciple by keeping the pole upright. At the same time, he hopes that the disciple will protect him by avoiding any jerky movement that will upset the pole's balance and make it difficult to keep the pole straight. The teacher's concern would also be that, whether he makes a mistake or the disciple makes a mistake, the one who falls down and risks injury is the disciple. So, as the teacher and with a natural attitude of concern, he expresses himself in terms of protecting the other.

The perspective introduced by the disciple that "we should each take care to protect ourselves" brings a refinement to the basic principle of harmonious cooperation by indicating that each of them should not just protect the other. This does not reject the need for both of them to be concerned about the other. Instead, it introduces the proper perspective for achieving smooth cooperation, namely being first of all centred oneself, as only then will one be able to protect the other.

If the teacher were to become excessively worried about the disciple, this might distract his attention from the need to keep his own balance and result in knocking over the whole set-up. Similarly, the disciple should not be overly concerned about the teacher, but needs to pay attention first of all to her own maintenance of balance, otherwise she risks falling off the pole.

In this way, the simile of the two acrobats introduces the theme of mutual protection into the image of *satipaṭṭhāna* as a form of balance. Being with mindfulness, one protects oneself and at the same time protects others. The significant indication here is that cultivating one's own practice is not a matter of selfishness, as it prepares the ground for truly being able to protect others. Without being established in mindfulness oneself, without having found the point of balance within, it is difficult to be of real assistance to others.[38]

---

38 Ñāṇaponika 1968/1986: 35 explains that "just as certain reflex movements automatically protect the body, similarly the mind needs spontaneous spiritual and moral self-protection. The practice of bare attention will provide this vital function." He adds (p.5) that such "self-protection will safeguard others, individuals and society, against our own unrestrained passions and selfish impulses … they will be safe from our reckless greed for possessions and power, from our unrestrained lust and sensuality, from our envy and jealousy; safe from the disruptive consequences of our hate and enmity." He then sums up (p.8) by saying that "he who earnestly devotes himself to moral self-improvement and spiritual self-development

Thus walking the path to liberation is for one's own benefit just as much as it is for the benefit of others.

XII.8 SATIPAṬṬHĀNA AND LIBERATION

The *Satipaṭṭhāna-sutta* and its *Madhyama-āgama* parallel list different periods of time within which the practice of *satipaṭṭhāna*, if it is undertaken properly, has the potential to lead to non-return or full awakening. The respective descriptions are as follows:

Majjhima-nikāya:

> If anyone should develop these four *satipaṭṭhāna*s in such a way for seven years, one of two fruits can be expected for him [or her]: either final knowledge here and now, or, if there is a trace of clinging left, non-returning … let alone seven years … six years … five years … four years … three years … two years … one year … seven months … six months … five months … four months … three months … two months … one month … half a month, if anyone should develop these four *satipaṭṭhāna*s in such a way for seven days, one of two fruits can be expected for him [or her]: either final knowledge here and now, or, if there is a trace of clinging left, non-returning.

Madhyama-āgama:

> If … with settled mind one properly dwells in the four *satipaṭṭhāna*s for seven years, then one will certainly attain one of two fruits: either final knowledge here and now, or, if there is a remainder [of clinging], the attainment of non-returning. Let alone seven years … six … five … four … three … two … one year… seven months … six … five … four … three … two … one month … seven days and nights … six … five … four … three … two … if with settled mind [one] properly dwells in the four *satipaṭṭhāna*s for one day and night, then one will certainly attain one of two fruits: either final

will be a strong and active force for good in the world", whereas "if we leave unresolved the actual or potential sources of social evil within ourselves, our external social activity will be either futile or markedly incomplete. Therefore, if we are moved by a spirit of social responsibility, we must not shirk the hard task of moral and spiritual self-development. Preoccupation with social activities must not be made an excuse or escape from the first duty, to tidy up one's own house first."

> knowledge here and now, or, if there is a remainder [of clinging], the attainment of non-returning. Let alone one day and night, if … with settled mind [one] properly dwells in the four *satipaṭṭhāna*s even for a short moment, then, practising in this way in the morning, one will certainly have made progress by the evening; practising in this way in the evening, one will certainly have made progress by the [next] morning.

The lists of time periods required to reach non-return or full awakening in the *Satipaṭṭhāna-sutta* range from seven years to seven days. The *Madhyama-āgama* parallel, which also explicitly mentions nuns alongside monks,[39] proceeds from seven days down to a single day and concludes with the statement that even practising properly just for a moment one will make progress. The two versions thus agree that the time it takes to reach the goal can vary considerably, yet, as the *Madhyama-āgama* version clarifies, every step taken along the path will be progress in the right direction and bring one closer to liberation.

The nature of progress to liberation finds illustration in a simile that employs the example of the gradual nature of the ocean. Here is the relevant part from the *Madhyama-āgama* version:[40]

> It is just as the ocean which becomes gradually more extensive, from the bottom to the surface and in circumference, evenly and uniformly increasing up to the surface, until it reaches the shore; and it is always full of water, never flowing out … like this my true Dharma and discipline is undertaken gradually, practised gradually, completed gradually, and taught gradually.

The *Aṅguttara-nikāya* parallel highlights that breakthrough to final knowledge does not take place in an abrupt manner.[41] Just as the ocean naturally deepens as long as one keeps moving away from the shore, so practice of *satipaṭṭhāna* has a natural tendency to deepen. Some beaches may be flat, others may be steep. So the time it takes to get into deep waters differs, in line with the indication in the *Satipaṭṭhāna-sutta* and its *Madhyama-āgama* parallel on the differing periods it can take to reach the goal of liberation. Yet, as long as

39 That some of the ancient nuns were proficient practitioners of *satipaṭṭhāna* is also highlighted in SN 47.10 at SN V 154,28 (translated Bodhi 2000: 1638) and its parallel SĀ 615 at T II 172b2.

40 MĀ 35 at T I 476b22 to 476b25.

41 AN 8.19 at AN IV 201,2 (translated Bodhi 2012: 1143). The quality of gradualness is not mentioned in another parallel, EĀ 42.4 at T II 753a20.

one keeps moving in the right direction, one's practice will become deeper and deeper.

Another set of three similes illustrating the nature of progress on the path occurs in a discourse in the *Saṃyutta-nikāya*. In what follows, I translate the parallel from the *Saṃyukta-āgama*:[42]

> It is just as a brooding hen which properly provides for her eggs by sheltering them and incubating them, properly regulating their temperature at the proper time. Even if she does not have the wish that the chickens, by making an effort, peck at the eggshells and come out on their own, nevertheless the chickens will be able to emerge safely from the eggshells by making an effort on their own. Why is that? Because that brooding hen has sheltered and incubated them, properly regulating their temperature at the proper time ...[43]
>
> It is just as a skilled master or his apprentice who takes the handle of a hatchet in his hand. Taking hold of it continuously, tiny impressions of the hand and the fingers become gradually visible in places. Even if he is not aware of the tiny impressions on the handle of the hatchet, the impressions become visible in places ...[44]
>
> It is just as a great ship that is [docked] on the seashore during the summer. For six months being blown on by the wind and exposed to the sun, its rigging gradually breaks apart.[45]

This series of similes suggests that, as long as one has the self-discipline to imitate the hen by sitting on one's cushion regularly, it is to be expected that eventually the desired result will come about. The progress of one's practice is not measurable by the day, but through

42 SĀ 263 at T II 67b12 to 67b27 (translated Anālayo 2013b).

43 The parallels, SN 22.101 at SN III 154,10 (translated Bodhi 2000: 960; cf. also AN 7.67 at AN IV 125,18, translated Bodhi 2012: 1088, given as AN 7.71), a Gāndhārī fragment parallel, Glass 2007: 207, and the *Bhaiṣajyavastu*, T 1448 at T XXIV 31c4, mention that the hen might have up to twelve eggs.

44 In SN 22.101 at SN III 154,31 (and in AN 7.67) the point of the simile is that the carpenter does not know how much of the handle has worn away today, how much the day before; yet, once it has worn away, he will know that this has happened.

45 According to SN 22.101 at SN III 155,6 (and AN 7.67), the rigging had already been affected when the ship was in the water for six months and is now further affected by sun and wind when the ship is hauled up onto land during the winter. The rigging then breaks apart when rain comes. The *Bhaiṣajyavastu*, T 1448 at T XXIV 32a11, also describes the ship being first in the water for six months and then hauled up onto the shore (although in its account this happens during the summer), where it is then affected by wind and sun. When great rain comes later, it naturally breaks apart.

long periods of dedicated practice the changes brought about become visible, like the wearing away of the handle of the hatchet. The fetters that hold one in bondage are bound to wither away and fall apart, as long as they are exposed to the wind of continuous practice and the sunlight of correct understanding.

Navigating the gradual path depicted in the above similes requires a fine sense of balance. The task one faces is the need to maintain the balance of a middle way that avoids two extremes. One extreme is excessive goal-orientation. Chasing after attainments will inevitably result in a sense of frustration that comes from the unbalanced attitude of sitting in order to get something out of it. This type of attitude can even lead to the self-deception of mistaking what are mere stepping stones along the path for being the final goal. The other extreme is pretending to be beyond the need for any aspiration. The erroneous belief that unwholesome desires can be overcome without having the wholesome desire to overcome them can result in mistaking stagnation for being a form of detachment, presuming that *satipaṭṭhāna* is nothing more than being in the present moment, full stop.

One way to achieve this middle-way balance would be by combining one's aspiration for complete liberation with awareness of momentary experiences of temporary liberation as a foretaste of the final goal.[46] In this way, instead of aspiring for something to be realized in the distant future, awareness turns to whatever in the present moment conforms to this aspiration.

The final goal of the gradual practice of *satipaṭṭhāna*, undertaken within the context of the noble eightfold path as the practical implementation of the fourth noble truth, is clearly the attainment of full awakening. Glimpses of what this means, however, can be seen in the most ordinary of situations, whenever the mind is not overcome by defilements even for a moment. Practising in this way one becomes ever more aware of the profundity of the teachings and of liberation through awakening as their fundamental "taste". Here is a simile that illustrates such qualities of the Dharma by comparing it to the ocean, based on the *Madhyama-āgama* version:[47]

> It is just as the depth of the great ocean's water which is unfathomably profound, being of utmost breadth and boundless ... in the same way the teachings in my right Dharma and discipline are unfathomably

46 See above p.162f.
47 MĀ 35 at T I 476c6 to 476c12.

> profound, being of utmost breadth and unlimited …
>
> It is just as the great ocean's water, which is salty and has the same flavour everywhere … in the same way my right Dharma and discipline has the flavour of dispassion, the flavour of realization, the flavour of appeasement, and the flavour of awakening.

The comparison with the depth of the ocean does not occur in the Pāli parallel found in the *Aṅguttara-nikāya*, although a comparable reference is preserved in an *Ekottarika-āgama* parallel.[48] This *Ekottarika-āgama* parallel continues by mentioning only a single flavour, which is the noble eightfold path.[49] The *Aṅguttara-nikāya* discourse also just mentions a single flavour, namely the taste of liberation.[50]

Every situation in life has the potential to be liberating; the taste of liberation can be found everywhere, if one is willing to look for it. In terms of the four noble truths, any situation has a potential relationship not only to *dukkha* and to its arising (first and second truth), but also to liberation and to what leads to liberation (third and fourth truth). As one proceeds by gradually liberating oneself, by keeping that "salty" taste of liberation on one's mental tongue, progress towards complete liberation of the irreversible type through awakening naturally unfolds.

Alongside the terms "liberation" and "awakening", the final goal has a range of other significant nuances that can be captured through various terms that bring out different aspects and connotations. To convey a sense of these complementary perspectives on the final goal, I conclude this study with a series of epithets of Nirvāṇa from the *Asaṅkhata-saṃyutta* of the *Saṃyutta-nikāya* and its *Saṃyukta-āgama* counterpart. These two parallels offer several alternative designations for the goal of practice, some more poetic, others more practical. In what follows, I list those epithets that are found in both versions.[51] I hope at least one of these terms will be able to capture the personal aspirations of the reader.

> Unconditioned … hard to see … unshakeable … deathless … influx-free … protection … island … shelter … sublime … peaceful … unailing … Nirvāṇa.

---

48 EĀ 42.4 at T II 753a20.
49 EĀ 42.4 at T II 753a28.
50 AN 8.19 at AN IV 203,7 (translated Bodhi 2012: 1144).
51 SĀ 890 at T II 224b7 to 224b10, with its parallel in SN 43 at SN IV 368,1 to 373,14 (translated Bodhi 2000: 1378).

XII.9 SUMMARY

The sixteen steps of mindfulness of breathing illustrate how the four *satipaṭṭhāna*s can be cultivated in such a way that the whole path to liberation unfolds based on a single object. A characteristic common to the three and the four *satipaṭṭhāna*s is a combination of being fully aware of what is happening with mental equipoise. Being mindful in this way protects oneself and at the same time protects others. Deepening one's practice by dedicatedly sitting in meditation like a hen that sits on her eggs, one's defilements wear away like the handle of a hatchet and one's mental bondage gradually falls apart like the rigging of a ship exposed to sun and wind. As one keeps the salty taste of liberation in mind, progress naturally unfolds towards final liberation.

XIII

THE SATIPAṬṬHĀNA-SUTTA

The present chapter contains translations of the *Satipaṭṭhāna-sutta* from the *Majjhima-nikāya* and its parallels from the *Madhyama-āgama* and the *Ekottarika-āgama*. While in the course of my study I have often heavily abbreviated excerpts to facilitate ease of reading and comparison with the parallel versions, here I give the text in full, even providing the parts that are abbreviated in the original, as indicated by the use of square brackets [ ]. In the case of the *Ekottarika-āgama* version this involves some degree of interpretation, as this translation can at times be somewhat irregular.

XIII.1 MAJJHIMA-NIKĀYA

THE DISCOURSE ON SATIPAṬṬHĀNA[1]

Thus have I heard. On one occasion the Blessed One was living among the Kurus, at a town of the Kurus called *Kammāsadhamma*. There the Blessed One addressed the monks: "Monks." The monks replied: "Venerable sir." The Blessed One said this:

"Monks, this is the direct path for the purification of beings, [56][2] for the surmounting of sorrow and lamentation, for the disappearance of *dukkha* and discontent, for acquiring the true method, for the realization of Nirvāṇa, namely, the four *satipaṭṭhāna*s. What are the four?

1 MN 10 at MN I 55,27 to 63,21 (translated Ñāṇamoli 1995: 145ff).

2 Here and below, numbers given in square brackets refer to the page of the translated original.

"Here, monks, in regard to the body a monk abides contemplating the body, diligent, clearly knowing, and mindful, free from desires and discontent with regard to the world. In regard to feelings he abides contemplating feelings, diligent, clearly knowing, and mindful, free from desires and discontent with regard to the world. In regard to the mind he abides contemplating the mind, diligent, clearly knowing, and mindful, free from desires and discontent with regard to the world. In regard to dharmas he abides contemplating dharmas, diligent, clearly knowing, and mindful, free from desires and discontent with regard to the world.

"And how, monks, does a monk in regard to the body abide contemplating the body? Here, monks, gone to the forest, or to the root of a tree, or to an empty hut, a monk sits down; having folded his legs crosswise, set his body erect and established mindfulness in front, he breathes in mindfully and he breathes out mindfully.

"Breathing in long, he knows: 'I breathe in long', breathing out long, he knows: 'I breathe out long.' Breathing in short, he knows: 'I breathe in short', breathing out short, he knows: 'I breathe out short.' He trains: 'I breathe in experiencing the whole body', he trains: 'I breathe out experiencing the whole body.' He trains: 'I breathe in calming the bodily formation', he trains: 'I breathe out calming the bodily formation.'

"Monks, it is just as a skilled turner or a turner's apprentice who knows, when making a long turn: 'I make a long turn'; he knows, when making a short turn: 'I make a short turn.'

"In the same way, monks, breathing in long, a monk knows: 'I breathe in long', [breathing out long, he knows: 'I breathe out long.' Breathing in short, he knows: 'I breathe in short', breathing out short, he knows: 'I breathe out short.' He trains: 'I breathe in experiencing the whole body', he trains: 'I breathe out experiencing the whole body.' He trains: 'I breathe in calming the bodily formation'], he trains: 'I breathe out calming the bodily formation.'

"In this way, in regard to the body he abides contemplating the body internally, or in regard to the body he abides contemplating the body externally, or in regard to the body he abides contemplating the body internally and externally. Or he abides contemplating the nature of arising in the body, or he abides contemplating the nature of passing away in the body, or he abides contemplating the nature of arising and passing away in the body. Or mindfulness that 'there is a body' is established in him just for the sake of bare knowledge and for the sake of continuous mindfulness. And he abides independent, not clinging to anything in the world. Monks, this is how a monk in regard to the body abides contemplating the body.

"Again, monks, when walking, a monk knows: 'I am walking'; or when standing, he knows 'I am standing'; or when sitting, [57] he knows 'I am sitting'; or when lying down, he knows: 'I am lying down'; or however his body is disposed, he knows it accordingly.

"In this way, in regard to the body he abides contemplating the body internally, [or in regard to the body he abides contemplating the body externally, or in regard to the body he abides contemplating the body internally and externally. Or he abides contemplating the nature of arising in the body, or he abides contemplating the nature of passing away in the body, or he abides contemplating the nature of arising and passing away in the body. Or mindfulness that 'there is a body' is established in him just for the sake of bare knowledge and for the sake of continuous mindfulness. And he abides independent, not] clinging [to anything in the world]. Monks, this is how a monk in regard to the body abides contemplating the body.

"Again, monks, when going forward and returning a monk acts clearly knowing; when looking ahead and looking away he acts clearly knowing; when flexing and extending [his limbs] he acts clearly knowing; when wearing his outer robe and [other] robes and [carrying] the bowl he acts clearly knowing; when eating, drinking, consuming food and tasting it he acts clearly knowing; when defecating and urinating he acts clearly knowing; when walking, standing, sitting, falling asleep, waking up, talking, and keeping silent he acts clearly knowing.

"In this way, in regard to the body he abides contemplating the body internally, [or in regard to the body he abides contemplating the body externally, or in regard to the body he abides contemplating the body internally and externally. Or he abides contemplating the nature of arising in the body, or he abides contemplating the nature of passing away in the body, or he abides contemplating the nature of arising and passing away in the body. Or mindfulness that 'there is a body' is established in him just for the sake of bare knowledge and for the sake of continuous mindfulness. And he abides independent, not] clinging [to anything in the world]. Monks, this is how a monk in regard to the body abides contemplating the body.

"Again, monks, a monk examines this same body up from the soles of the feet and down from the top of the hair, enclosed by skin and full of many kinds of impurity: 'In this body there are head hairs, body hairs, nails, teeth, skin, flesh, sinews, bones, bone marrow, kidneys, heart, liver, diaphragm, spleen, lungs, bowels, mesentery, contents of the stomach, faeces, bile, phlegm, pus, blood, sweat, fat, tears, grease, spittle, snot, oil of the joints, and urine.'

"Monks, it is just as a man with good eyes who has opened a double-mouthed bag full of different sorts of grain, such as hill rice, red rice, beans, peas, millet, and white rice, which he would examine: 'This is hill rice, this is red rice, these are beans, these are peas, this is millet, and this is white rice.'

"In the same way, monks, a monk examines this same body up from the soles of the feet and down from the top of the hair, enclosed by skin and full of many kinds of impurity: 'In this body there are head hairs, body hairs, nails, teeth, skin, flesh, sinews, bones, bone marrow, kidneys, heart, liver, diaphragm, spleen, lungs, bowels, mesentery, contents of the stomach, faeces, bile, phlegm, pus, blood, sweat, fat, tears, grease, spittle, snot, oil of the joints, and urine.'

"In this way, in regard to the body he abides contemplating the body internally, [or in regard to the body he abides contemplating the body externally, or in regard to the body he abides contemplating the body internally and externally. Or he abides contemplating the nature of arising in the body, or he abides contemplating the nature of passing away in the body, or he abides contemplating the nature of arising and passing away in the body. Or mindfulness that 'there is a body' is established in him just for the sake of bare knowledge and for the sake of continuous mindfulness. And he abides independent, not] clinging [to anything in the world]. Monks, this is how a monk in regard to the body abides contemplating the body.

"Again, monks, a monk examines this same body, however it is placed, however disposed, by way of the elements: 'In this body there are the earth element, the water element, the fire element, and the wind element.' [58]

"Monks, it is just as a skilled butcher or a butcher's apprentice who, having killed a cow, were to be seated at a crossroads with it cut up into pieces.

"In the same way, monks, a monk examines this same body, however it is placed, however disposed, by way of the elements:

'In this body there are the earth element, the water element, the fire element, and the wind element.'

"In this way, in regard to the body he abides contemplating the body internally, [or in regard to the body he abides contemplating the body externally, or in regard to the body he abides contemplating the body internally and externally. Or he abides contemplating the nature of arising in the body, or he abides contemplating the nature of passing away in the body, or he abides contemplating the nature of arising and passing away in the body. Or mindfulness that 'there is a body' is established in him just for the sake of bare knowledge and for the sake of continuous mindfulness. And he abides independent, not] clinging [to anything in the world]. Monks, this is how a monk in regard to the body abides contemplating the body.

"Again, monks, as though a monk were to see a corpse thrown away in a charnel ground that is one, two, or three days dead, being bloated, livid, and oozing matter, and he compares this same body with it: 'This body too is of the same nature, it will be like that, it is not exempt from that fate.'

"In this way, in regard to the body he abides contemplating the body internally, [or in regard to the body he abides contemplating the body externally, or in regard to the body he abides contemplating the body internally and externally. Or he abides contemplating the nature of arising in the body, or he abides contemplating the nature of passing away in the body, or he abides contemplating the nature of arising and passing away in the body. Or mindfulness that 'there is a body' is established in him just for the sake of bare knowledge and for the sake of continuous mindfulness. And he abides independent, not] clinging [to anything in the world]. Monks, this is how a monk in regard to the body abides contemplating the body.

"Again, monks, as though a monk were to see a corpse thrown away in a charnel ground that is being devoured by crows, hawks, vultures, dogs, jackals, or various kinds of worms, and he compares this same body with it: 'This body too is of the same nature, it will be like that, it is not exempt from that fate.'

"In this way, in regard to the body he abides contemplating the body internally, [or in regard to the body he abides contemplating the body externally, or in regard to the body he abides contemplating the body internally and externally. Or he abides contemplating the nature of arising in the body, or he abides contemplating the nature of passing away in the body, or he abides contemplating the nature of arising and passing away in the body. Or mindfulness that 'there is a body' is established in him just for the sake of bare knowledge and for the sake of continuous mindfulness. And he abides independent, not] clinging [to anything in the world]. Monks, this is how a monk in regard to the body abides contemplating the body.

"Again, monks, as though a monk were to see a corpse thrown away in a charnel ground, a skeleton with flesh and blood, held together by the sinews, [and he compares this same body with it: 'This body too is of the same nature, it will be like that, it is not exempt from that fate.'

"In this way, in regard to the body he abides contemplating the body internally, or in regard to the body he abides contemplating the body externally, or in regard to the body he abides contemplating the body internally and externally. Or he abides contemplating the nature of arising in the body, or he abides contemplating the nature of passing away in the body, or he abides contemplating the nature of arising and passing away in the body. Or mindfulness that 'there is a body' is established in him just for the sake of bare knowledge and for the sake of continuous mindfulness. And he abides independent, not clinging to anything in the world. Monks, this is how a monk in regard to the body abides contemplating the body.

"Again, monks, as though a monk were to see a corpse thrown away in a charnel ground], a skeleton without flesh, smeared with blood and held together by the sinews, [and he compares this same body with it: 'This body too is of the same nature, it will be like that, it is not exempt from that fate.'

"In this way, in regard to the body he abides contemplating the body internally, or in regard to the body he abides contemplating the body externally, or in regard to the body he abides contemplating the body internally and externally. Or he abides contemplating the nature of arising in the body, or he abides contemplating the nature of passing away in the body, or he abides contemplating the nature of arising and passing away in the body. Or mindfulness that 'there is a body' is established in him just for the sake of bare knowledge and for the sake of continuous mindfulness. And he abides independent, not clinging to anything in the world. Monks, this is how a monk in regard to the body abides contemplating the body.

"Again, monks, as though a monk were to see a corpse thrown away in a charnel ground], a skeleton without flesh and blood, held together by the sinews, [and he compares this same body with it: 'This body too is of the same nature, it will be like that, it is not exempt from that fate.'

"In this way, in regard to the body he abides contemplating the body internally, or in regard to the body he abides contemplating the body externally, or in regard to the body he abides contemplating the body internally and externally. Or he abides contemplating the nature of arising in the body, or he abides contemplating the nature of passing away in the body, or he abides contemplating the nature of arising and passing away in the body. Or mindfulness that 'there is a body' is established in him just for the sake of bare knowledge and for the sake of continuous mindfulness. And he abides independent, not clinging to anything in the world. Monks, this is how a monk in regard to the body abides contemplating the body.

"Again, monks, as though a monk were to see a corpse thrown away in a charnel ground], disconnected bones scattered in the main and intermediate directions, here a hand bone, elsewhere a foot bone, elsewhere a shin bone, elsewhere a thigh bone, elsewhere a hip bone, elsewhere a back bone, and elsewhere a skull,[3] and he compares this same body with it: 'This body too is of the same nature, it will be like that, it is not exempt from that fate.'

"In this way, in regard to the body he abides contemplating the body internally, [or in regard to the body he abides contemplating the body externally, or in regard to the body he abides contemplating the body internally and externally. Or he abides contemplating the nature of arising in the body, or he abides contemplating the nature of passing away in the body, or he abides contemplating the nature of arising and passing away in the body. Or mindfulness that 'there is a body' is established in him just for the sake of bare knowledge and for the sake of continuous mindfulness. And he abides independent, not] clinging [to anything in the world]. Monks, this is how a monk in regard to the body abides contemplating the body.

"Again, monks, as though a monk were to see a corpse thrown away in a charnel ground, bones bleached white, the colour of shells, [and he compares this same body with it: 'This body too is of the same nature, it will be like that, it is not exempt from that fate.'

3 The Burmese and Siamese editions list additional types of bones.

"In this way, in regard to the body he abides contemplating the body internally, or in regard to the body he abides contemplating the body externally, or in regard to the body he abides contemplating the body internally and externally. Or he abides contemplating the nature of arising in the body, or he abides contemplating the nature of passing away in the body, or he abides contemplating the nature of arising and passing away in the body. Or mindfulness that 'there is a body' is established in him just for the sake of bare knowledge and for the sake of continuous mindfulness. And he abides independent, not clinging to anything in the world. Monks, this is how a monk in regard to the body abides contemplating the body.

"Again, monks, as though a monk were to see a corpse thrown away in a charnel ground], bones heaped up, more than a year old, [and he compares this same body with it: 'This body too is of the same nature, it will be like that, it is not exempt from that fate.'

"In this way, in regard to the body he abides contemplating the body internally, or in regard to the body he abides contemplating the body externally, or in regard to the body he abides contemplating the body internally and externally. Or he abides contemplating the nature of arising in the body, or he abides contemplating the nature of passing away in the body, or he abides contemplating the nature of arising and passing away in the body. Or mindfulness that 'there is a body' is established in him just for the sake of bare knowledge and for the sake of continuous mindfulness. And he abides independent, not clinging to anything in the world. Monks, this is how a monk in regard to the body abides contemplating the body.

"Again, monks, as though a monk were to see a corpse thrown away in a charnel ground], bones rotten and crumbling to dust, [59] and he compares this same body with it: 'This body too is of the same nature, it will be like that, it is not exempt from that fate.'

"In this way, in regard to the body he abides contemplating the body internally, or in regard to the body he abides contemplating the body externally, or in regard to the body he abides contemplating the body internally and externally. Or he abides contemplating the nature of arising in the body, or he abides contemplating the nature of passing away in the body, or he abides contemplating the nature of arising and passing away in the body. Or mindfulness that 'there is a body' is established in him just for the sake of bare knowledge and for the sake of continuous mindfulness. And he abides independent, not clinging to anything in the world. Monks, this is how a monk in regard to the body abides contemplating the body.

"And how, monks, does a monk in regard to feelings abide contemplating feelings? Here, monks, when feeling a pleasant feeling, a monk knows: 'I feel a pleasant feeling'; when feeling a painful feeling, he knows: 'I feel a painful feeling'; when feeling a neutral feeling, he knows: 'I feel a neutral feeling.'

"When feeling a worldly pleasant feeling, he knows: 'I feel a worldly pleasant feeling'; [when feeling] an unworldly pleasant [feeling, he knows: 'I feel an unworldly pleasant feeling'; when feeling] a worldly painful [feeling, he knows: 'I feel a worldly painful feeling'; when feeling] an unworldly painful [feeling, he knows: 'I feel an unworldly painful feeling'; when feeling] a worldly neutral [feeling, he knows: 'I feel a worldly neutral feeling']; when feeling an unworldly neutral feeling, he knows: 'I feel an unworldly neutral feeling.'

"In this way, in regard to feelings he abides contemplating feelings internally, or in regard to feelings he abides contemplating feelings externally, or in regard to feelings he abides contemplating feelings internally and externally. Or he abides contemplating the nature of arising in feelings, or he abides contemplating the nature of passing away in feelings, or he abides contemplating the nature of arising and passing away in feelings. Or mindfulness that 'there is feeling' is established in him just for the sake of bare knowledge and for the sake of continuous mindfulness. And he abides independent, not clinging to anything in the world. Monks, this is how a monk in regard to feelings abides contemplating feelings.

"And how, monks, does a monk in regard to the mind abide contemplating the mind? Here, monks, a monk knows a mind with lust to be 'a mind with lust'; or he knows a mind without lust to be 'a mind without lust'; [or he knows a mind] with anger [to be 'a mind with anger'; or he knows a mind] without anger [to be 'a mind without anger'; or he knows a mind] with delusion [to be 'a mind with delusion'; or he knows a mind] without delusion [to be 'a mind without delusion'; or he knows] a contracted [mind to be 'a contracted mind'; or he knows a] distracted [mind to be 'a distracted mind'.

"Or he knows a mind that has] become great [to be 'a mind that has become great'; or he knows a mind that has] not become great [to be 'a mind that has not become great'; or he knows a] surpassable [mind to be 'a surpassable mind'; or he knows an] unsurpassable [mind to be 'an unsurpassable mind'; or he knows a] concentrated [mind to be 'a concentrated mind'; or he knows a] not concentrated [mind to be 'a not concentrated mind'; or he knows a] liberated [mind to be 'a liberated mind']; or he knows a not liberated mind to be 'a not liberated mind'.

"In this way, in regard to the mind he abides contemplating the mind internally, or in regard to the mind he abides contemplating the mind externally, or in regard to the mind he abides contemplating the mind internally and externally. He abides contemplating the nature of arising in the mind, [60] or he abides contemplating the nature of passing away in the mind, or he abides contemplating the nature of arising and passing away in the mind. Or mindfulness that 'there is a mind' is established in him just for the sake of bare knowledge and for the sake of continuous mindfulness. And he abides independent, not clinging to anything in the world. Monks, this is how in regard to the mind a monk abides contemplating the mind.

"And how, monks, does a monk in regard to dharmas abide contemplating dharmas? Here, monks, in regard to dharmas a monk abides contemplating dharmas with regard to the five hindrances. And how, monks, does a monk in regard to dharmas abide contemplating dharmas with regard to the five hindrances?

"Here, monks, if sensual desire is present within, a monk knows: 'sensual desire is present within me'; or if sensual desire is not present within, he knows: 'sensual desire is not present within me'; and he knows how unarisen sensual desire arises, he knows how arisen sensual desire is removed, and he knows how removed sensual desire does not arise in the future.

"If anger is present within, he knows: 'anger is present within me'; [or if anger is not present within, he knows: 'anger is not present within me'; and he knows how unarisen anger arises, he knows how arisen anger is removed, and he knows how removed anger does not arise in the future].

"If sloth-and-torpor is present within, he knows: 'sloth-and-torpor is present within me'; [or if sloth-and-torpor is not present within, he knows: 'sloth-and-torpor is not present within me'; and he knows how unarisen sloth-and-torpor arises, he knows how arisen sloth-and-torpor is removed, and he knows how removed sloth-and-torpor does not arise in the future].

"If restlessness-and-worry is present within, he knows: 'restlessness-and-worry is present within me'; [or if restlessness-and-worry is not present within, he knows: 'restlessness-and-worry is not present within me'; and he knows how unarisen restlessness-and-worry arises, he knows how arisen restlessness-and-worry is removed, and he knows how removed restlessness-and-worry does not arise in the future].

"If doubt is present within, he knows: 'doubt is present within me'; or if doubt is not present within, he knows: 'doubt is not present within me'; and he knows how unarisen doubt arises, he knows how arisen doubt is removed, and he knows how removed doubt does not arise in the future.

"In this way, in regard to dharmas he abides contemplating dharmas internally, or in regard to dharmas he abides contemplating dharmas externally, or in regard to dharmas he abides contemplating dharmas internally and externally. Or he abides contemplating the nature of arising in dharmas, or he abides contemplating the nature of passing away in dharmas, or he abides contemplating the nature of arising and passing away in dharmas. Or mindfulness that 'there are dharmas' is established in him just for the sake of bare knowledge and for the sake of continuous mindfulness. And he abides independent, not clinging to anything in the world. Monks, this is how in regard to dharmas a monk abides contemplating dharmas with regard to the five hindrances.

"Again, monks, in regard to dharmas a monk abides contemplating dharmas with regard to the five aggregates of clinging. [61] And how, monks, does a monk in regard to dharmas abide contemplating dharmas with regard to the five aggregates of clinging?

"Here, monks, a monk knows: 'such is material form', 'such is the arising of material form', 'such is the passing away of material form'; 'such is feeling', 'such is the arising of feeling', 'such is the passing away of feeling'; 'such is perception', 'such is the arising of perception', 'such is the passing away of perception'; 'such are volitional formations', 'such is the arising of volitional formations', 'such is the passing away of volitional formations'; 'such is consciousness', 'such is the arising of consciousness', 'such is the passing away of consciousness.'

"In this way, in regard to dharmas he abides contemplating dharmas internally, [or in regard to dharmas he abides contemplating dharmas externally, or in regard to dharmas he abides contemplating dharmas internally and externally. Or he abides contemplating the nature of arising in dharmas, or he abides contemplating the nature of passing away in dharmas, or he abides contemplating the nature of arising and passing away in dharmas. Or mindfulness that 'there are dharmas' is established in him just for the sake of bare knowledge and for the sake of continuous mindfulness. And he abides independent, not] clinging [to anything in the world]. Monks, this is how in regard to dharmas a monk abides contemplating dharmas with regard to the five aggregates of clinging.

"Again, monks, in regard to dharmas a monk abides contemplating dharmas with regard to the six internal and external sense-spheres. And how, monks, does a monk in regard to dharmas abide contemplating dharmas with regard to the six internal and external sense-spheres?

"Here, monks, a monk knows the eye, he knows forms, and he knows the fetter that arises dependent on both; and he knows how an unarisen fetter arises, he knows how an arisen fetter is removed, and he knows how a removed fetter does not arise in the future.

"He knows the ear, he knows sounds, [and he knows the fetter that arises dependent on both; and he knows how an unarisen fetter arises, he knows how an arisen fetter is removed, and he knows how a removed fetter does not arise in the future].

"He knows the nose, he knows odours, [and he knows the fetter that arises dependent on both; and he knows how an unarisen fetter arises, he knows how an arisen fetter is removed, and he knows how a removed fetter does not arise in the future].

"He knows the tongue, he knows flavours, [and he knows the fetter that arises dependent on both; and he knows how an unarisen fetter arises, he knows how an arisen fetter is removed, and he knows how a removed fetter does not arise in the future].

"He knows the body, he knows tangibles, [and he knows the fetter that arises dependent on both; and he knows how an unarisen fetter arises, he knows how an arisen fetter is removed, and he knows how a removed fetter does not arise in the future].

"He knows the mind, he knows mind-objects, and he knows the fetter that arises dependent on both; and he knows how an unarisen fetter arises, he knows how an arisen fetter is removed, and he knows how a removed fetter does not arise in the future.

"In this way, in regard to dharmas he abides contemplating dharmas internally, [or in regard to dharmas he abides contemplating dharmas externally, or in regard to dharmas he abides contemplating dharmas internally and externally. Or he abides contemplating the nature of arising in dharmas, or he abides contemplating the nature of passing away in dharmas, or he abides contemplating the nature of arising and passing away in dharmas. Or mindfulness that 'there are dharmas' is established in him just for the sake of bare knowledge and for the sake of continuous mindfulness. And he abides independent, not] clinging [to anything in the world]. Monks, this is how in regard to dharmas a monk abides contemplating dharmas with regard to the six internal and external sense-spheres.

"Again, monks, in regard to dharmas a monk abides contemplating dharmas with regard to the seven awakening factors. And how, monks, does a monk in regard to dharmas abide contemplating dharmas with regard to the seven awakening factors?

"Here, monks, if the mindfulness awakening factor is present within, a monk knows: 'the mindfulness awakening factor is present within me'; or if the mindfulness awakening factor is not present within, he knows: 'the mindfulness awakening factor is not present within me'; [62] and he knows how the unarisen mindfulness awakening factor arises, and he knows how the arisen mindfulness awakening factor is perfected by development.

"If the investigation-of-dharmas awakening factor is present within, [he knows: 'the investigation-of-dharmas awakening factor is present within me'; or if the investigation-of-dharmas awakening factor is not present within, he knows: 'the investigation-of-dharmas awakening factor is not present within me'; and he knows how the unarisen investigation-of-dharmas awakening factor arises, and he knows how the arisen investigation-of-dharmas awakening factor is perfected by development].

"If the energy awakening factor is present within, [he knows: 'the energy awakening factor is present within me'; or if the energy awakening factor is not present within, he knows: 'the energy awakening factor is not present within me'; and he knows how the unarisen energy awakening factor arises, and he knows how the arisen energy awakening factor is perfected by development].

"If the joy awakening factor is present within, [he knows: 'the joy awakening factor is present within me'; or if the joy awakening factor is not present within, he knows: 'the joy awakening factor is not present within me'; and he knows how the unarisen joy awakening factor arises, and he knows how the arisen joy awakening factor is perfected by development].

"If the tranquillity awakening factor is present within, [he knows: 'the tranquillity awakening factor is present within me'; or if the tranquillity awakening factor is not present within, he knows: 'the tranquillity awakening factor is not present within me'; and he knows how the unarisen tranquillity awakening factor arises, and he knows how the arisen tranquillity awakening factor is perfected by development].

"If the concentration awakening factor is present within, [he knows: 'the concentration awakening factor is present within me'; or if the concentration awakening factor is not present within, he knows: 'the concentration awakening factor is not present within me'; and he knows how the unarisen concentration awakening factor arises, and he knows how the arisen concentration awakening factor is perfected by development].

"If the equanimity awakening factor is present within, he knows: 'the equanimity awakening factor is present within me'; or if the equanimity awakening factor is not present within, he knows: 'the equanimity awakening factor is not present within me'; and he knows how the unarisen equanimity awakening factor arises, and he knows how the arisen equanimity awakening factor is perfected by development.

"In this way, in regard to dharmas he abides contemplating dharmas internally, [or in regard to dharmas he abides contemplating dharmas externally, or in regard to dharmas he abides contemplating dharmas internally and externally. Or he abides contemplating the nature of arising in dharmas, or he abides contemplating the nature of passing away in dharmas, or he abides contemplating the nature of arising and passing away in dharmas. Or mindfulness that 'there are dharmas' is established in him just for the sake of bare knowledge and for the sake of continuous mindfulness. And he abides independent, not] clinging [to anything in the world]. Monks, this is how in regard to dharmas a monk abides contemplating dharmas with regard to the seven awakening factors.

"Again, monks, in regard to dharmas a monk abides contemplating dharmas with regard to the four noble truths. And how, monks, does a monk in regard to dharmas abide contemplating dharmas with regard to the four noble truths?

"Here, monks, a monk knows as it really is: 'this is *dukkha*'; he knows as it really is: 'this is the arising of *dukkha*'; he knows as it really is: 'this is the cessation of *dukkha*'; he knows as it really is: 'this is the path leading to the cessation of *dukkha*.'

"In this way, in regard to dharmas he abides contemplating dharmas internally, or in regard to dharmas he abides contemplating dharmas externally, or in regard to dharmas he abides contemplating dharmas internally and externally. Or he abides contemplating the nature of arising in dharmas, or he abides contemplating the nature of passing away in dharmas, or he abides contemplating the nature of arising and passing away in dharmas. Or mindfulness that 'there are dharmas' is established in him just for the sake of bare knowledge and for the sake of continuous mindfulness. And he abides independent, not clinging to anything in the world. Monks, this is how in regard to dharmas a monk abides contemplating dharmas with regard to the four noble truths.

"Monks, if anyone should develop these four *satipaṭṭhāna*s in such a way for seven years, one of two fruits can be expected for him: either final knowledge here and now, or, if there is a trace of clinging left, non-returning.

"Monks, let alone seven years, if anyone should develop these four *satipaṭṭhāna*s in such a way for six years, [63] [one of two fruits can be expected for him: either final knowledge here and now, or, if there is a trace of clinging left, non-returning.

"Monks, let alone six years, if anyone should develop these four *satipaṭṭhāna*s in such a way] for five years, [one of two fruits can be expected for him: either final knowledge here and now, or, if there is a trace of clinging left, non-returning.

"Monks, let alone five years, if anyone should develop these four *satipaṭṭhāna*s in such a way] for four years, [one of two fruits can be expected for him: either final knowledge here and now, or, if there is a trace of clinging left, non-returning.

"Monks, let alone four years, if anyone should develop these four *satipaṭṭhāna*s in such a way] for three years, [one of two fruits can be expected for him: either final knowledge here and now, or, if there is a trace of clinging left, non-returning.

"Monks, let alone three years, if anyone should develop these four *satipaṭṭhāna*s in such a way] for two years, [one of two fruits can be expected for him: either final knowledge here and now, or, if there is a trace of clinging left, non-returning.

"Monks, let alone two years, if anyone should develop these four *satipaṭṭhāna*s in such a way] for one year, [one of two fruits can be expected for him: either final knowledge here and now, or, if there is a trace of clinging left, non-returning].

"Monks, let alone one year, if anyone should develop these four *satipaṭṭhāna*s in such a way for seven months, one of two fruits can be expected for him: either final knowledge here and now, or, if there is a trace of clinging left, non-returning.

"Monks, let alone seven months, if anyone should develop these four *satipaṭṭhāna*s in such a way for six months, [one of two fruits can be expected for him: either final knowledge here and now, or, if there is a trace of clinging left, non-returning.

"Monks, let alone six months, if anyone should develop these four *satipaṭṭhāna*s in such a way] for five months, [one of two fruits can be expected for him: either final knowledge here and now, or, if there is a trace of clinging left, non-returning.

"Monks, let alone five months, if anyone should develop these four *satipaṭṭhāna*s in such a way] for four months, [one of two fruits can be expected for him: either final knowledge here and now, or, if there is a trace of clinging left, non-returning.

"Monks, let alone four months, if anyone should develop these four *satipaṭṭhāna*s in such a way] for three months, [one of two fruits can be expected for him: either final knowledge here and now, or, if there is a trace of clinging left, non-returning.

"Monks, let alone three months, if anyone should develop these four *satipaṭṭhāna*s in such a way] for two months, [one of two fruits can be expected for him: either final knowledge here and now, or, if there is a trace of clinging left, non-returning.

"Monks, let alone two months, if anyone should develop these four *satipaṭṭhāna*s in such a way] for one month, [one of two fruits can be expected for him: either final knowledge here and now, or, if there is a trace of clinging left, non-returning.

"Monks, let alone one month, if anyone should develop these four *satipaṭṭhāna*s in such a way] for half a month, [one of two fruits can be expected for him: either final knowledge here and now, or, if there is a trace of clinging left, non-returning].

"Monks, let alone half a month, if anyone should develop these four *satipaṭṭhāna*s in such a way for seven days, one of two fruits can be expected for him: either final knowledge here and now, or, if there is a trace of clinging left, non-returning.

"So it was with reference to this that it was said: 'Monks, this is the direct path for the purification of beings, for the surmounting of sorrow and lamentation, for the disappearance of *dukkha* and discontent, for acquiring the true method, for the realization of Nirvāṇa, namely, the four *satipaṭṭhāna*s.'"

This is what the Blessed One said. The monks were glad and delighted in the Blessed One's words.

XIII.2 MADHYAMA-ĀGAMA

THE DISCOURSE ON SATIPAṬṬHĀNA[4]

Thus have I heard. On one occasion the Buddha was living among the Kurus, at a town of the Kurus [called] Kammāsadhamma.

At that time the Blessed One told the monks: "There is one path for the purification of beings, for going beyond sorrow and fear, for eradicating *dukkha* and distress, for abandoning weeping and tears, for attaining the right Dharma, namely the four *satipaṭṭhāna*s.

"Whatever Tathāgatas there were in the past, free from attachment and fully awakened, they all attained unsurpassable and complete awakening by abandoning the five hindrances, which defile the mind and weaken wisdom, by dwelling with the mind well established in the four *satipaṭṭhāna*s, and by cultivating the seven factors of awakening.

"Whatever Tathāgatas there will be in the future, free from attachment and fully awakened, they will all attain unsurpassable and complete awakening by abandoning the five hindrances, which defile the mind and weaken wisdom, by dwelling with the mind well established in the four *satipaṭṭhāna*s, and by cultivating the seven factors of awakening.

"Now I, being the Tathāgata of the present, free from attachment and fully awakened, have attained unsurpassable and complete awakening by abandoning the five hindrances, which defile the mind

4 MĀ 98 at T I 582b7 to 584b28; which has already been translated into English by Minh Chau 1964/1991: 87–95, Saddhāloka 1983: 9–15, Nhat Hanh 1990: 151–67, and Kuan 2008: 146–54.

and weaken wisdom, by dwelling with the mind well established in the four *satipaṭṭhānas*, and by cultivating the seven factors of awakening.

"What are the four? [They are] the *satipaṭṭhāna* of contemplating the body as a body, in the same way [the *satipaṭṭhāna*] of contemplating feelings [as feelings], [the *satipaṭṭhāna* of contemplating] mind [as mind], and the *satipaṭṭhāna* of contemplating dharmas as dharmas.

"What is the *satipaṭṭhāna* of contemplating the body as a body? Walking a monk knows he is walking, standing he knows he is standing, sitting he knows he is sitting, lying down he knows he is lying down, [falling] asleep he knows he is [falling] asleep, waking up he knows he is waking up, [falling] asleep [or] waking up he knows he is [falling] asleep [or] waking up.

"In this way a monk contemplates the body as a body internally and contemplates the body as a body externally. He establishes mindfulness in the body and is endowed with knowledge, vision, understanding, and penetration. This is reckoned how a monk contemplates the body as a body.

"Again a monk contemplates the body as a body: a monk clearly knows he is going out and coming in, he contemplates and discerns it well; bending, stretching, lowering, or raising [any of his limbs], he does it with appropriate deportment; wearing his outer robe and [other] robes, and [carrying his] bowl, he does it properly; walking, standing, sitting, lying down, [falling] asleep, waking up, talking and keeping silent – all this he clearly knows.

"In this way a monk contemplates the body as a body internally and contemplates the body as a body externally. He establishes mindfulness in the body and is endowed with knowledge, vision, understanding, and penetration. This is reckoned how a monk contemplates the body as a body.

"Again a monk contemplates the body as a body: [582c] [when] evil and unwholesome thoughts arise, a monk rectifies, abandons, eradicates, and stops them by recollecting wholesome states.

"It is just as a carpenter or a carpenter's apprentice who might apply an inked string to a piece of wood [to mark a straight line] and then cut the wood with a sharp adze to make it straight. In the same way, [when] evil and unwholesome thoughts arise, a monk rectifies, abandons, eradicates, and stops them by recollecting wholesome states.

"In this way a monk contemplates the body as a body internally and contemplates the body as a body externally. He establishes mindfulness in the body and is endowed with knowledge, vision, understanding, and penetration. This is reckoned how a monk contemplates the body as a body.

"Again a monk contemplates the body as a body: with teeth clenched and tongue pressed against his palate a monk uses [the will-power of his own] mind to rectify his mind, to rectify, abandon, eradicate, and stop [evil thoughts].

"It is just as two strong men who might grab a weak man and, turning him this way and that way, might beat him up as they wish. In the same way with teeth clenched and tongue pressed against his palate a monk uses [the will-power of his own] mind to rectify his mind, to rectify, abandon, eradicate, and stop [evil thoughts].

"In this way a monk contemplates the body as a body internally and contemplates the body as a body externally. He establishes mindfulness in the body and is endowed with knowledge, vision, understanding, and penetration. This is reckoned how a monk contemplates the body as a body.

"Again a monk contemplates the body as a body: a monk is mindful of breathing in and knows he is breathing in mindfully; he is mindful of breathing out and knows he is breathing out mindfully.

"Breathing in long, he knows he is breathing in long; breathing out long, he knows he is breathing out long. Breathing in short, he knows he is breathing in short; breathing out short, he knows he is breathing out short. He trains [in experiencing] the whole body when breathing in; he trains [in experiencing] the whole body when breathing out. He trains in calming bodily formations when breathing in; he trains in calming bodily formations when breathing out.[5]

"In this way a monk contemplates the body as a body internally and contemplates the body as a body externally. He establishes mindfulness in the body and is endowed with knowledge, vision, understanding, and penetration. This is reckoned how a monk contemplates the body as a body.

"Again a monk contemplates the body as a body: a monk completely drenches and pervades his body with joy and happiness

---

5 The present passage actually speaks of the "verbal formations" when breathing out, which clearly seems to be a textual error, hence I have emended this to read "bodily formations", in line with what is to be experienced when breathing in.

born of seclusion [experienced in the first absorption], so that there is no part within his body that is not pervaded by joy and happiness born of seclusion.

"It is just as a bath attendant who, having filled a vessel with bathing powder, mixes it with water and kneads it, so that there is no part [of the powder] that is not completely drenched and pervaded with water.

"In the same way a monk completely drenches and pervades his body with joy and happiness born of seclusion, so that there is no part within his body that is not pervaded by joy and happiness born of seclusion.

"In this way a monk contemplates the body as a body internally and contemplates the body as a body externally. He establishes mindfulness in the body and is endowed with knowledge, vision, understanding, and penetration. This is reckoned how a monk contemplates the body as a body.

"Again a monk contemplates the body as a body: a monk completely drenches and pervades his body with joy and happiness born of concentration [experienced in the second absorption], so that there is no part within his body that is not pervaded by joy and happiness born of concentration.

"It is just as a mountain spring that is full and overflowing with clear and clean water, [583a] so that water coming from any of the four directions cannot enter it, with the spring water welling up from the bottom on its own, flowing out and flooding the surroundings, completely drenching every part of the mountain so that there is no part that is not pervaded by it.

"In the same way a monk completely drenches and pervades his body with joy and happiness born of concentration so that there is no part within his body that is not pervaded by joy and happiness born of concentration.

"In this way a monk contemplates the body as a body internally and contemplates the body as a body externally. He establishes mindfulness in the body and is endowed with knowledge, vision, understanding, and penetration. This is reckoned how a monk contemplates the body as a body.

"Again a monk contemplates the body as a body: a monk completely drenches and pervades his body with happiness born of the absence of joy [experienced in the third absorption], so that there is no part within his body that is not pervaded by happiness born of the absence of joy.

"It is just as a blue, red, or white lotus, being born in the water and having come to growth in the water, remains submerged in water, with every part of its roots, stem, flower, and leaves completely drenched and pervaded [by water], so that there is no part that is not pervaded by it.

"In the same way a monk completely drenches and pervades his body with happiness born of the absence of joy so that there is no part within his body that is not pervaded by happiness born of the absence of joy.

"In this way a monk contemplates the body as a body internally and contemplates the body as a body externally. He establishes mindfulness in the body and is endowed with knowledge, vision, understanding, and penetration. This is reckoned how a monk contemplates the body as a body.

"Again a monk contemplates the body as a body: a monk mentally resolves to dwell having accomplished a complete pervasion of his body with mental purity [experienced in the fourth absorption], so that there is no part within his body that is not pervaded by mental purity.

"It is just as a man who covers himself from head to foot with a cloth measuring seven or eight units, so that no part of his body is not covered.

"In the same way a monk completely pervades his body with mental purity [experienced in the fourth absorption], so that there is no part within his body that is not pervaded by mental purity.

"In this way a monk contemplates the body as a body internally and contemplates the body as a body externally. He establishes mindfulness in the body and is endowed with knowledge, vision, understanding, and penetration. This is reckoned how a monk contemplates the body as a body.

"Again a monk contemplates the body as a body: a monk is mindful of the perception of light, properly taking hold of it, properly retaining it, and properly recollecting what he is mindful of, [so that] what is behind is like what is in front, what is in front is like what is behind, night is like day, day is like night, what is above is like what is below, and what is below is like what is above. In this way he cultivates an undistorted and undefiled mind, a mind that is bright and clear, a mind that is not at all obscured by impediments.

"In this way a monk contemplates the body as a body internally and contemplates the body as a body externally. He establishes mindfulness in the body and is endowed with knowledge, vision, understanding, and penetration. This is reckoned how a monk contemplates the body as a body.

"Again a monk contemplates the body as a body: a monk properly holds [in mind] the reviewing sign, recollecting properly what he is mindful of.

"It is just as a person who is seated and contemplates another person who is lying down, [583b] or while lying down contemplates another person who is seated. In the same way a monk properly holds [in mind] the reviewing sign, recollecting properly what he is mindful of.

"In this way a monk contemplates the body as a body internally and contemplates the body as a body externally. He establishes mindfulness in the body and is endowed with knowledge, vision, understanding, and penetration. This is reckoned how a monk contemplates the body as a body.

"Again a monk contemplates the body as a body: a monk contemplates this body, according to its position and according to what is attractive and what is repulsive, from head to foot, seeing that it is full of various kinds of impurities: 'Within this body of mine there are head hairs, body hairs, nails, teeth, rough and smooth epidermis,[6] skin, flesh, sinews, bones, heart, kidneys, liver, lungs, large intestine, small intestine, spleen, stomach, lumps of faeces, brain and brain stem,[7] tears, sweat, saliva,[8] pus, blood, fat, marrow, mucus, phlegm,[9] and urine.'

"It is just as a clear-sighted person who, on seeing a vessel full of various seeds, clearly distinguishes them all, that is, 'rice, millet seed, turnip seed, or mustard seed'.

---

6 Regarding the present reference to "rough and smooth epidermis", Glass 2007: 153ff suggests the original sense could have been "tendons and vein network".

7 Kuan 2008: 211 n.28 notes an explanation according to which the characters rendered above as "brain stem" would refer to the occipital bone.

8 My rendering follows a suggestion by Glass 2007: 162 to read as one anatomical part what according to the punctuation in the Taishō edition would be two parts.

9 With the translation "phlegm" I follow Kuan 2008: 211 n.29.

"In the same way a monk contemplates this body from head to foot, according to its position and according to what is attractive and what is repulsive, seeing that it is full of various kinds of impurities: 'Within this body of mine there are head hairs, body hairs, nails, teeth, rough and smooth epidermis, skin, flesh, sinews, bones, heart, kidneys, liver, lungs, large intestine, small intestine, spleen, stomach, lumps of faeces, brain and brain stem, tears, sweat, mucus, saliva, pus, blood, fat, marrow, mucus, phlegm, and urine.'

"In this way a monk contemplates the body as a body internally and contemplates the body as a body externally. He establishes mindfulness in the body and is endowed with knowledge, vision, understanding, and penetration. This is reckoned how a monk contemplates the body as a body.

"Again a monk contemplates the body as a body: a monk contemplates the body's elements: 'Within this body of mine there are the earth element, the water element, the fire element, the wind element, the space element, and the consciousness element.'

"It is just as a butcher who, on having slaughtered and skinned a cow, divides it into six parts and spreads them on the ground [for sale].

"In the same way a monk contemplates the body's elements: 'Within this body of mine there are the earth element, the water element, the fire element, the wind element, the space element, and the consciousness element.'

"In this way a monk contemplates the body as a body internally and contemplates the body as a body externally. He establishes mindfulness in the body and is endowed with knowledge, vision, understanding, and penetration. This is reckoned how a monk contemplates the body as a body.

"Again a monk contemplates the body as a body: a monk contemplates a corpse dead for one or two days, or up to six or seven days, that is being pecked at by crows, devoured by jackals and wolves, burned by fire, or buried in the earth, or that is completely rotten and decomposed. Having seen this, he compares himself to it: 'This present body of mine is also like this. It is of the same nature and in the end cannot escape [this fate].'

"In this way a monk contemplates the body as a body internally and contemplates the body as a body externally. He establishes mindfulness in the body and is endowed with knowledge, vision, understanding, and penetration. This is reckoned how a monk contemplates the body as a body.

"Again a monk contemplates the body as a body: [583c] similar to what he has formerly seen in a charnel ground, so a monk [recollects] a carcass of bluish colour, decomposed and half eaten [by animals], with the bones lying on the ground still connected together. Having seen this, he compares himself to it: 'This present body of mine is also like this. It is of the same nature and in the end cannot escape [this fate].'

"In this way a monk contemplates the body as a body internally and contemplates the body as a body externally. He establishes mindfulness in the body and is endowed with knowledge, vision, understanding, and penetration. This is reckoned how a monk contemplates the body as a body.

"Again a monk contemplates the body as a body: similar to what he has formerly seen in a charnel ground, so a monk [recollects a skeleton] without skin, flesh, or blood, held together only by sinews. Having seen this, he compares himself to it: 'This present body of mine is also like this. It is of the same nature and in the end cannot escape [this fate].'

"In this way a monk contemplates the body as a body internally and contemplates the body as a body externally. He establishes mindfulness in the body and is endowed with knowledge, vision, understanding, and penetration. This is reckoned how a monk contemplates the body as a body.

"Again a monk contemplates the body as a body: similar to what he has formerly seen in a charnel ground, so a monk [recollects] disconnected bones scattered in all directions: foot bones, shin bones, thigh bones, a hip bone, vertebrae, shoulder bones, neck bones, and a skull, all in different places. Having seen this, he compares himself to it: 'This present body of mine is also like this. It is of the same nature and in the end cannot escape [this fate].'

"In this way a monk contemplates the body as a body internally and contemplates the body as a body externally. He establishes mindfulness in the body and is endowed with knowledge, vision, understanding, and penetration. This is reckoned how a monk contemplates the body as a body.

"Again a monk contemplates the body as a body: similar to what he has formerly seen in a charnel ground, so a monk [recollects] bones white like shells, or bluish like the colour of a pigeon, or red as if smeared with blood, rotting and decomposing, crumbling to dust. Having seen this, he compares himself to it: 'This present body of mine is also like this. It is of the same nature and in the end cannot escape [this fate].'

"In this way a monk contemplates the body as a body internally and contemplates the body as a body externally. He establishes mindfulness in the body and is endowed with knowledge, vision, understanding, and penetration. This is reckoned how a monk contemplates the body as a body.

If a monk or a nun contemplates the body as a body in this way even for a short time, then this is what is reckoned to be the *satipaṭṭhāna* of contemplating the body as a body.

"What is the *satipaṭṭhāna* of contemplating feelings as feelings? At the time of experiencing a pleasant feeling, a monk then knows he is experiencing a pleasant feeling; at the time of experiencing a painful feeling, he then knows he is experiencing a painful feeling; at the time of experiencing a neutral feeling, he then knows he is experiencing a neutral feeling.

"At the time of experiencing a pleasant bodily feeling, [he then knows he is experiencing a pleasant bodily feeling; at the time of experiencing] a painful bodily [feeling, he then knows he is experiencing a painful bodily feeling; at the time of experiencing] a neutral bodily [feeling, he then knows he is experiencing a neutral bodily feeling; at the time of experiencing] a pleasant mental [feeling, he then knows he is experiencing a pleasant mental feeling; at the time of experiencing] a painful mental [feeling, he then knows he is experiencing a painful mental feeling; at the time of experiencing] a neutral mental [feeling, he then knows he is experiencing a neutral mental feeling.

"At the time of experiencing] a pleasant worldly [feeling, he then knows he is experiencing a pleasant worldly feeling; at the time of experiencing] a painful worldly [feeling, he then knows he is experiencing a painful worldly feeling; at the time of experiencing] a neutral worldly [feeling, he then knows he is experiencing a neutral worldly feeling; at the time of experiencing] a pleasant unworldly [feeling, he then knows he is experiencing a pleasant unworldly feeling; at the time of experiencing] a painful unworldly [feeling, he then knows he is experiencing a painful unworldly feeling; at the time of experiencing] a neutral unworldly [feeling, he then knows he is experiencing a neutral unworldly feeling.

"At the time of experiencing] a pleasant sensual [feeling, he then knows he is experiencing a pleasant sensual feeling; at the time of experiencing] a painful sensual [feeling, he then knows he is experiencing a painful sensual feeling; [584a] at the time of experiencing] a neutral sensual [feeling, he then knows he is experiencing a neutral sensual feeling; at the time of experiencing] a pleasant non-sensual [feeling, he then knows he is experiencing a pleasant non-sensual feeling; at the time of experiencing] a painful non-sensual feeling, [he then knows he is experiencing a painful non-sensual feeling], at the time of experiencing a neutral non-sensual feeling, he then knows he is experiencing a neutral non-sensual feeling.

"In this way a monk contemplates feelings as feelings internally and he contemplates feelings as feelings externally. He establishes mindfulness in feelings and is endowed with knowledge, vision, understanding, and penetration. This is reckoned how a monk contemplates feelings as feelings. If a monk or a nun contemplates feelings as feelings in this way even for a short time, then this is reckoned the *satipaṭṭhāna* of contemplating feelings as feelings.

"What is the *satipaṭṭhāna* of contemplating mind as mind? Having a mind with sensual desire a monk knows, as it really is, that he has a mind with sensual desire; having a mind without sensual desire he knows, as it really is, that he has a mind without sensual desire.

"Having a mind with anger, [he knows, as it really is, that he has a mind with anger]; having [a mind] without anger, [he knows, as it really is, that he has a mind without anger].

"Having a mind with delusion, [he knows, as it really is, that he has a mind with delusion]; having [a mind] without delusion [he knows, as it really is, that he has a mind without delusion].

"Having a defiled [mind he knows, as it really is, that he has a defiled mind]; having an undefiled [mind he knows, as it really is, that he has an undefiled mind].

"Having a contracted [mind he knows, as it really is, that he has a contracted mind]; having a distracted [mind he knows, as it really is, that he has a distracted mind].

"Having an inferior [mind he knows, as it really is, that he has an inferior mind]; having a superior [mind he knows, as it really is, that he has a superior mind].

"Having a narrow [mind he knows, as it really is, that he has a narrow mind]; having a great [mind he knows, as it really is, that he has a great mind.

"Having a] cultivated [mind he knows, as it really is, that he has a cultivated mind; having an] uncultivated [mind he knows, as it really is, that he has an uncultivated mind.

"Having a] concentrated [mind he knows, as it really is, that he has a concentrated mind; having a] not concentrated [mind he knows, as it really is, that he has a not concentrated mind].

"Having a not liberated mind he knows, as it really is, that he has a not liberated mind; having a liberated mind he knows, as it really is, that he has a liberated mind.

"In this way a monk contemplates the mind as mind internally and he contemplates the mind as mind externally. He establishes mindfulness in the mind and is endowed with knowledge, vision, understanding, and penetration. This is reckoned how a monk contemplates mind as mind. If a monk or a nun contemplates the mind as mind in this way even for a short time, then this is reckoned the *satipaṭṭhāna* of contemplating mind as mind.

"What is the *satipaṭṭhāna* of contemplating dharmas as dharmas? In dependence on the eye and forms a fetter arises internally. Actually having a fetter internally, a monk knows, as it really is, that he has a fetter internally; actually not having a fetter internally, a monk knows, as it really is, that he does not have a fetter internally. He knows, as it really is, how an unarisen fetter arises internally; and he knows, as it really is, how an internally arisen fetter ceases and does not arise again.

"In the same way [in dependence on] the ear [and sounds a fetter arises internally. Actually having a fetter internally, a monk knows, as it really is, that he has a fetter internally; actually not having a fetter internally, a monk knows, as it really is, that he does not have a fetter internally. He knows, as it really is, how an unarisen fetter arises internally; and he knows, as it really is, how an internally arisen fetter ceases and does not arise again.

"In dependence on] the nose [and odours a fetter arises internally. Actually having a fetter internally, a monk knows, as it really is, that he has a fetter internally; actually not having a fetter internally, a monk knows, as it really is, that he does not have a fetter internally. He knows, as it really is, how an unarisen fetter arises internally;

and he knows, as it really is, how an internally arisen fetter ceases and does not arise again.

"In dependence on] the tongue [and flavours a fetter arises internally. Actually having a fetter internally, a monk knows, as it really is, that he has a fetter internally; actually not having a fetter internally, a monk knows, as it really is, that he does not have a fetter internally. He knows, as it really is, how an unarisen fetter arises internally; and he knows, as it really is, how an internally arisen fetter ceases and does not arise again.

"In dependence on] the body [and tangibles a fetter arises internally. Actually having a fetter internally, a monk knows, as it really is, that he has a fetter internally; actually not having a fetter internally, a monk knows, as it really is, that he does not have a fetter internally. He knows, as it really is, how an unarisen fetter arises internally; and he knows, as it really is, how an internally arisen fetter ceases and does not arise again].

"In dependence on the mind and mind-objects a fetter arises internally. Actually having a fetter internally, a monk knows, as it really is, that he has a fetter internally; actually not having a fetter internally, a monk knows, as it really is, that he does not have a fetter internally. He knows, as it really is, how an unarisen fetter arises internally; and he knows, as it really is, how an internally arisen fetter ceases and does not arise again.

"In this way a monk contemplates dharmas as dharmas internally and contemplates dharmas as dharmas externally. He establishes mindfulness in dharmas and is endowed with knowledge, vision, understanding, and penetration. This is reckoned how a monk contemplates dharmas as dharmas, namely [in relation] to the six internal [sense-]spheres.

"Again a monk contemplates dharmas as dharmas: actually having sensual desire internally, a monk knows, as it really is, that he has sensual desire; actually having no sensual desire internally, he knows, as it really is, that he has no sensual desire. He knows, as it really is, how unarisen sensual desire arises; and he knows, as it really is, how arisen sensual desire ceases and does not arise again.

"In the same way, [actually having] anger [internally he knows, as it really is, that he has anger; actually having no anger internally, he knows, as it really is, that he has no anger. He knows, as it really is, how unarisen anger arises; and he knows, as it really is, how arisen anger ceases and does not arise again.

"Actually having] sloth-and-torpor [internally he knows, as it really is, that he has sloth-and-torpor; actually having no sloth-and-torpor internally, he knows, as it really is, that he has no sloth-and-torpor. He knows, as it really is, how unarisen sloth-and-torpor arises; and he knows, as it really is, how sloth-and-torpor ceases and does not arise again.

"Actually having] restlessness-and-worry [internally he knows, as it really is, that he has restlessness-and-worry; actually having no restlessness-and-worry internally, he knows, as it really is, that he has no restlessness-and-worry. He knows, as it really is, how unarisen restlessness-and-worry arises; and he knows, as it really is, how arisen restlessness-and-worry ceases and does not arise again].

"Actually having doubt internally, he knows, as it really is, that he has doubt; actually having no doubt internally, he knows, as it really is, that he has no doubt. He knows, as it really is, how unarisen doubt arises; and he knows, as it really is, how arisen doubt ceases and does not arise again. [584b]

"In this way a monk contemplates dharmas as dharmas internally and he contemplates dharmas as dharmas externally. He establishes mindfulness in dharmas and is endowed with knowledge, vision, understanding, and penetration. This is reckoned how a monk contemplates dharmas as dharmas, namely [in relation] to the five hindrances.

"Again a monk contemplates dharmas as dharmas: actually having the mindfulness awakening factor within, a monk knows, as it really is, that he has the mindfulness awakening factor; actually not having the mindfulness awakening factor within, he knows, as it really is, that he does not have the mindfulness awakening factor. He knows, as it really is, how the unarisen mindfulness awakening factor arises; and he knows, as it really is, how the arisen mindfulness awakening factor is maintained without loss or deterioration, and how it is further developed and increased.

"In the same way, actually having the investigation-of-dharmas [awakening factor within, he knows, as it really is, that he has the investigation-of-dharmas awakening factor; actually not having the investigation-of-dharmas awakening factor within, he knows, as it really is, that he does not have the investigation-of-dharmas awakening factor. He knows, as it really is, how the unarisen investigation-of-dharmas awakening factor arises; and he knows, as it really is, how the arisen investigation-of-dharmas awakening factor is maintained without loss or deterioration, and how it is further developed and increased.

"Actually having] the energy [awakening factor within, he knows, as it really is, that he has the energy awakening factor; actually not having the energy awakening factor within, he knows, as it really is, that he does not have the energy awakening factor. He knows, as it really is, how the unarisen energy awakening factor arises; and he knows, as it really is, how the arisen energy awakening factor is maintained without loss or deterioration, and how it is further developed and increased.

"Actually having] the joy [awakening factor within, he knows, as it really is, that he has the joy awakening factor; actually not having the joy awakening factor within, he knows, as it really is, that he does not have the joy awakening factor. He knows, as it really is, how the unarisen joy awakening factor arises; and he knows, as it really is, how the arisen joy awakening factor is maintained without loss or deterioration, and how it is further developed and increased.

"Actually having] the tranquillity [awakening factor within, he knows, as it really is, that he has the tranquillity awakening factor; actually not having the tranquillity awakening factor within, he knows, as it really is, that he does not have the tranquillity awakening factor. He knows, as it really is, how the unarisen tranquillity awakening factor arises; and he knows, as it really is, how the arisen tranquillity awakening factor is maintained without loss or deterioration, and how it is further developed and increased.

"Actually having] the concentration [awakening factor within, he knows, as it really is, that he has the concentration awakening factor; actually not having the concentration awakening factor within, he knows, as it really is, that he does not have the concentration awakening factor. He knows, as it really is, how the unarisen concentration awakening factor arises; and he knows, as it really is, how the arisen concentration awakening factor is maintained without loss or deterioration, and how it is further developed and increased].

"Actually having the equanimity awakening factor within, a monk knows, as it really is, that he has the equanimity awakening factor; actually not having the equanimity awakening factor within, he knows, as it really is, that he does not have the equanimity awakening factor. He knows, as it really is, how the unarisen equanimity awakening factor arises; and he knows, as it really is, how the arisen equanimity awakening factor is maintained without loss or deterioration, and how it is further developed and increased.

"In this way a monk contemplates dharmas as dharmas internally and he contemplates dharmas as dharmas externally. He establishes mindfulness in dharmas and is endowed with knowledge, vision, understanding, and penetration. This is reckoned how a monk contemplates dharmas as dharmas, namely [in relation] to the seven factors of awakening. If a monk or a nun contemplates dharmas as dharmas in this way even for a short time, then this is reckoned the *satipaṭṭhāna* of contemplating dharmas as dharmas.

"If a monk or a nun with settled mind properly dwells in the four *satipaṭṭhāna*s for seven years, then they will certainly attain one of two fruits: either final knowledge here and now, or, if there is a remainder [of clinging], the attainment of non-returning.

"Let alone seven years, [if a monk or a nun with settled mind properly dwells in the four *satipaṭṭhāna*s for] six years, [then they will certainly attain one of two fruits: either final knowledge here and now, or, if there is a remainder of clinging, the attainment of non-returning.

"Let alone six years, if a monk or a nun with settled mind properly dwells in the four *satipaṭṭhāna*s for] five [years, then they will certainly attain one of two fruits: either final knowledge here and now, or, if there is a remainder of clinging, the attainment of non-returning.

"Let alone five years, if a monk or a nun with settled mind properly dwells in the four *satipaṭṭhāna*s for] four [years, then they will certainly attain one of two fruits: either final knowledge here and now, or, if there is a remainder of clinging, the attainment of non-returning.

"Let alone four years, if a monk or a nun with settled mind properly dwells in the four *satipaṭṭhāna*s for] three [years, then they will certainly attain one of two fruits: either final knowledge here and now, or, if there is a remainder of clinging, the attainment of non-returning.

"Let alone three years, if a monk or a nun with settled mind properly dwells in the four *satipaṭṭhāna*s for] two [years, then they will certainly attain one of two fruits: either final knowledge here and now, or, if there is a remainder of clinging, the attainment of non-returning.

"Let alone two years, if a monk or a nun with settled mind properly dwells in the four *satipaṭṭhāna*s for] one year, [then they will certainly attain one of two fruits: either final knowledge here and now, or, if there is a remainder of clinging, the attainment of non-returning.

"Let alone one year], if a monk or a nun with settled mind properly dwells in the four *satipaṭṭhāna*s for seven months, then they will certainly attain one of two fruits: either final knowledge here and now, or, if there is a remainder [of clinging], the attainment of non-returning.

"Let alone seven months [if a monk or a nun with settled mind properly dwells in the four *satipaṭṭhāna*s for] six [months, then they will certainly attain one of two fruits: either final knowledge here and now, or, if there is a remainder of clinging, the attainment of non-returning.

"Let alone six months, if a monk or a nun with settled mind properly dwells in the four *satipaṭṭhāna*s for] five [months, then they will certainly attain one of two fruits: either final knowledge here and now, or, if there is a remainder of clinging, the attainment of non-returning.

"Let alone five months, if a monk or a nun with settled mind properly dwells in the four *satipaṭṭhāna*s for] four [months, then they will certainly attain one of two fruits: either final knowledge here and now, or, if there is a remainder of clinging, the attainment of non-returning.

"Let alone four months, if a monk or a nun with settled mind properly dwells in the four *satipaṭṭhāna*s for] three [months, then they will certainly attain one of two fruits: either final knowledge here and now, or, if there is a remainder of clinging, the attainment of non-returning.

"Let alone three months, if a monk or a nun with settled mind properly dwells in the four *satipaṭṭhāna*s for] two [months, then they will certainly attain one of two fruits: either final knowledge here and now, or, if there is a remainder of clinging, the attainment of non-returning.

"Let alone two months, if a monk or a nun with settled mind properly dwells in the four *satipaṭṭhāna*s for] one month, [then they will certainly attain one of two fruits: either final knowledge here and now, or, if there is a remainder of clinging, the attainment of non-returning.

"Let alone one month], if a monk or a nun with settled mind properly dwells in the four *satipaṭṭhāna*s for seven days and nights, then they will certainly attain one of two fruits: either final knowledge here and now, or, if there is a remainder [of clinging], the attainment of non-returning.

Let alone seven days and nights, [if a monk or a nun with settled mind properly dwells in the four *satipaṭṭhāna*s for] six [days and nights, then they will certainly attain one of two fruits: either final knowledge here and now, or, if there is a remainder of clinging, the attainment of non-returning.

Let alone six days and nights, if a monk or a nun with settled mind properly dwells in the four *satipaṭṭhāna*s for] five [days and nights, then they will certainly attain one of two fruits: either final knowledge here and now, or, if there is a remainder of clinging, the attainment of non-returning.

Let alone five days and nights, if a monk or a nun with settled mind properly dwells in the four *satipaṭṭhāna*s for] four [days and nights, then they will certainly attain one of two fruits: either final knowledge here and now, or, if there is a remainder of clinging, the attainment of non-returning.

Let alone four days and nights, if a monk or a nun with settled mind properly dwells in the four *satipaṭṭhāna*s for] three [days and nights, then they will certainly attain one of two fruits: either final knowledge here and now, or, if there is a remainder of clinging, the attainment of non-returning.

Let alone three days and nights, if a monk or a nun with settled mind properly dwells in the four *satipaṭṭhāna*s for] two [days and nights, then they will certainly attain one of two fruits: either final knowledge here and now, or, if there is a remainder of clinging, the attainment of non-returning.

Let alone two days and nights, if a monk or a nun with settled mind properly dwells in the four *satipaṭṭhāna*s for one day and night, then they will certainly attain one of two fruits: either final knowledge here and now, or, if there is a remainder of clinging, the attainment of non-returning].

"Let alone one day and night, if a monk or a nun with settled mind properly dwells in the four *satipaṭṭhāna*s even for a short moment, then, practising in this way in the morning, they will certainly have made progress by the evening; practising in this way in the evening, they will certainly have made progress by the [next] morning."

This is what the Buddha said. The monks who had heard what the Buddha had said were delighted and received it respectfully.

XIII.3 EKOTTARIKA-ĀGAMA

TWELFTH CHAPTER [ENTITLED] ON THE ONE-GOING PATH, [DISCOURSE] ONE[10]

Thus have I heard. On one occasion the Buddha was staying at Sāvatthī in Jeta's Grove, Anāthapiṇḍika's Park.

At that time the Blessed One told the monks: "There is a one-going path for the purification of the actions of living beings, for removing worry and sorrow, for being without vexations, for attaining great knowledge and wisdom, for accomplishing the realization of Nirvāṇa. That is: the five hindrances should be abandoned and the four *satipaṭṭhāna*s should be attended to.[11]

"What is the significance of 'one-going'? That is, it is unification of the mind. This is reckoned to be 'one-going'. What is the 'path'? That is, it is the noble eightfold path: [factor] one is called right view, [factor] two is called right thought, [factor] three is called right action, [factor] four is called right livelihood, [factor] five is called right effort, [factor] six is called right speech, [factor] seven is called right mindfulness, and [factor] eight is called right concentration. This is the significance of the 'path'. This is reckoned to be the 'one-going path'.

"What are the five hindrances that should be abandoned? That is, the hindrance of lustful sensual desire, the hindrance of ill will, the hindrance of restlessness[-and-worry], the hindrance of sloth-and-torpor, and the hindrance of doubt. These are reckoned to be the five hindrances that should be abandoned.

"How to attend to the four *satipaṭṭhāna*s? Here [in regard to] his own body a monk contemplates [the body] internally, and by removing evil thoughts and being free from worry and sorrow [he

10 EĀ 12.1 at T I 568a1 to 569b12, which has already been translated into English by Nhat Hanh 1990: 168–77 and Pāsādika 1998: 495–502.

11 The two Chinese characters used here in EĀ 12.1 literally mean "settlings of the mind", though they do seem to translate what in the Indic original would have been a term paralleling the Pāli *satipaṭṭhāna*; cf. Hirakawa 1997: 491.

experiences joy in himself;[12] in regard to the body] he contemplates the body externally,[13] and by removing evil thoughts and being free from worry and sorrow [he experiences joy in himself; and in regard to the body] he contemplates the body internally and externally, and by removing evil thoughts and being free from worry and sorrow [he experiences joy in himself].

"[In regard to] feelings he contemplates feelings internally and [by removing evil thoughts and being free from worry and sorrow] he experiences joy in himself; [in regard to] feelings he contemplates feelings externally, and [by removing evil thoughts and being free from worry and sorrow he experiences joy in himself; and in regard to] feelings he contemplates feelings internally and externally [and by removing evil thoughts and being free from worry and sorrow he experiences joy in himself].

"[In regard to the mind] he contemplates the mind internally and [by removing evil thoughts and being free from worry and sorrow] he experiences joy in himself; [in regard to the mind] he contemplates the mind externally and [by removing evil thoughts and being free from worry and sorrow he experiences joy in himself; and in regard to the mind] he contemplates the mind internally and externally and [by removing evil thoughts and being free from worry and sorrow he experiences joy in himself].

"[In regard to dharmas] he contemplates dharmas internally and [by removing evil thoughts and being free from worry and sorrow he experiences joy in himself; in regard to dharmas] he contemplates dharmas externally and [by removing evil thoughts and being free

12 My supplementation of "experiencing joy in himself" is oriented on several occurrences of this phrase as the result of being free from worry and sorrow later in the text.

13 The text at this point actually repeats the qualification "his own" in regard to external contemplation. The same qualification is not found, however, in regard to internal and external contemplation. Yet if "internal" and "external" are applicable to oneself, the same would hold for a form of contemplation that combines the two. This suggests that a textual error may have occurred, in that the qualification "his own" would originally have been applied to internal contemplation only. The present condition of the text could have come about through an error that is quite common in oral transmission, whereby the qualification "his own" was accidentally applied to the next item in the description. This assumption finds confirmation towards the end of the description of body contemplation, where the qualification "his own" is indeed applied only to internal contemplation. Therefore I have emended the present passage and translate it as if already here the second instance regarding external contemplation did not carry the qualification "his own".

from worry and sorrow he experiences joy in himself; and in regard to dharmas] he contemplates dharmas internally and externally, and [by removing evil thoughts and being free from worry and sorrow] he experiences joy in himself.

"How does a monk contemplate the body internally and [by removing evil thoughts and being free from worry and sorrow] experience joy in himself? Here a monk contemplates this body according to its nature and functions, from head to feet and from feet to head, contemplating all in this body that is of an impure [nature] as not worth being attached to.

"He then contemplates that in this body there are body hairs, head hairs, nails, teeth, skin, flesh, tendons, bones, bone marrow, brain, fat, intestines, stomach, heart, liver, spleen, kidneys, he contemplates and knows them all. [There are also] faeces, urine, [whatever else] is produced by digestion in the two receptacles, tears in the eyes, spittle, mucus, blood in the veins, fat, and gall; he contemplates and knows them all as not worth being attached to.

"In this way, monks, he should contemplate the body, experiencing joy in himself by removing evil thoughts and being free from worry and sorrow.

"Again, a monk contemplates [reflecting]: 'In this body, is there the earth element, the water [element], the fire [element], and the wind element?' In this way a monk contemplates this body.

"Again, [when] a monk contemplates this body by distinguishing the elements in this body as being the four elements, [then] this is just like a capable cow butcher or the apprentice of a cow butcher who divides a cow [into pieces by cutting through] its tendons. While dividing it he contemplates and sees for himself that 'these are the feet', 'this is the heart', 'these are the tendons', and 'this is the head.'

"In this way the monk distinguishes the elements, contemplating and examining himself that in this body there are the earth, water, fire, and wind elements. In this way a monk contemplates the body and experiences joy in himself [by removing evil thoughts and being free from worry and sorrow]. [568b]

"Again, a monk contemplates the orifices that are found in this body that discharge impurity.

"It is just as a person who, contemplating a bamboo garden, contemplates clumps of reeds. In this way a monk contemplates the orifices that are found in this body and that discharge impurity.

"Again, a monk contemplates a corpse that has been dead for one day, two days, three days, four days, five days, six days, or seven days, the body being bloated, a fetid place of impurity. He then contemplates that his own body is not different from that: 'My body will not escape from this calamity.'

"Again, a monk contemplates a corpse that has visibly been fed on by crows, magpies, and owls, or that has visibly been fed on by tigers, wolves, dogs, worms, and [other] beasts. He then contemplates that his own body is not different from that: 'My body is not free from this calamity.' This is reckoned how a monk contemplates the body and experiences joy in himself [by removing evil thoughts and being free from worry and sorrow].

"Again, a monk contemplates a corpse that has been about half eaten and left scattered on the ground, a fetid place of impurity. He then contemplates that his own body is not different from that: 'My body is not free from this condition.'

"Again, he contemplates a corpse whose flesh has disappeared, with only the bones remaining, smeared with blood. Again, he contemplates that this body is not different from that body. In this way a monk contemplates the body.

"Again, a monk contemplates a corpse [whose bones] are held together by the tendons, [like] a bundle of firewood. He then contemplates that his own body is not different from that. In this way a monk contemplates the body.

"Again, a monk contemplates a corpse whose joints have come apart, [with its parts] scattered in different places, here a hand bone, there a foot bone, or a shin bone, or the pelvis, or the coccyx, or an arm bone, or a shoulder bone, or ribs, or the spine, or the neck bones, or the skull. Again he uses the contemplation that his body is not different from that: 'I will not escape from this condition. My body will also be destroyed.' In this way a monk contemplates the body and experiences joy in himself [by removing evil thoughts and being free from worry and sorrow].

"Again, a monk contemplates a corpse [whose bones] have become white, the colour of white agate. Again he contemplates that his own body is not different from that: 'I am not free from this condition.' This is reckoned how a monk contemplates his own body.

"Again, a monk sees a corpse whose bones have become bluish, appearing as if they have been bruised, or of a colour that is indistinguishable from that of ash, as not worth being attached to.

"In this way a monk contemplates his own body and [experiences joy in himself] by removing evil thoughts and being free from worry and sorrow: 'This body is impermanent, of a nature to fall apart.' In this way a monk contemplates his own body internally, he contemplates the body externally, and he contemplates the body internally and externally, understanding that there is nothing in it that he owns.

"How does a monk [in regard to] feelings contemplate feelings internally? Here, at the time of having a pleasant feeling, a monk is aware of it and knows of himself: 'I am having a pleasant feeling.' At the time of having a painful feeling, he is aware of it and knows of himself: 'I am having a painful feeling.' At the time of having a neutral feeling, [568c] he is aware of it and knows of himself: 'I am having a neutral feeling.'

"At the time of having a worldly pleasant feeling, he is aware of it and knows of himself: 'I am having a worldly pleasant feeling.' At the time of having a worldly painful feeling, he is aware of it and knows of himself: 'I am having a worldly painful feeling.' At the time of having a worldly neutral feeling, he is also aware of it and knows of himself: 'I am having a worldly neutral feeling.' At the time of having an unworldly pleasant feeling, he is aware of it and knows of himself: 'I am having an unworldly pleasant feeling.' At the time of having an unworldly painful feeling, he is also aware of it and knows of himself: 'I am having an unworldly painful feeling.' At the time of having an unworldly neutral feeling, he is also aware of it and knows of himself: 'I am having an unworldly neutral feeling.' In this way, [in regard to feelings] a monk contemplates feelings internally.

"Again, at the time when a monk then has a pleasant feeling, at that time he does not have a painful feeling; at that time he is aware and knows of himself: 'I am experiencing a pleasant feeling.' At the time when he has a painful feeling, at that time he does not have a pleasant feeling; he is aware and knows of himself: 'I am experiencing a painful feeling.' At the time when he has a neutral feeling, at that time there is no pain or pleasure; he is aware and knows of himself: 'I am experiencing a neutral feeling.'

"He [contemplates] their nature of arising, experiencing joy in himself [by removing evil thoughts and being free from worry and sorrow], he also contemplates their nature of ceasing, [experiencing joy in himself by removing evil thoughts and being free from worry and sorrow], and he then contemplates their nature of arising and ceasing [experiencing joy in himself by removing evil thoughts and being free from worry and sorrow].

"Further, he is able to know and able to see that these are feelings that manifest here and now, giving attention to their origination. Not depending on anything, he experiences joy in himself [by removing evil thoughts and being free from worry and sorrow], not arousing worldly perceptions.

"Herein he is also not agitated, and because of not being agitated he attains Nirvāṇa, knowing as it really is that 'birth and death have been extinguished, the holy life has been established, what had to be done has been done, there is no more experiencing of [another] existence.'

"In this way a monk contemplates his own feelings internally, discarding distracted thoughts and [experiencing joy in himself by removing evil thoughts and] being free from worry and sorrow; he contemplates feelings externally, [discarding distracted thoughts and experiencing joy in himself by removing evil thoughts and being free from worry and sorrow]; he contemplates feelings internally and externally, discarding distracted thoughts [and experiencing joy in himself by removing evil thoughts and] being free from worry and sorrow. In this way a monk contemplates feelings internally and externally.

"How does a monk [in regard to the mind] contemplate the nature of the mind, experiencing joy in himself [by removing evil thoughts and being free from worry and sorrow]? Here on having a mind with craving for sensual pleasures, a monk is aware of it and knows of himself that he has a mind with craving for sensual pleasures. Having a mind without craving for sensual pleasures, he is aware of it and knows of himself that he has a mind without craving for sensual pleasures.

"Having a mind with anger, he is aware of it and knows of himself that he has a mind with anger. Having a mind without anger, he is aware of it and knows of himself that he has a mind without anger.

"Having a mind with delusion, he is aware of it and knows of himself that he has a mind with delusion. Having a mind without delusion, he is aware of it and knows of himself that he has a mind without delusion.

"Having a mind with thoughts of craving, he is aware of it and knows of himself that he has a mind with thoughts of craving. Having a mind without thoughts of craving, he is aware of it and knows of himself that he has a mind without thoughts of craving.

"Having a mind that has reached an attainment, he is aware of it and knows of himself that he has a mind that has reached an attainment. Having a mind that has not reached an attainment, he is aware of it and knows of himself that he has a mind that has not reached an attainment.

"Having a mind that is distracted, he is aware of it and knows of himself that he has a mind that is distracted. [569a] Having a mind that is not distracted, he is aware of it and knows of himself that he has a mind that is not distracted.

"Having a mind that is scattered, he is aware of it and knows of himself that he has a mind that is scattered. Having a mind that is not scattered, he is aware of it and knows of himself that he has a mind that is not scattered.

"Having a mind that is pervasive, he is aware of it and knows of himself that he has a mind that is pervasive. Having a mind that is not pervasive, he is aware of it and knows of himself that he has a mind that is not pervasive.

"Having a mind that is great, he is aware of it and knows of himself that he has a mind that is great. Having a mind that is not great, he is aware of it and knows of himself that he has a mind that is not great.

"Having a mind that is boundless, he is aware of it and knows of himself that he has a mind that is boundless. Having a mind that is not boundless, he is aware of it and knows of himself that he has a mind that is not boundless.

"Having a mind that is concentrated, he is aware of it and knows of himself that he has a mind that is concentrated. Having a mind that is not concentrated, he is aware of it and knows of himself that he has a mind that is not concentrated.

"Having a mind that is not liberated, he is aware of it and knows of himself that he has a mind that is not liberated. Having a mind that is already liberated, he is aware of it and knows of himself that he has a mind that is already liberated.

"In this way a monk [in regard to the mind] contemplates the characteristics of the mind as a *satipaṭṭhāna*. He contemplates their nature of arising, he contemplates their nature of ceasing, and he contemplates conjointly their nature of arising and ceasing. He gives attention to contemplating their nature, experiencing joy in himself [by removing evil thoughts and being free from worry and sorrow].

"He is able to know, able to see, able to give attention [instead of] not being able to give attention, he does not depend on anything and does not give rise to worldly perceptions. Not having given rise to [worldly] perceptions he is not agitated, not being agitated he has no remainder [of grasping], not having a remainder [of grasping] he [attains] Nirvāṇa, knowing as it really is that 'birth and death have been extinguished, the holy life has been established, what had to be done has been done, there is no more experiencing of [another] existence.'

"In this way a monk [in regard to the] mind contemplates his own mind internally as a *satipaṭṭhāna*, discarding distracted thoughts and [experiencing joy in himself by removing evil thoughts and] being free from worry and sorrow; he contemplates the mind externally, [discarding distracted thoughts and experiencing joy in himself by removing evil thoughts and being free from worry and sorrow]; and [in regard to the] mind he contemplates the mind internally and externally as a *satipaṭṭhāna* [discarding distracted thoughts and experiencing joy in himself by removing evil thoughts and being free from worry and sorrow]. In this way a monk [in regard to the] mind contemplates the characteristics of the mind as a *satipaṭṭhāna*.

"How does a monk in regard to dharmas contemplate the characteristics of dharmas as a *satipaṭṭhāna*? Here a monk cultivates the mindfulness awakening factor supported by insight, supported by dispassion, and supported by cessation, discarding evil states.

"He cultivates the [investigation-of-]dharmas awakening factor [supported by insight, supported by dispassion, and supported by cessation, discarding evil states].

"He cultivates the energy awakening factor [supported by insight, supported by dispassion, and supported by cessation, discarding evil states].

"He cultivates the joy awakening factor [supported by insight, supported by dispassion, and supported by cessation, discarding evil states].[14]

14 The text at this point refers again to the mindfulness awakening factor, an obvious error. I have therefore replaced this with a reference to the awakening factor of joy that according to the standard description of the

"He cultivates the tranquillity awakening factor [supported by insight, supported by dispassion, and supported by cessation, discarding evil states].

"He cultivates the concentration awakening factor [supported by insight, supported by dispassion, and supported by cessation, discarding evil states].

"He cultivates the equanimity awakening factor supported by insight, supported by dispassion, and supported by cessation, discarding evil states. In this way a monk [in regard to] dharmas contemplates the characteristics of dharmas as a *satipaṭṭhāna*.

"Again, free from craving for sensual pleasures, removing evil and unwholesome states, with [directed] awareness and [sustained] contemplation, being tranquil and mindful, a monk enjoys the first absorption and experiences joy in himself. In this way, [in regard to] dharmas a monk contemplates the characteristics of dharmas as a *satipaṭṭhāna*.

"Again, discarding [directed] awareness and [sustained] contemplation, arousing joy within, the mind being unified, without [directed] awareness or [sustained] contemplation, being mindful and tranquil, with joy and at ease, a monk dwells in the second absorption and experiences joy in himself. In this way, [in regard to] dharmas a monk contemplates the characteristics of dharmas as a *satipaṭṭhāna*.

"Again, mindfully discarding [joy] a monk cultivates equanimity in this respect,[15] he constantly knows and experiences pleasant feelings himself with the body, [569b] as sought after by noble ones, with purity of equanimity and mindfulness,[16] he engages in the third absorption. In this way, [in regard to] dharmas a monk contemplates the characteristics of dharmas as a *satipaṭṭhāna*.

"Again, discarding mental states of pain and pleasure and also being without sadness and joy, without pain and without pleasure, with purity of equanimity and mindfulness, a monk enjoys the fourth

---

seven awakening factors should come at this place, found in this way also elsewhere in the *Ekottarika-āgama*, cf., e.g., T II 741b3.

15 That the point at stake is the discarding of joy can be seen from other descriptions of the four absorptions in the *Ekottarika-āgama* at T II 582b8 or at T II 696c15, each of which shows some variations when compared with the present description.

16 This reference to purity of equanimity and mindfulness appears to be the result of an accidental copying of the phrasing appropriate for the fourth absorption.

absorption. In this way, [in regard to] dharmas a monk contemplates the characteristics of dharmas as a *satipaṭṭhāna*.

"He dwells [contemplating] their nature of arising, he dwells [contemplating] their nature of ceasing, and he dwells [contemplating] conjointly their nature of arising and ceasing, experiencing joy in himself [by removing evil thoughts and being free from worry and sorrow]. He gains the *satipaṭṭhāna* of dharmas and keeps it present in front [of himself].

"He is able to know, able to see, discarding distracted perceptions, he does not depend on anything and does not give rise to worldly perceptions. Not having given rise to such perceptions he is not agitated, not being agitated he knows as it really is that 'birth and death have been extinguished, the holy life has been established, what had to be done has been done, there is no more experiencing of [another] existence.'

"Monks, supported by the one-going path living beings attain purification, are removed from worry and sorrow, no longer delight in perceptions, reach knowledge and wisdom, and attain the realization of Nirvāṇa, that is, by abandoning the five hindrances and cultivating the four *satipaṭṭhāna*s."

At that time the monks, who had heard what the Buddha had said, were delighted and received it respectfully.

REFERENCES

Agostini, Giulio 2010: "'Preceded by Thought Are the Dhammas': The Ancient Exegesis on Dhammapada 1–2", in *Buddhist Asia 2, Papers from the Second Conference of Buddhist Studies Held in Naples in June 2004*, G. Orofino and S. Vita (ed.), 1–34, Kyoto: Italian School of East Asian Studies.

Anacker, Stefan 1984/2005: *Seven Works of Vasubandhu: The Buddhist Psychological Doctor*, Delhi: Motilal Banarsidass.

Anālayo 2003a: "Nimitta", in *Encyclopaedia of Buddhism*, W.G. Weeraratne (ed.), 7/1: 177–9, Sri Lanka: Department of Buddhist Affairs.

Anālayo 2003b: *Satipaṭṭhāna: The Direct Path to Realization*, Birmingham: Windhorse Publications.

Anālayo 2007a: "The Divine Messengers", in *Buddhist Studies in Honour of Venerable Kirindigalle Dhammaratana*, S. Ratnayaka (ed.), 15–26, Colombo: Felicitation Committee.

Anālayo 2007b: "Mindfulness of Breathing in the Saṃyukta-āgama", *Buddhist Studies Review*, 24/2: 137–50.

Anālayo 2009: *From Craving to Liberation: Excursions into the Thought-world of the Pāli Discourses (1)*, New York: Buddhist Association of the United States.

Anālayo 2010a: "Channa's Suicide in the Saṃyukta-āgama", *Buddhist Studies Review*, 27/2: 125–37.

Anālayo 2010b: *From Grasping to Emptiness: Excursions into the Thought-world of the Pāli Discourses (2)*, New York: Buddhist Association of the United States.

Anālayo 2010c: "Saccaka's Challenge: A Study of the Saṃyukta-āgama Parallel to the Cūḷasaccaka-sutta in Relation to the Notion of Merit Transfer", *Chung-Hwa Buddhist Journal*, 23: 39–70.

Anālayo 2010d: "Teachings to Lay Disciples: The Saṃyukta-āgama Parallel to the Anāthapiṇḍikovāda-sutta", *Buddhist Studies Review*, 27/1: 3–14.

Anālayo 2011a: *A Comparative Study of the Majjhima-nikāya*, Taipei: Dharma Drum Publishing Corporation.

Anālayo 2011b: "The Tale of King Ma(k)hādeva in the Ekottarika-āgama and the Cakravartin Motif", *Journal of the Centre for Buddhist Studies, Sri Lanka*, 9: 43–77.

Anālayo 2012a: "The Dynamics of Theravāda Insight Meditation", in *Fojiao chanzuo chuantong guoji xueshu yantaohui lunwenji [Buddhist Meditation Traditions: An International Symposium]*, K. Chuang (ed.), 23–56, Taiwan: Dharma Drum Publishing Corporation.

Anālayo 2012b: *Excursions into the Thought-world of the Pāli Discourses*, Onalaska, WA: Pariyatti.

Anālayo 2012c: "The Historical Value of the Pāli Discourses", *Indo-Iranian Journal*, 55: 223–53.

Anālayo 2012d: *Madhyama Āgama Studies*, Taipei: Dharma Drum Publishing Corporation.

Anālayo 2012e: "Protecting Oneself and Others through Mindfulness: The Acrobat Simile in the Saṃyukta-āgama", *Sri Lanka International Journal of Buddhist Studies*, 2: 1–23.

Anālayo 2012f: "Purification in Early Buddhist Discourse and Buddhist Ethics", *Bukkyō Kenkyū*, 40: 67–97.

Anālayo 2013a: "Defying Māra: Bhikkhunīs in the Saṃyukta-āgama", in *Women in Early Indian Buddhism: Comparative Textual Studies*, A. Collett (ed.), 116–39, Oxford: Oxford University Press.

Anālayo 2013b: "On the Five Aggregates (2): A Translation of Saṃyukta-āgama Discourses 256 to 272", *Dharma Drum Journal of Buddhist Studies*, 12: 1–68.

Anālayo forthcoming 1: *The Dawn of Abhidharma*, Hamburg: Hamburg University Press.

Anālayo forthcoming 2: "Perspectives on the Body in Early Buddhist Meditation", in *Proceedings of the International Conference on Buddhist Meditative Traditions*, K. Chuang (ed.), Taipei: Dharma Drum Publishing Corporation.

Anālayo in preparation: "Asubha Gone Overboard: A Comparative Study of the Mass Suicide of Monks".

Arch, Joanna J. and M.G. Craske 2006: "Mechanisms of Mindfulness: Emotion Regulation Following a Focused Breathing Induction", *Behaviour Research and Therapy*, 44: 1849–58.

Baba, Norihisa 2004: "On Expressions regarding 'śūnya' or 'śūnyatā' in the Northern Āgamas and the Pali Commentaries", *Journal of Indian and Buddhist Studies*, 52/2: 946–4.

Bapat, P.V. 1926: "The Different Strata in the Literary Material of the Dīgha Nikāya", *Annals of the Bhandarkar Oriental Research Institute*, 8: 1–16.

Bareau, André 1962: "La légende de la jeunesse du Buddha dans les Vinayapiṭaka anciens", *Oriens-Extremus*, 9/1: 6–33.

Barua, Dipak Kumara 1971/2003: *An Analytical Study of Four Nikāyas*, Delhi: Munshiram Manoharlal.

Bechert, Heinz and K. Wille 2000: *Sanskrithandschriften aus den Turfanfunden*, 8, Wiesbaden: Franz Steiner.

Bechert, Heinz and K. Wille 2004: *Sanskrithandschriften aus den Turfanfunden*, 9, Wiesbaden: Franz Steiner.

Bendall, Cecil 1902/1970: *Çikshāsamuccaya: A Compendium of Buddhist Teaching Compiled by Çāntideva, Chiefly from Earlier Mahāyāna-Sūtras*, Osnabrück: Biblio Verlag.

Bernhard, Franz 1965: *Udānavarga*, 1, Göttingen: Vandenhoeck & Ruprecht.

Bingenheimer, Marcus 2011: *Studies in Āgama Literature, with Special Reference to the Shorter Chinese Saṃyuktāgama*, Taiwan: Shi Weng Feng Print Co.

Bishop, Scott R., M. Lau, S. Shapiro, L. Carlson, N.D. Anderson, J. Carmody, Z.V. Segal, S. Abbey, M. Speca, D. Velting, and G. Devins 2004: "Mindfulness: A Proposed Operational Definition", *Clinical Psychology: Science and Practice*, 11/3: 230–41.

Bodhi, Bhikkhu 2000: *The Connected Discourses of the Buddha: A New Translation of the Saṃyutta Nikāya*, Boston: Wisdom Publications.

Bodhi, Bhikkhu 2011: "What Does Mindfulness Really Mean? A Canonical Perspective", *Contemporary Buddhism*, 12/1: 19–39.

Bodhi, Bhikkhu 2012: *The Numerical Discourses of the Buddha: A Translation of the Aṅguttara Nikāya*, Boston: Wisdom Publications.

Bowker, John 1991: *The Meanings of Death*, Cambridge: Cambridge University Press.

Brough, John 1962/2001: *The Gāndhārī Dharmapada, Edited with an Introduction and Commentary*, Delhi: Motilal Banarsidass.

Brown, Kirk Warren, R.J. Goodman, and M. Inzlicht 2013: "Dispositional Mindfulness and the Attenuation of Neural Responses to Emotional Stimuli", *Social Cognitive and Affective Neuroscience*, 8/1: 93–9.

Brown, Kirk Warren, R.M. Ryan, and J.D. Creswell 2007: "Mindfulness: Theoretical Foundations and Evidence for Its Salutary Effects", *Psychological Inquiry*, 18/4: 211–37.

Bühler, G. 1886: *The Laws of Manu, Translated with Extracts from Seven Commentaries*, Oxford: Clarendon Press.

Choong, Mun-keat 2000: *The Fundamental Teachings of Early Buddhism: A Comparative Study Based on the Sūtrāṅga Portion of the Pāli Saṃyutta-Nikāya and the Chinese Saṃyuktāgama*, Wiesbaden: Otto Harrassowitz.

Chun, Marvin M. and N.B. Turk-Browne 2007: "Interactions Between Attention and Memory", *Current Opinion in Neurobiology*, 17: 177–84.

Cone, Margaret 1989: "Patna Dharmapada", *Journal of the Pali Text Society*, 13: 101–217.

Creswell, J.D., B.M. Way, N.I. Eisenberger, and M.D. Lieberman 2007: "Neural Correlates of Dispositional Mindfulness during Affect Labelling", *Psychosomatic Medicine*, 69: 560–5.

Deleanu, Florin 1992: "Mindfulness of Breathing in the Dhyāna Sūtras", *Transactions of the International Conference of Orientalists in Japan*, 37: 42–57, Tokyo: Institute of Eastern Culture.

Deo, Shantaram Bhalchandra 1956: *History of Jaina Monachism, from Inscriptions and Literature*, Poona: Deccan College, Postgraduate and Research Institute.

de Silva, Padmal 2001: "A Psychological Analysis of the Vitakkasaṇṭhāna Sutta", *Buddhist Studies Review*, 18/1: 65–72.

Devacandra 1996: *Gang po la sogs pa'i rtogs pa brjod pa brgya pa*, Xining.

Dhammajoti, Bhikkhu K.L. 1995: *The Chinese Version of Dharmapada, Translated with Introduction and Annotations*, Colombo: University of Kelaniya, Postgraduate Institute of Pali and Buddhist Studies.

Dhammajoti, Bhikkhu K.L. 2009: "The aśubhā Meditation in the Sarvāstivāda", *Journal of the Centre for Buddhist Studies, Sri Lanka*, 7: 248–95.

Dutt, Nalinaksha 1934/2000: *Pañcaviṃśatisāhasrika Prajñāpāramitā, Edited with Critical Notes and Introduction*, Calcutta: Bhattacharya.

Eimer, Helmut 1983: *Rab tu 'byuṅ ba'i gźi: Die Tibetische Übersetzung des Pravrajyāvastu im Vinaya der Mūlasarvāstivādins*, 2, Wiesbaden: Otto Harrassowitz.

Enomoto, Fumio 1989: "Śarīrārthagāthā: A Collection of Canonical Verses in the Yogācārabhūmi", in *Sanskrit-Texte aus dem Buddhistischen Kanon: Neuentdeckungen und Neueditionen Folge 1*, 1: 17–35, Göttingen: Vandenhoeck & Ruprecht.

Enomoto, Fumio 1994: *A Comprehensive Study of the Chinese Saṃyuktāgama, Indic Texts Corresponding to the Chinese Saṃyuktāgama as Found in the Sarvāstivāda-Mūlasarvāstivāda Literature*, 1: *Saṃgītanipāta*, Kyoto: Kacho Junior College.

Enomoto, Fumio 1997: "Sanskrit Fragments from the Saṃgītanipāta of the Saṃyuktāgama", in *Bauddhavidyāsudhākaraḥ: Studies in Honour of Heinz Bechert on the Occasion of his 65th Birthday*, J.U. Hartmann et al. (ed.), 91–105, Swisstal-Odendorf: Indica et Tibetica.

Gethin, Rupert 1992: *The Buddhist Path to Awakening: A Study of the Bodhi-Pakkhiyā Dhammā*, Leiden: E.J. Brill.

Gethin, Rupert 2011: "On Some Definitions of Mindfulness", *Contemporary Buddhism*, 12/1: 263–79.

Ghosa, Pratāpacandra 1914: *Çatasāhasrikā-prajñā-pāramitā-sūtra: A Theological and Philosophical Discourse of Buddha with His Disciples*, Calcutta: Asiatic Society.

Glass, Andrew 2007: *Four Gāndhārī Saṃyuktāgama Sūtras: Senior Kharoṣṭhī Fragment 5*, Seattle: University of Washington Press.

Gnoli, Raniero 1977 (part 1), 1978 (part 2): *The Gilgit Manuscript of the Saṅghabhedavastu, Being the 17th and Last Section of the Vinaya of the Mūlasarvāstivādin*, Rome: Istituto Italiano per il Medio ed Estremo Oriente.

Gombrich, Richard F. 2009: *What the Buddha Thought*, London: Equinox.

Griffiths, Paul J. 1992: "Memory in Classical Indian Yogācāra", in *In the Mirror of Memory: Reflections on Mindfulness and Remembrance in Indian and Tibetan Buddhism*, J. Gyatso (ed.), 109–31, Albany: State University of New York Press.

Gunaratana, Henepola 1991/1992: *Mindfulness in Plain English*, Boston: Wisdom Publications.

Hamilton, Sue 1995: "From the Buddha to Buddhaghosa: Changing Attitudes towards the Human Body in Theravāda Buddhism", in *Religious Reflections on the Human Body*, J.M. Law (ed.), 46–63, Bloomington: Indiana University Press.

Hamilton, Sue 1996: *Identity and Experience: The Constitution of the Human Being according to Early Buddhism*, London: Luzac Oriental.

Harmon-Jones, Eddie, L. Simon, J. Greenberg, T. Pyszczynski, S. Solomon, and H. McGregor 1997: "Terror Management Theory and Self-Esteem: Evidence that Increased Self-Esteem Reduces Mortality Salience Effects", *Journal of Personality and Social Psychology*, 72/1: 24–36.

Harrison, Paul 1997: "The Ekottarikāgama Translations of An Shigao", in *Bauddhavidyāsudhākaraḥ: Studies in Honour of Heinz Bechert on the Occasion of his 65th birthday*, J.U. Hartmann et al. (ed.), 261–84, Swisstal-Odendorf: Indica et Tibetica.

Harrison, Paul 2007: "A Fragment of the *Saṃbādhāvakāśasūtra from a Newly Identified Ekottarikāgama Manuscript in the Schøyen Collection", *Annual Report of the International Research Institute for Advanced Buddhology at Soka University*, 10: 201–11.

Hirakawa, Akira 1997: *Buddhist Chinese–Sanskrit Dictionary*, Tokyo: Reiyukai.

Hoffmann, Wilhelm and L. Van Dillen 2012: "Desire: The New Hot Spot in Self-control Research", *Current Directions in Psychological Science*, 21/5: 317–22.

Hölzel, Britta K., S.W. Lazar, T. Gard, Z. Schuman-Olivier, D.R. Vago, and U. Ott 2011: "How Does Mindfulness Meditation Work? Proposing Mechanisms of Action from a Conceptual and Neural Perspective", *Perspectives on Psychological Science*, 6/6: 537–59.

Ireland, John D. 1990: *The Udāna, Inspired Utterances of the Buddha*, Kandy: Buddhist Publication Society.

Jaini, Padmanabh S. 1979/1998: *The Jaina Path of Purification*, Delhi: Motilal Banarsidass.

Jayawickrama, N.A. 1990: *The Story of Gotama Buddha: The Nidāna-kathā of the Jātakaṭṭhakathā*, Oxford: Pali Text Society.

Jones, Dhivan Thomas 2009: "New Light on the Twelve Nidānas", *Contemporary Buddhism*, 10/2: 241–59.

Jones, J.J. 1952/1976: *The Mahāvastu, Translated from the Buddhist Sanskrit*, 2, London: Pali Text Society.

Jurewicz, J. 2000: "Playing with Fire: The Pratītyasamutpāda from the Perspective of Vedic Thought", *Journal of the Pali Text Society*, 26: 77–103.

Kabat-Zinn, Jon 2011: "Some Reflections on the Origins of MBSR, Skillful Means, and the Trouble with Maps", *Contemporary Buddhism*, 12/1: 281–306.

Kabat-Zinn, Jon, L. Lipworth, and R. Burney 1985: "The Clinical Use of Mindfulness Meditation for the Self-Regulation of Chronic Pain", *Journal of Behavioral Medicine*, 8/2: 163–90.

Karunadasa, Y. 1967/1989: *Buddhist Analysis of Matter*, Singapore: Buddhist Research Society.

Karunadasa, Y. 2010: *The Theravāda Abhidhamma: Its Inquiry into the Nature of Conditioned Reality*, Hong Kong: University of Hong Kong, Centre of Buddhist Studies.

Kuan, Tse-Fu 2001: "The Four Satipaṭṭhānas in Early Buddhism", *Satyābhisamaya*, 17: 154–209.

Kuan, Tse-Fu 2008: *Mindfulness in Early Buddhism: New Approaches through Psychology and Textual Analysis of Pali, Chinese and Sanskrit Sources*, London: Routledge.

Kudo, Noriyuki 2009: "Or. 15009/101–150", in *Buddhist Manuscripts from Central Asia: The British Library Sanskrit Fragments*, S. Karashima et al. (ed.), 2: 169–98, Tokyo: International Research Institute for Advanced Buddhology, Soka University.

Lamotte, Étienne 1970: *Le Traité de la grande vertu de sagesse de Nāgārjuna (Mahāprajñāpāramitāśāstra)*, 3, Louvain-la-Neuve: Institut Orientaliste.

Lamotte, Étienne 1973/1993: "Three Sūtras from the Saṃyuktāgama Concerning Emptiness", S. Webb-Boin (trsl.), *Buddhist Studies Review*, 10/1: 1–23.

Lévi, Sylvain 1925: *Vijñapatimātratāsiddhi: deux traités de Vasubandhu: Viṃśatikā (la Vingtaine), accompagnée d'une explication en prose et Triṃśikā (la Trentaine) avec le commentaire de Sthiramati, original sanscrit publié pour la première fois d'après des manuscrits rapportés du Népal*, Paris: Librairie Ancienne Honoré Champion.

Lévi, Sylvain 1932: *Mahākarmavibhaṅga (La Grande Classification des actes) et Karmavibhaṅgopadeśa (Discussion sur le Mahā Karmavibhaṅga): textes sanscrits rapportés du Népal, édités et traduits avec les textes parallèles en sanscrit, en pali, en tibétain, en chinois et en koutchéen*, Paris: Ernest Leroux.

Liu, Zhen 2010: *Dhyānāni tapaś ca*, Shanghai: Guji chubanshe.

Lutz, Antoine, H.A. Slagter, J.D. Dunne, and R.J. Davidson 2008: "Attention Regulation and Monitoring in Meditation", *Trends in Cognitive Sciences*, 12/4: 163–9.

Minh Chau, Thich 1964/1991: *The Chinese Madhyama Āgama and the Pāli Majjhima Nikāya*, Delhi: Motilal Banarsidass.

Muzzio, Isabel A., C. Kentros, and E. Kandel 2009: "What Is Remembered? Role of Attention on the Encoding and Retrieval of Hippocampal Representations", *The Journal of Physiology*, 587/12: 2837–54.
Ñāṇamoli, Bhikkhu 1956/1991: *The Path of Purification (Visuddhimagga) by Bhadantācariya Buddhaghosa*, Kandy: Buddhist Publication Society.
Ñāṇamoli, Bhikkhu 1982: *The Path of Discrimination (Paṭisambhidāmagga) Translated from the Pali*, London: Pali Text Society.
Ñāṇamoli, Bhikkhu 1995: *The Middle Length Discourses of the Buddha: A Translation of the Majjhima Nikāya*, Bhikku Bodhi (ed.), Boston: Wisdom Publications.
Ñāṇaponika Thera 1949/1985: *Abhidhamma Studies: Researches in Buddhist Psychology*, Kandy: Buddhist Publication Society.
Ñāṇaponika Thera 1968/1986: *The Power of Mindfulness*, Kandy: Buddhist Publication Society.
Ñāṇaponika Thera 1983: *Contemplation of Feeling: The Discourse-Grouping on the Feelings (Vedana-Saṃyutta) Translated from the Pali with an Introduction*, Kandy: Buddhist Publication Society.
Nattier, Jan 2007: "'One Vehicle' (yi cheng) in the Chinese Āgamas: New Light on an Old Problem in Pāli", *Annual Report of the International Research Institute for Advanced Buddhology at Soka University*, 10: 181–200.
Nhat Hanh, Thich 1990: *Transformation & Healing: The Sutra on the Four Establishments of Mindfulness*, Berkeley: Parallax Press.
Norman, K.R. 1969: *The Elders' Verses: Theragāthā, Translated with an Introduction and Notes*, 1, Oxford: Pali Text Society.
Norman, K.R. 1992: *The Group of Discourses (Sutta-nipāta), Revised Translation with Introduction and Notes*, Oxford: Pali Text Society.
Norman, K.R. 1997/2004: *The Words of the Doctrine (Dhammapada), Translated with an Introduction and Notes*, Oxford: Pali Text Society.
Olendzki, Andrew 2009: "Mindfulness and Meditation", in *Clinical Handbook of Mindfulness*, F. Didonna (ed.), 37–44, New York: Springer.
Olendzki, Andrew 2010: *Unlimiting Mind: The Radically Experiential Psychology of Buddhism*, Boston: Wisdom Publications.
Olendzki, Andrew 2011: "The Construction of Mindfulness", *Contemporary Buddhism*, 12/1: 55–70.
Olivelle, Patrick 2002: "Deconstruction of the Body in Indian Asceticism", in *Asceticism*, V.L. Wimbush et al. (ed.), 188–210, New York: Oxford University Press.
Pāsādika, Bhikkhu 1998: "The Smṛtyupasthānasūtra of the Ekottarāgama (EĀ), Translated from the Chinese Version", in *Facets of Indian Culture: Gustav Roth Felicitation Volume, Published on the Occasion of his 82nd Birthday*, C.P. Sinha (ed.), 494–502, Patna: Bihar Puravid Parishad.
Pe Maung Tin 1976: *The Expositor (Atthasālinī): Buddhaghosa's Commentary on the Dhammasaṅgaṇī, the First Book of the Abhidhamma Piṭaka*, C.A.F. Rhys Davids (ed.), London: Pali Text Society.

Pischel, Richard 1904: "Bruchstücke des Sanskritkanons der Buddhisten aus Idyuktšari Chinesisch-Turkestān" and "Neue Bruchstücke des Sanskritkanons der Buddhisten aus Idyuktšari, Chinesisch-Turkestān", *Sitzungsbericht der Königlich Preussischen Akademie der Wissenschaften, Berlin*, 25: 807–27 and 1138–45.

Potter, Karl H. 1996: "A Few Early Abhidharma Categories", in *Encyclopaedia of Indian Philosophies, 7: Abhidharma Buddhism to 150 AD*, K. Potter et al. (ed.), 121–33, Delhi: Motilal Banarsidass.

Pradhan, P. 1967: *Abhidharmakośabhāṣya of Vasubandhu*, Patna: K.P. Jayaswal Research Institute.

Pyszczynski, Tom, J. Greenberg, S. Solomon, J. Arndt, and J. Schimel 2004: "Why Do People Need Self-Esteem? A Theoretical and Empirical Review", *Psychological Bulletin*, 130/3: 435–68.

Radhakrishnan, S. 1953/1992: *The Principal Upaniṣads, Edited with Introduction, Text, Translation and Notes*, New York: Humanity Books.

Rahder, J. 1926: *Daśabhūmika et Bodhisattvabhūmi: chapitres Vihāra et Bhūmi, publiés avec une introduction et des notes*, Paris: Paul Geuthner.

Ronkin, Noa 2005: *Early Buddhist Metaphysics: The Making of a Philosophical Tradition*, London: RoutledgeCurzon.

Rupp, Heather A. and K. Wallen 2008: "Sex Differences in Response to Visual Sexual Stimuli: A Review", *Archives of Sexual Behaviour*, 37: 206–18.

Saddhāloka, Bhikkhu 1983: "The Discourse on the Foundations of Mindfulness", *Buddhist Friendship*, 12–13: 9–22.

Sakaki, Ryōzaburō 1926/1962: *Hon'yaku myōgi taishū* [*Mahāvyutpatti*], Tokyo: Suzuki Research Foundation.

Salmon, Paul, S. Sephton, I. Weissbecker, K. Hoover, C. Ulmer, and J.L. Studts 2004: "Mindfulness Meditation in Clinical Practice", *Cognitive and Behavioral Practice*, 11: 434–46.

Samtani, N.H. 1971: *The Arthaviniścaya-Sūtra and Its Commentary (Nibandhana) (Written by Bhikṣu Vīryaśrīdatta of Śrī-Nālandāvihāra), Critically Edited and Annotated for the First Time with Introduction and Several Indices*, Patna: K.P. Jayaswal Research Institute.

Sander, Lore and E. Waldschmidt 1985: *Sanskrithandschriften aus den Turfanfunden*, 5, Stuttgart: Franz Steiner.

Schlingloff, Dieter 1964: *Ein Buddhistisches Yogalehrbuch*, Berlin: Akademie Verlag.

Schmidt-Leukel, Perry 1984: *Die Bedeutung des Todes für das menschliche Selbstverständnis im Pali-Buddhismus*, Munich: Missio Verlags- und Vertriebsgesellschaft.

Schmithausen, Lambert 1976: "Die vier Konzentrationen der Aufmerksamkeit, zur geschichtlichen Entwicklung einer spirituellen Praxis des Buddhismus", *Zeitschrift für Missionswissenschaft und Religionswissenschaft*, 60: 241–66.

Schmithausen, Lambert 2012: "Achtsamkeit 'innen', 'außen' und 'innen wie außen'", in *Achtsamkeit: ein buddhistisches Konzept erobert die Wissenschaft, mit einem Beitrag S.H. des Dalai Lama*, M. Zimmermann et al. (ed.), 291–303, Bern: Hans Huber.
Senart, Émile 1890: *Le Mahāvastu: texte sanscrit publié pour la première fois et accompagné d'introductions et d'un commentaire*, 2, Paris: Imprimerie Nationale.
Shaoyong, Ye 2009: "Or. 15009/201–250", in *Buddhist Manuscripts from Central Asia: The British Library Sanskrit Fragments*, S. Karashima et al. (ed.), 2: 227–57, Tokyo: International Research Institute for Advanced Buddhology, Soka University.
Sheng Yen 2006: *Attaining the Way: A Guide to the Practice of Chan Buddhism*, Boston: Shambhala.
Shukla, Karunesha 1973: *Śrāvakabhūmi of Ācārya Asaṅga*, Patna: K.P. Jayaswal Research Institute.
Skilling, Peter 1993: "Theravādin Literature in Tibetan Translation", *Journal of the Pali Text Society*, 19: 69–201.
Skilling, Peter 1997: *Mahāsūtras: Great Discourses of the Buddha*, 2, Oxford: Pali Text Society.
Skilling, Peter 2007: "'Dhammas Are as Swift as Thought ...': A Note on Dhammapada 1 and 2 and Their Parallels", *Journal of the Centre for Buddhist Studies, Sri Lanka*, 5: 23–50.
Speyer, J.S. 1909/1970: *Avadānaçataka: A Century of Edifying Tales Belonging to the Hīnayāna*, 2, Osnabrück: Biblio Verlag.
Sujato, Bhikkhu 2005: *A History of Mindfulness: How Insight Worsted Tranquility in the Satipatthana Sutta*, Taipei: Corporate Body of the Buddha Educational Foundation.
Ṭhānissaro Bhikkhu 1996: *The Wings to Awakening: An Anthology from the Pali Canon*, Massachusetts: Barre Center for Buddhist Studies.
Ṭhānissaro Bhikkhu 2012: *Right Mindfulness: Memory & Ardency on the Buddhist Path*, California: Metta Forest Monastery.
Thiṭṭila, P.A. 1969: *The Book of Analysis (Vibhaṅga): The Second Book of the Abhidhammapiṭaka, Translated from the Pāḷi of the Burmese Chaṭṭasaṅgīti Edition*, London: Pali Text Society.
Thomas, E.J. 1927/2003: *The Life of Buddha as Legend and History*, Delhi: Munshiram Manoharlal.
Tripāṭhī, Chandrabhāl 1962: *Fünfundzwanzig Sūtras des Nidānasaṃyukta*, Berlin: Akademie Verlag.
Tripāṭhī, Chandrabhal 1995: *Ekottarāgama-Fragmente der Gilgit-Handschrift*, Reinbek: Verlag für Orientalistische Fachpublikationen.
Vetter, Tilmann 2000: *The "Khandha Passages" in the Vinayapiṭaka and the Four Main Nikāyas*, Vienna: Österreichische Akademie der Wissenschaften.
von Gabain, Annemarie 1954: *Türkische Turfan-Texte*, 8, Berlin: Akademie Verlag.

von Hinüber, Oskar 1996/1997: *A Handbook of Pāli Literature*, Delhi: Munshiram Manoharlal.

von Rospatt, Alexander 1995: *The Buddhist Doctrine of Momentariness: A Survey of the Origins and Early Phase of This Doctrine up to Vasubandhu*, Stuttgart: Franz Steiner.

Waldschmidt, Ernst 1950: *Das Mahāparinirvāṇasūtra: Text in Sanskrit und Tibetisch, verglichen mit dem Pāli nebst einer Übersetzung der chinesischen Entsprechung im Vinaya der Mūlasarvāstivādins, auf Grund von Turfan-Handschriften herausgegeben und bearbeitet*, 1, Berlin: Akademie Verlag.

Waldschmidt, Ernst 1953: *Das Mahāvadānasūtra: ein kanonischer Text über die sieben letzten Buddhas, Sanskrit, verglichen mit dem Pāli nebst einer Analyse der in chinesischer Übersetzung überlieferten Parallelversion, auf Grund von Turfan-Handschriften herausgegeben*, 1, Berlin: Akademie Verlag.

Waldschmidt, Ernst 1965: *Sanskrithandschriften aus den Turfanfunden*, 1, Wiesbaden: Franz Steiner.

Waldschmidt, Ernst 1967: "Zu einigen Bilinguen aus den Turfan-Funden", in *Von Ceylon bis Turfan, Schriften zur Geschichte, Literatur, Religion und Kunst des indischen Kulturraums, Festgabe zum 70. Geburtstag am 15. Juli 1967 von Ernst Waldschmidt*, 238–57, Göttingen: Vandenhoeck & Ruprecht.

Waldschmidt, Ernst 1971: *Sanskrithandschriften aus den Turfanfunden*, 3, Wiesbaden: Franz Steiner.

Walshe, Maurice 1987: *Thus Have I Heard: The Long Discourses of the Buddha*, London: Wisdom Publications.

Wayman, Alex 1982: "The Religious Meaning of Concrete Death in Buddhism", in *Sens de la mort dans le christianisme et les autres religions*, M. Dhavamony et al. (ed.), 273–95, Rome: Università Gregoriana Editrice.

Weber, Claudia 1994: *Wesen und Eigenschaften des Buddha in der Tradition des Hīnayāna Buddhismus*, Wiesbaden: Harrassowitz.

Wille, Klaus 1990: *Die handschriftliche Überlieferung des Vinayavastu der Mūlasarvāstivādin*, Stuttgart: Franz Steiner.

Wille, Klaus 2008: *Sanskrithandschriften aus den Turfanfunden*, 10, Stuttgart: Franz Steiner.

Winternitz, Moriz 1920/1968: *Geschichte der Indischen Literatur*, 2: *Die Buddhistische Literatur und die heiligen Texte der Jainas*, Stuttgart: K.F. Koehler.

Xuezhu, Li and E. Steinkellner 2008: *Vasubandhu's Pañcaskandhaka*, Beijing/Vienna: China Tibetology Publishing House/Austrian Academy of Sciences Press.

Zysk, Kenneth G. 1991: *Asceticism and Healing in Ancient India: Medicine in the Buddhist Monastery*, New York: Oxford University Press.

LIST OF ABBREVIATIONS

AN	*Aṅguttara-nikāya*
As	*Atthasālinī*
CBETA	Chinese Buddhist Electronic Text Association
D	Derge edition
DĀ	*Dirgha-āgama* (T 1)
Dhp	*Dhammapada*
Dhp-a	*Dhammapada-aṭṭhakathā*
DN	*Dīgha-nikāya*
EĀ	*Ekottarika-āgama* (T 125)
EĀ[2]	*Ekottarika-āgama* (T 150A)
Jā	*Jātaka*
MĀ	*Madhyama-āgama* (T 26)
MN	*Majjhima-nikāya*
Mp	*Manorathapūraṇī*
Paṭis	*Paṭisambhidāmagga*
Ps	*Papañcasūdanī*
Q	Qian-long (Peking) edition
SĀ	*Saṃyukta-āgama* (T 99)
SĀ[2]	*Saṃyukta-āgama* (T 100)
SHT	Sanskrithandschriften aus den Turfanfunden
Si	Sichuan Tanjur edition
Sn	*Sutta-nipāta*
SN	*Saṃyutta-nikāya*
Spk	*Sāratthappakāsinī*
T	Taishō (CBETA)
Th	*Theragāthā*
Ud	*Udāna*
Vibh	*Vibhaṅga*
Vin	*Vinayapiṭaka*

INDEX OF SUBJECTS

INDEX LOCORUM

WINDHORSE PUBLICATIONS

Windhorse Publications is a Buddhist charitable company based in the UK. We place great emphasis on producing books of high quality that are accessible and relevant to those interested in Buddhism at whatever level. We are the main publisher of the works of Sangharakshita, the founder of the Triratna Buddhist Order and Community. Our books draw on the whole range of the Buddhist tradition, including translations of traditional texts, commentaries, books that make links with contemporary culture and ways of life, biographies of Buddhists, and works on meditation.

As a not-for-profit enterprise, we ensure that all surplus income is invested in new books and improved production methods, to better communicate Buddhism in the 21st century. We welcome donations to help us continue our work – to find out more, go to www.windhorsepublications.com.

The Windhorse is a mythical animal that flies over the earth carrying on its back three precious jewels, bringing these invaluable gifts to all humanity: the Buddha (the 'awakened one'), his teaching, and the community of all his followers.

Windhorse Publications
169 Mill Road
Cambridge
CB1 3AN
UK
info@windhorsepublications.com

Perseus Distribution
210 American Drive
Jackson TN 38301
USA

Windhorse Books
PO Box 574
Newtown NSW 2042
Australia

THE TRIRATNA BUDDHIST COMMUNITY

Windhorse Publications is a part of the Triratna Buddhist Community, which has more than sixty centres on five continents. Through these centres, members of the Triratna Buddhist Order offer classes in meditation and Buddhism, from an introductory to a deeper level of commitment. Members of the Triratna community run retreat centres around the world, and the Karuna Trust, a UK fundraising charity that supports social welfare projects in the slums and villages of South Asia.

Many Triratna centres have residential spiritual communities and ethical Right Livelihood businesses associated with them. Arts activities and body awareness disciplines are encouraged also, as is the development of strong bonds of friendship between people who share the same ideals. In this way Triratna is developing a unique approach to Buddhism, not simply as a set of techniques, but as a creatively directed way of life for people living in the modern world.

If you would like more information about Triratna please visit www.thebuddhistcentre.com or write to:

London Buddhist Centre
51 Roman Road
London E2 0HU
UK

Aryaloka
14 Heartwood Circle
Newmarket NH 03857
USA

Sydney Buddhist Centre
24 Enmore Road
Sydney NSW 2042
Australia